D1741364

JEWS AND PORT CITIES, 1590–1990

Parkes-Wiener Series on Jewish Studies
Series Editors: David Cesarani and Tony Kushner
ISSN 1368-5449

The field of Jewish Studies is one of the youngest, but fastest growing and most exciting areas of scholarship in the academic world today. Named after James Parkes and Alfred Wiener, this series aims to publish new research in the field and student materials for use in the seminar room, to disseminate the latest work of established scholars and to re-issue classic studies which are currently out of print.

The selection of publications reflects the international character and diversity of Jewish Studies; it ranges over Jewish history from Abraham to modern Zionism, and Jewish culture from Moses to post-modernism. The series also reflects the inter-disciplinary approach inherent in Jewish Studies and at the cutting edge of contemporary scholarship, and provides an outlet for innovative work on the interface between Judaism and ethnicity, popular culture, gender, class, space and memory.

Other Books in the Series

Jews and Port Cities 1590–1990

Commerce, Community and Cosmopolitanism

Editors

David Cesarani
and Gemma Romain

VALLENTINE MITCHELL
LONDON • PORTLAND, OR

First published in 2006 in Great Britain by
VALLENTINE MITCHELL
Suite 314 Premier House, 112–114 Station Road,
Edgware, Middlesex HA8 7BJ

and in the United States of America by
VALLENTINE MITCHELL
c/o ISBS, 920 N.E. 58th Street, Suite 300
Portland, Oregon 97213-3786

*Website:*www.vmbooks.com

Copyright © 2006 Vallentine Mitchell

British Library Cataloguing in Publication Data

Jews and port cities, 1590–1990 : commerce, community and
cosopolitanism. – (Parkes-Wiener series on Jewish studies)
1. Jews – History – Congresses 2. Jews – Commerce – History –
Congresses 3. Jews – Social networks – Congresses 4. Jews –
Economic conditions – Congresses 5. Jewish merchants –
History – Congresses 6. City and town life – History – Congresses
I. Cesarani, David II. Romain, Gemma
909'.04924

ISBN 0 85303 681 0 (cloth)
ISBN 0 85303 682 9 (paper)
ISSN 1368-5449

Library of Congress Cataloging-in-Publication Data:

A catalog record has been applied for

This group of studies first appeared in a special issue of *Jewish Culture and History*,
Vol.7/1–2 [ISSN 1462-169X]
published by Vallentine Mitchell & Co. Ltd.

*All rights reserved. No part of this publication may be reproduced, stored in or introduced into a
retrieval system, or transmitted, in any form or by any means, electronic, mechanical, photocopying,
recording or otherwise, without the prior written permission of the publisher of this book.*

Printed in Great Britain by
Antony Rowe Ltd, Chippenham, Wilts

Contents

Introduction

DAVID CESARANI

In October 2000 the AHRB Parkes Centre for the Study of Jewish/non-Jewish Relations at the University of Southampton launched a five-year research programme into the phenomena of port Jews. The programme was inspired by the concept that Lois Dubin and David Sorkin had earlier developed and elaborated, with individual modulations, in previous monographs and articles. Both participated in the first international symposium on port Jews held at Southampton University in June 2001, the proceedings of which subsequently appeared in a collection edited by David Cesarani. The discussions during the symposium and the papers that appeared in the subsequent publication revealed a considerable range of opinion about the applicability of the concept of the port Jew as a 'social type' and the directions in which it might be developed.[1]

In David Sorkin's now classic formulation this 'social type' was confined to Sephardim, originating as *conversos* or New Christians in the Iberian peninsular, who settled in port cities on the Atlantic seaboard between the late sixteenth and mid-eighteenth century. These Sephardim were permitted to emerge and live openly as Jews by virtue of the economic benefits that they brought with them, attributes that were valued by local authorities with a mercantilist outlook that valued the concentration of commercial acumen more highly than the strict preservation of religious homogeneity. Sorkin noted that in many cases once these Jewish merchants were permitted to establish communities the new elite tended to favour 'modernised' forms of Jewish religious observance and education. Many had previously lived a double life as secret Jews or even as non-Jews and had a distanced or sceptical view of Judaism. Others were keen to meld in with their hospitable surroundings and so softened the elements of Judaism that tended to preserve difference. Thanks to the absence of 'Jewry laws' membership of Jewish communities tended to be voluntary, a fact that weakened the control of the rabbinate and lay leadership. Consequently, communities of port Jews provided a fertile soil for individual innovation, intellectual questioning that in many ways anticipated the *haskalah*, the Jewish enlightenment. Thanks to the tolerant, pragmatic atmosphere in these cosmopolitan maritime trading centres and the willingness, and ability, of the Jews in question to acculturate, port cities also tended to offer Jews civic inclusion earlier than other regions. The superior legal status they enjoyed offered a distinctive stepping-stone to emancipation. In these ways the Sephardi port Jews followed a singular path into Jewish modernity, one that has been overshadowed in Jewish historiography due to the emphasis on central European, predominantly Ashkenazi, court Jews and the *haskalah* as the model for modernisation in Jewish history.[2]

In her study of the Jews of Trieste, Lois Dubin pioneered the notion of port cities offering to Jews in the eighteenth century a specific model of civic inclusion based on the principle of commercial utility. Dubin's approach challenged the standard view that the modernisation of Jewish communities necessarily had an intellectual impulse, the Enlightenment and its Jewish variant. The case of Trieste indicated that pragmatic considerations could be responsible for creating a situation of tolerance and an improvement in the legal status of Jews. Indeed, Trieste provided Jewish intellectuals in central Europe with an example of Jews and non-Jews interacting as equals on the basis of shared values: utility.[3]

At the 2001 symposium in Southampton, held in cooperation with the Kaplan Centre for Jewish Studies, University of Cape Town, Dubin pleaded for the port Jew concept to be broadened beyond the eighteenth-century Sephardi type. Otherwise it excluded Ashkenazi and mixed communities, such as the Triestine Jews, and paradoxically also marginalised Sephardi Jews in port cities that did not follow the trajectory of those on the Atlantic littoral. Yet, she argued, similar traits might be found amongst Jews in port cities of the Ottoman Empire or even further afield. Since much research was being conducted on Jewish populations in maritime centres during the era of mass migration between the 1870s and the 1920s, a period well beyond the range and relevance of Sorkin's 'social type', yet nevertheless distinctive social formations thanks to their port location, she also ventured that the term port Jewry or port Jewish community might be more appropriate.[4]

Other contributions to the symposium reinforced the contention that port cities, with their unusual social, economic and political and cultural properties, are a key to the transformation of Jewish populations and the evolution of distinctive relations with other ethnic-faith groups. For this reason the characteristics of the port should be fore-grounded when examining the Jews who inhabit them rather than the other way around. Shifting the point of departure from a pre-defined type of Jew to a particular milieu does not negate the value of Sorkin's concept. Instead, it was agreed that the term port Jewry or port Jewish community was a better descriptor and offered a broader and more inclusive definition that recognised the applicability of the concept in different eras and regions.[5]

The symposium helped to crystallise an agenda for future research into cosmopolitan trading centres with Jewish populations that displayed common features, including: migration; commercial activity; local commercial ethos; positive legal status of Jews; programmes of improvement within the Jewish community; and changing ethnic identity. The aims of this research programme were set out in a call for papers for a follow-up conference in 2003:

- to clarify the applicability of the concepts of 'port Jew,' 'port Jewry' and 'Jews in port cities' and to resolve whether there is a distinct 'social type' or social formation that can be called a port Jew or port Jewry in the nineteenth and twentieth centuries;
- to determine whether the 'social type' of the port Jew can be applied to cases and eras in the Mediterranean and Atlantic regions independently of the transition to modernity;
- to explore diversification of the concept, leaving the original definition intact while adding a variant that incorporates such issues as transmigration, diasporic connections and the changing image and perception of Jews in ports;
- to explore the changing perceptions of the port city and its Jewish inhabitants; and
- to engage in comparative studies that embrace non-Jews in port cities.[6]

On 5–8 January 2003 several of the participants in the now well-established port Jews network reconvened at an international conference in Cape Town hosted by the Kaplan Centre for Jewish Studies, University of Cape Town. They were joined by many more researchers who had responded to the call for papers, whose work had been inspired by the first volume of studies or whose independently conducted research chimed with the programmes' objectives. The result was a stimulating and challenging event that pushed the boundaries of the port Jew concept, explored the value of port Jewry and port Jewish community as an analytical tool, and interrogated the specific ingredients of the port city milieu.

In her keynote lecture, Lois Dubin drew attention to the importance of the constant movement and migration of Jewish merchants between trading hubs and within the Jewish diaspora. Dubin challenged the formerly rather static notion of the port city and port Jew, stressing that thanks to commercial practice and trading necessity some Jews were in constant motion. Certain Jews (not just those engaged in commerce) were perpetually crossing geographical, political, linguistic and cultural boundaries. The patterns of mobility and the networks they followed and the implications of this fluidity call for as careful study as their bases of operation and the ethos fostered in these places. To encapsulate her message for researchers Dubin cited the description of merchants by Joseph Penso de la Vega's in the seventeenth century: 'Mercury, the god of merchants, is rightly portrayed with wings on head and feet. For, although some merchants have neither head nor feet, most seem to have wings on their feet witnessing the speed with which they move about and wings on their head considering the flight of their thoughts …'.[7]

Dubin's admonition was reflected in a number of the papers delivered at the conference, several of which are published here for the first time. Indeed, it became clear that researchers working autonomously, as well as those whose work was informed by the port Jews network, had reached a similar conclusion about the importance of seeing port Jews and port Jewish communities in a dynamic context. It has to be noted here that the verb 'seeing' is both problematic and poignant since the velocity of Jews, and the nature of transmigrancy, often rendered Jews individually and collectively invisible. The challenge posed by this unconscious or deliberate imperceptibility is a theme explored below. A number of other thematic strands emerged by way of qualifying or enlarging the original notion of the port Jew. As the following chapters demonstrate, ports have not always been tolerant milieux and, ironically, when they have lived up to their cosmopolitan reputation they may actually have been inimical to Jewish continuity. New research, presented here, shows that port Jews frequently clung to the sort of corporate identity associated with pre-modern Jewish communities, seeking to insulate themselves from the rampant individualism and intermixing that flourished in some cosmopolitan ports during certain periods.

In her study of Livorno, Francesca Trivellato argues for the extension of the port Jew concept beyond the Sephardi classical type that appeared in the Atlantic ports. The rulers of Livorno offered generous charters to Jews fleeing the Iberian peninsular in the late sixteenth century, with the result that Jews settled there in such large numbers that 150 years later they formed 10–15 per cent of the city's population. Livorno actually offered inspiration for Trieste and other ports seeking to attract entrepreneurial immigrants regardless of their confessional or national allegiances. However, the Jews of Livorno formed a community that was quite unlike the voluntary association typical of Sorkin's port Jews: Jews who wished to settle there were obliged to join the community and the Jewish elite was able to exercise strict control over Jewish immigration. Ironically, the well-established Jews of Iberian origin displayed a marked coolness towards Italian Jews especially if they were poor. Despite the bad memories of persecution, Iberian Jews retained close ties with family and business partners in the peninsular, while intermarriage with Italian Jews was rare. Yet, at the same time as they guarded their Spanish and Portuguese heritage, the Sephardim of Livorno crossed boundaries in the pursuit of profit and happily dealt with Ashkenazi Jews in other parts of Italy and Europe. The Hindus of Goa were crucial business partners in the trade in diamonds and coral – a trade in which the Livornese Jews played a hugely important role. Trivellato concludes by virtually standing the port Jew concept on its head.

Although they may be seen following the classic 'port Jew' path to modernity in a port environment that could be a case study of benevolence, the Jews of Livorno were oriented towards the eastern Mediterranean and Asia rather than the Atlantic. They had little intercourse with the New World. Moreover, while the Livornese merchants travelled extensively and were at ease with cross-cultural exchanges, they preserved their distinct identity as part of a *Sephardi diaspora* and resisted assimilation or creolisation.

Thorsten Wagner addresses a seaport community of Jews on the other side of the continent of Europe, in Copenhagen, and also finds that the classic port Jew concept has valuable but limited applicability. As in Livorno, the Jewish community founded by Sephardim was neither wholly mercantile nor voluntary. Jewish economic activity, if not residence, was subjected to extensive oversight and legal regulation. The small core of Sephardim was quickly overwhelmed by an influx of Ashkenazi Jews for whom they had paved the way by securing privileges on the basis of commercial utility. Initially these two groups did not mix well. The Ashkenazim tended more towards the model of court Jews rather than port Jews. The Sephardim were irked by their doctrinaire and rigid forms of Judaism. However, over time a hybrid community developed. Certain elite members of the Ashkenazi community crossed over to the Sephardim who were more 'modern'. This process of adjustment was mainly pragmatic, even though several Copenhagen Jews were part of the network of enlightened Jews whose intellectual hub lay in Berlin. Wagner shows that the transformation of the Jews in Denmark resulted from a blend of factors which go well beyond the port milieux and the contribution of Sephardi port Jews.

The extraordinary mobility of Jews in the early modern period is underlined by Evelyne Oliel-Grausz in her study of networks and communication in the Sephardi diaspora. But while Jews may have been agile, Oliel-Grausz reveals, like Trivellato, that velocity did not negate constancy of identity. She demonstrates that networks of ethnicity and kin were of far greater importance than merely providing commercial channels. They were also the ligaments that held a diaspora together, that enabled the circulation of policy, people, religious ideas and artefacts. Oliel-Grausz stresses that research should avoid focusing too heavily on either individual port communities or the networks between them. Rather, the study of port Jewish communities should encompass the dynamic relationship between settlements and show how developments in once place had an impact on another, how a metropolitan community affected the fortunes of a 'colony'. Through four delightful case studies or vignettes, she illustrates the complexity of decision-making by Jews moving around the diaspora for a multitude of reasons, the importance of communal policy affecting the circulation of poor Jews, and the importance of hubs such as Amsterdam for religious education and leadership throughout the

Sephardi disapora. Thanks to her search for sources and her assiduous use of difficult texts, Oliel-Grausz achieves a densely textured depiction of diaspora that sets a benchmark for aspiring historians of dispersed, transnational communities.

However, the image of the successfully functioning diaspora hinged on hub communities that enjoyed benign living and trading conditions cannot pass without qualification. Some port Jewish communities simply failed. But why? Klaus Weber sets out to explain the fate of the Sephardim of Hamburg, a community that appears in the 1590s, flourishes and peaks in the 1660s, but has been all but extinguished by 1730. Weber shows that despite the evident benefits that the immigrants brought to Hamburg, the city's Christian population was bitterly divided over the merits of their presence. The mercantile elite in the municipal senate repeatedly had to defend the Jews from the representatives of the burgers or citizens who demanded the curtailment of their rights and even their expulsion. These citizens were routinely inflamed by local Lutheran preachers who vilified the Jews, thereby adding spiritual fervour to commercial jealousy. Even so, Weber challenges the received wisdom that intolerance was responsible for the decline and fall of the Hamburg Sephardim. He locates the community's fortunes in the context of trading patterns as they were influenced by wars, the emergence of new commercial relationships between entrepôts, the arrival of new immigrants and internal dissension. The Sephardic community of Hamburg atrophied because it never achieved the demographic critical mass for continual reproduction, while the arrival of Huguenots after 1694 created competition that limited the wealth and benefits that the Jews could attain. Sheer malice towards Jews could not have been responsible for the extinction of the port Jews because Ashkenazi Jews from the German lands clung on and eventually prospered. Weber's study is a sanguine reminder that port cities were a place of volatile fortunes: the very commercial base that made life possible for Jews could shift and slide for reasons of trade and cut the ground from under their feet.

Port cities could be treacherous terrain for Jewish continuity for other, more benign reasons too. Adam Sutcliffe shows that the intensity of commercial exchange in port cities brought with it an unprecedented degree of social and cultural interchange which could be inimical to the preservation of an individual group identity. One of the first to undergo this challenge was the Sephardi community of Amsterdam and its offshoot in London. Commercial practices and pragmatic attitudes generated a new, common culture that enabled individuals from different backgrounds to meet, combine and find a 'cross-cultural identity'. Sutcliffe remarks that 'the cosmopolitan conditions that enabled these communities to gain acceptance and to prosper also insistently challenged and threatened to undermine these boundaries of cultural separateness'. Faced by the conditions of transience and potential anonymity in the bustling, densely populated port city of Amsterdam, the communal leadership, the *Mahamad*, struggled to impose its control. Out of fear that uncontrolled contact could spark conflict or allow Jews to sink into licentiousness, it tried to use the draconian device of the *herem*, expulsion from the community, to regulate the interaction between Jews and non-Jews. It was a loosing battle, especially in London where there were more Jews who, having recently fled Spain or Portugal, were barely integrated into Jewish life in any case. When wealthy Jewish merchants moved to suburban and rural residences the rabbinate lost any hold over them it ever had. Economic opportunity and spatial divergence were a fateful combination, the effect of which runs counter to many assumptions about the positive role of the port city in modern Jewish history. Sutcliffe concludes that 'The desire to be distinctive, and therefore also to some extent separate, strained against the contrary desire to take full advantage of the cosmopolitan possibilities offered in these unprecedentedly interactive environments'.

A symptom of this interaction was creolisation. One of the most remarkable instances of this phenomenon is the emergence of Papiementu, a Creole language used in Curaçao and its environs from the mid-eighteenth century until today. Linda Rupert excavates the origins of Papiementu, explaining that it probably originated in the diurnal relations between Sephardi merchants and free blacks in the port settlement of Willemstad. The language may have spread thanks to their extensive trading activity and their crucial place in the local economy. Yet the interaction between Jews and blacks begs the question of what role Jews played in the slave-based economies of the Americas in the eighteenth and nineteenth centuries.

Gemma Romain's study of Jews and non-Jews in Charleston is a revealing and at times shocking dissection of these relations. She remarks that in both the historiography of the American South and in Jewish historiography Jews who lived and functioned in the interstices of a slave-owning society have either been uncritically celebrated as a part of the White South or marginalised for fear of exposing them to the stigma of a hated system. However, her research on Charleston uncovers a diverse Jewish community that does not easily fit the port Jew type. It was more occupationally differentiated, mobile and operated in a diasporic rather than a solely local context. Charleston was, for the South, a cosmopolitan and progressive port city and historians have tended to echo the self-promoting testimony of locals who depicted Jews fitting into this benign framework. Yet Romain has discovered documents that suggest a much more ambivalent picture. In private communications and occasionally in the public sphere Jews were constructed as neither wholly 'white' nor 'black'. Indeed, the fluidity of Jewish identity undermines the value of these rigid, racialised categories. Jews, for their part, did not conform uniformly to patterns of behaviour towards blacks and while most wholeheartedly endorsed slavery a few worked around it or undermined its preservation.

Until recently slavery was largely written out of the history of Jewish communities, even in localities where the economy depended on it. This historiographical vacuum was then filled by polemicists who accused Jews of having had a dominant role in the transatlantic slave trade. Research, including Romain's work on Charleston, has exposed the hollowness of such charges. However, proof of the limited nature of direct Jewish involvement in the slave trade does not negate the evidence of its indirect impact on Jewish life – or the way that many Jews benefited from slavery albeit at one remove. In his chapter, David Cesarani observes that Jews arrived in Bristol and Liverpool in England during the period of rapid economic expansion that was buoyed up by the profits of the 'triangular trade'. While they entered the local economy too late to invest in or gain directly from the transportation of slaves, they inevitably benefited from the 'multiplier effect' of the trade. The gentrification of Jewish communities, symbolised by the building of fine new synagogues, paralleled the civic improvements in both towns – embellishments that were ultimately funded by inflows of wealth from the plantation economy in the West Indies and the southern states of America. During the boom years of the slave trade the citizens of Bristol and Liverpool gained a reputation for hard-headed commercialism. By virtue of being ports their cities had a patina of cosmopolitanism. Yet this did not exclude the frequent display of prejudice and discrimination. In 1753–54, Bristol merchants railed against extending the civic inclusion of Jews via the practice of naturalisation. The profits of slavery and unsavoury traditions of sectarianism cast these cities in a dimmer light. On this basis, Cesarani questions whether ports ruled by the doctrine of profit and utility were always and unambiguously friendly to entrepreneurial Jewish newcomers.

The ambiguities of the port city in the history of Jewish emancipation are laid bare by Carlotta Ferrara degli Uberti, who returns us to Livorno. Uberti notes that civic inclusion in Livorno rested on privileges that were originally granted in the sixteenth century – the Letters Patent and the accompanying system of *ballotazione* or naturalisation. Unlike the classic port Jew model, the Jewish community of Livorno, the Nation, was allowed to retain internal jurisdiction according to Jewish law and, crucially, to control its own membership. The Jews were afforded privileges collectively and the community was a mandatory body. This was the complete opposite of developments in Bordeaux, Amsterdam, Hamburg and London. Moreover, in contrast to what would be expected from the model developed by Sorkin, the Jews remained deeply attached to this arrangement throughout the first half of the nineteenth century despite the promise of full emancipation and civic equality. Jewish leaders vacillated between seeking full equality and negotiating the preservation of communal autonomy. Change came to Livorno precisely because the conditions that made port cities and port Jews so distinctive began to fade. Jewish privileges rested on their utility and their mercantile functions. With the rise of the hinterland and the growth of a local bourgeoisie that looked inland rather than overseas for business opportunities and cultural validation, Jews adjusted their activities and image. They began to diversify away from trade, educated their sons into the liberal professions, and bruited their civic virtues as against their commercial acuity. When in 1868 Livorno lost its status as a Free Port, the transformation was all but complete. Spatial diffusion completed the process. When well to do Livornese Jews started moving to grand villas on the outskirts of the city the *Massari*, the equivalent of the *Mahamad*, lost its influence and the rationale for the mandatory community that ran counter to full emancipation was eroded. Thus the Jews of Livorno travelled the path to modernity and emancipation in, literally, the opposite direction to that suggested by the port Jew model. In the classic era of the port Jew, when they were at the height of mercantile activity, they clung to a pre-modern identity; at the moment that they turned their backs to the sea they embraced a modern individualistic identity and full civic equality.

Further evidence that the hard-headed ethos and diversity of port cities were no guarantee of civic inclusion and emancipation comes from the example of Corfu port, the subject of the chapter by Sakis Gekas. This research importantly takes on a port city in the eastern Mediterranean that was under Venetian rule from 1386 to 1797 and British rule from 1815 until 1864 when it was handed over the Greece. Jews had been on the island since the 1380s and their fortunes had ebbed and flowed. Under the Venetians they were subjected to residential segregation and many other restrictions. They only began to enjoy improved legal status from the 1790s. When Greek rule began the Jewish population numbered 2,000, ranging in status and occupation from rich merchants to poor tailors and peddlers. Gekas emphasises the occupational range of Corfu port Jews as revealed by the 1864 census: despite many myths, this was not a community exclusively composed of wealthy traders. Until 1891, Jews moved steadily towards full civic equality and relations with the Greek population were good. Then a blood libel case erupted that resulted in violence, a blockade of the Jewish district, and finally the exodus of most of the Jewish population. Gekas traces the origins of the explosion to economic tensions flowing from the decline of the port and the importation of Greek nationalism from the mainland. It was also rooted in traditional antipathies towards the Jews that were articulated in the local press with increasing openness from the 1880s. Like Odessa and Salonika, Corfu is an example of a port city that both embraced Jews and enabled them to progress economically and socially, only to frustrate the development of its Jewish community because of the commercial rivalries that mercantile activity engendered. When the economy went into depression, the lines of national or ethnic-faith diversity that had once been so easily crossed in a spirit of pragmatic cooperation and respect became bitter cleavages.

The era of mass migration in the late nineteenth and early twentieth century tends to throw up more and more examples of port cities transformed into sites of tension and ethnic conflict. However, this is not the only feature that requires a reconceptualisation of the port Jew concept. In modern times the port city was not simply a hub for the shipment and trans-shipment of commodities and goods: it was a nodal point for waves of migration, too. Port cities acquired huge transient populations that enjoyed at best ambivalent relations with the settled communities. Even long-established Jews were no exception to this rule and looked askance at their transmigrating co-religionists. Ports in the industrial age were no less cosmopolitan than they were in the age of sail, and continued to manifest a rational, can-do, business-minded ethos. They still offered more opportunities to entrepreneurial immigrants than old-established urban centres or many industrial cities in the interior. But the problematic that attracts the attention of historians had changed fundamentally, thus warranting the appellation port Jewry or port Jewish community to distinguish the subject at hand.[8]

Nick Evans begins his study of the Jews of Libau by noting that they were quite unlike the small, mercantile communities of the eighteenth century. Only a tiny elite were wealthy and acculturated: most were poor, working-class Jews who were still very traditional in their outlook and mores. Yet the Libau Jews resemble the classic model insofar as they were given greater freedom than Jews in the Pale of Settlement and did foster a more liberal approach to Jewish education, typified by the state-run Libau rabbinical school. Thanks to the port's excellent rail links to the interior, running into the heart of the Pale, Libau Jews exercised a far-flung cultural influence. However, the very same rail net enabled Jews from within the Pale to travel to the port and embark directly on ships going to the west without having to struggle through numerous border posts. This made Libau a favourite point of embarkation from the 1880s when mass Jewish emigration gathered pace in response to the fear of pogroms, discrimination and the pressure of population on jobs. Libau's Jewish merchants began to organise and profit from the trade in their co-religionists with the same vigour and commercial ruthlessness that they had shown in the export of grain, timber and ponies to England. The mass transportation of Jews on unsuitable ships resulted in the arrival at UK ports of bedraggled and frequently sick passengers. Such an influx of ill and ragged Jews added impetus to anti-alien sentiment and fuelled the backlash against Jewish mass migration to Britain.

Industrialisation and mass migration transformed the face of port cities such as Glasgow. As William Kenefick shows, they sucked in immigrants from the region and globally to create teeming multinational, multi-ethnic and religiously diverse populations. At the same time, the class solidarity that came with the massive docks and their associated industries could act as a counterweight to this social fragmentation. Kenefick argues that immigrant Jews in the Gorbals district of Glasgow and the local Irish managed to maintain harmonious relations in part thanks to a shared working-class identity (and even militancy) and partly due to enlightened religious leadership in the city. However, the Jews, who numbered 6,500 at the most, may have been spared sectarian conflict because the flashpoint was between the huge Sots and Irish Catholic population and the dominant Protestant community.

More typically, perhaps, mass immigration and industrialisation helped to transform ethnic and race relations in Cape Town in the late nineteenth century. As Milton Shain, Richard Mendelsohn and Vivian Bickford-Smith explain, Jews suffered from exclusion and severe discrimination while the Cape was under Dutch Protestant rule – a surprising inversion of the pattern evident in the metropolis. It was only under the benevolent aegis of the British that Jews began to immigrate in significant numbers. Jewish life in Cape Town flowered under the benign conditions of British rule. Indeed, this was less a result of the peculiar characteristics of a port and more a product of policy. 'Cape Town's status as a colonial port city was at best marginal to its tolerance of cultural and religious difference, in particular its acceptance of Jews. More significant in this regard was its character as an outpost of liberal empire'. The British promoted a limited form of diversity and pluralism, but even this could not hold sway against social and economic changes, least of all after a significant shift of local political power. The establishment of white-only rule in 1872 coincided with mass immigration and a bourgeois panic about health and sanitation. The influx of Jewish refugees from the hinterland during the Boer War accentuated the anxiety about the 'alien' presence and generated calls for immigration restriction. Jews were spared the worst racist laws because they were white and thanks to the intervention of pro-Jewish voices such as Olive Schreiner. But anti-Jewish stereotypes put down deep roots and antipathies built up. Shain, Mendelsohn and Bickford-Smith thus qualify the unreservedly positive image of the cosmopolitan colonial port city. They also note that antagonistic currents came from the hinterland (in the shape of a reaction to the refugees) and from England. In an admonitory conclusion they remark that 'Modernity, it would seem, erodes the social space within which Sorkin's and Dubin's port Jew thrives; that was unique to the self-contained port city of the early modern period. The close integration of modern port cities with society at large, including their hinterlands, precludes this'.

Tony Kushner echoes many of these themes in his dissection of Southampton, a study that fittingly opens with the description of the panic engendered when the SS Cheshire arrived from South Africa in February 1900 with 350 Jewish migrants on board. The immigrants were brought ashore as discreetly as possible and with the aid of the local Jewish community dispersed to London and beyond. Kushner argues that Southampton had proved a haven for Jews in the nineteenth century but only on its terms: that the Jews remained relatively few in number and conformed to the expectations of the local middle classes by demonstrating commercial utility and civic virtue – constantly assuring the dominant community of their worthiness. Poor immigrant Jews and refugees disrupted this image and had to be hidden from sight in specially constructed hostels prior to their on-migration. The experience of the transmigrants, penned in these holding centres and regularly subjected to rough and humiliating medical checks, has eluded most historians of Jewish migration and barely features at all in accounts of port Jews. Kushner insists that especially for the period of mass migration it is essential to recover the experience of the transient populations that at moments far outnumbered local Jewish communities. While established local Jews might be feted, the conditions of the transmigrants were more likely to be foetid. There is a connection between the two conditions: the security and permanence of local Jews depended on the insecurity and transience of the migrant population. A total history of port Jewish communities needs to bring these parts together.

The myth of the tolerant, cosmopolitan port city that was so important to the public image of Cape Town and Southampton was precious also for Hamburg. Post-1945, the burgers of Hamburg liked to maintain that their city had never been in favour of the Nazis and the late arrival of 'Aryanisation', the confiscation of Jewish businesses, might seem to confirm this. This alibi does not withstand scrutiny by Rainer Liedtke. He shows that about half of the Jewish population had emigrated by 1941 in response to unremitting legal pressure emanating from the municipal authorities as much as from Berlin, discrimination, prejudice and violence. The pogrom against the Jews known as *Kristallnacht* was no less severe in Hamburg than in other cities. Indeed, the rate of prosecutions launched against Jews accused of 'race defilement' was higher in Hamburg than in comparable urban centres. Since these often originated in denunciations, Liedtke concludes that there must have been a deep and broad pool of animosity towards the Jews. 'Aryanisation' may indeed have come relatively late to Hamburg, but this was largely for local and pragmatic reasons. Since so many Jewish-owned businesses had outlets or partners overseas, the local business elite was reluctant to unleash a policy that might provoke a foreign backlash. Once 'Aryanisation' was instigated on a large scale by the local Nazi Party bosses in 1938, German firms swooped on their previous competitors – if only to prevent them falling into the hands of rivals. Hamburg's history of diversity and cosmopolitanism did not withstand the racism unleashed by the Third Reich: instead the city did its best to profit from the destruction of its venerable and much vaunted Jewish community.

Such examples of a port city acting as a negative factor in Jewish history need to be seen in their specific context. This volume ends with Jonathan Goldstein's survey of Jewish communities in the Far East in which he applies the classic Dubin-Sorkin model to a series of ports. He finds that the model of benevolence and improvement works quite well even in such a culturally different milieu. However, he ends with a stimulating examination of the Jews of inland Harbin. This community, he maintains, comes closest to the Sorkin 'social type' – although it is hundreds of miles for the coast! Goldstein thereby raises the question of whether there is anything specific about the land–sea interface or whether landlocked transport hubs can fulfil the same function. The extension of the port Jew concept to the Far East, and the examination of Jewish community within the distinctive framework of the port city in the era of mass migration show the immense flexibility and heuristic value of these approaches. There are still many ports crying out for investigation and there is much still to be achieved in research on Jewish population that established themselves where *terra firma* meets the ocean.

NOTES

1. David Cesarani (ed.), *Port Jews: Jewish Communities in Cosmopolitan Maritime Trading Centres, 1550–1950* (London: Frank Cass, 2002).
2. David Sorkin, 'The Port Jew: Notes Towards a Social Type', *Journal of Jewish Studies* 50.1 (Spring 1999), 87–97; and idem, 'Port Jews and the Three Regions of Emancipation', in Cesarani (see note 1), pp.31–46.
3. Lois Dubin, *The Port Jews of Habsburg Trieste* (Stanford, CA: Stanford University Press, 1999); and idem, 'Trieste and Berlin: The Italian Role in the Cultural Politics of the Haskalah', in J. Katz (ed.), *Towards Modernity: The European Jewish Model* (New Brunswick, NJ: Associated University Press of America, 1987), pp.189–224. See also idem, 'Researching Port Jews and Port Jewries: Trieste and Beyond', in Cesarani (see note 1), pp.47–58.
4. See also Dubin, 'Researching Port Jews and Port Jewries' (note 3), pp.47–58.
5. See David Cesarani, 'Conclusion: Future Research on Port Jews', in Cesarani (see note 1), pp.197–8.
6. See ibid.
7. Lois Dubin, 'Port Jewry in the Collective: Reflections on Individual, Community and Nation in the Study of Port Jews', keynote lecture at the conference on 'Port Jews and Jewish Communities in Cosmopolitan and Maritime Trading Centres', Kaplan Centre, Cape Town, 5 January 2003. See also her contribution to this volume: '"Wings on their feet … and wings on their head": Reflections on the Study of Port Jews', pp.14–30.
8. See David Cesarani, 'The Forgotten Port Jews of London: Court Jews Who Were Also Port Jews', in Cesarani (see note 1), pp.111–24.

'Wings on their feet ... and wings on their head': Reflections on the Study of Port Jews

LOIS C. DUBIN

Introduction

Reflecting yet again on port Jews evokes a number of arresting images and phrases about commerce, merchants and the sea. In 1807, a French émigré to the Habsburg free port of Trieste described its busy merchants and ship-owners pursuing their 'steady work ... in the shade of the caduceus of Mercury and the trident of Neptune', that is, as inspired and protected by the Roman gods of commerce and the sea.[1] Mercury's particular qualities were highlighted by Joseph Penso de la Vega in his treatise on the Amsterdam stock exchange, *Confusion de Confusiones* (1688):

> Mercurius, the god of merchants, is rightly portrayed with wings on head and feet. For, although some merchants have neither head nor feet, most seem to have wings on their feet witnessing the speed with which they move about and wings on their head considering the flight of their thoughts ...[2]

The winged sandals and hat of Mercury thus represent movement and speed, of both foot and of mind, as quintessential qualities of merchants.

Indeed, movement and speed, and distance and strangeness, lie at the heart of the commercial enterprise. The *Oxford English Dictionary* offers a seventeenth-century usage (1631) for 'merchant' that stresses the sea and travel: 'He is properly called a Marchant ... who passeth over the Seas ... and from thence transports merchandise'. We may recall the sea voyages of medieval Jewish merchants: in real life, those of David son of Maimon (brother of the better-known scholar Moses Maimonides), who lost his life at sea in 1173 while plying the family business between Cairo and Indian Ocean ports; and in fiction, in A.B. Yehoshua's *A Journey to the End of the Millennium* (1998), the commercial voyages of Ben Attar and Raphael Abulafia from Tangiers all the way round Spain to the distant, vastly different northern world of Paris and the Rhineland.[3] The early modern English phrases 'merchant traveller', 'merchant venturer' and 'merchant stranger' highlight two salient facts about merchant life in the past: (1) merchants often travelled long distances to convey their goods to places where these would be scarce, and hence precious and profitable; (2) it was the merchant's job to take the near far and to bring the far near; in so doing, merchant-travellers often ventured afar, or came from afar, as strangers or foreigners. In the wide-ranging *Cross-Cultural Trade in World History*, Philip Curtin noted that the Greek Hermes, many of whose qualities Mercury inherited, was god both of trade and of the boundary stones that separated one city from another.[4] Merchants were often boundary-crossers, and communities of merchants in trade diasporas were often cross-cultural brokers: as they brought goods from one zone to another, they also mediated between one culture and another.

By piquing our imaginations, these images can help stimulate some fresh thinking about port Jews. My goal is to place in perspective what David Sorkin and I respectively had in mind in our first formulations of the port Jew concept; to reflect upon the ensuing work done by others in this burgeoning sub-field of Jewish history; and to draw attention to some hitherto neglected elements.[5] In my view, we ought to distinguish more clearly, if possible, between the respective roles of Neptune and Mercury, that is, between the sea and commerce, in the experience of port Jews. We ought to focus more on the 'wings on their feet', that is, on movement and distance, exchange and networks, which are the nitty-gritty of international commerce.[6] And we ought to raise questions about the 'wings on their head' and the 'flight of their thoughts', that is, about the often perplexing relations between commerce, culture and cosmopolitanism. Does further analysis of port Jews show that mercantile societies foster particular habits of mind or values? Does it suggest that mercantile societies promote open-mindedness toward Others? Finally, we ought to pay attention to the communal dimensions of port Jew existence, that is, to *port Jews* and *port Jewries* in the collective and not only to *the port Jew* in the singular, for the structure and status of the Jewish communities in which port Jews lived were important. At this stage, I aim to open up more questions than answers as we think about what might be involved in the study of port Jews.

Port Jews: Definitions and Delineation

Let's refresh our memories with the concept of port Jews that arose a few years ago in conversations between David Sorkin and myself. In the course of writing my book, *The Port Jews of Habsburg Trieste: Absolutist Politics and Enlightenment Culture*,[7] I coined the term 'port Jews' to refer to the acculturated Jewish merchants in dynamic port cities who seemed to tread a distinctive path toward integration in early modern Europe. I intended the term to highlight both the location and function of Jews engaged in international maritime commerce, in settings in which commerce was valued and their commercial prowess appreciated. I hoped that the rhyme port–court, as more than a mere play on words, would stimulate comparison and contrast with the well-known court Jews. Later, Tullia Catalan of Trieste highlighted the play on words in German: *Hofjuden* and *Hafenjuden*, court Jews and port Jews.

Through my detailed case study of the free port of Trieste, I analysed how the perceived utility of Jewish merchants, and the commercial and communal structures instituted by the Habsburg state, led to significant benefits and privileges for Jews. Their particularly favourable civil and legal status was encapsulated by the phrase 'almost all the privileges and equalities with the rest of the population' used by Governor Karl von Zinzendorf of Trieste in 1781.[8] I considered the continuum with other early modern port Jew communities significant, but my primary concern was to elucidate the relations between this port Jewry and civil improvement in the circumstances of late eighteenth-century Enlightenment and reforming absolutism.

In his seminal article 'The Port Jew: Notes Toward a Social Type', David Sorkin drew broad implications from the notion of port Jews on the canvas of modern Jewish history. Focusing mainly on the western Sephardic diaspora in the emerging Atlantic ports of Amsterdam, Hamburg, Bordeaux and London, he explicitly contrasted these mercantile societies and their Jewish merchants to the more agrarian north-central European ones and their Ashkenazic court Jews. He argued that the port Jew represented 'a particular experience of early modern Europe and a particular path to modernity'.[9] In his later article 'Port Jews and the Three Regions of Emancipation', he argued that the benefits port Jews enjoyed from the economic and political freedoms of commercial cities and societies provided an early and distinctive path to Emancipation, a path that was characteristic of and distinctive to western Europe, and fundamentally different from those of central and eastern Europe.[10]

In his delineation of the port Jew as a social type, David Sorkin abstracted five distinguishing factors from the western Sephardic experience: (1) migration and commerce; (2) the valuation of commerce; (3) legal status: he generalised that port Jews did not live in autonomous Jewish communities, but rather in voluntary associations or merchant corporations; (4) re-education and *haskalah* (Enlightenment) *avant la lettre*, that is, education of former *conversos* about normative rabbinic Judaism and intellectual-cultural involvement with surrounding non-Jewish society; and (5) identity and belief: that is, adherence to ethnic identity and non-religious forms of communal solidarity rather than strict religious observance, an identity at times accompanied by sceptical, rationalist, even deistic challenges to Jewish belief of the sort associated with Uriel Da Costa and Benedict Spinoza.

However, I think it important to sound some cautionary notes about these five characteristics as a definition of port Jews. To my mind, the last three features are critically important when describing early modern west European Sephardic communities comprised substantially of Iberian former New Christians, but they are not necessarily integral to port Jews as such. For example, concerning the third characteristic, the Jewish community in Trieste was not voluntary, nor was it in Livorno, Salonica or Constantinople, to name but a few other obvious examples. Concerning the fourth characteristic, re-education into normative Judaism was necessary only among former New Christians. Concerning the fifth, might not the combination of ethnic solidarity and rationalist scepticism be seen primarily as a result of the former New Christian experience? Would it be as likely to arise in other port Jew communities and circumstances? Indeed, when we look for common elements among other port Jewries, it might make sense to separate the two aspects, ethnic solidarity and rationalist scepticism, and to search for each independently. In general, we should not equate port Jews with western Sephardim *tout court*. Nor can we forget the port Jews who were Italians or Sephardim in the eastern Mediterranean.

Drawing on my research on Trieste and reflecting on other port Jewries, I propose a somewhat different list of features to define early modern port Jews. I would highlight:

(1) location in a dynamic maritime trading centre that was part of a society or polity that valued international commerce;
(2) perception by others of Jewish commercial aptitude and hence utility;
(3) invitation or acceptance of Jewish merchants along with other non-Jewish merchants for the purpose of developing commerce;
(4) a relatively favourable legal and civil status for Jewish merchants, roughly comparable to that of other merchant groups, though not necessarily in all respects; and
(5) a Jewish self-consciousness with a strong degree of relation, that is, (a) a keen sense of connection to, and network with, other Jewish merchants living elsewhere, merchants who were kin or business partners, often both, and also sometimes potential immigrants, and (b) also a keen sense of interaction and comparison to other non-Jewish merchants in the given port city.

A similar methodological question confronts these efforts to define port Jews: how to generalise from particular cases? How to abstract the common and general from individual cases which always have distinctive elements to them? In other words, how to take the Sephardic former New Christian or the Habsburg-Mediterranean Triestine out of the port Jew admixture? The plan of this volume is to multiply individual examples so as to provide a greater base for comparison and contrast, clarification and generalisation.

Port Jews: Roots and Routes

Though with somewhat differing emphases, David Sorkin and I had shared similar concerns. From our perspectives as historians of modern Jewish culture and politics, we had seen port Jews through the prism of Jewish integration in early modern Europe and the related issues of acculturation and emancipation. We discerned a phenomenon not described in most standard works of modern Jewish historiography: that is, a positive evaluation of Jewish merchants for their commercial activities that was translated into a favourable civil and legal status, and acceptance of their socio-cultural behaviour.[11] In a sense, in viewing Jewish merchants in Trieste and the great Atlantic ports, we unwittingly echoed Isaac Euchel's imaginary Jewish traveller who exclaimed about eighteenth-century Livorno:

> The Jews in Livorno live together in calm and security in fine houses amidst the nobles of the land, and their houses are stone-built and most of its people are merchants and notables. Most of them shave their beards and style their hair, there is no difference between their dress and that of the [other] inhabitants. They speak the language of the people correctly and eloquently like one of their orators ... They dwell peacefully and quietly, and they pursue every occupation and business their hearts desire. My heart gladdens and I am proud to see my brothers living securely amidst the Gentiles without foe or troublemaker.[12]

In certain commercial societies, we saw a relatively favourable status for Jews, obtained by way of *ancien régime* privilege yet constituting a significant route toward parity and eventual legal equality. Indeed, the first Emancipation decreed by the French National Assembly in January 1790, that of the Sephardic Jews of south-western France, predicated the rights of active citizenship upon *ancien régime* privilege: '[T]hey shall continue to enjoy the same rights they have hitherto enjoyed, and which have been granted to them by letters of patent'.[13] Sorkin argued that Emancipation in western Europe simply cannot be understood without the concept or social type of the port Jew.

Scholarly response has been positive to the concept of port Jews as a significant phenomenon in early modern Jewish history and to the claim of their distinctive path toward becoming rooted, integrated and emancipated. But now, beckoned by the active and versatile Hermes-Mercury – god of commerce, messenger of the gods, the god on the move with winged sandals and winged hat – I am led to a somewhat paradoxical reflection. What had powerfully struck David Sorkin and me about early modern port Jews was their positive image and trajectory to improved civil-legal standing. In other words, we were concerned with how Jewish merchants settled down and became permanent residents, recognised subjects and ultimately citizens in a given city or polity. In effect, we were viewing port Jews as resident subjects or citizens in the making. We were not concerned primarily with the ongoing migration or movement of Jewish merchants and their goods or with the nitty-gritty of commercial exchange and travel.

Thus, in emphasising the processes by which port Jews became rooted and integrated, we may have neglected some fundamental features of the mercantile world and experience: movement, fluidity, travel, strangeness, crossing regions and bridging cultures. We may have seen port Jews too much as settled and fixed in a given locale rather than as travellers, strangers, boundary-crossers and cultural brokers, as purveyors of products and often much more between different points, between far and near. We ought to remember the 'wings on the feet' of port Jews.

The Trident of Neptune or the Caduceus of Mercury?

At the first Port Jew conference in Southampton, a debate arose whether to limit the port Jew concept to the original early modern European paradigm or to extend it to Jewish merchants in port cities in other times and places. The question was also raised whether there ought to be a distinction between 'port Jews' and 'Jews in port cities', in other words between international Jewish merchants and Jews who pursued other occupations in port cities.[14] I am among those who seek to broaden our investigations of port Jews beyond early modern Europe. To do so responsibly, I urge us to think beyond the initial categories of integration and emancipation. If we recognise the relevance of several other subjects and disciplines to the study of port Jews – for example, geography, maritime history, urban history, trade and commerce, communication and technology, minorities in plural societies, and diaspora studies – then we can draw on these fields to fructify our thinking and to spur us in developing new questions in our analyses of port Jews.[15]

At the outset, I propose that we address a fundamental issue: Neptune or Mercury? Though seaport location and international commerce were intricately connected for port Jews, is it possible for heuristic purposes to separate the two elements of sea and commerce? If we try to do so, toward which issues will the trident of Neptune beckon, and toward which the staff of Mercury?

If we focus on maritime location, that is, Jews in port cities or Jews at sea, then we might consider Jews of diverse circumstances and social strata whose lives and livelihoods were affected by the sea in different ways. If we focus on seaports as such, then Jewish dockworkers and stevedores come into our purview, especially in cities such as Salonica, Odessa, Haifa and Ashdod. Besides international merchants, we would investigate Jews as seafarers and Jews as ship-builders.[16] As Tony Kushner suggested with regard to Jews in Portsmouth and Southampton, we might wish to consider transmigrants during the mass migrations of the nineteenth and twentieth centuries, and those who managed and serviced this vast shipping enterprise of human cargo.[17] We might also pay attention to the role of Jews in the international slave trade, and to the so-called white slave trade, that is, the transport of women for prostitution.

If we attend seriously to the location of port Jews in port cities and to the organisation of space in port cities, then we would heed the advice of geographer Brian Hoyle to consider changing patterns of interface between ports and cities and also to evolving stages of technology and communications.[18] While still in Neptune's watery domain, we might consider river and lake ports – in addition to seaports – as possible venues for port Jewries. And venturing beyond water currents to those of air and wind above, might we find it useful to think also about cities that serve as hubs of air transport?

With this last speculation, we have perhaps begun to transfer our allegiance from Neptune to Mercury, insofar as we focus our considerations of port Jews less on the site of the sea and more on the function of exchange. Are there aspects of port Jewish communities that seem due more to commerce and exchange per se rather than to maritime location? My intention here is not to rehearse the well-known subjects of Jews and commerce, Jews as middlemen, or Jews and capitalism. Rather, it is to urge us to pay attention to port cities as entrepôts and hubs of exchange, primarily of goods, but also of people, ideas and information.

Let us remember that Hermes-Mercury was god of the boundary stones as well as god of commerce. Trade always brings together at least two disparate worlds, the world of one product with a world that does not have it but has something else to give in exchange. Trade often takes place at boundaries between different worlds: between different physical worlds, and between the states of having and not having, between possession and desire. When we think of trade as crossing boundaries and bridging worlds, then we are tempted to think of land as well as sea, that is, of the interface of desert and cultivated area at desert ports as well as the interface of sea and shore at seaports.

Ancient, medieval and modern Jewish history offers many examples of Jews engaged in long-distance trade both on land and on sea, and trading at different kinds of commercial crossroads. What comparisons and contrasts can be drawn between port Jews and long-distance Jewish land traders? Jonathan Goldstein finds many features of Sorkin's port Jew model in the inland Siberian trading centre of Harbin rather than in Far Eastern seaports.[19] Perhaps we should also look at inland commercial cities such as Aleppo, Brody, Tashkent and Samarkand. We might compare free ports to inland free trade cities. And we might contrast both of these to cities that hosted annual trade fairs, and thereby served intermittently as commercial entrepôts. Finally, if we remember Mercury's function as messenger of the gods, purveyor of information, and consider the function of ports as sites for the exchange of information, then we might want to think of today's electronic ports and portals. We might ask: have Jews played a significant role in the Silicon Valleys, in the centres that built and sustain the virtual networks of our contemporary world? Can there be electronic port Jews?

'Wings on their feet': Commerce, Movement and Networks

From these wide-ranging questions, some offered in a spirit of playful speculation, let us return to the empirical realities of commercial exchange. Whether conducted by strangers bearing wares from afar, or by venturers heading off to do the same, or by financiers organising the merchant-travellers, international commerce involves the conveying of goods from one point to another, from a here to a there. Commerce generates movement: of goods, financial instruments, services and information. Colin Renfrew has defined trade as 'action at a distance'.[20] Jeremy Adelman and Stephen Aron state that 'Commerce sets worlds in motion', in effect echoing Joseph Penso de la Vega's comment on speed, flight and movement.[21]

When we look again at the early modern Sephardic port Jews, we cannot help but be struck by the constancy of movement in their lives. As exiles and refugees, many moved restlessly from one home to another: variously back and forth in Christian lands, Muslim lands; in the Mediterranean ranging from Iberia, to Italy, to North Africa, to the Levant; to the west European Atlantic seaboard; to colonial possessions in the New World or the Far East. With families far-flung across countries and continents, the Sephardic world was one of both people and goods on the move.[22]

The movement of commerce involves at least one dyadic relationship, for there must be a trading partner at the other end with whom to exchange goods. Indeed, international commerce involves many connections and requires a whole network of relationships, both at home and abroad. One network is comprised of those in ancillary occupations such as brokerage, record keeping, finance and insurance. Even more fundamentally, a merchant needs reliable trading partners. As Adelman and Aron put it, connections were important: 'In worlds without formal institutions of credit, business practices rested on personal ties. No trader was better than his or her reputation or networks'.[23] In medieval and early modern times, family was often the connecting tissue of commercial networks; kinship and ethnic-religious ties were those that structured patterns of commerce and forged trading diasporas. For example, Evelyne Oliel-Grausz's work on the Sephardic diaspora has stressed networks of family and communication, while Benjamin Braude has highlighted the ethnic division of trade in the sixteenth and seventeenth-century Ottoman Balkans.[24]

How can greater attention to movement, connections and networks inform our study of port Jews? Let us remember that it was precisely their networks that made port Jews valuable, that is, networks of commerce forged by kin and community at home and abroad. Accordingly, I would suggest that we not limit our purview solely to the local dimension of port Jewries, that is, to a port Jewry 'embedded' within its own locale or polity.[25] Rather, bearing movement and relationship always in mind, we should see a port Jewry as a node in a broader network. For example, Daniel Swetchinski urged that Portuguese Jews in seventeenth-century Amsterdam be viewed sometimes as part of an Amsterdam–Hamburg–Antwerp–London–Rouen network; at other times as part of the Amsterdam–Italy (Florence–Livorno)–Iberian (Madrid–Lisbon) network; and yet at others as part of the networks linking western Europe to Dutch colonial possessions in the Caribbean, Africa and Asia.[26] Some Jewish networks comprised Jews of different ethnic origins. In contrast, some of the Portuguese networks were religiously diverse insofar as they included Jews, New Christians and people whose religious-communal affiliation fluctuated somewhere between the two. And as Francesca Trivellato has demonstrated, a network could maintain long-lasting commercial ties across religious, communal and cultural lines, as in the case of the coral–diamond trade conducted by Jews, Italian Catholics and Hindus in seventeenth and eighteenth-century Livorno, Lisbon and Goa.[27]

Awareness of distance, movement, communication and networks takes us beyond the fixedness and embeddedness of a port Jewry in its local environment. Thus our perspective on port Jews needs a dual focus: both on the locality and on the larger networks at sea and on land. We cannot understand the world of a particular port Jewry without its hinterland and without its broad networks of kin and commerce. In the study of port Jews, we should be prepared to connect the local, the regional and the global.

Community and Communities

Attention to networks reinforces the emphasis I place on community or the collective in the study of port Jews.[28] As Sorkin argued, the port Jew as an individual does stand out as a distinct social type when compared to a court Jew or a *maskil* (enlightened Jew). Still, in my view, we also need to consider port Jews in the plural, and the agglomeration of port Jews in a given city as a collective port Jewry.

First, to be effective commercially, a Jewish merchant needed a community and a network. Further, as stated above, though the western Sephardic communities tended to be structured legally as voluntary communities, many other port Jew communities in the early modern period were not, notably Livorno, Trieste, Salonica and Constantinople. Moreover, in Livorno, the

Jewish lay leaders exercised some of the most extensive powers of self-government ever accorded a Jewish community.[29] Community – as both a legal and social reality – was vitally important for early modern Jews generally and was certainly not anachronistic or irrelevant for port Jews. Thus, we ought to look at how diverse kinds of legal arrangements in different polities and periods allowed Jewish communities to structure the lives of port Jews. Did differing legal forms of community – autonomous, voluntary or some combination – contribute to significant variations in port Jewries?

Reflections on networks of commerce and kin raise a different set of questions about community. Of course, Jews were not the only merchants organized in ethnic trading networks. Nor were they the only merchant communities in thriving port cities in early modern Europe.[30] Should we not compare port Jews to other groups engaged in maritime commerce, especially to those also defined as religious-ethnic minorities, such as the Greek Orthodox in eastern and south-eastern Europe and the Chinese in Southeast Asia?[31] Indeed, for comparison and contrast with port Jews, we can entertain thoughts not only of port Greeks and port Chinese but also port Lombards, port Huguenots, port Armenians, port Lebanese and port Indians – and no doubt others – from different times and places. And, besides the inevitable competition between merchant groups, we should, as mentioned above, be alert to the possibility of inter-ethnic commercial networks.

Such comparative work may help us address a difficult and thorny question in Jewish history. Daniel Swetchinski analysed the self-perception of the Portuguese Jews in Amsterdam as both an 'association of religious exiles' and as a 'colony of foreign merchants'.[32] His formulation points to a fundamental issue: what is attributable to Jews being a religious-ethnic group, and what is attributable to their frequent economic and social role as merchants? For most Jewish historians, religious-ethnic categories tend to predominate. Perhaps our investigations of port Jews and other mercantile groups will enable us to deploy more deftly both sets of categories: Jews as merchants as well as Jews as religious believers/communal members.

'Wings on their head': Commerce, Culture and Cosmopolitanism

Let us return to the image of 'wings on their head' and the 'flight of their thoughts'. How can we understand the wings on merchants' heads? To put it in slightly different terms, do such wings foster particular habits of mind, values or culture among merchants? Do mercantile societies produce certain kinds of culture? And if so, what might be the connection between mercantile cultures and benevolent, tolerant or inclusive attitudes toward Others? We should note that at the first Port Jew conference, several scholars cautioned against hasty assumptions in such matters.[33]

'Wings on their head' implies consciousness of the distant. Merchants always have distant places on their minds, the origin or destination for their goods. Maritime merchants' horizons also include the perils of the vast and often storm-tossed sea. As *The Merchant of Venice* put it: 'Your mind is tossing on the ocean'.[34] Whether through experience, report or imagination, a merchant's consciousness contains the sights and smells, the manners and mores, of distant markets and cultures. Merchants must ask: what's happening there? How do they do things there? In our day, the trader in New York must know what has happened in Tokyo and London and Frankfurt before making the first move of the day.

Thus, awareness of distance and difference are givens for international merchants. Might a merchant's broad commercial horizons lead to other kinds of broad horizons? How might awareness of distance translate into consciousness and appreciation of difference? How might commerce foster cosmopolitanism?

First, however, we must address the question of merchants and culture: do merchants tend to have particular styles of culture? We will dispense with the criticism of those who argue – usually in anti-modernist terms – that merchants are too materialistic or fast-paced, in fact that they lack soul or culture altogether. Rather, let's consider the observations of Edward Whiting Fox in his book *History in Geographic Perspective: The Other France*, in which he distinguished between two kinds of society in France: one based on large land areas and subsistence farming, and the other based in port cities and on maritime commerce such as Bordeaux. He argued that commerce does produce its own kind of culture because it

> depends on written records and instructions, which require literacy; involves travel, which invites observation, discussion, and comparison; and deals with other independent and frequently distant merchants, which encourages negotiation and compromise.[35]

Yes, Hermes was messenger of the gods and the god of eloquence, with words and by extension literacy certainly his tools. Fox characterised the cultural styles prevalent in commercial cities as 'urbane, tolerant, skeptical, and pragmatic'.[36] Parenthetically, are not coastal port cities, notably New York and San Francisco to cite two obvious American examples, often considered more open and liberal, sophisticated and cutting-edge, than most inland cities not enmeshed in webs of international commerce?

The features identified by Fox as characteristic of commercial cities – literacy, urbanity and scepticism – dovetail with those cited by Robin Cohen as necessary survival skills for diasporic communities, both past and present: awareness and sensitive antennae to surrounding currents. In his view, these qualities of awareness and knowledge often enable diasporas 'to act as a bridge between the particular and the universal ... [and] as interlocutors in commerce and administration'; they may also result in 'cosmopolitanism or humanism' and may lead to over-representation in the arts, media and entertainment worlds.[37] It would seem that both commerce and diaspora might foster cultural life and production.

We might apply some of these considerations to port Jews when we approach the questions of Jewish enlightenment and acculturation pursued by Steven Zipperstein on Odessa, Robert Cohen on Surinam, and Daniel Swetchinski on Amsterdam.[38] In such mercantile communities, these considerations are surely relevant to the analysis of knowledge of languages, patterns of cultural consumption and production, inventories of private libraries, educational choices, patterns of dress, behaviour, leisure time and social activities. Further, we may ask: to what degree did port Jews actively pursue non-economic contact with non-Jews? How similar were the cultural profile and behaviour of a particular port Jewry to those of other merchants in their city?

Moreover, port Jews did sometimes function as cultural mediators or brokers. For example, in Amsterdam, the Sephardim had the linguistic skills and cultural experience to be a bridge between Iberians and Dutch, and in the Ottoman Empire between Europeans and Ottoman authorities. Like Mercury, these Jewish merchants were classic boundary-crossers and cross-cultural brokers. Difference was a daily feature of their lives and worlds.

Still, I wonder: when the behaviour of port Jews resembled that of other groups, how aware were they of such similarities and how did they evaluate them? How much commonality across group lines were they prepared to admit? Do cross-cultural brokers necessarily have positive evaluations of the different bridged cultures, or might they have merely pragmatic utilitarian views towards them? If they became cosmopolitans – if for example a Triestine Jewish merchant followed the advice of Italo Svevo's father to learn four languages – did they become so out of necessity, or with enthusiasm? Should we not put aside facile assumptions of deliberate or enthusiastic cosmopolitanism, and at least try to grasp what purely pragmatic, matter-of-fact or indeed 'reluctant cosmopolitanism' might mean?[39]

Commerce, Cosmopolitanism and Politics

Having asked how cultural brokering may be viewed by those engaged in it, let us now consider how others may view it. When might boundary crossing be seen as positive and pioneering, and when rather as negative and transgressive? At the outset, I reminded us that a merchant was often a stranger. When is the stranger exotic and exciting, and when rather frightening or alien? Curtin notes that dislike of merchants has often been tied to distrust of foreigners, and that 'the interests of the hosts and the strangers alike suggest that a slightly distant contact was the most desirable relationship'.[40] Thus it was not surprising that merchants were often segregated in their own quarters. Where such distrust existed in early modern European port cities, how was it managed? And what kinds of situations, structures and dynamics tended to activate distrust of the Other in multi-ethnic settings? In other words, when, for example, in a city such as Odessa or Salonica, would Jews and Greeks cooperate with one another in commercial enterprises? And when might they shun one another, or worse?

Several demographic, economic and political factors are relevant to these questions of inter-group cooperation, competition or fear among merchants. Is the plural mercantile stratum of a city or society comprised of one majority and one minority, or of several different religious-ethnic minorities? Is the economy growing or contracting, both in reality and perception? Of prime importance are political factors: does one group enjoy particular proximity or access to the ruling authorities? Does the port city develop as a planned economic venture by the state? If the state is a prime actor in the commercial sphere, then what is the nature of the state: a local city state independent of other jurisdictions, such as Venice and Hamburg, or is the port city also the capital, such as London, or is the port city governed by a distant imperial centre, as were Trieste and Odessa?[41] Or indeed, does the state appear as a foreign power making inroads by negotiated concession, or by conquest, or by importing a foreign ethnic community sometimes to the detriment of the indigenous population? Crucially, is the political order a pre-modern dynastic empire, or a modern nation state, or an emerging nation state – often the most sensitive of all? Is the state one that aspires toward ethnic homogeneity or toward ethnic diversity?

It is beyond the scope of this essay to answer these many questions about commerce, culture and cosmopolitanism. For the moment, I would say that merchants must have 'wings on their heads', but those wings do not automatically put them benevolently inside others' heads or hearts, or enable them to take flight from the realities of their earthbound society and polity. We must always contextualise the question of commerce and cosmopolitanism. What was the touchstone of tolerance at the time: the absence of persecution, or the absence of discrimination?[42] Attitudes toward Others is surely one of the ways in which merchants, port Jews and those around them remained most earthbound and most embedded in their particular time and place, society and ideology. For example, Jonathan Schorsh's findings that Sephardic Jews in the early modern Atlantic world shared many of the racialist assumptions prevalent in their day should not be surprising; these attitudes could be seen as a sign of their acculturation.[43] Cosmopolitanism does not necessarily mean tolerance or preclude racism.

Conclusions

I hope these many questions have not produced another *Confusion de Confusiones*. Rather, my goal has been analysis: to break up the subject of port Jews into many discrete pieces, to spin out questions and speculations so that we can ponder together how to extend our notions of port Jews. As important as the original port Jew concept is for early modern European Jewish history, I think it is a fecund concept beyond that. If extending it produces variation, so be it. I do not think we need one single model of port Jews.

As we begin to accumulate several diverse examples of port Jewries and to engage in wide-ranging comparisons, we are moving beyond the particulars of western Sephardic former New Christians and of free port Habsburg Trieste. We will need to sort out the dualities of Neptune's sea and Mercury's commerce, of roots and routes, of localities and broader webs of relation. We will have to pay more attention to fluidity, movement, communication and networks. And we shall be obliged to probe further the interrelations between commerce, politics, culture and cosmopolitanism so that we can better contextualise and understand mercantile attitudes and relations. The challenge is to grasp the connections between Mercury's winged sandals and winged hat, between the wings on port Jews' feet and the wings on their heads.

NOTES

This written text generally preserves the flavour of the original oral version, delivered as the keynote lecture at the conference in Cape Town. I would like to thank Holly Snyder and Francesca Trivellato for bibliographic guidance on the study of trade, and Kenneth Stow for suggestions for revisions. I am especially grateful to my husband and colleague Benjamin Braude for his close reading of this essay, and for his sharing many thoughts on Jewish economic history with me over the years.

1. Charles Albert Comte de Moré, in Oscar de Incontrera, *Trieste e l'America* (Trieste: Edizioni dello Zibaldone, 1960), pp.99–101.

2. Daniel M. Swetchinski, *Reluctant Cosmopolitans: The Portuguese Jews of Seventeenth-Century Amsterdam* (London and Portland, OR: Littman Library of Jewish Civilization, 2000), p.278.

3. On David Maimonides, see Isadore Twersky, *A Maimonides Reader* (New York: Behrman House, 1972), pp.4–5; A.B. Yehoshua, *A Journey to the End of the Millennium: A Novel of the Middle Ages* [1998], trans. Nicholas De Lange (San Diego, New York, London: Harcourt, 1999). More generally, see S.D. Goitein (ed. and trans.), *Letters of Medieval Jewish Traders* (Princeton, NJ: Princeton University Press, 1974).

4. Philip D. Curtin, *Cross-Cultural Trade in World History* (Cambridge: Cambridge University Press, 1984), p.2.

5. Our first formulations appeared in David Sorkin, 'The Port Jew: Notes Toward a Social Type', *Journal of Jewish Studies* 50.1 (1999), 87–97; and Lois C. Dubin, *The Port Jews of Habsburg Trieste: Absolutist Politics and Enlightenment Culture*, Stanford Studies in Jewish History and Culture (Stanford, CA: Stanford University Press, 1999). The University of Southampton conference on Port Jews held in June 2001 resulted in David Cesarani (ed.), *Port Jews: Jewish Communities in Cosmopolitan Maritime Trading Centres, 1550–1950*, published both as a special issue of *Jewish*

Culture and History 4.2 (2001), and as a separate volume (London and Portland, OR: Frank Cass, 2002). For further elaborations of the Port Jew concept, see Lois Dubin, 'Researching Port Jews and Port Jewries: Trieste and Beyond', and David Sorkin, 'Port Jews and the Three Regions of Emancipation', both in Cesarani (ed.), *Port Jews*, pp.47–58 and 31–46, respectively. This keynote address refers throughout to the several valuable case studies in this volume.

6. See now the section on merchant networks, 'Réseaux marchands', *Annales* 58:3 (2003), 567–672, especially the introduction by Anthony Molho and Diogo Ramada Curto, 'Les réseaux marchands à l'époque moderne', pp.569–79.

7. See note 5 above.

8. Lois Dubin, 'Between Toleration and 'Equalities': Jewish Status and Community in Pre-Revolutionary Europe', *Jahrbuch des Simon-Dubnow-Instituts / Simon Dubnow Institute Yearbook* 1 (2002), 219–34.

9. Sorkin, 'The Port Jew' (see note 5), p.97.

10. Sorkin, 'Port Jews and the Three Regions of Emancipation' (see note 5).

11. Salo W. Baron did of course call attention to the role of economic factors, commerce and modern capitalism: see *A Social and Religious History of the Jews*, 3 vols. (New York: Columbia University Press, 1937), vol.2, pp.164–90; and 'Newer Approaches to Jewish Emancipation', *Diogenes* 29 (1960), 56–81. See also Jonathan I. Israel, *European Jewry in the Age of Mercantilism 1550–1750*, 3rd edn. (London and Portland, OR: Littman Library of Jewish Civilization, 1998).

12. [Isaac Euchel], 'Igrot Meshulam ben Uriah ha-Eshtemoi' [Letters of Meshulam son of Uriah the Eshtamoan] *Ha-Measef* 6 (1789–90), 173–4.

13. 28 January 1790 decree, in Paul Mendes-Flohr and Jehuda Reinharz (eds.), *The Jew in the Modern World: A Documentary History*, 2nd edn. (New York and Oxford: Oxford University Press, 1995), p.117.

14. See, for example, David Cesarani, 'Port Jews: Concepts, Cases and Questions', and 'Conclusion: Future Research on Port Jews', both in Cesarani (see note 5), esp. pp.4–5, 9–10, 197.

15. To cite but a few pertinent works on trade and cities: Karl Polanyi, 'Traders and Trade', in Jeremy A. Sabloff and C.C. Lamberg-Karlovsky (eds.), *Ancient Civilization and Trade* (Albuquerque, NM: School of American Research, University of New Mexico Press, 1975), pp.133–54; Karl Polanyi, Conrad M. Arensberg and Harry W. Pearson (eds.), *Trade and Market in the Early Empires: Economies in History and Theory* (Glencoe: The Free Press, and Falcon's Wing Press, 1957); Abner Cohen, 'Cultural Strategies in the Organization of Trading Diasporas', in Claude Meillassoux (ed.), *The Development of Indigenous Trade and Markets in West Africa* (Oxford: Oxford University Press, for the International African Institute, 1971), pp.266–81; Richard Lawton and Robert Lee (eds.), *Population and Society in Western European Port-Cities c.1650–1939* (Liverpool: Liverpool University Press, 2002); Richard Fox, *Urban Anthropology: Cities in their Cultural Settings* (Englewood Cliffs, NJ: Prentice-Hall, 1977), on ports of entry and mercantile cities, discussed in David R. Ringrose, 'Capital Cities and their Hinterlands: Europe and the Colonial Dimension', in Peter Clark and Bernard Lepetit (eds.), *Capital Cities and their Hinterlands in Early Modern Europe* (Aldershot and Brookfield, VT: Scolar Press and Ashgate, 1996), pp.219–23; Franklin W. Knight and Peggy K. Liss (eds.), *Atlantic Port Cities: Economy, Culture, and Society in the Atlantic World, 1650–1850* (Knoxville, TN: University of Tennessee Press, 1991).

16. Nadav Kashtan, *Seafaring and the Jews* (London and Portland, OR: Frank Cass, 2001); and therein Benjamin Arbel, 'Shipping and Toleration: The Emergence of Jewish Shipowners in the Early Modern Period', pp.56–71.

17. Tony Kushner, 'A Tale of Two Port Jewish Communities: Southampton and Portsmouth Compared', in Cesarani (see note 5), pp.87–110; see also his contribution to this volume, 'From Atlantic Hotel to Atlantic Park: Anglo-America, Port Jews and the Invisible Transmigrant', pp.247–60.

18. Brian Hoyle, 'Fields of Tension: Development Dynamics at the Port-City Interface', in Cesarani (see note 5), pp.12–30.

19. Jonathan Goldstein, 'The Sorkin and Golab Theses and Their Applicability to South, Southeast, and East Asian Port Jewry', in Cesarani (see note 5), pp.179–96.

20. Colin Renfrew, 'Trade as Action at a Distance: Questions of Integration and Communication',

in Sabloff and Lamberg-Karlovsky (see note 15), pp.3–59.

21. Jeremy Adelman and Stephen Aron (eds.), *Trading Cultures: The Worlds of Western Merchants*, Shelby Cullom Davis Center for Historical Studies, Princeton University (Turnhout, Belgium: Brepols, 2001), 'Introduction', pp.1–6.

22. Jonathan I. Israel, *Diasporas within a Diaspora: Jews, Crypto-Jews and the World Maritime Empires (1540–1740)* (Leiden, Boston, Köln: E.J. Brill, 2002).

23. Adelman and Aron, 'Introduction' (see note 21).

24. See, for example, Evelyne Oliel-Grausz's essay in this volume, 'Networks and Communication in the Sephardi Diaspora: An Added Dimension to the Concept of Port Jews and Port Jewries', pp.61–76; Benjamin Braude, 'Venture and Faith in the Commercial Life of the Ottoman Balkans, 1500–1650', *International History Review* 7.4 (1985), 519–42.

25. Adelman and Aron, 'Introduction' (see note 21).

26. Swetchinski (see note 2), pp.105–30.

27. Francesca Trivellato, 'Juifs de Livourne, Italiens de Lisbonne, hindous de Goa', *Annales* 58:3 (2003), pp.581–603. And see her contribution to this volume, 'The Port Jews of Livorno and their Global Networks of Trade in the Early Modern Period', pp.31–48.

28. Dubin, 'Researching Port Jews and Port Jewries' (see note 5), p.56.

29. See, for example, Carlotta Ferrara degli Uberti's essay in this volume, 'The "Jewish Nation" of Livorno: A Port Jewry on the Road to Emancipation', pp.157–70.

30. See, for example, Frédéric Mauro, 'Merchant Communities, 1350–1750', in James D. Tracy (ed.), *The Rise of Merchant Empires: Long-Distance Trade in the Early Modern World, 1350–1750* (Cambridge and New York: Cambridge University Press, 1990), pp.255–86; Roberta Garruccio, 'Il comportamento economico delle minoranze in prospettiva storica: un'introduzione metodologica', and Silvia Marzagalli, 'Città portuali e minoranze etniche: Amburgo, Bordeaux e Livorno tra Sette e Ottocento', *Archivi e imprese* 16 (1997), 231–44 and 365–83, respectively.

31. Maria Vassilikou, 'Greeks and Jews in Salonika and Odessa: Inter-ethnic Relations in Cosmopolitan Port Cities', in Cesarani (see note 5), 155–72; Daniel Chirot and Anthony Reid (eds.), *Essential Outsiders: Chinese and Jews in the Modern Transformation of Southeast Asia and Central Europe* (Seattle, WA and London: University of Washington Press, 1997).

32. Swetchinski (note 2 above), pp.184–5. Cf. Gershon Hundert's discussion of categories and terms for commercially active ethnic groups, 'An Advantage to Peculiarity? The Case of the Polish Commonwealth', *AJS Review* 6 (1981), 21–38.

33. See especially the essays by Jonathan Schorsch, 'Portmanteau Jews: Sephardim and Race in the Early Modern Atlantic World'; Rainer Liedtke, 'Germany's Door to the World: A Haven for the Jews? Hamburg, 1590–1933'; Tony Kushner (see note 17); David Cesarani, 'The Forgotten Port Jews of London: Court Jews Who Were Also Port Jews'; Mark Levene, 'Port Jewry of Salonika, Between Neo-colonialism and Nation-state'; and Maria Vassilikou (note 31); all in Cesarani (see note 5), pp.59–74, 75–86, 87–110, 111–24, 125–54 and 155–72, respectively. For more recent critical perspectives on cosmopolitanism, see now *History and Anthropology* 16.1 (2005), based on the conference 'Mediterranean Conundrums' (held at Freie Universität, Berlin, 2003), which appeared too late for me to incorporate into this essay.

34. William Shakespeare, *The Merchant of Venice*, Act I, Scene 1, cited in Braude (see note 24), p.519.

35. Edward Whiting Fox, *History in Geographic Perspective: The Other France* (New York: Norton, 1971), p.65.

36. Ibid., p.65.

37. Robin Cohen, *Global Diasporas: An Introduction* (Seattle, WA: University of Washington Press, 1997), p.170. Cf. Steven Vertovec and Robin Cohen (eds.), *Migration, Diasporas and Transnationalism* (Cheltenham and Northampton, MA: Elgar Reference Collection, International Library of Studies on Migration, 1999); and Robin Cohen and Steven Vertovec (eds.), *Conceiving Cosmopolitanism: Theory, Context, and Practice* (Oxford and New York: Oxford University Press, 2002).

38. Steven J. Zipperstein, The Jews of Odessa: A *Cultural History, 1794–1881* (Stanford, CA: Stanford University Press, 1985); Robert Cohen, *Jews in Another Environment: Surinam in the Second Half of the Eighteenth Century* (Leiden and New York: E.J. Brill, 1991); and Swetchinski (see note 2).

39. I am of course borrowing and transposing Swetchinski's phrase.
40. Curtin (see note 4), p.38.
41. Liedtke (see note 33); Cesarani (see note 33); Dubin, 'Researching Port Jews and Port Jewries (see note 5); John D. Klier, 'A Port, Not a Shtetl: Reflections on the Distinctiveness of Odessa'; and Maria Vassilikoui (see note 31); all in Cesarani (see note 5), pp.75–86, 111–24, 47–58, 173–78 and 155–72, respectively. See also Patricia Herlihy, 'Port Jews of Odessa and Trieste – A Tale of Two Cities', *Jahrbuch des Simon-Dubnow-Instituts/Simon Dubnow Institute Yearbook* 2 (2003), 183–98. On the impact of the state and politics, see also the wide-ranging M.N. Pearson, 'Merchants and States', in James D. Tracy (ed.), *The Political Economy of Merchant Empires: State Power and World Trade 1350–1750* (Cambridge: Cambridge University Press, 1991), pp.41–116; Perry Gauci, *The Politics of Trade: The Overseas Merchant in State and Society, 1660–1720* (Oxford and New York: Oxford University Press, 2001); and Levene (see note 33).
42. Benjamin Braude and Bernard Lewis (eds.), *Christians and Jews in the Ottoman Empire: The Functioning of a Plural Society*, 2 vols. (New York and London: Holmes and Meier, 1982), vol.1, Introduction.
43. Schorsch (see note 33).

The Port Jews of Livorno and their Global Networks of Trade in the Early Modern Period

FRANCESCA TRIVELLATO

In September 1767 Abraham, son of Jacob Baruch Carvaglio, a wealthy Sephardic merchant of Livorno, was about to marry Esther, daughter of Josef Belilios from Venice. Both the Baruch Carvaglio and the Belilios had moved from Venice to Livorno some 50 years before, and members of these two Jewish families had since then intermarried, thus consolidating the links between the two most important Sephardic communities of the Italian peninsula. In addition, the Belilios had relatives and business partners in Aleppo, and the Carvaglio sent one of their scions there in the 1740s. While the marriage of Abraham and Esther was being arranged, Jacob Baruch Carvaglio dictated his last will to a Christian notary of Livorno. He named as his heirs all sons born from the union of Abraham and Esther or 'from any other marriage that he [Abraham] would contrive with a woman of the Jewish Nation, of Portuguese or Spanish descent, born from parents living in Livorno, Venice, London, Amsterdam or Aleppo'.[1]

Baruch Carvaglio's will leaves us a strikingly precise and self-conscious definition of the ethnic and geographical boundaries of the group to which he belonged. Would the expression 'port Jews' have described his relatives and friends? And if so, who among his co-religionists involved in long-distance trade could be included in such a category – those in Italy and western Europe (Livorno, Venice, London and Amsterdam), or also those living in the Ottoman territories (Aleppo)? Available sources do not allow us to enter the mental world of these Sephardic merchants in search of straightforward answers, but they do provide us with indirect evidence of the creation and dissolution of several networks within the Sephardic diaspora that help us address these questions. In so doing, such evidence further complicates the concept of 'port Jews' as it has recently emerged in historiographical debates.

This expression appeared in works published by Lois Dubin and David Sorkin more or less simultaneously in the late 1990s. Dubin used the terms 'port Jews' and 'port Jewry' to capture some essential characteristics of the Jewish community of Trieste in the eighteenth century. By that time, the Jews in Trieste were no longer a tiny group of families who were given *ad personam* privileges (according to the court Jew model), but had become a larger settlement which negotiated their collective rights with the Habsburg rulers in light of the perceived economic utility of elite Jewish merchants.[2] The Jewish population of Trieste grew during the eighteenth century primarily because of immigration from neighbouring Venice and other localities: at the end of the century, with little over a thousand members, the Jewish community of Trieste comprised mostly Italian and Ashkenazi Jews, and only a small though increasing number of Sephardim.[3] Sorkin focused instead on European Atlantic ports such as Bordeaux, Hamburg, Amsterdam and London, and described the 'port Jew' (in the singular form) as a 'social type' who represents a particular form of Jewish modernisation and acculturation.[4] More recently, Dubin urged us to test the validity of these concepts regarding vital Sephardic settlements in other European as well as Ottoman port cities.[5] In taking up her exhortation, I will focus here on the Jewish community of Livorno in the period before emancipation, and stress both the striking similarities to and fundamental differences from the north-western European settlements examined by Sorkin. I will also call attention to the close ties that the Sephardim of Livorno forged with the Levant and North Africa, as well as the durable business relations that they entertained with non-Jews in the Portuguese commercial empire.

Indeed, no Sephardic community of the early modern period can be studied in isolation. If the legal, demographic and even socio-economic traits that it came to acquire largely derived from specific arrangements with local power and dominant society, the lives of Sephardic individuals, families and communities were closely interwoven into those of their relatives and co-religionists in places both near and far.[6] In attempting to articulate the experience of 'port Jews', we thus need to place more emphasis on the disaporic dimension of their social, economic and cultural existence. The commercial networks developed by the Sephardim of Livorno included lasting economic relations with merchants of different ethnic, religious and national origins. These cross-cultural business relations derived much of their solidity from the individual and communitarian interconnectedness of the Sephardim who participated in them. As I will try to show, concepts of 'trading diasporas' and 'trading networks' need to be integrated into a global vision of 'port Jews'.

The Port Jews of Early Modern Livorno

Livorno in the late seventeenth and early eighteenth centuries was both the most important Mediterranean port (before the rise of Marseilles in the 1720s) and home to the largest Sephardic settlement in the West together with Amsterdam. Its inclusion in any theoretical and empirical reflection about the notion of 'port Jews' is therefore imperative.

In 1591 and 1593 the Medici grand dukes of Tuscany issued two charters (known as *livornine*) granting Jewish families of Iberian descent willing to settle in Livorno privileges that had no equal in Christian Europe at the time, including tax exemptions, the right to own real estate in a town with no official ghetto, and (in 1593) extensive autonomy in self-government and administration of justice. These charters also forbade the Inquisition from interrogating Iberian refugees arriving in Livorno about their previous religious allegiance.[7] After an initial period of fluidity, this provision helped dispel crypto-Judaism. Between 1545 and 1591, attracted by special initiatives of the Medici, Portuguese New Christians had entered Tuscan society as Catholics and mingled with the Florentine elite, but after the *livornine* were issued, they mostly came to Livorno as Jews.[8] The rabbinical authorities of Livorno, seeking to enforce religious conformity among Iberian immigrants, required that boys or men not yet circumcised be sent to North Africa before they were to be accepted into the community.[9] In 1634 the departure of Antonio Dias Pinto, a Portuguese New Christian who had become an influential judge in Florence but eventually left for the ghetto of Venice, marked the end of the presence of Portuguese *marranos* professing to be Catholic in Tuscany.[10] During the following century and a half, uninterrupted relations with Iberia (especially via immigration and commerce) kept questions of religious affiliation alive, but crypto-Judaism ceased to be a pressing social phenomenon.

During the second half of the sixteenth century, the Medici transformed Livorno from a small fishermen's village into a fortified port-city. The *livornine* of 1591 and 1593 called for various ethnic and religious trading diasporas (Jews of various regions, Greeks, Armenians, Persians, Moors and Turks) to inhabit the newly founded town. But the invitation was really intended for the Sephardim. Accordingly, the patents of 1593 contained two special provisions for Jews alone. First, all members of the 'Jewish nation' of Livorno became Tuscan subjects.[11] The right to admit new members to the 'Jewish nation' was conferred upon its elected officials (through a procedure called *ballottazione*); the latter thus had the unique authority of conferring or denying Tuscan citizenship to potential applicants.[12] Tuscan citizenship, in turn, came with other advantages, including the protection of French consuls in the Levant (and after 1748 the protection of Habsburg consuls) – an assistance that was particularly attractive to merchants active across the Mediterranean. Citizenship, however, was linked to residence, as only those Jews who permanently resided in Livorno were entitled to it.[13] For a highly mobile population, this nexus between citizenship and residence provided an incentive to become rooted in Livorno. The second novelty introduced by the patents of 1593 consisted in granting the 'Jewish nation' of Livorno a mandate to adjudicate civil and criminal disputes among its members, which were brought before a court of lay elected officials who ruled in light of Jewish Law (*Halakhah*) except in commercial matters, when local and customary legislation was applied. The office of the Governor of Livorno (and occasionally other Tuscan tribunals) functioned as a court of appeal for cases involving Jews alone, and as an ordinary court for all trials involving Jews and non-Jews.[14] Overall, substantial power was delegated to the Jewish community of Livorno to self-govern, which contributed to its stability over time.

The combination of the generous privileges established by the *livornine* and the burgeoning role of Livorno in Mediterranean trade made the Tuscan port a favourite haven for Iberian exiles. From but 134 in 1601, the Jews in Livorno numbered 711 by 1622, and by then represented at least eight per cent of the total population. The community counted about 1,250 members in 1643, and more than 2,000 fifty years later. In the eighteenth century, the Jewish inhabitants continued to expand: 3,476 in 1738, 3,687 twenty years later, and 4,327 in 1784. Meanwhile, Livorno's total population grew from less than a thousand to over 40,000. Thus from the mid-seventeenth to the end of the eighteenth century, Jews comprised between 10 and 15 per cent of the resident population of Livorno.[15] The only other Jewish settlement in Italy comparable in size to that of Livorno was Rome, but there the Sephardim were not many and mostly of Spanish rather than Portuguese descent. The Jews of Venice (home to a large Sephardic community) reached their demographic zenith of 2,500 before the plague of 1630–31, and then steadily declined.[16] Of the largest Sephardic centres in Europe, in the 1660s Hamburg grew to a maximum of about 600 (plus 200 Ashkenazim).[17] Bayonne and Bordeaux, with only two or three hundred Portuguese New Christians in 1637, counted 1,100 Jews in 1728, and 1,500 by 1751 respectively.[18] The Spanish and Portuguese nation of Amsterdam comprised as many as 3,000 members (if not 4,500) in the 1680s, and apparently did not decrease in number until after 1735, while Ashkenazi immigrants rapidly outnumbered the Sephardim.[19] In 1695, London counted only 548 Sephardim and 203 Ashkenazim. Fifty years later, the English capital was home to 6,000 Jews, who numbered 15,000 after half a century. The Sephardim, however, were about 1,050 by 1720, grew to 1,700 as refugees from Portugal arrived in the 1720s and 30s, and later peaked at a little more than 2,000.[20]

Large Sephardic settlements existed in the Balkans and other parts of the Ottoman Empire, but these prospered from the mid-sixteenth to the early seventeenth century and had since developed cultural traditions and economic networks distinct from those of the Western Sephardim.[21] During the early eighteenth century, the Sephardic communities in the Caribbean were those that grew most rapidly in the world, but they were still less populated than those in Amsterdam and Livorno: in Jamaica Jews numbered 7–800 in 1735 and 900 in 1770; in Curaçao they counted about 600 in 1702 and between

1,200 and 1,500 in the second half of the eighteenth century; in Barbados in 1750 there were about 400 Jews; in Suriname, the Jewish population of the port of Paramaribo was 1,050 in 1791 and more Jews lived in the inland plantations.[22] In sum, from the mid-seventeenth to the late eighteenth century, the Sephardic community of Livorno rivalled that of Amsterdam as the largest in the West. Livorno was also the European city with the highest percentage of Jewish inhabitants.[23]

The basis for the existence and growth of the Jewish settlement in Livorno resided in policies inspired by what has been called 'philosemitic mercantilism'.[24] The *livornine* of the 1590s also established the model later used by the Habsburgs in Trieste.[25] Other Italian port cities, and notably Venice, had pursued analogous (though less liberal) policies in the previous decades.[26] Unlike in the north-western European port cities discussed by Sorkin, however, membership in all these Italian Jewish communities was mandatory, not 'voluntary'.[27] The *livornine* not only promoted but also required the return to Judaism of the New Christian refugees. Similarly, in Venice, Jews were presumed to live according to the prerogatives of their co-religionists, and by the mid-seventeenth century most of them did so.[28] The concept of voluntary membership was strictly linked to local norms and their implementation, especially when it came to the issue of religious practices and allegiances. In south-western France, for example, the patents issued by the king of France to the Portuguese and Spanish immigrants to Bordeaux in 1574 explicitly forbade 'any inquiry whatsoever into their lives'. Most of these immigrants were indeed crypto-Jews, but only in 1684 did Louis XIV recognise the Jewish presence as such and New Christians slowly reverted to the open practice of Judaism in the eighteenth century.[29] In Amsterdam, the city magistrates tolerated the construction of new, imposing synagogues in the 1630s, although Jews were still denied full rights as citizens (they were, for example, forbidden from entering craft guilds and had to obtain special dispensations if they wished to follow their own customs with regard to prescribed degrees of kinship in marriage).[30] Neither in the Netherlands nor in England, however, did secular authorities ever persecute New Christians. Community leaders, especially in Amsterdam, attempted to impose conformity, but the primary role of Dutch Sephardim in the commercial relations between the United Provinces and Spain in the seventeenth and early eighteenth centuries acted as an incentive to dissimulation among prominent merchants, bankers and diplomats.[31] After Jews were tacitly readmitted to England in 1656, many Sephardim, the most privileged in particular, had only a loose affiliation with their co-religionists, and quickly embraced the outlook and values of the upper echelon of English society.[32]

In Italy, the presence of the Inquisition left little or no room for fluidity in religious behaviours and affiliations, and made New Christians' membership in the Jewish communities all but 'voluntary'. Nonetheless, Sephardic communities in Italy and north-western Europe experienced similar phenomena of acculturation. Until the early eighteenth century, the Jewish 'nation' of Livorno remained almost exclusively Sephardic. Immigrants from other parts of Italy (mostly Rome) and North Africa increasingly challenged the Sephardic oligarchy, and in 1715 the grand duke admitted Italian and Ashkenazi Jews to the governing body of the 'nation'.[33] The gulf between the Italian and Sephardic Jews in Livorno persisted throughout the eighteenth century. In the 1760s, reciprocal hostility was expressed in both socio-economic and religious terms. The Sephardim looked down on the Italians as poor and unrefined. Italian Jews, in contrast, still used the argument about the religious heterodoxy of their Iberian co-religionists in order to demean them.[34] Within the community, the arrival of these less prosperous and 'foreign' immigrants gave rise to a process of aristocratisation in the manners and style of affluent Sephardim, who dressed more and more like Christian aristocrats, acquired villas in the countryside and regularly attended the opera – all phenomena that bear resemblance to those noted for the Sephardic merchant-bankers of Amsterdam, Bordeaux and London.[35] Sephardic Jews often used Iberian noble titles and coats of arms to recollect a more or less imaginary aristocratic descent. In seventeenth-century Amsterdam, heraldic emblems favoured assimilation into the local dominant society and at the same time shaped the profile of rich Sephardim in relation to the Jewish diaspora at large.[36] Dutch Sephardim also shared the same concepts and practices as Christian elites with regard to black slaves both in Amsterdam and the Caribbean.[37] In Livorno, Jews had been given privileges that fostered social pre-eminence and social climbing, such as the right to become physicians and treat Christian patients, to receive degrees from the university, including the nearby, important athenaeum of Pisa, to bear standard arms, to have Muslim servants and slaves, and even Christian servants and wet nurses.[38] Such privileges, uncommon for Jews in Italy, fostered aspirations to other forms of cultural prestige and, at least for its wealthiest members, promoted what, in describing the status of their co-religionists of Trieste, Dubin has called 'civil inclusion' (rather than equality or simply toleration).[39]

At the same time, the Sephardim of Livorno were not ready or willing to repudiate entirely forms of kinship relations, such as levirate union and bigamy, which had been abandoned by Ashkenazim and were incompatible with the canon law prescriptions about marriage.[40] Those well-to-do and acculturated Sephardim who shared visits to the thermal springs of Tuscany with local aristocrats and tourists did not experience any contradiction between their economic ethos and kinship structures in ways that would puzzle sociologists two centuries later. Moreover, prompted by attractive commercial opportunities (especially in the booming cotton exports from the Levant) some Sephardic families of Livorno resettled in the Levant under French diplomatic protection occasionally after 1670 and regularly after 1682.[41] The majority of them went to Aleppo, where in 1672 the male heads of household comprised 377 Arab Jews and 73 West European Sephardim, and where by 1695 the number of adult Jewish men grew to 875 as a result of immigration from both southern Anatolia and Europe.[42] There was not much mingling between the two groups: the Western Sephardim recently immigrated in the Ottoman Empire enjoyed special status, wore European cloths and spoke Spanish, Portuguese, French and Italian rather than Ladino. In Tunis, a Spanish and Portuguese community separate from those of the native co-religionists was formed between 1685 and 1710.[43] These recent Sephardic immigrants to the Ottoman lands negotiated their daily lives, family strategies and economic activities between three worlds: one which kept them connected with the 'port Jews' of Livorno and north-western Europe, one which was immersed in the local Muslim society, and one in which they competed against and cooperated with other European merchants in the same Ottoman ports.

A Cross-Cultural Merchant Network

As Dubin and Sorkin initially defined it, the category of 'port Jews' is markedly European (and West European in particular), and the characteristics of different 'port Jews' were shaped by specific local conditions. It should be clear that neither the experience nor the self-representation of elite Sephardic merchant families can be extricated from their close personal and collective links to the diaspora at large, and to their own circles within it. The ways in which these flourishing Sephardic merchants tightened their commercial relations with non-Jews in long-distance trade constitute an important point of entry into the complex diasporic life of Sephardic communities. If Jews could gain the trust of non-Jews and monitor their conduct at a distance, thus minimising the risks of trading overseas even where they lacked legal protection, it was thanks to the diaspora's ability to gather and transmit information about the performance of various agents involved in the exchange. In what follows, I will show that the organisation of informal cross-cultural merchant networks is revelatory of the global dimension of European 'port Jews', including Livorno 'port Jews'.

The demographic size and geographic dispersal of the Western Separdic diaspora made it attractive to both state authorities and other private merchants interested in expanding their financial and commercial activities. When referring to the cross-cultural nature of this diaspora, we should not limit ourselves to observing and examining the interdependence of individuals, families and communities that resided in far-away locations.[44] The ability to integrate markets that were both geographically and culturally distant derived from the unity and dispersion of the diaspora as much as from its capacity to engage in sustained business relations with outsiders, which was itself a by-product of this unity and dispersion. The effectiveness of these informal ties between Jews and non-Jews is particularly visible in some specialised trade that the Sephardim continued to dominate in Iberian mainland and overseas territories where their presence and activities were prohibited and actively persecuted by the Inquisition.

After the middle of the seventeenth century, when trade with Iberia ceased to be an attraction for most Italian merchants and bankers, the Sephardim of Livorno maintained vital commercial and financial relations with Portugal, from where they imported colonial goods such as tobacco, dyestuff, sugar and precious stones. The use of pseudonyms in dealing with Iberia was a common and legally accepted practice, but was not always sufficient to grant safety to their partners and their goods, especially after the fall of the count duke of Olivares, who had protected New Christian financiers in Madrid from 1627 to 1643, or when the Spanish and Portuguese Inquisitions renewed their attack (possibly their fiercest) against the Jews in the 1720s and 1730s.[45] The Sephardim of Livorno thus resorted to the mediation of other merchant communities, who did not decline their services to entrepreneurial Jews. It was the cohesion of Sephardic trading networks that made these cross-cultural trading relations possible.

On 9 September 1743, writing to Benjamin Alvarenga in London, the Sephardic partnership Ergas & Silvera thanked God that the exchange of Mediterranean coral and Indian diamonds was mostly in the hands of what they called 'our nation'.[46] Various branches of the Ergas family had been prominent among the Jewish community of Livorno since its early days. During the first half of the eighteenth century, some Ergas intermarried with the Silvera of Aleppo, one of the principal families of European Jews who resided and operated there under French protection. Together, Ergas and Silvera sold colonial goods on both sides of the Mediterranean, exported Levantine cotton and fine Italian silk textiles to central and northern Europe, offered third parties maritime insurance, and speculated on currency exchange rates. In 1735 David Ergas (one of the principals of Ergas & Silvera) married Ricca Baruch Carvaglio, sister of Jacob's father (with whose will I opened this essay).[47] Ricca's brothers Abraham and Moses Baruch Carvaglio were well-known in coral trade and processing, two of the most profitable activities in Livorno at the time.[48] As was often the case, marriage between Ergas and Baruch Carvaglio consolidated economic alliances, and women's dowries were added to the partnership's liquid capital. Ergas & Silvera were among the affluent Sephardim of Livorno engaged in the intercontinental barter of Mediterranean coral and Indian diamonds, which they conducted mostly via Lisbon and Goa, and from the 1740s increasingly via London and Madras.

This apparently bizarre exchange was then a vital component of Euro-

Asian commerce. The geography of the Sephardic diaspora gave it a competitive advantage in this branch of trade, while the geography of the coral–diamond trade contributed to more Sephardic migrations. In the seventeenth and eighteenth centuries the Sephardic capitals of Christian Europe coincided with the capitals of the coral–diamond trade: Livorno was the centre of an annual coral fair, and of coral processing; Amsterdam remained the site of most diamond cutting and polishing; and once London became the world market for rough diamonds, it also began to attract entrepreneurial Sephardim, including some families from Livorno. A speciality of European Sephardim, and to some extent of the Armenian diaspora, the diamond trade has been studied mostly from a Dutch and especially from an English perspective.[49] Indeed, from the late seventeenth eighteenth century, the English East India Company came to dominate this branch of trade with India, thanks both to special provisions that favoured private trade and to its increasingly powerful position in the Indian Ocean. Until the 1730s, however (that is, before Brazilian diamonds invaded Europe, and before the English achieved supremacy in India), the Jews of Livorno continued to trade in coral and diamonds extensively through Portugal rather than London. To do so, they had to circumvent legal restrictions and Inquisition persecution that endangered their affairs in the Iberian territories (both in the mainland and overseas). Notarial records and private business correspondence of leading Sephardim of Livorno document how they relied on Italian merchants in Lisbon and Hindu traders in Goa as their agents. The persistence of the same names among these agents proves the existence of a stable cross-cultural network of merchants belonging to different religious and ethnic communities.

During the seventeenth century, the Italian merchant-bankers resident in Lisbon began to supply essential economic and financial services to the Sephardim of Livorno, Venice and Amsterdam. After having contributed to Portuguese maritime expansion, by the early sixteenth century the Italians of Lisbon had been increasingly replaced by Flemish and German competitors. Nonetheless, a resident community of Italian (mostly Genoese and Florentine) merchant families continued to enjoy a certain status in the Portuguese capital and to play a role as intermediaries with the Italian port cities. Coral was a primary item exported from Livorno to Lisbon. From there, coral was taken to Goa, which until the 1730s remained a centre of the diamond trade.

Jews and New Christians were banned from Portuguese India, where the Inquisition was also established in 1560. In Goa, after a wave of Inquisitorial persecution in the 1620s, Hindu traders increasingly replaced New Christians as important agents of both the crown and private European merchants. The Portuguese legislation that discriminated against non-Christians in all economic activities was never fully implemented because there were insufficient numbers of resident Portuguese, and because the empire was increasingly unable to enforce its monopoly. As a result, Hindu merchants rose to primacy in Goa.

The cross-cultural network that connected the Sephardim of Livorno to the Italians of Lisbon and the Hindus of Goa had several remarkable qualities. First of all, it was primarily linked to the exchange of coral and diamonds, but also served to channel other financial transactions. Moreover, scattered evidence indicates that this network was in place for over a century and a half between the early seventeenth and the late eighteenth century. Finally, a prosopographic analysis shows that the same Italians and Hindus who served the Sephardim of Livorno were also correspondents of the Sephardim of Amsterdam, and occasionally of London.

How did the Sephardic merchants (who by then no longer travelled in person to India) make sure that their orders were faithfully delivered by agents who lived in distant regions and were not related to them by blood ties or other 'natural' forms of loyalty? How did they know on whom to rely? And if cheated, how did they punish a dishonest agent? Scholars of long-distance trade frequently address these questions. Economic historians tend to emphasise the importance of institutions in minimising risks and putting contracts into place. Anthropologists and sociologists, on the other hand, generally stress the assistance that members of trading diasporas offered their members across space. But the case we are examining here challenges both these approaches because business relations traversed ethnic and religious boundaries, and it was virtually impossible to bring a distant correspondence to court for alleged omissions.

Given the geographical distance involved in the intercontinental trade of coral and diamonds, and the lack of military or legal instruments of coercion at the disposal of the merchant communities involved in it, reputation was the only effective instrument of control. Both recruitment into and expulsion from the network depended on the circulation of information about an agent's ability and honesty. If a Hindu merchant of Goa tried to cheat one of his Jewish correspondents in Livorno, for example, the information would soon reach the Jews of Amsterdam and London, as well as their Italian intermediaries in Lisbon.

As stated in an anonymous late seventeenth-century English treatise, 'wealth is the result of credit and credit is the effect of fair dealing'.[50] This general rule acquires an even greater meaning when we consider that it not only applied to each single merchant, but also had a collective dimension. A trading diaspora such as the Sephardim was best equipped to develop cross-cultural trading relations because they used communitarian organisation to enforce good conduct, and were able to disseminate information among a variety of agents across distant areas. Many elements that cannot be fully recapitulated here account for the predominance of the Sephardim in the diamond trade, including their flexible organisation and their exclusion from other branches of English colonial trade. Certainly their ability to act as a unified trading diaspora across vast geographical areas enabled them to engage in prolonged and risky business relations with members of communities who had neither 'natural' nor institutional incentives to remain loyal business partners. The interconnectedness of the Sephardic diaspora was a decisive factor in facilitating the circulation of information, including information concerning the reputation of both co-religionists and outsiders. For sure, the Sephardim of Livorno involved in the exchange of coral and diamonds conceived themselves as part of a transnational network within the Jewish diaspora. In 1722, when the Portuguese ship *Nossa Senhora do Cabo* was captured by pirates on its way from Goa to Lisbon and the diamonds carried on board seemed lost, Ergas & Silvera lamented the suffering that the ship's loss would cause their 'nation' in both Livorno and Amsterdam – '*que el Dio tenga piedad y restaure a los perdientes que bastantes ai de nostra nacion aqui y Amsterdam*', they wrote to their agent Abraham Lusena in Genoa.[51]

The Local and Global Worlds of Sephardic Port Jews

Throughout this essay, I have used the expression 'Sephardic diaspora' rather generically. Today we nonetheless acknowledge that long after most New Christians and *marranos* openly reverted to Judaism, divisions within the Sephardic diaspora persisted –divisions that developed along religious, socio-economic and geographical lines. The involvement of the Sephardim of Livorno in the coral–diamond trade helps us to elucidate the boundaries and workings of one these sub-groups of the Sephardic diaspora in more specific terms.[52] Partnerships like Ergas & Silvera and the Baruch Carvaglio, among the first to open up new connections with London, also continued to trade in the Levant. To them and other affluent Sephardic families, Aleppo and Izmir in the Levant, Livorno and Venice in Italy, Bordeaux, Amsterdam and London in western and northern Europe were the capitals of the Portuguese Jewish diaspora, and the centres of a triangular trading system that connected the western and eastern Mediterranean to northern Europe. This geography naturally poses questions about the concept of 'port Jews' as currently understood. Can we include the Levantine ports of Aleppo and Izmir, homes to established communities of westernised Sephardic merchants, under the rubric of 'port Jews'? That is, can we apply this typology to the Ottoman Empire, although the concept of 'port Jews' has been coined in reference to precocious processes of modernisation and acculturation that occurred in north-western Europe?

Jewish society was invariably heterogeneous and stratified, and this was particularly true of these Ottoman cities. According to Matthias Lehmann, the category of 'port Jews' can only be used to refer to those Sephardim who, like Silvera or Baruch Carvaglio, moved to the Ottoman Empire from the late seventeenth to the mid-eighteenth century.[53] They undoubtedly formed a separate enclave, and their lives and self-representations were grounded in a sense of separate identity. But even more distinctive was the simultaneous local and global dimensions that characterised the experience and self-perception of all Sephardic Jews. The Sephardim of Livorno lived in multiple and overlapping universes. Their aristocratic manners made them better accepted by their fellow townspeople. Their solid business relations with non-Jews built on common economic interests and derived strength from their community organisation. Meanwhile, they fully participated and saw themselves as part of a diaspora whose networks cut across conventional divisions between East and West. Bigamy, for example, which was still practised in Livorno in the seventeenth and eighteenth centuries, hardly conformed to contemporary practices of Catholic societies or to today's images of the modern nuclear family as it developed in western Europe. Marriage alliances and philanthropic associations highlight the Sephardim's sense of belonging to a diasporic, ethnic community. The goal of the *Santa companhia de dotar orfans e donzelas pobres*, founded in Amsterdam in 1615, for example, was to support less fortunate girls by providing 'orphans and poor maidens of this Portuguese nation, and the Castilian, among residents [in the region stretching] from St. Jean de Luz to Danzig, including France and the Netherlands, England and Germany' as long as they married a circumcised man.[54] The analogous institution founded in Livorno in 1644 only allowed Sephardim to sit on its board, but did not discriminate against any Jewish women on the basis of their origin. Between 1670 and 1704, ten per cent of its beneficiaries were Italian or Ashkenazi girls, while 14 per cent resided in other Sephardic centres (Alexandria, Jerusalem, Amsterdam, Izmir, Aleppo, Tunis, Venice and Genoa).[55] Similarly, the *Zedaqà* of Livorno gave charity primarily to poor Jews who emigrated to other Sephardic capitals – not only Amsterdam and London, but also Tunis, Izmir and Alexandria.[56] And yet emigration did not mean cutting all ties to Livorno. In 1700 Rachel Rodrigues Diaz continued to receive her subsidy of 12 pieces (to which she was entitled because of her destitute state), even though she resided in London; and an extra allowance of 25 pieces was granted her at her daughter's marriage.[57] In 1678, Abraham son of Israel Passarinho (alias Rafael Vega), who had arrived in Livorno from Amsterdam, left a separate fund of 4,000 pieces to provide dowries for three poor girls every year in either Livorno, Venice, Amsterdam or Hamburg.[58]

Recent literature has emphasised the degree of interconnection among the Sephardic communities in early modern Europe, the Mediterranean and the Atlantic world.[59] Further examination of marriage practices and commercial activities of the Sephardic elite will allow us to map various intra-diasporic networks. The Jews of Livorno remained marginal to the Sephardic expansion in the New World.[60] Instead, they maintained close ties with the Levant, and strengthened those with Tunis and Algiers as the axis between Marseille and North Africa became central in Mediterranean trade throughout the eighteenth century.[61]

The Sephardim of Livorno were ideal intermediaries in Mediterranean commerce between the Levant and northern Europe because they could rely on relatives and co-religionists in both regions. Whenever necessary or helpful, they could also resort to the services of non-Jews because the internal cohesion of their networks was both an attraction to outsiders and a threat against dishonest behaviours. The intercontinental exchange of Mediterranean coral and Indian diamonds examined here makes clear how the Sephardic diaspora was able to deploy informal mechanisms of reputation control sufficient to minimise risks even in the absence of an overarching legal or military authority. Business cooperation between Jews and non-Jews, however, occurred in the framework of corporate societies where assimilation and creolisation were the exceptions rather than the rule, and did not entail direct social interaction (conversion, intermarriage and in the case of intercontinental trade even personal contact). Cross-cultural networks developed precisely out of strong divides, and the need for mediation in a world where collective identities and rights were more rigidly defined than they are today.[62] Analysis of the sources of reputation control that made this cooperation possible therefore permits us to historicise concepts such as toleration and cosmopolitanism, which sometimes carry an anachronistic overtone and imply a process of modernisation that was less linear than often thought.

In conclusion, the case of Livorno allows us to understand better the coexistence of tradition and innovation in the experience of early modern Sephardim. Crucial in this revision are the concepts of 'trading diasporas' and 'trading networks', which we need to take into account when evaluating the analytical potential of 'port Jews'. We can more effectively capture the self-representations of Sephardic merchants, their marriage practices and business relations with non-Jews by focusing on the global and yet close-knit nature of this diaspora. The lives of Sephardic men and women, even when spent for the longest part in a European city where they held fairly secure rights and were respected members of the host society, were linked in multiple ways to diasporic networks that traversed predictable geopolitical and cultural lines, and thus cannot be reduced to a single process of acculturation.

NOTES

1. Archivio di Stato, Florence (hereafter ASF), *Notarile Moderno: Testamenti*, notary Giovanni Lorenzo Meazzoli, 26541, fols.28v–34r. On the Belilios of Aleppo and Venice, see Vera Costantini, 'Il commercio veneziano ad Aleppo nel Settecento', *Studi veneziani* XLII (2001), 143–211. Manuel Baruch Carvaglio in Aleppo arrived in 1746; Thomas Philipp, 'French Merchants and Jews in the Ottoman Empire during the Eighteenth Century', in Avigdor Levy (ed.), *The Jews of the Ottoman Empire* (Princeton, NJ: Darwin Press, 1994), pp.315–25 (p.323).
2. Lois C. Dubin, *The Port Jews of Habsburg Trieste: Absolutist Politics and Enlightenment Culture* (Stanford, CA: Stanford University Press, 1999).
3. In the 1780s and 1790s, Sephardic services in Trieste were held only in private houses, with the first 'public' Sephardic synagogue opening in 1798; Dubin (see note 2), pp.21–3, 237 n.54.
4. David Sorkin, 'The Port Jew: Notes Towards a Social Type', *Journal of Jewish Studies* 50.1 (1999), 87–97. An earlier, sketchy formulation of the concept in idem, 'Into the Modern World', in Nicholas de Lange (ed.), *The Illustrated History of the Jewish People* (New York, San Diego and London: Harcourt Brace, 1997), pp.199–253 (pp.205–9).
5. Lois Dubin, 'Researching Port Jews and Port Jewries: Trieste and Beyond', in David Cesarani (ed.), *Port Jews: Jewish Communities in Cosmopolitan Maritime Trading Centres, 1550–1950* (London and Portland, OR: Frank Cass, 2002), pp.47–58 (pp.48, 56).
6. See also the essay by Evelyne Oliel-Grausz in this volume, 'Networks and Communication in the Sephardi Diaspora: An Added Dimension to the Concept of Port Jews and Port Jewries', pp.61–76.
7. In 1497 King Manuel of Portugal ordered the forced conversion of all Jews, including those who had come as refugees from Spain five years earlier. Therefore, after 1497 all Jews who left Iberia had necessarily been baptised and lived as Christians. Once they reverted to Judaism in Italy they were thus subject to accusations of apostasy by the Inquisition. The secular rulers of Venice and Livorno chose to grant Iberian Jews immunity from their past conversion in order to secure their safety. For textual and historical analysis of the *livornine*, see Bernard Dov Cooperman, *Trade and Settlement: The Establishment and Early Development of the Jewish Communities of the Jewish Communities in Leghorn and Pisa (1591–1626)* (unpublished Ph.D. Dissertation, Harvard University, 1976); and Renzo Toaff, *La nazione ebrea a Livorno e Pisa (1591–1700)* (Firenze: Olschki, 1990).
8. Lucia Frattarelli Fischer, 'Cristiani nuovi e nuovi ebrei in Toscana fra Cinque e Seicento: Legittimazioni e percorsi individuali', in Pier Cesare Ioly Zorattini (ed.), *L'identità dissimulata. Giudaizzanti iberici nell'Europa cristiana dell'età moderna* (Firenze: Olschki, 2000), pp.99–149.
9. Lucia Frattarelli Fischer, 'Ebrei a Pisa fra Cinquecento e Settecento', in Michele Luzzati (ed.), *Gli ebrei di Pisa (secoli IX–XX): Atti del convegno internazionale, Pisa 3–4 ottobre 1994* (Ospitaletto, Pisa: Pacini Editore, 1998), pp.89–115 (p.100).
10. Ibid. p.92; and Frattarelli Fischer (see note 8), p.142.
11. In *ancien régime* Europe, the term 'nation' indicated any collective group whose status was legally recognised in the framework of a corporate society, but was mostly used in reference to foreigners and ethno-religious minorities.
12. The term 'citizenship' is used here according it the meaning it had at the time. In a pre-French Revolution context, different individuals and groups might be 'citizens' of a certain state, but did not enjoy the same civil and political rights.
13. Except between 1758 and 1761, if Jews wanted to leave for a few months, they had to obtain permission to do so; Toaff (see note 7), pp.408–9.
14. Ibid. pp.47, 205–40.
15. Ibid. pp.119–23.
16. Data on the Jewish population of all Italian towns with a ghetto are collected in Alan Charles Harris, 'La demografia del ghetto in Italia, 1516–1797 circa', *La rassegna mensile di Israel* 33.1–5 (1967), Appendix, 3–68. Livorno is excluded from this list because formally it did not have a ghetto. New data for Venice in Giovanni Favero and Francesca Trivellato, 'Gli abitanti del ghetto di Venezia (1516–1797): dati e ipotesi', *Zakhor: Rivista di storia degli ebrei d'Italia* 7 (2004), 9–50.
17. Hermann Kellenbenz, 'History of the Sephardim of Germany', in R.D. Barnett and W.M. Schwab (eds.), *The Sephardi Heritage*, vol. II: *The Western Sephardim* (Grendon: Gibraltar Books, 1989), pp.26–40 (p.34).

18. For the figures of 1637, see Israel (see note 6), p.262. On Bayonne, see Simon Schwartzfuchs, 'Notes sur les juifs de Bayonne au XVIIIe siècle', *Revue des études juives* 125.3 (1966), 353–64 (p.355). On Bordeaux, see Jean Cavignac, *Les israélites bordelais de 1780 à 1850: Autour de l'émancipation* (Paris: Publisud, 1991), p.15. At the outbreak of the French Revolution, Bayonne and Bordeaux housed 2,500–3,500 and 1,500–2,000 Jews respectively; Simon Schwartzfuchs, *Les Juifs de France* (Paris: Albin Michel, 1975), p.146.

19. Conservative figures in Miriam Bodian, *Hebrews of Portuguese Nations: Conversos and Community in Early Modern Amsterdam* (Bloomington, IN: Indiana University Press, 1997), p.156 (2,800 members in 1683); and Daniël M. Swetschinski, *Reluctant Cosmopolitans: The Portuguese Jews of Seventeenth-Century Amsterdam* (London and Portland, OR: Littman Library of Jewish Civilisation, 2000), p.91. Figures of more than 4,500 for 1681–85 in H.P.H. Nusteling, 'The Jews in the Republic of the United Provinces: Origins, Numbers and Dispersion', in Jonathan Israel and Reiner Salverda (eds.), *Dutch Jewry: Its History and Secular Culture* (Leiden, Boston and Köln: E.J. Brill, 2002), pp.43–62 (pp.51–3). A few Ashkenazim began to arrive in Amsterdam after the end of the Thirty Years' War (1648), more from the 1670s onwards, and the great bulk after 1726. In 1795 there were about 25,000 Jews in a city of 221,000 inhabitants: 22,000 were Ashkenazim and 3,000 Sephardim; ibid., pp.45 n.3, 54–5; and R.G. Fuks-Mansfeld, 'Enlightenment and Emancipation from c.1750 to 1814', in J.C.H. Blom, R. G. Fuks-Mansfeld, I. Schöffer (eds.), *The History of the Jews in the Netherlands* (Oxford and Portland, OR: Littman Library of Jewish Civilisation, 2002), pp.164–91 (p.171).

20. V.D. Lipman, 'Sephardi and Other Jewish Immigrants in England in the Eighteenth Century', in *Migration and Settlement (Proceedings of the Anglo-American Jewish Historical Conference, 1970)* (London: Jewish Historical Society of England, 1971), pp.37–62; Todd M. Endelman, *The Jews of Britain, 1656 to 2000* (Berkeley, CA, Los Angeles and London: University of California Press, 2002), p.41.

21. Bernard Lewis, *The Jews of Islam* (Princeton, NJ: Princeton University Press, 1984), pp.107–53 (p.118 on the demographic figures for the 1520s–1530s); Jonathan I. Israel, *European Jewry in the Age of Mercantilism, 1550–1750*, 3rd edn. (London and Portland, OR: Littman Library for Jewish Civilisation, 1998), pp.20–21, 26–7; Esther Benbassa and Aron Rodrigue, *Sephardi Jewry: A History of the Judeo-Spanish Community, 14th–20th Centuries* (Berkeley, CA, Los Angeles and London: University of California Press, 2000).

22. Isaac S. and Suzanne A. Emmanuel, *History of the Jews of the Netherlands Antilles* (Cincinnati: American Jewish Archives, 1970), pp.234, 277; Cornelis Ch. Goslinga, *The Dutch in the Caribbean and the Guineas, 1680–1791* (Assen, Maastricht and Dover, NH: Van Gorcum, 1985), pp.209, 519; Mordecai Arbell, *The Portuguese Jews of Jamaica* (Kingston, Jamaica: Canoe Press, University of the West Indies, 2000), p.36; Jonathan Israel, 'The Jews of Dutch America', in Paolo Bernardini and Norman Fiering (eds.), *The Jews and the Expansion of Europe to the West, 1450 to 1800* (New York and Oxford: Berghahn Books, 2001), pp.335–49 (p.337). Overall, by 1700 there were roughly 4,000 Sephardim in the West Indies, most of them in Dutch colonies; Israel (see note 21), p.128.

23. Israel (see note 21), p.93.

24. Ibid., pp.46–7, 90. On considerations of *raison d'état* as distinctive elements in the notion of 'port Jews', see Sorkin, 'The Port Jew' (note 4), p.90; and Dubin (note 2), pp.11, 199–203, 231 n.7, and *passim*.

25. Ibid., p.61.

26. Benjamin Ravid, 'A Tale of Three Cities and their *Raison d'État*: Ancona, Venice, Livorno, and the Competition for Jewish Merchants in the Sixteenth Century', in Alisa Meyuhas Ginio (ed.), *Jews, Christians, and Muslims in the Mediterranean World after 1492* (London and Portland, OR: Frank Crass, 1992), pp.138–62.

27. Sorkin, 'The Port Jew' (see note 4), pp.90–92. Dubin now suggests that we downplay the importance of 'voluntary membership' as a prerequisite for the definition of 'port Jews', and instead inquire into whether and how different legal arrangements made Jewish communities of various port cities different; see the essay by Lois Dubin in this volume, '"Wings on their feet … and wings on their head": Reflections on the Study of Port Jews', pp.14–30.

28. Brian Pullan, '"A Ship with Two Rudders": "Righetto Marrano" and the Inquisition in Venice', *Historical Journal* 20 (1977), 25–58; idem, *The Jews of Europe and the Inquisition of Venice, 1550–1670* (Totowa, NJ: Barnes & Nobles Book, 1983); Federica Ruspio, 'Una comunità di marrani a Venezia', *Zakhor: Rivista di storia degli ebrei d'Italia* 5 (2000–01), 53–85.

29. Israel (see note 21), p.96; Gérard Nahon, *Juifs et Judaïsme à Bordeaux* ([Bordeaux]: Mollat, 2003).

30. Arend H. Huusen, 'The Legal Position of the Jews in the Dutch Republic c.1590–1796', in Israel and Salverda (see note 19), pp.25–41 (pp.34–6).

31. Jonathan Israel has written extensively on the subject. See now his *Diasporas within a Diaspora: Jews, Crypto-Jews and the World Maritime Empires, 1540–1740* (Leiden, Boston and Köln: E.J. Brill, 2002), pp.185–244, 533–66.

32. Todd M. Endelman, *Radical Assimilation in English Jewish History, 1656–1945* (Bloomington, IN: Indiana University Press, 1990), pp.9–33. For an interesting comparison of Christian–Jewish relations in Amsterdam and London, see also the essay by Adam Sutcliffe in this volume, 'Identity, Space and Intercultural Contact in the Urban Entrepôt: The Sephardic Bounding of Community in Early Modern Amsterdam and London', pp.93–108.

33. Toaff (see note 7), pp.180–82. In 1721 official documents referred to a 'Spanish nation' and an 'Italian nation'; ASF, *Mediceo del Principato*, 2475, fols.79, 92.

34. Archivio di Stato, Livorno (hereafter ASL), *Governo*, 961, fol.33. At the extinction of the Medici dynasty in 1737, Tuscany passed under the rule of the house of Lorraine, and in 1765 under direct Habsburg rule. But the 'Jewish nation' continued to be governed by the *livornine*. Galasso argues that socio-economic inequality counted more than ethnic divisions among the Jews of Livorno in the seventeenth century. Indeed, in Livorno we do not encounter discriminatory provisions analogous to those that characterised the Spanish and Portuguese community in Amsterdam (where inter-ethnic marriages were penalised in 1671, and non-Sephardim excluded from brotherhoods and charity). Nonetheless, ethnic tensions grew in Livorno too, especially as Italian and North African immigrants became more numerous in the eighteenth century. If they never escalated to the same level, it was perhaps also because immigration flows never reached the size they did in Amsterdam, nor created the same emergencies in terms of poor relief. Compare Cristina Galasso, *Alle origini di una comunità: Ebree ed ebrei a Livorno nel Seicento* (Firenze: Olschki, 2002), pp.19, 41–4; Yosef Kaplan, 'The Portuguese Community of Amsterdam in the 17th Century and the Ashkenazi World', in Jozeph Michman (ed.), *Dutch Jewish History: Proceedings of the Fourth Symposium on the History of the Jews in the Netherlands (7–10 December – Tel-Aviv and Jerusalem, 1986)* (Van Gorcum, Assen and Maastricht: Tel-Aviv University, Hebrew University of Jerusalem, Institute for Research on Dutch Jewry, 1989), pp.23–45; idem, 'The Self-Definition of the Sephardic Jews of Western Europe and Their Relation to the Alien and the Stranger', in Benjamin R. Gampel (ed.), *Crisis and Creativity in the Sephardic World, 1391–1648* (New York: Columbia University Press, 1997), pp.121–45.

35. Compare with Sorkin, 'The Port Jew' (see note 4), p.95.

36. Miriam Bodian, '"Men of the Nation": The Shaping of *Converso* Identity in Early-Modern Europe', *Past and Present* 143 (1994), 48–76 (pp.66–7); and Bodian (see note 19), p.90.

37. Jonathan Schorsch, *Jews and Blacks in the Early Modern World* (Cambridge: Cambridge University Press, 2004).

38. On the debated right of Jewish doctors to treat non-Jewish patients, see Cooperman (note 7), pp.296–8; and Toaff (note 7), pp.114, 200. Permission to have Christian servants and wet nurses was rescinded in 1620, but the prohibition was largely unattended. See Cooperman (note 7), pp.298–300; Toaff (note 7), pp.542–3; Cristina Galasso, '"Solo il loro servigio si brama, sia fedel, accurato, sincer": Il servizio domestico nella comunità ebraica di Livorno (secoli XVII–XVIII)', *Società e storia* 97 (2000), 457–74.

39. Dubin (see note 2), pp.198–225; David Sorkin, 'Port Jews and the Three Regions of Emancipation', in Cesarani (see note 5), pp.31–46 (pp.37–8).

40. Galasso (see note 34), pp.31–4.

41. Attilio Milano, *Storia degli ebrei italiani nel Levante* (Firenze: Casa Editrice Israel, 1949), p.172; Simon Schwarzfuchs, 'La "nazione ebrea" livournaise au Levant', *La rassegna mensile di Israel* 50 (1984), 707–24 (p.709).

42. Bruce Masters, *Christians and Jews in the Ottoman Arab World: The Roots of Sectarianism* (Cambridge: Cambridge University Press, 2001), pp.55–6.

43. In 1685 there were 49 Jewish families from Livorno in Tunis. See Paul Sebag, *Histoire des Juifs de Tunisie des origines à nos jours* (Paris: L'Harmattan, 1991), pp.82, 95–96; and Lionel Lévy, *La nation juive portugaise: Livourne, Amsterdam, Tunis, 1591–1951* (Paris: L'Harmattan, 1999), pp.65–7.

44. Philip D. Curtin, *Cross-Cultural Trade in World History* (Cambridge: Cambridge University Press, 1984).

45. Israel (see note 31), pp.566–9.
46. ASF, *Libri di commercio e famiglia*, 1957 (ex 1636). Unless noted, in this section I summarise the findings that I have presented more extensively in Francesca Trivellato, 'Juifs de Livourne, Italiens de Lisbonne et hindous de Goa: réseaux marchands et échanges interculturels à l'époque moderne', *Annales HSS* 3 (2003), 581–603.
47. ASL, *Capitano, poi Governatore, poi Auditore vicario: Atti civili spezzati*, 2245, no.953.
48. In 1743 the Baruch Carvaglio opened a large coral-manufacturing workshop in Pisa, which operated for more than 20 years, and sold large quantities of coral beads in Livorno as well as shipped them to London. See ASF, *Arte dei Giudici e Notai*, 608; and *Ruota Civile*, 4802, fols.383r–392r.
49. For England, see Holden Furber, *Rival Empires of Trade in the Orient 1600–1800* (Minneapolis: University of Minnesota Press, 1976), pp.133–4, 260–62; Gedalia Yogev, *Diamonds and Coral: Anglo-Dutch Jews and Eighteenth-Century Trade* (Leicester: Leicester University Press, 1978); Søren Mentz, 'English Private Trade on the Coromandel Coast, 1660–1690: Diamonds and Country Trade', *Indian Economic and Social History Review* 33.2 (1996), 155–73; Edgar Samuel, 'Diamonds and Pieces of Eight: How Stuart England won the Rough-Diamond Trade', *Jewish Historical Studies* 38 (2003), 23–40. On Amsterdam, see idem, 'Manuel Levy Duarte (1631–1714): An Amsterdam Merchant Jeweller and His Trade with London', *Transactions of the Jewish Historical Society of England* 27 (1978–80), 11–31.
50. Quoted in Nuala Zahedich, 'Making Mercantilism Work: London Merchants and Atlantic Trade in the Seventeenth Century', *Transactions of the Royal Historical Society* 9 (1999), 143–58 (151).
51. ASF, *Libri di commercio e famiglia*, 1938 (ex 1631).
52. In his recent, remarkable monograph, Israel acknowledges the 'pre-eminence of Amsterdam and Livorno in the western Sephardic world', which stood on 'a unique category to which neither Hamburg nor London … ever managed to attain'; Israel (see note 31), p.36. But he devotes little attention to Livorno and disregards entirely the activities of Western Sephardim in the eighteenth-century Mediterranean.
53. Matthias B. Lehmann, 'How to Westernize Ottoman Jews: The Eighteenth Century', Paper presented at the Association for Jewish Studies in Boston, 21 December 2003, and 'A Livornese "Port Jew" and the Sephardim of the Ottoman Empire', *Jewish Social Studies* 11.2 (2005), 51–76.
54. St Jean de Luz is small town on the south-western French Atlantic coast. *Marranos* were expelled from there in 1619, while more New Christians settled in nearby Bayonne. On the statutes of the *Santa companhia* of Amsterdam, see I.S. Révah, 'Le premier réglement imprimé de la "Santa Companhia de dotar orfans e donzelas pobres"', *Boletim internacional de bibliografia luso-brasileira* 4 (1963), 650–91 (635); Miriam Bodian, 'Amsterdam, Venice and the Marrano Diaspora in the Seventeenth Century', in Michman (see note 34), pp.47–66; Daniel M. Swetschinski, 'Kinship and Commerce: The Foundation of Portuguese Jewish Life in Seventeenth-Century Holland', *Studia Rosenthaliana* 15 (1981), 52–74.
55. Galasso (see note 34), pp.126–7.
56. Toaff (see note 7), pp.253–8; Galasso (see note 34), pp.135–7.
57. Galasso (see note 34), pp.140–41.
58. Toaff (see note 7), p.263; Galasso (see note 34), p.130.
59. Among an increasingly large literature, see Gérard Nahon, *Métropoles et périphéries sefardes d'Occident: Kairouan, Amsterdam, Bayonne, Bordeaux, Jérusalem* (Paris: Les éditions du Cerf, 1993); Lévy (see note 43); Evelyne Oliel-Grausz, 'A Study in Intercommunal Relations in the Sephardi Diaspora: London and Amsterdam in the Eighteenth Century', in Chaya Brasz and Yosef Kaplan (eds.), *Dutch Jews as Perceived by Themselves and by Others: Proceedings of the Eighth International Symposium on the History of the Jews in the Netherlands* (Leiden, Boston and Köln: E.J. Brill, 2000), pp.41–58.
60. Several poor Jewish families left Livorno for the Dutch Caribbean between 1645 and the 1660s; Israel (see note 21), p.133; and idem (see note 31), pp.401–2. Emigration continued thereafter, but the Sephardic merchants of Livorno relied on the their intermediaries in Iberia, Marseilles and Amsterdam to import American goods.
61. Minna Rozen, 'The Leghorn Merchants in Tunis and their Trade with Marseilles at the End of the 17th Century', in Jean-Louis Meige (ed.), *Les relations intercommunautaires juives en Méditerranée occidentale, XIIIe–XXe siècles* (Paris: CNRS, 1984), pp.51–9; Jean-Pierre Filippini, 'Les Juifs

d'Afrique du Nord et la communauté de Livourne au XVIIIe siècle', in ibid., pp.60–69; idem, 'La "nation juive" de Livourne et le Royaume de France au XVIIIe siècle', in Irad Malkin (ed.), *La France et la Méditerranée: vingt-sept siècles d'interdependance* (Leiden and New York: E.J. Brill, 1990), pp.259–71; Boubaker Sadok, *La Régence de Tunis au XVIIe siècle: ses relations commerciales avec les ports de l'Europe méditerranéenne, Marseilles et Livourne* (Tunis: Ceroma, Zaghouan, 1987); Lévy (see note 43).

62. Anthropologist Fredrik Barth has examined how ethnic boundaries do not necessarily dissolve as a result of stable economic exchanges. Fredrik Barth, 'Ecological Relationship of Ethnic Groups in Swat, North Pakistan', *American Anthropologist* 58.6 (1956): 1079–89; idem (ed.), *Ethnic Groups and Boundaries: The Social Organization of Cultural Differences* (Bergen, Oslo and London: Universitets Forlaget and George Allen & Unwin, 1969).

Port Jews in Copenhagen:
The Sephardi Experience and its Influence on the Development of a Modern Jewish Community in Denmark

THORSTEN WAGNER

Introduction

When a couple of missionaries from the Institutum Judaicum in Halle in 1734 embarked on the first of a series of missionary journeys to Denmark's Jews in the course of the 1730s and 1740s, their diaries were soon marked by a sombre tone of resignation.[1] The Kingdom's Jews had allegedly turned out to be unusually stubborn and resistant, and both the missionaries and their local partners supporting the project agreed that the reason for their failure to convert more than a tiny number of the Kingdom's Jews was their privileged status: their situation was all too good, they were treated as other citizens, they were not supposed to pay special taxes (*Schutzgeld*) or other extraordinary fees, and they had become rich.[2]

Whether this explanation is convincing might be debatable, but the perception points towards an important aspect of the Danish-Jewish experience: the status of the Jews of the Kingdom of Denmark did not fit the conventional criteria of central European Jewish life. To what degree might this be attributed to the presence of port Jews, especially in Copenhagen? And how might this have affected the path of Denmark's Jews into 'modernity'? Arguably, the concept of the port Jew seems applicable to some degree to the transformation of Jewish life in late eighteenth and early nineteenth-century Denmark. Jews first settled in the Duchies, and from the late sixteenth century also in the Kingdom itself; but it was only in the course of the eighteenth century that Copenhagen became the centre of almost all Danish-Jewish cultural and political activity. At the turn of the century, the number of Jews living in Copenhagen was approximately 2,400, which amounted to more than 80 per cent of the Jewish population residing in the Kingdom and around 2 per cent of the capital's inhabitants.

Especially in Copenhagen the general appreciation of commerce seems to have contributed significantly to an early rapprochement between Jews and non-Jews, preparing the ground for social inclusion. The 'Portuguese' community played a crucial role in the formative beginnings of a modern Jewish culture in Denmark as well: Sephardi merchants constituted the core of a counter-elite challenging the rabbinic establishment from the 1780s.

Applying the criteria and definitions of the port Jew phenomenon set out by David Sorkin, it might seem debatable to suggest Copenhagen could be a case of port Jewish life, however: situated on the Baltic sea – and not on the Atlantic Ocean or the Mediterranean – and in a society economically and politically dominated by agrarian interests, it does not fulfil the preconditions of the concept as defined by Sorkin – and even less so, as the number of Jews remained limited and the community did not have the status of a merchant corporation or of a voluntary religious association.[3] By way of contrast to port Jewish settlements like Amsterdam or London, David Sorkin even makes mention of Copenhagen as an example of a post-1648 'northern court settlement' (like Vienna and especially Berlin and Königsberg), marked by the tensions deriving from the state's attempt to graft mercantilist, commercial policy onto a primarily agrarian society, in which the economic utility of the Jews was both prized and condemned.[4]

But in spite of the fact that after the military defeats of the sixteenth century Copenhagen had turned into a culturally rather isolated backwater almost devoid of ethnic or confessional minorities, with conspicuous limits to its cosmopolitanism, pluralism and tolerance, (partially worsened by Pietist influences in the early eighteenth century), it nevertheless was the metropolis and uncontested centre of a multilingual and multi-ethnic Commonwealth consisting of Schleswig-Holstein, Norway, Iceland, the Faroes, Greenland and some colonial territories, stretching from the North Cape to the Elbe. Furthermore, in the course of the eighteenth century, Denmark's maritime trade saw a dramatic upsurge, primarily caused by the advantages of remaining neutral in the military conflicts of the age. This resulted in the burgeoning new bourgeoisie accumulating substantial wealth and growing social influence. Especially from the late eighteenth century, an experimenting reform absolutist regime attempted to cater to these new forces by pursuing a policy of wide-ranging agrarian and social reforms.[5]

This complex constellation affected the process of social inclusion and cultural transformation of Danish Jewry in multiple ways. Research on Danish-Jewish history has been scarce so far,[6] the *lacunae* are legion, and even fewer scholars have appreciated the importance of the Portuguese segment of Danish-Jewish life.[7] But when Per Katz, in his authoritative work on the early period of Danish-Jewish history, concludes that the Portuguese influence in the seventeenth and eighteenth century was a transitory phenomenon without any significant impact on the trajectory of Danish-Jewish history,[8] he seems to underestimate both its predetermining and lasting effect on the terms of settlement and the modes of cultural change, let alone appreciate the broader implications of these processes highlighted by more recent research on port Jewish settlements in early modern Europe and their impact on Jewish emancipation and acculturation.[9]

It will be argued here that Copenhagen is a case in point, both illustrating the usefulness of the port Jew category and at the same time requiring an approach that does not push the dichotomies between court Jews and port Jews too far, but rather focuses on the interplay and simultaneity of these phenomena. Three related issues will be discussed below: the conditions of settlement, the role of a 'modernising' counter-elite, and the modes of Danish-Jewish acculturation and religious reform.

Terms of Settlement and Legal Status of the Jewish Communities in Copenhagen

The beginning of a Jewish presence in the Danish Commonwealth dates back to the seventeenth century, when Portuguese Jews in the Duchies of Schleswig and Holstein such as Alvaro Dinis and the families de Lima und Texeira, after first having established commercial relations with the Royal Court in Copenhagen, attained freedom of movement and, later on, residence permits for the Kingdom of Denmark. Gabriel Gomez, an influential Court Jew serving Christian IV and Frederick III, was able to attain a privilege in 1657 that exempted all Portuguese Jews from the law that barred Jews from entering the Kingdom proper. In 1667 this exemption was even extended to include all protected Jews of Altona – and this group was now explicitly granted the privilege to enter the Kingdom and carry on trade here. Thus, while Jews from Glückstadt and Altona, protected by the Danish King, enjoyed freedom of travel and trade, other Ashkenazi Jews still needed a *Geleitbrief* (safe conduct pass).[10]

The first Jews to carry on trade in Copenhagen were Portuguese Jews, who provided the Court with financial services and luxury goods such as jewelry. The 'second or third generation' of Iberian émigrés had often migrated to Denmark via Amsterdam and Hamburg or Altona.[11] But as it became increasingly difficult for the authorities to differentiate between Portuguese and Ashkenazi Jews, the attempt to keep Jews out of the Kingdom was undermined: the incrementally extended Portuguese privileges prepared the ground for Jewish immigration from the Duchies to Denmark proper in the last decades of the seventeenth century. Towards the end of the seventeenth century, still more Ashkenazi Jews trickled into the Kingdom, taking advantage of the generous privileges already granted to Sephardi merchants and bankers as individuals. Israel Fürst, Court Jew in Hamburg, was granted a residence permit for Copenhagen in 1673, but did not use it; whereas Simon Hartvig in

1673 and Isaac Joseph in 1674 actually did settle in Ribe, as did Jacob Sostman in Nakskov in the same year – all of them were involved in tobacco manufacturing. In 1682 Israel David, an Ashkenazi Jew providing the Court with jewelry, was allowed to settle in the capital and to practice 'the Jewish ceremonies in peace', as was Meyer Goldschmidt in 1683. Finally, in 1684 the Ashkenazi Jews' status as a community in Copenhagen was legalised as 'Jews of the German Nation', when they received the permission to hold synagogue services in their private homes. For the first time the right to settle in the capital was linked to freedom of religion.

Furthermore, the young community was allowed to employ its first rabbi, Abraham Salomon from Moravia in 1687, and to establish a cemetery in 1694. In spite of their pioneering role, the Sephardi immigrants only obtained the privilege to form a community and to conduct services in their homes 11 years later, presumably due to their small numbers. In 1682, 11 Jewish families in Copenhagen officially resided in Copenhagen, three jewellers and four tobacco manufacturers. Three of these families were Portuguese.[12]

This successive liberalisation of settlement regulations that created the preconditions for a significant Jewish presence from the late seventeenth century onwards might have come too late for a major immigration of port Jews, as their economic and territorial expansion in the north had already passed its climax. The number of Portuguese families remained low, and the sources remain ambiguous as to the exact legal status of this group. It seems clear, however, that their distinctiveness went beyond the status of a synagogue fellowship, as the Portuguese community had established and administered its own cemetery from 1715. On the other hand, there is not much mention of Portuguese community elders or other community functions in the course of these first decades.

In the course of the following decades the Ashkenazim soon outnumbered the Portuguese, who remained a distinct but small community of a maximum of 20–30 families, existing alongside the dominant Ashkenazi community. The growth of the Ashkenazi presence implied a certain broadening of the Jews' economic activities in the capital, as the 'German' Jews were also involved in manufacturing and mercantile activities without any direct relationship to the Court. Nevertheless, the concentration in (wholesale and petty) trade, commerce and banking was overwhelming, even more so, as the Jews were not allowed to own land or to enter the artisans' guilds. The Jewish minority in general remained socially and culturally separated, and anti-Jewish attitudes among the clergy and broad segments of Danish society were widespread. But Jews were nevertheless granted a comparably favourable legal status by a mercantilist regime that increasingly subordinated theological and fiscal concerns to trade interests and hopes for mercantile and manufacturing development. While the port Jew privileges of the seventeenth century were partially transferred to the predominantly Ashkenazi Court Jews of later years, these external distinctions lost their importance in the course of the eighteenth century.

In contrast to the worsening legal status of Jews in Prussia during the eighteenth century, in Denmark regulations of acceptance were even eased over time, as were other restrictions on Jewish activities. Thus a hybrid Jewish presence consisting of an Ashkenazi and a Sephardi community developed, with separate religious institutions and social networks, and arguably the elite of Copenhagen Jewry came to consist of court Jews as well as of port Jews. To what degree the community was perceived by contemporaries as being hybrid remains unclear. State authorities had shared high hopes regarding the chances of a Sephardi port Jewish settlement in Copenhagen, but these never materialised in any substantial way, and soon the Ashkenazim inherited this goodwill and took control of Jewish lay leadership in the capital. Nevertheless this takeover never came to mean either the complete abolishment of Portuguese distinctiveness or the end of the port Jewish undercurrent in Danish-Jewish history.

To be sure, in spite of the relatively favourable terms of settlement enjoyed by Jews in Denmark, certain regulations continued to curtail Jewish life. Economic activities were strictly limited, and in case of a conflict of interests with the guilds, the latter's protest was often heeded. And as so often in early modern Europe the immigration of Jews, especially of poor Jews, was harshly controlled; state authorities both enforced tough policing of towns and roads, and put pressure on Jewish lay leaders to report offenders. Corporations, (Christian) schools and the university remained barred to Jews for more than a century, and the oath *more judaico* – formalised in 1747 – was no less condescending and marked by anti-Jewish suspicion than in German lands.

But on the other hand, residential segregation was not enforced, the privilege to settle and pursue trade was granted individually, and collective liability only pertained to the community elders regarding the fight against illegal immigrants. The Jewish population in Copenhagen – in contrast to the Ashkenazi community in Altona – was neither constituted as an autonomous community nor was it to be ruled by some body of Jewry laws. The community structures were neither defined by compulsory membership nor by voluntary association. Furthermore, no comprehensive jurisdiction was granted, for example, relating to the *cherem*. As became evident from a series of conflicts in the first decades of eighteenth century, when the Elders applied for permission to use the *cherem* against reluctant taxpayers, the community leadership had no such general authority, and had to request permission to issue a ban in each case. In 1722 the King decided to allow the issue of the light *cherem*, but only with respect to internal, ceremonial issues and in order to enforce internal taxation.[13] In general, there was no exchange of legal authority for the remission of state taxes: Jews only had to contribute individually to the municipal welfare system and to the local parish priest (as did members of the Calvinist Reformed and the Catholics), and *Schutzgeld* was only paid by the first generation of Ashkenazi Jews – as a one-time fee for tax exemption.

A law temporarily prohibited Jews from employing Christians, and diverse suggestions – to establish a ghetto, to force Jews to wear a coloured badge, to deport them to Greenland,[14] to confiscate Jewish capital, to introduce collective legal liability and a Jew tax – were all turned down by the authorities. The remarkably self-assertive Portuguese reaction to the short period of forced missionary sermons in 1728 might point towards the fact that to some degree this social and legal status was to be accounted for by the appreciation of the Sephardi presence – an appreciation that had been partially transferred to the community as a whole. While the Ashkenazi protests against the missionaries referred to the freedom of conscience and primarily asked for compassion towards the Jews, who were being scorned in the street and were risking economic disaster, the Portuguese spokesman Isaac Granada in a resolute statement threatened to withdraw capital invested in the East Indian (Trade) Company. The effect of this statement cannot be discerned, but the missionary project was discontinued a short time later.[15]

Juxtaposing the two most conspicuous individuals of the period in question illustrates the duality of the Danish-Jewish trajectory at the end of the seventeenth century. It was the court Jew *par excellence*, Meyer Goldschmidt, who dominated Danish-Jewish affairs around 1700 due to his control of the synagogue service and the lay leadership of the Ashkenazi community over the course of almost five decades. But it was a port Jew, the wealthy merchant and owner of about 15 merchant ships, Jacob Abensur, who first officially attained the privilege of trade (*at løse borgerskab*), and soon it became customary to do so as a 'Jew'. This implied that the applicants in question were granted the specific right of commercial activity as merchant. This designation turned the 'Jewish nation' into something more like a merchant corporation than a *kehilla*.[16]

In spite of its small size, the port Jewish presence – that had helped to double Copenhagen's merchant fleet in the last decade of the seventeenth century – seems to have had a decisive influence in creating a social and legal setting that ended up determining crucial dimensions of the process of Jewish emancipation and social inclusion: When civic equality was discussed for the first time in the Danish context in the 1790s, it took shape as a debate on whether the general Civic Law should pertain to the Jews of the Kingdom as well. Thus, there was no Jewry law to be abolished and no fully fledged autonomous community to be dismantled or at least radically reformed in order to attain a new legal status. Here, there seem to be some similarities to the controversy about the extension of Sephardi privileges in revolutionary

France in 1790–91. Furthermore, one might speculate whether the fact that this discourse on the terms of emancipation did not include a *quid pro quo* of acculturation as a precondition for emancipation to some degree was caused by the hybrid character of the community.[17]

Copenhagen Port Jews and the Challenge to 'Baroque Judaism' in the Late Eighteenth Century

The presence of port Jews seems to have had some significance regarding the internal dimensions of cultural change as well. To be sure, there is not much evidence to substantiate the notion of a '*haskalah avant la lettre*' in the case of the port Jews of Copenhagen.[18] Nevertheless, there seem to be three aspects in which the port Jewish dimension of Jewish life in Copenhagen did accelerate acculturation or new ways of thinking in the Jewish minority.

The first aspect to be mentioned here is that already decades before the radical, politicised *haskalah* marked a turning point in central European Jewish intellectual life, the Portuguese community of Copenhagen brought forth several significant harbingers of cultural change that ended up challenging the baroque Judaism prevalent in the local Ashkenazi community. Salomon Abraham de Meza (1727–1800), a Sephardi physician from Amsterdam settling in Copenhagen in 1753, was to become one prominent example of this.[19] All of his sons studied medicine at the university, and in the 1760s, in cooperation with his tutee, the educated Ashkenazi manufacturer Marcus Salomonsen Nyeborg, whom he had introduced to secular studies, languages and philosophy, he pursued an energetic debate in Danish language public journals, celebrating the Sephardi civilisation of London and Amsterdam, promoting Mendelssohn and Berlin Jewry as the role model for Europe, and demanding a more tolerant and benevolent attitude towards the Jews of Denmark. He maintained that more refined nations such as Great Britain, Italy and the Netherlands had granted their Jews access to artisanry and the professions, while the Danish state denied its Jews such privileges. He pointed to both Dutch and British Jewries as well as the educated and noble Jews of Berlin to illustrate how only *politesse*, tolerance and civic liberties would lead to Jewish refinement.[20]

Two details seem relevant in this context as well: the Portuguese community in 1770 succeeded with its plea to the Chancellery to be allowed to employ as many teachers as necessary – and only after that did the 'High German' community follow the example set by the Sephardi Jews. And when in 1788 it became possible for Jews to take a doctoral degree at the University of Copenhagen, a Sephardi Jew, Samuel Frederik Henriques was the first to pass the exam as surgeon in 1797, becoming a government-employed surgeon at the Surgical Academy a year later.

In spite of the acculturating pioneer function of port Jews, as asserted by Sorkin and Dubin, it might seem doubtful whether these observations regarding the Danish case can truly be interpreted as expressions of 'acculturation being a *fait accompli*'. They might rather constitute a specific mode of acculturation, determined by the preconditions of port Jewish existence.[21] In other words, the acculturation of the Portuguese community in Copenhagen is very much a process as well, but different in nature from the Ashkenazi path of acculturation.

A second dimension that highlights the importance of the port Jewish dimension of Copenhagen Jewry was that, during the same decade, the Sephardi community was gradually turned into the institutional basis of a counter-elite, an avant garde challenging the 'traditionalists' for control of the Ashkenazi-dominated community. Already in the beginning of the eighteenth century, there were instances of Jews attempting to become 'Sephardi by choice', be it in order to evade taxes and community control, to achieve better privileges, or simply due to 'mixed' marriages. (This phenomenon in itself seems to underline the necessity not to reduce the phenomenon of port Jews to a purely ethnic issue – in terms of the 'western Sephardi experience'.) One of the potential legal ways to achieve this was illustrated by the Copenhagen merchant Nathanael Wallich's request to the civic authorities in 1786 to be allowed to leave the Ashkenazi and join the Portuguese community. His harsh criticism focused on the financial administration (the *Plettenwesen*) and the taxation policy of the community leadership. Wallich charged that they wanted to employ another superfluous 'Polish Rabbi' and Polish *melamdim* 'devoid of any education [*Bildung*] and good manners', and concluded that only by joining the Portuguese community would he be able to avoid their 'despotic rule' and ensure a satisfying education for his children. Wallich's protest set off a series of petitions that not only accused the *parnassim* of fiscal mismanagement, but categorically denied them the power of coercion. East European *melamdim* were scorned and the education of the neighbouring Sephardi community hailed as an alternative to the present Ashkenazi curriculum. Many of these contentions are well-known from other *haskalah*-inspired voices, but in this case there is no evidence of a direct reference to or connection with the centres of *haskalah* activity. Furthermore, there seems to be a specific twist to this criticism, as Wallich not only cultivated the Sephardi ideal of learning, but very specifically presented the Portuguese community as an alternative for emulation and affiliation.

The most obvious example of the function of the Portuguese community as a safe haven and a base for those forces spearheading acculturation and social inclusion may have been the Society for the Promotion of Vocational Training among Jews (*Prämiengesellschaft für die Anstellung der jüdischen Jugend bei Künstlern und Handwerkern*). It had been initiated in 1792 – as a reaction to the law that had opened the guilds to Jews in 1788 – by Heiman Isaac and Levin

Isaac Cantor, two wholesale merchants belonging to the Portuguese community, who already in the years immediately preceding the foundation of the Society had challenged the Ashkenazi community leadership and their 'despotic' practice. Consisting of both Christian and Jewish members, the Society became instrumental in creating a public sphere transcending ethnic and religious cleavages, thus preparing the ground for the process of social inclusion and cultural rapprochement that gained momentum during these years. In this context, it seems worth noting that the Society found its staunchest patrons among the port Jews of the capital, whereas the Elders of the Ashkenazi community refused to support the project in any way.[22]

When the terms of Jewish emancipation were negotiated from the late 1790s, it comes as no surprise that the representative of the Portuguese community, Jeremias Henriques, repeatedly argued against a fusion of the communities and against the state endowing a new community leadership with administrative authority over educational and other institutions. On the contrary, the state should refrain from interference, the congregation was to have a purely confessional character and civic and religious functions had to be strictly separated.

A third and final aspect deserves to be mentioned here: the question of whether the Danish setting did contribute in some way to the *haskalah* and its appreciation for the Sephardi tradition and curriculum. As has been pointed out before, the early *maskil* Solomon Hanau served as private tutor to the young Naphtali Herz Wessely during Hanau's stay in Copenhagen around 1735 and contributed to Wessely's interest in grammar and scripture. Both Gottlieb and Isaac Euchel had been living there for some time, and Moses Mendelssohn's brother-in-law, Joseph Guggenheim, as well as Fromet's brother-in-law, Moses Fürst, had settled here.[23] Furthermore, the *Bi'ur*, Mendelssohn's project of a Bible translation and commentary, was safeguarded against traditionalist attacks by having the Danish Court and a number of Copenhagen scholars subscribe to it – and so did a significantly high number of Copenhagen Jews.[24]

Nevertheless, it remains hard to find evidence that the Copenhagen setting and its cultural configuration had any clear influence on the *haskalah* – let alone its port Jewish dimension. Copenhagen did generate a couple of *maskilim*, but as a Jewish community, it was more into 'consuming' than 'producing' *haskalah*. In this respect, it is significant that no comprehensive counter-ideology favouring acculturation or integration was developed, let alone by a wholesale adoption of the Berlin *haskalah*.

Conclusion: The Hybrid Path of Danish-Jewish Acculturation and Religious Reform

The port Jewish legacy in the Danish case of a hybrid community seems primarily to have consisted of a rather moderate course of reform and acculturation, neither of which is to be described as an ideological import – in the sense of Jacob Katz – nor as non-intellectual or non-reflective in terms of how Todd Endelman has described the path of England's Jews into modernity. The transformation of Denmark's Jews then was neither caused nor controlled by an 'import' of German-Jewish reform ideology nor did it represent another case of purely pragmatic, non-ideological change.[25] Judaism was consciously redefined by a small group of acculturated Copenhagen Jews – partially influenced by a port Jewish experience and outlook – that adopted, transformed and applied arguments from the German-Jewish discourse during the 1790s. This conflict had started out with an attack by a group of acculturated merchants and bankers on the traditional elders' authority, questioning their right to define the legitimate degree of acculturation,[26] but had quickly developed into a major discussion on the nature of Judaism.[27]

The cultural transformation of Danish Jewry definitely did not occur without intellectual reflection, and from early on the frame of reference was German Jewry and the Berlin *haskalah*. There was, thus, a clear and articulated awareness of the implications and ramifications of this change, but this was not equivalent with taking over some *haskalah* blueprint of reform ideology. This is true for the situation at the outset of the community conflict as well. In spite of the often-cited family relations connecting figures of the Berlin *haskalah* such as Moses Mendelssohn or Isaac Euchel to Copenhagen, and in spite of the high number of subscribers to the *Bi'ur*, until 1785 no clear group of *haskalah* supporters had emerged, let alone in terms of its now radicalising Berlin variant.[28] It took the dynamics of local controversies over authority and acculturation to set the stage for an adaptation of *haskalah* arguments in the Danish-Jewish community, with far-reaching consequences for the understanding of Jewish religion.

It was the gradual implementation of subsequent institutional reforms, however, that came to constitute the backbone of modern Danish Judaism from the early nineteenth century onwards. In spite of a diminishing degree of observance, the loyal identification with the – now both Ashkenazi and Portuguese – community and its institutional infrastructure remained by and large intact, preparing the ground for a segmental Jewish life and identity in Denmark. By way of conclusion, it might be argued that the establishment of 'modern' community schools for boys and girls and the middle path of moderate synagogue reforms at the beginning of the nineteenth century, contributing significantly to the continued cohesion of Danish-Jewish life, was to a considerable degree indebted to a specific interplay between what has been designated as the social types of the court Jew, the *haskalah* affiliate and the port Jew of a Danish variant.

NOTES

I am grateful to Lois Dubin and David Sorkin for their useful comments.

1. These diaries constitute an invaluable source for Danish-Jewish affairs in the eighteenth century, especially as most of the Jewish community records were destroyed by fire in 1795 and 1807.
2. Martin Schwarz Lausten, *De fromme og jøderne: Holdninger til jødedom og jøder i Danmark i pietismen (1700–1760)* (Copenhagen: Akademisk Forlag, 2000), p.327.
3. On the other hand, even agrarian societies can have a port city or cities that function as urban maritime exceptions to the predominantly agrarian society. For an example of agrarian inland France versus commercial coastal Bordeaux, see Edward Whiting Fox, *History in Geographic Perspective: The Other France* (New York: Norton 1971).
4. David Sorkin, 'Enlightenment and Emancipation: German Jewry's Formative Age in Comparative Perspective', in Todd M. Endelman (ed.), *Comparing Jewish Societies* (Ann Arbor, MI: University of Michigan Press, 1997), p.104.
5. Here it might be worth noting that Lois Dubin has stressed the potential of experimenting reform absolutism against an emphasis on the role of less feudally structured states, young democracies and colonies as harbingers of emancipation in other works. Cf. Lois Dubin, *The Port Jews of Habsburg Trieste: Absolutist Politics and Enlightenment Culture* (Stanford, CA: Stanford University Press, 1999).
6. This essay draws on my dissertation research on the acculturation and emancipation of Danish Jewry 1750–1850 in a comparative European perspective.
7. See, for example, Theodor Hauch-Fausbøll, 'Jødernes Færden og Ophold i den danske Stat i det 17de Aarhundrede', *Tidsskrift for jødisk historie og literatur* II (1919–21), pp.106–79, 201–40, 307–26; Michael Hartvig, *Jøderne i Danmark i tiden 1600–1800* (Copenhagen: G.E.C. Gad, 1951).
8. Per Katz, *Jøderne i Danmark i det 17. århundrede* (Copenhagen: C.A. Reitzel, 1981), p.94 and passim.
9. See David Cesarani, 'Introduction', pp.1–13, for further reference.
10. Cf. for this and the following: Hartvig (see note 7), p.33ff.; Arthur Arnheim, 'De første jødiske bosættelser i København', *Rambam* 5 (1996), 43–8.
11. Cf. Hermann Kellenbenz, *Sephardim an der unteren Elbe: Ihre wirtschaftliche und politische Bedeutung vom Ende des 16. bis zum Beginn des 18. Jahrhunderts*, Beiheft No.40, Vierteljahrsschrift für Sozial- und Wirtschaftsgeschichte (Wiesbaden: Franz Steiner, 1958), pp.72ff. and 323–419.
12. Katz (see note 8), p.74.
13. Schwarz Lausten (see note 2), p.147.
14. In 1727, three private citizens suggested to the Copenhagen Magistrate to threaten the Jews with forced colonisation. Schwarz Lausten (see note 2), 210.
15. Schwarz Lausten (see note 2), p.277 n.14.
16. Katz, (see note 8), pp.86f. and 91–3.
17. For the *quid pro quo* of the German-Jewish emancipation contract, cf. David Sorkin, *The Transformation of German Jewry 1780–1840* (Oxford: Oxford University Press, 1987), pp.13–21 and passim.
18. For the term '*haskalah avant la lettre*', see David Sorkin, 'The Port Jew: Notes towards a Social Type', *Journal of Jewish Studies* 50.1 (1999).
19. For the notion of an early modern 'baroque Judaism', characterised by a neglect of Jewish philosophy and Hebrew language and grammar, as well as by a glaring cultural insularity, see David Sorkin, *The Berlin Haskalah and German Religious Thought* (London: Vallentine Mitchell, 2000), p.38.
20. See the pamphlets by Marcus Salomonsen Nyeborg, *Forsvarsskrift for den jødiske Nation eller Kritiske Betragtninger over det første Capitel i den VII. Tome af Voltaire Verker i Anledning af Jøderne.Oversat af Fransk* (Copenhagen 1765); *Svar til Philaletos paa hans Brev til Oversetteren af Forsvarsskriftet for Jøderne* (Copenhagen 1766); *Andet Svar til Philaletos* (Copenhagen, 1766).
21. Sorkin (see note 19), p.128.
22. See Georg Simon, *Præmieselskabet for den jødiske Ungdoms Anbringelse til Kunster og Håndværk* (Copenhagen: C.A. Reitzel, 1999).
23. Both Naphtali Herz (Hartwig) Wessely and the brothers Isaac and Gottlieb Euchel were raised in Copenhagen and spent some decades of their life there – though their activity as promoters

of *haskalah* did not begin until later. Joseph Guggenheim was a brother-in-law to Mendelssohn (i.e. married to his sister), and Moses Fürst was married to a sister of Mendelssohn's wife Fromet. But: Mendelssohn's letter of recommendation for I. Euchel to Fürst does implicate that in 1784 the Copenhagen relatives are not familiar with these activists of the *haskalah*. Cf. Alexander Altmann, *Moses Mendelssohn: A Biographical Study* (Tuscaloosa: University of Alabama Press, 1973), pp.329–45.

24. Of 515 subscribers altogether, 47 Jews (and six Christians) were residents of Copenhagen.

25. In this sense, the Danish case is to be situated within the trend to allow for more nuances, variations and shades in the drama of European Jewish acculturation, cf. the recent works of Lois Dubin, Frances Malino, David Ruderman and Josef Kaplan.

26. Three main issues were dominant in this early phase of conflict: the management of the community's financial matters by the Elders; the distribution of meal vouchers for poor migrants, and how people had to be dressed – and what wig to wear – when participating in the synagogue service.

27. One might speculate, why this took place so early: it might have been due to a combination of the dynamics of local conflict and the availability of alternative models and patterns of Jewish life.

28. A case in point seems to be that the above-mentioned subscribers cannot be differentiated in terms of a traditionalism–modernisation cleavage: they belong to both factions that might not have yet fully developed. Furthermore, August v. Hennings complains about the Jewish community in his letters to Mendelssohn: Copenhagen Jewry seemed not to be a potential source of support for *haskalah* projects, cf. Altmann (see note 23), p.491.

Networks and Communication in the Sephardi Diaspora: An Added Dimension to the Concept of Port Jews and Port Jewries

EVELYNE OLIEL-GRAUSZ

The relevance of Sephardi history to the concept of Port Jews or Port Jewries during the early modern era defined, discussed and refined by Lois Dubin and David Sorkin, does not need restating because the very characteristics of this diaspora were instrumental to the conceptualisation process in the first place.[1] The Sephardi diaspora, particularly the western diaspora, with which the present essay will be concerned, offers a paradigm for depicting Port Jewries.[2]

However, although the relevance and utility of the concept from both a historiographical and heuristic point of view is beyond discussion, one dimension is absent from the Sorkin–Dubin dialogue. The missing dimension is the focus on the relations between port Jewries, on the multifaceted networks shaping the diasporic space, and ultimately on the issue of communication. This general statement immediately needs to be qualified and embroidered. First, the core emphasis of both authors on commerce does imply commercial links and networks. However, these commercial links are only one aspect of the complex set of relations and the forms of communication at work in the early modern Sephardi diaspora. Secondly, these networks are usually mentioned as a historical *topos*, the difficulty residing precisely in the passage from the *topos* or cliché to historical depiction and analysis of concrete phenomena. Thirdly, this absence echoes the state of historiography on the subject at the time when the port Jews concept was crafted. Since then, the growing interest in the network approach has produced a number of fine scholarly works, primarily concerned with economic history and private merchant networks.[3] Nevertheless, except for a few pioneering studies, and histories of communication and networks in the Jewish world, despite signs of a growing interest in the question little, or at least insufficient, attention has been paid to the issue of inter-communal history.[4]

Among the reasons for these historiographical *lacunae* is the often restrictive perspective of monographs, which sometimes act as the mythological Procrustean bed. Local monographs are indispensable, but with few exceptions they rarely foster an active interest in inter-communal history.[5] The issues involving other parts of the Jewish world are often overlooked, or underestimated, or relegated to a minor section when dealt with at all. Many of the numerous titles published around or in the wake of the commemoration of the fifth centenary of the expulsion from Spain bear testimony to these *lacunae* and limitations. While aiming at a global history of the Sephardi diaspora, these collections often offer a similar pattern: a juxtaposition of essays dealing with separate portions of the diaspora, which is thus sliced into as many regional, national or community sections.[6] Yet the sum of local micro-analyses of port Jewries does not equal the total history of that diaspora: it ignores a fundamental dimension that deserves to be addressed as such – that of communication, of relations, connections, conflicts and more generally circulation between the various poles and port Jewries, whether of persons, material or immaterial goods.

In the last few years the field of Jewish Studies, and the sub-field of Sephardi studies, bear witness to a growing interest in these issues. In the enlightening introduction to the volume entitled *Communication in the Jewish Diaspora*, Sophia Menache reviews major theories and definitions of communication and their relevance to the historian, and draws both from these theories and from her work as a specialist on communication in the Middle Ages, to present a number of useful guidelines and categories.[7] However, the only article in the volume devoted to early modern history is a classical contribution on the spread of the Sabbatean movement. And in his concluding statement Daniel Gutwein questions the traditional view associating the advent of modern communication in the Jewish diaspora and the development of the Jewish press to the Damascus Affair.[8] Undoubtedly, elaborate networks of communication did exist in the diaspora before the Damascus Affair, the formation of the Alliance Israelite and the emergence of a Jewish press that, when needed, offered a basis for international action. An example of is the reaction of the diaspora to the expulsion of Bohemian Jewry by Maria Theresa in 1744.[9]

Among the richest and most impressive bodies of material available for the analysis of these networks is the correspondence of the Amsterdam *Mahamad*, or governing board, of the Portuguese nation. Barring a few gaps, the outgoing correspondence of *Kahal Kadosh Talmud Torah* community (*copiador de cartas*) has been preserved from 1702 onwards and contains over 5,000 letters from the eighteenth century alone, addressed to a large number of communities as well as to a wide range of private persons.[10] The prolixity of the Amsterdam *Mahamad* is best emphasised though a comparison with the official correspondence of a middle-sized French town, Bayonne, which also hosted a port Jewry. Bayonne's outgoing correspondence for the eighteenth century (up to the French Revolution), numbers, approximately 10,000 letters, that is, only twice the amount of letters sent by the *Mahamad*, a board governing a nation of two or three thousand individuals at most.[11]

In order to incorporate the critical dimension of communication, movement and interaction into our understanding of port Jewries, and more generally of Jewish history, it is necessary to confront a multiplicity of sources, stemming from various port societies or communities, of various natures – official, private and communal sources – none of which will individually suffice to sketch the full scope of these interactions. Furthermore it is essential to utilise an interdisciplinary approach, combining demography, social, economic and religious history, as well as the history of material culture and representations.[12]

The focus of this essay will be limited to a global sketch of these networks and interactions, through an examination of three major issues. First, it will explore the issue of mobility and private networks in order to identify specific patterns of mobility within the Sephardi maritime diaspora which may be of use for a reflection on the concept of port Jewries as a whole. Secondly, it will delineate the main features of inter-communal networks, with an emphasis on the diversity of these evolving networks. Finally, it will raise the question of the articulation between the various forms and levels of interactions and the need to consider them globally and interdependently.

Mobility and Private Networks

Four examples or scenes of Sephardi mobility in the eighteenth century will serve as a departure point.

In the first, a vignette from 1754, a young Amsterdam widow, Ester Levy Flores, embarks aboard a ship bound for Surinam. Her marriage to Joseph Arias Carvalho had remained childless, and upon her husband's death she is required by Jewish law either to marry her brother-in-law or to be freed from this obligation through the ceremony of *halitza* (divorce). Her brother-in-law, Jeosuah Menahem Arias, lives in Surinam. Unfortunately, when she finally reaches her destination, the brother-in-law has vanished from the colony, and no one knows his whereabouts. The episode is documented through a collection of letters exchanged between the *parnassim* of the *Talmud Torah* of Amsterdam and *Beraha vesalom* of the Jodensavannah. Two years of difficulties and pressure from the communal authorities will pass before she can recover her freedom to marry whom she chooses.[13]

The second example is taken from a certificate of Sephardic ancestry, also in Amsterdam Portuguese archives, which describes an interesting itinerary.

The certificate is written in Livorno, in the year 1700, in favour of two sisters, Lea and Jael Cohen, daughters of Moseh and Ester Cohen Azevedo. They were born in Amsterdam, and from there left for Salé in Berberia. After their mothers' death in Salé, they settled in Livorno. At the time the document is written one is a widow and the other one has apparently been abandoned by her husband, who is presently in Smyrna. In preparation for their voyage to Amsterdam they have this certificate drawn up, a sort of identification document for internal use within the Sephardi diaspora, which is of the first importance if they want to be granted financial and institutional help in Amsterdam.[14]

The third scenario is the life and career of a very interesting character, Abraham Gabay Isidro. He is the subject of countless letters and memoranda exchanged between Surinam and Amsterdam. Abraham Gabay Isidro was born in Spain at the very end of the seventeenth century and escaped to London when part of his family, including his wife, was imprisoned by the Inquisition. He is circumcised in London around 1721, and thereafter settles in Amsterdam where he becomes a brilliant student of Ets Haim. Following his studies he is appointed as *Haham* of the Surinam community, but after a lengthy and violent conflict with the *parnassim* during the 1730s he leaves Surinam to serve as *Haham* of the Barbadoes community. He dies in London. His widow commissions from Bayonne, her 'hometown', the posthumous publication of his *Sefer yad Avraham* published in 1763. The diasporic peregrinations of his posthumous work add to the intricacy of his life and itinerary.[15]

The last illustration centres on the figure of Samuel Peixotto, son to a prosperous Bordeaux family of merchants and bankers. In 1762, together with his uncle and chaperon, he undertakes a lengthy trip to Holland and England which is designed to serve a double purpose. First, it is intended to train him in commerce by introducing him to his relatives and correspondents. Second, it is hoped to find him a suitable wife. He attains the latter aim in London when he marries Sarah Mendes da Costa. But their divorce case will make him both famous and notorious a decade later, and become a *cause célèbre*.[16]

These instances were not chosen haphazardly. Each of them exemplifies one or several features of Sephardi mobility. The *halitza* case illustrates the westward movement of Sephardim toward the New World and the dispersion of close kin across vast expanses. The young Peixotto embarking upon his *bildungsreise* and his matrimonial quest illustrates how kinship and commerce networks functioned as active agents of mobility. The experience of the Cohen sisters illustrates the high degree of mobility among the less affluent while, by contrast, Haham Gabay Isidro shows the equally high mobility of rabbinical graduates of the Ets Haim seminary in Amsterdam.

For Haham Gabay Isidro, and not only for planters, merchants and paupers, the New World is a land of professional opportunity. More to the point, these cases demonstrate the variety of profiles, motives and routes of the Sephardi migrants: the rich and the not-so-rich, those seeking economic opportunity, those moving out of the prospect of betterment or due to dire necessity, educational mobility, *Halakhic*/matrimonial mobility. Unlike the epics of the greater figures of the seventeenth century, these case studies exemplify both the extraordinary and the ordinary dimensions of Sephardi mobility. Only one of these migrants/travellers fled the Iberian peninsular and all of them illustrate movement from one community to another – a very important and much neglected aspect of the history of Sephardi migrations and mobility.

The deliberate juxtaposition of these examples is intended to recreate the feeling of dizziness one sometimes experiences when reading through communal or personal archives from the Sephardi communities of London, Amsterdam, Bordeaux or the Caribbean. The criss-crossing of individual or family itineraries resembles some Brownian movement informed by such complex patterns of migration and remigration, routes and motives that it is difficult to make any sense of it.

In this context, the eighteenth century is of particular interest because it combines, for a large part, the persistence of mobility throughout the Jewish diaspora and a definite pattern whereby Sephardi groups emulate mobility within their national environment.

This kind of investigation into individual mobility is necessary for a better understanding of the Jewish World in the era before statistical records were kept. However, such research is arduous because the available material it confronts is very slight and it is difficult to devise a method of analysis that takes into account the heterogeneity of the sources. The possibilities and difficulty of such research can be illustrated by one example: I proposed a typology of travellers and patterns of Sephardi mobility based on a beautiful series of passport registers in Bordeaux that covered most of the eighteenth century. The passports originated in the desire of the French monarchy to control all passengers leaving Bordeaux in the years immediately after the revocation of the Edict of Nantes so as to prevent the covert emigration of Protestants from an area where they were particularly numerous. The exact title of these documents is '*certificats d'identité et de catholicité, soumissions et passeports des passagers*'. From this series of 14 registers we identified 1,078 Jews, most of whom were Sephardi, out of a total of approximately 33,000 passengers between the years 1713 and 1787 (with a few gaps). The search for 'equivalent' sources that would enable a comparative perspective, mobility through Amsterdam or London for example, led to a vast collection of passport registers in the State Papers of the National Archives (formerly the Public Records Office) in London.[17] After a lengthy process of sifting through the whole series, about 1,500 Jews were extracted from this archival magma, sometimes with a precise description of age, origin, destination and travelling motive, which matches the information of the Bordeaux passports, but more often just carrying the designation 'poor Jews'. The main conclusion from this research, though, was more relevant to a comparative history of French and British administrative history than to the study of Jewish migrations. The lack of chronological continuity, the heterogeneity of contents of these multi-purpose registers, and the change of data every time the secretary of state in charge of a specific area changed, created huge obstacles in the way of using what at first appeared like a promising source for comparative history.

When trying to devise a conceptual system to analyse Sephardi mobility and migrations, we are confronted with the same basic difficulty that arises in the study of migrations in general, namely the difficulty of combining a general framework that takes into account major trends and factors (religious, political, economic) and the complex decision-making process that causes an individual or a group to migrate, and that shapes the timing and the direction of their migration. It is necessary to bring together the macro- and micro-historical perspectives in the study of these migration patterns, not only to describe the migration trends, but also to understand the migration project and its implementation more broadly.

The various agents and factors prompting migration and mobility can be analysed going from the macro to the micro perspective on three main levels. The first level of analysis belongs to the macro-historical perspective, and encompasses general religious, political and economic factors. Here a distinction can be drawn between long-term, chronic factors and immediate causes such as persecution by the Inquisition in Spain and Portugal. Another example is the prolonged economic crisis affecting a community like Venice, as against the sudden expulsion of the Jews from Oran in 1669 or the collapse of the political-religious system which had protected Hamburg Sephardi Jewry at the end of the seventeenth century. A second set of factors that play a different but decisive role in the mobility patterns of the Sephardi diaspora consists of community institutions and policy. The most obvious dimension of community-triggered mobility is the systematic policy of sending away the 'supernumerary' poor. All Sephardi communities, with varying means and methods, implemented the same policy – Livorno, Bordeaux, London, Hamburg, Altona, Surinam, Curaçao, New York – and only a global, comparative optic can embrace them. Half of the coerced migration generated by this policy was multidirectional, sending poor Jews to the New World. Sometimes it was circular: the comparative study of community sources shows the existence of an intricate ballet of Sephardi *Betteljuden*. Their destination was often the result of a combination of elements: the financial means of the community, the emigration policy of the nation (because sometimes Jewish communal policy resembled of a larger scheme like the extrusion of Jews to Georgia in England in the early 1730s or the Amsterdam scheme to alleviate the burden of the community by establishing settlements for the poor in Surinam), and the personal desire and family connections of the *despachado* themselves.[18] Alongside this communally-prompted mobility, the wealth of the Amsterdam Portuguese community exerted a power of attraction, the measure of which is not easy to estimate. For example, the Aby Yetomim, the orphanage and orphan school, regularly received children from throughout the diaspora. The third and final level of analysis is that of the migrant himself, within a sometimes-limited choice of options. Here the role of the family in the decision-making process supplies a crucial dimension that is often underestimated.

The idea here is not to assume the dispersion of families as a given, but to see how kinship and family networks act as potent mobility agents. Daniel Swetchinski's analysis of kinship and commerce is very helpful for examining a good part of the eighteenth century. For example, the history of the Colaço family is one of movement back and forth between Bayonne and Amsterdam with offshoots in Curaçao and Hamburg. Similarly, the construction of the diamond and coral networks of the Franco and Castro families, between Livorno, London, India, Amsterdam and Curaçao was a result of the planned dispersion of close family members. Economic strategy and family mobility interacted in a complex and often self-perpetuating cycle. The expansion of Sephardi colonial trade in the Caribbean finds its expression in the dispatching of agents and partners who are often close kin.[19]

It needs to be emphasised is that kinship acted as an activating agent far beyond the circle of the merchant elite. The family dimension of the emigration from Spain and Portugal has been rightly emphasised. It can be seen from the names of merchants recorded on the freight bills presented by ship captains to the treasurer of the Portuguese community in London. Within the limits of other constraints bearing on potential emigrants, the establishment of kin in Amsterdam, London and Bordeaux operated as a strong attractive factor and sometimes created a migratory chain. The various Brandão mentioned in the 1803 Bevis Marks *Aliens List*, arriving from Portugal between 1762 and 1798, suggests that their move to England was partly motivated by the desire to join their relatives.[20] Among the destitute and others migrants, joining the family is the second motive listed in the Bordeaux passports.

Yet it is essential to add that simply describing the composition, chronology and directions of Sephardi migration and mobility (the classical pull and push perspective), and more generally using the cognitive approach to the act of migration, are not sufficient to highlight the specificity of the Sephardi diaspora.

It is important to analyse the long-term traces of the migration decision in the biography of the migrants: how closely connected are they to the sending area or areas and do they remain for the short term or long term? The renewal of migration studies during the last decade has laid a special emphasis on what happens after the actual migration, and the relationship between the migrant and his/her place of origin or former residence. This suggests many useful analytical tools for application to Sephardi migration patterns.[21] Pointing to the mechanical and over-determined causality of the push and pull factors explanatory framework, a French historian and demographer suggested a clever distinction between two major kinds of migrations, '*migrations de maintien*' and '*migrations de rupture*'.[22]

In the case of the '*migrations de rupture*', the migrant turns his back on the old country or sending area and invests intensely in the new homeland. In the case of '*migrations de maintien*', the migrant remains closely linked and attached to the original group, through his way of life and through the intensity of exchange and communication with them. Sephardi mobility and migration are undoubtedly typical of the '*migrations de maintien*', with the maintenance of a strong link with some of the original group. The expression of this link is multifaceted. It can be an intense communication between family clusters and Portuguese communities, institutional interaction between the communities, the use of a common liturgical and linguistic background, as well as more formal and diverse links between the communities.

Inter-Communal Networks and Communication

If the question of inter-communal networks and communication is not the *terra incognita* it was two decades ago, there is still a striking discrepancy between the effort and space devoted to the issue in the historiography and its historical centrality. Fernand Braudel's statement about the essence of the Mediterranean unity being not the sea but the links, movement and circulation, may well apply to the concept of port Jewry.[23]

This research originated in a dissertation, a revised monograph on Bordeaux Jewry in the early modern era. The awareness of the intense links and exchanges between that community and the rest of the Sephardi and Jewish world shifted the emphasis to a study of inter-communal relations, the scope of which gradually expanded. In order to avoid the limits of a local study, a multi-lens approach was adopted utilising contrasting viewpoints and archives from several key communities. Using correspondence and community registers, an attempt was made to map the networks of relations of communities of various sizes and importance, including Amsterdam,

London, Hamburg, Altona and Bordeaux.[24] Each of these communities is the centre of a specific network, which varies greatly in terms of the size of the community, its geographical location and its historical links with the other communities. The important idea is that space in the Sephardic diaspora is not to be measured only in terms of distance. It contracts thanks to intensive exchanges and close links. An illustration comes from a letter written by a Curaçoan Jew in 1755, Jacob de Jeudah Leao, to the Amsterdam *parnassim* in which he complains that his son was denied the honour of reading a passage from the Prophets in synagogue on Yom Kippur. In the context of the constant exchanges between the Curaçoan 'nation' and its metropolis, and of the extensive conflicts within the island community, the Amsterdam *parnassim* were appealed to for arbitration in a matter of little importance. The distance in space and time was erased by the closeness of both communities.

The in-depth study of these networks cannot be summarised within the scope of this essay, so it will outline a few distinctive features. First, whatever viewpoint is adopted, it appears that the word 'network' has to be used in the plural sense. The networks are multi-stranded and constantly in flux. For instance, the expulsion of Bohemian Jewry led to the mobilisation of numerous, varied circuits of information, financial support and diplomatic action. At the same time, despite that plasticity, the network is constituted by the existence of major hubs, a definite polarisation around key nations, and visible hierarchies. I have analysed elsewhere the metropolitan functions played by the *Talmud Torah* community in the Sephardi diaspora: it served as an institutional model and reference point, and it was resorted to by western Portuguese nations to solve internal conflicts of minor or major importance (such as the accusation of deism levelled by several congregants at the London *Haham*, David Nieto, in 1705).[25] Indeed, the Amsterdam *parnassim* often referred to the legitimacy and necessity of their intervention as deriving from their duty of patronage toward other Portuguese nations.

But the polarisation of Sephardi space goes far beyond a simple model of centre/periphery as suggested by the image of Amsterdam as the Sephardi metropolis. With the westward expansion of the Sephardi diaspora and the European turn to the Atlantic, the newer Portuguese 'nations' such as those in London, Curaçao and Jamaica took on an added weight in this spatial organisation, while communities like the ones in London and Curaçao developed their own sphere of influence and their own metropolitan role.[26]

A particular case may serve as a paradigm for the polarisation of the diasporic space and enable us to depart from general considerations. This was the process of hiring rabbinical and para-rabbinical staff, whether they be *Haham* (fully fledged rabbi), cantor or cantor in second, Rabbi or Ruby (school or academy teacher). That process is widely documented in community registers and correspondence. Where the communities turn to when no local candidate is available is indicative of the relationships they enjoy, the patterns of allegiance, existing hierarchies as well as self-image and representation. The selection of the candidates, as well as the recruitment process matter as much as the final choice. In many instances, the Amsterdam *parnassim* were required by their counterparts of the London, Hamburg, Curaçao and Surinam 'nations' to select a candidate from the graduates of the Ets Haim seminary. But here again, the simple model of the metropolis/colony fails because the selection process was often two-tiered. The communities Nidhe Israel of Barbados, Shaar Hashamayim of Jamaica, and Shearith Israel of New York, when in need of a rabbi or a *hazan*, resorted to the London *Mahamad*, which in turn asked the Amsterdam *parnassim* for a suitable candidate from Ets Haim. Curaçao provided some of the *hazanim* and schoolteachers needed in the Caribbean area, and their careers reflect the local hierarchy.

For example, Josuah Hisquiau de Cordovah, born in Amsterdam and trained in Ets Haim, was sent to Curaçao to be a teacher at the request of Mikve Israel. By 1755 he very much wanted to leave Curaçao and the irascible Samuel Mendes de Solla, rabbi of the community, so he turned to the Jamaican 'nation'. His appointment there, to what was a lesser community, led to a significant promotion, since he became a fully fledged *Haham*. The London community, when it did not appeal to Amsterdam, turned to Italy and once, in 1765, to Smyrna to find suitable candidates. In 1760, when no eligible candidate was to be found locally, the Amsterdam *Mahamad* itself turned to the East, to Constantinople and entrusted the selection of a rabbi to the Deputies of the Holy Land.[27]

The Sephardi diaspora was thus criss-crossed by numerous routes and circuits which delineated networks of varying nature and permanence, the combination of which constitutes the idea of a people in communication. The explicit rationality of these forms of interaction is organised around three major functions: the perpetuation of the structure of the Portuguese community; the defence and protection of local or foreign Jews and their activities, whether Sephardi or not; and the implementation and transmission of *halakhah*. The pursuit of these ends accounts for the multiplicity and the variety of the networks and circulation process: networks of information, financial networks, diplomatic networks and networks of a more religious nature. In this last category can be included such different matters as the circulation of rabbinical and pseudo-rabbinical personnel, the channels of liturgical innovation, the networks of *halakhic* authority (as reflected by the sphere of influence of the various rabbinical courts), and also the circulation of 'sacred *realia*', or ritual objects connected with religious observance.

Two instances of the latter will be briefly considered here. The circulation of information forms the basis of this inter-communal communication. It is carried out through a number of media, of which letters ranks as most important. Indeed, they merit a sharper interest among historians of Jewish societies.[28] The lay leadership was the main channel for normative communication, but it did not have an exclusive monopoly. Apart from the official correspondence between communities, information was also channelled through the private merchant and family networks. Emissaries from the Holy Land or from communities in trouble were also important vectors of information, as well naturally as private travellers, whether merchants, students or paupers. Letters were sometimes sent twice, through different routes or aboard different ships.

Reconstructing the route followed by individual pieces of information is a fascinating task, and can be illustrated by one example. In 1691, the London *parnassim* dispatched to the British Caribbean news that the Jerusalem *kahal* was in dire poverty, relaying the description that they themselves had received from Amsterdam. Two years later, information travelled back from the New World to the Holy Land when the London *parnassim* inform the Safed community about a disastrous earthquake in Jamaica.[29] In the latter case, the communication did not aim at collecting funds, but was purely informational. These routes and hubs were not fortuitous, but point to hierarchical networks for the communities transmitting the letters and requests also serving an authentification purpose. In 1776 the Tetuan community faced severe financial troubles and set about requesting help from the major Portuguese 'nations'. One letter was sent to London, via Gibraltar, accompanied by a letter of recommendation from the Gibraltar community, which numbered many Portuguese Jews, and a second letter was sent to Amsterdam via Livorno. In this instance, Livorno worked both as a permanent epistolary hub and as a certification authority. The mediation of Gibraltar on the Tetuan–London route guaranteed the legitimacy of the request, but also gave leverage to the cry for help, because of the close institutional and personal links between the London and Gibraltar communities.[30]

A second instance is the circulation of sacred *realia*, or the '*choses du sacré*', which is one aspect of the religious-*halakhic* networks. Far from being trifling the existence and the forms of this circulation are important markers of inter-communal networks of communication. These sacred paraphernalia included Torah scrolls and the whole gamut of Torah and synagogue ornaments; kosher foods such as wine, meat, cheese; specific and precious liturgical items like the *lulav* and *etrog* fruit used during the festival of Succot; and items related to deceased individuals, including bodies, bones and tombstones.[31] One example of this circulation may stand for many. It was customary to bury a small quantity of soil from the Holy Land with a deceased person and the Amsterdam *parnassim* ordered shipments of soil either directly from Safed or through the mediation of the deputies of the Holy Land in Constantinople. It was then sent through Smyrna. We know that in 1786 the Jamaican community turned to London for a fresh supply, but the London community was itself in short supply, and thus turned to its Italian correspondents to renew its stock and enable London to comply with the Jamaican request.[32]

Interactions of Individual, Group and Community Strategies

It is arduous to separate the various agents at work in the diaspora but individual, sub-group and community strategies have to be analysed in the same way, using documents critically.

Community strategies are deeply intertwined with sub-group or individual social and economic strategies. One obvious locus of this interaction is the communal treatment of poverty. The communal policy of sending the local and foreign poor to other Portuguese 'nations', either within western Europe or westward toward the Caribbean or North America, contributed significantly to intra-diasporic mobility and was, of course, important relative to the demography of these modestly-sized Jewish communities.

Another level of interaction between the private, communal and inter-communal realms, far less obvious, is how the threads of communal and private network communication strategies were intricately intertwined. Of this interconnection, we shall provide but an example: the commercial correspondence of Abraham da Costa's firm, in the 1720s, mainly addressed to Surinam. It is interspersed with official letters to the Surinam *Mahamad*, which appear side by side with letters to local trading partners. These letters are dated both in the civil and the Jewish calendar, whereas the strictly business-centred letters only bear the civil date. This imbrication indicates that the lay leadership recruited its agents largely among the merchant elite. More interesting, however, is the fact that official information is channelled in various forms through merchant networks. But the da Costa firm does not only act as postal service: it also serves the implementation of community strategies. The combination of community and business interest reached a climax with da Costa being asked to sell shipments of sugar for the benefit of the Surinamese charity fund or *Tzedaka*.[33]

Our hypothesis, which calls for further investigation, is that the interaction between these various agents and levels of communication is a specific feature of the Sephardi diaspora. In conclusion, it appears from the present survey that researching both dimensions is necessary for the study of the Sephardi diaspora, and that one of the most interesting aspects is the interaction between individuals, social sub-groups and communities or 'nations'. This approach is necessary in order to understand the dynamics of local port Jewries, as Lois Dubin has emphasised,[34] but also that of the connections between the various Jewish entities. Working with the Sephardi diaspora as a distinctive sub category of Port Jews and Port Jewries compels the historian to combine and confront three historical dimensions: the local; the comparative or pan-diasporic; and the dynamic or interactive dimension.[35]

NOTES

1. David Sorkin, 'The Port Jew: Notes toward a Social Type', *Journal of Jewish Studies* 50 (1999), 87–97; idem, 'Port Jews and the Three Regions of Emancipation', in David Cesarani (ed.), *Port Jews: Jewish Communities in Cosmopolitan Maritime Trading Centre, 1550–1950* (London: Frank Cass, 2002), pp.31–46; Lois Dubin, 'Researching Port Jews and Port Jewries: Trieste and Beyond', in ibid., pp.47–58.

2. On the western Diaspora, see for recent references Yosef Kaplan, *An Alternative Path to Modernity: The Sephardi Diaspora in Western Europe* (Leiden: E.J. Brill, 2001); Jonathan Israel, *Diasporas within a Diaspora* (Leiden: E.J. Brill, 2001); and also Gérard Nahon, *Métropoles et périphéries séfarades d'Occident: Kairouan, Amsterdam, Bayonne, Bordeaux, Jérusalem* (Paris: Cerf, 1993).

3. Daniel Snydacker, *Traders in Exile: Quakers and Jews of New York and Newport in the New World Economy, 1650-1776* (Ph.D. dissertation, John Hopkins University, 1982); Israel (see note 2); idem, 'El comercio de los judíos sefardíes de Amsterdam con los conversos de Madrid a través del suroeste francés', in Jaime Contreras *et al.* (eds.), *Familia, religión y negocio: El Sephardismo en las relaciones entre el mundo ibérico y los Países Bajos en la Edad Moderna* (Fundación Carlos Amberes, 2003), pp.373–90; and for a enlightening cross-cultural perspective, Francesca Trivellato, 'Juifs de Livourne, Italiens de Lisbonne, Hindous de Goa: Réseaux marchands et échanges interculturels à l'époque moderne', *Annales HSS* (2003), 581–603.

4. Gérard Nahon, 'Les rapports des communautés judéo-portugaises de France avec celles d'Amsterdam aux XVII et XVIIIe siècles', *Studia Rosenthaliana* 10 (1976), 37–78, 151–88; idem, 'Les relations entre Amsterdam et Constantinople au XVIIIe siècle d'après le Copiador de Cartas de la Nation Juive Portugaise d'Amsterdam', in Jozeph Michman (ed.), *Dutch Jewish History: Proceedings of the Symposium on the History of the Jews in the Netherlands* (Jerusalem: Institute for Research on Dutch Jewry, 1986), pp.157–84; idem, 'Amsterdam and Jerusalem in the 18th Century: the State of the Sources and Some Questions', in Jozeph Michman (ed.), *Dutch Jewish History: Proceedings of the Fourth Symposium on the History of the Jews in the Netherlands, 7–10 décembre 1986, Jerusalem* (Jerusalem and Assen: Van Gorcum, 1986), pp.95–116; Jonathan Israel, 'The Jews of Venice and their links with Holland and with Dutch Jewry (1600-1710)', in Gaetano Cozzi (ed.), *Gli Ebrei e Venezia, secoli XIV–XVIII* (Milan: Edizioni Comunita, 1987), pp.95–116; Miriam Bodian, 'Amsterdam, Venice and the Marrano Diaspora in the Seventeenth Century', in J. Michman (ed.), *Dutch Jewish History* (Jerusalem: Van Gorcum, 1989), pp.47–65; Yosef Kaplan, 'The Curaçao and Amsterdam Jewish Communities in the 17th and 18th Centuries', *American Jewish History* (1982), 172–92; Yosef Haim Yerushalmi, 'Between Amsterdam and New Amsterdam: The Place of Curaçao and the Caribbean in Early Modern Jewish History', *American Jewish History* 72 (1982), 172–92; Evelyne Oliel-Grausz, 'Relations, coopération et conflits intercommunautaires dans la diaspora séfarade: l'affaire Nieto, Londres, Amsterdam, Hambourg (1704-1705)', in Henry Mechoulan and Gérard Nahon (eds.), *Mémorial I.-S. Révah: Etudes sur le marranisme, l'hétérodoxie juive et Spinoza*, (Paris and Louvain: E. Peeters, 2001), pp.335–64, idem, 'Study in Intercommunal Relations

in the Sephardi Diaspora: London and Amsterdam in the XVIIIth Century', in Yosef Kaplan, Chaya Brasz (eds.), *Dutch Jews as Perceived by Themselves and by Others* (Leiden, Boston and Cologne: E.J. Brill, 2001), pp.41–58; idem, *Relations et réseaux intercommunautaires dans la diaspora séfarade d'Occident au XVIIIe siècle* (unpublished dissertation, Université Paris I Sorbonne, 2000); Sophia Menache (ed.), *Communication in the Jewish Diaspora: The Pre-Modern World* (Leiden and New York: E.J. Brill, 1996).

5. Shlomo Simonsohn, *History of the Jews in the Duchy of Mantua* (Jerusalem: Kiryath Sepher, 1977), pp.413–98; Tullia Catalan, *La comunita ebraica di Trieste, 1781–1914: politica, societa e cultura* (Trieste: LINT, 2000).

6. See, for instance, Richard Barnett and Walter Schwab (eds.), *The Western Sephardim* (Northants: Gibraltar, 1989); Henry Méchoulan (ed.), *Les juifs d'Espagne: Histoire d'une diaspora, 1492–1992* (Paris: Liana Lévi, 1992).

7. Sophia Menache, 'The "Pre-History" of Communication', in Menache (see note 4), pp.2–13; idem, 'Communication in the Jewish Diaspora: A Survey', in ibid., pp.14–56. See also the series of volumes edited by Shmuel Trigano, *La société juive à travers l'histoire* (Paris: Fayard, 1993), vols.3 and 4, especially Zeev Gries, 'L'imprimerie comme moyende communication entre les communautés juives: prolégomènes à une analyse d'après des exemples du XVIe siècle', pp.229–44; see also, *The Book as an Agent of Culture: 1700–1900 [ha-Sefer ke-sokhen tarbut: ba-shanim 460–660 (1700–1900)]* (Tel Aviv: ha-Kibuts ha-meuhad, 2002).

8. Daniel Gutwein, 'Traditional and Modern Communication: The Jewish Context', in Menache (see note 4), pp.409–26.

9. Baruch Mevorach, 'The Intercommunal and Diplomatic Activity Undertaken by the Hamburg Community to Prevent the Expulsion of the Jews of Bohemia, 1745', in B. Mevorach *et al.* (eds.), *Studies in the History of the Jewish People and the Land of Israel* (Haifa: University of Haifa, 1970), pp.187–232; Evelyne Oliel-Grausz, 'Les communautés séfarades d'Europe occidentale et l'expulsion des juifs de Prague en 1745', *Yod* 1–2 (1995–96), pp.49–58.

10. Gérard Nahon, 'Une source pour l'histoire de la diaspora séfarade au XVIIIe siècle: le *Copiador de Cartas* de la communauté portugaise d'Amsterdam', *Proceedings of the First International Congress for the Study of the Sephardi and Oriental Jewry* (Jerusalem: 1981), pp.109–22.

11. Anne Zink, 'La ville de Bayonne et ses correspondants au XVIIIe siècle', in Pierre Albert (ed.), *Correspondre Jadis et Naguère*, actes du 120e congrès national des Sociétés historiques et scientifiques, Aix en Provence, 23–29 October 1995 (Paris: Comité des travaux historiques et scientifiques, 1997), pp.243–44.

12. Our previous research was conducted mainly with sources emanating from the Amsterdam, London, Hamburg and south-west France communities; we are currently working on several additional observatories, Livorno, Surinam and Curaçao.

13. This Atlantic *halitza* case is narrated in a series of letters exchanged between the communities of Amsterdam and Surinam, Gemeente Archief Amsterdam (hereafter GAA), PA 334 93, *Copiador de cartas*, fos.227–9 11 July 1755, fos.262–4, 305, 14 mai 1756, fos.323–4, 7 September 1756; PA 334 66, fos.858–9.

14. GAA, PA 334 503, no.7.

15. Cecil Roth, 'The Remarkable Career of Haham Abraham Gabay Izidro', *Transactions of the Jewish Historical Society of England* XXIV, Miscellanies IX (1970–73), 211–13; Zvi Loker, *Jews in the Caribbeans* (Jerusalem: Misgav Yerushalayim, 1991), pp.82–3. We are currently working on the conflict involving Haham Gabay Isidro, the Surinam *Parnassim* and the Amsterdam *Mahamad* as a case study in inter-communal interaction.

16. Archives Départementales de la Gironde, 3E 21678, Notarial archives, Etude de Maitre Rauzan, 13 April 1763.

17. Public Record Office, SP 386–413.

18. Richard D. Barnett, 'Dr Samuel Nunes Ribeiro and the Settlement of Georgia', in *Migration and Settlement: Proceedings of the Anglo-American Jewish Historical Conference held in London jointly by the Jewish Historical Society of England and the American Jewish Historical Society, July 1970* (London:

Jewish Historical Society of England, 1971), pp.63–101; Robert Cohen, 'Passage to a New World: The Sephardi Poor of Eighteenth Century Amsterdam', in Lea Dasberg et J.N. Cohen (eds.), *Neveh Yaakov: Jubilee volume presented to Dr Jaap Meijer on the occasion of his seventieth birthday* (Assen: Van Gorcum, 1982), pp.31–42.

19. Jean de Maupassant, *Un grand armateur de Bordeaux: Abraham Gradis (1699?–1780)* (Bordeaux: Féret et fils, 1917), pp.10–11, 21ff.; on the Gradis kin and trade networks, see Richard Menkis, *The Gradis Family of Eighteenth Century Bordeaux: A Social and Economic Study* (unpublished dissertation, Brandeis University, 1988); idem, 'Patriarchs and Patricians: The Gradis Family of Eighteenth Century Bordeaux', in Frances Malino and David Sorkin (ed.), *From East and West: Jews in a Changing Europe, 1750–1850* (Oxford: Basil Blackwell, 1990), pp.11–45; Paul Butel, 'Comportements familiaux dans le négoce bordelais au XVIIIe siècle', *Annales du Midi* 88 (1976), 139–57; idem, *Les négociants bordelais, l'Europe et les Iles au XVIIIe siècle* (Paris: Aubier, 1974).

20. Vivian D. Lipman, 'Sephardi and Other Jewish Immigrants in England in the Eighteenth Century', in *Migration and Settlement* (see note 18), pp.47–58.

21. David Cressy, *Coming Over: Migration and Communication between England and New England in the Seventeenth Century* (Cambridge: Cambridge University Press, 1987).

22. Paul-André Rosental, 'Maintien/rupture: un nouveau couple pour l'analyse des migrations', *Annales ESC* 45 (1990), pp.1403–31.

23. Fernand Braudel, 'La Mediterranée n'a d'unité que par le mouvement des hommes, les liaisosn qu'il implique, les routes qui le conduisent', *La Méditerranée et le monde méditerranéen à l'époque de Philippe II* (Paris: Armand Colin, 1966), édition Livre de Poche, vol.1, p.338.

24. Oliel-Grausz, *Relations et réseaux intercommunautaires* (see note 4), pp.326–43.

25. Oliel-Grausz, 'Relations, coopération et conflits intercommunautaires' (see note 4).

26. For the Caribbean area, see Jonathan Israel (note 2), pp.511–32; Oliel-Grausz, *Relations et réseaux intercommunautaires* (see note 4), pp.693–700.

27. For a first cursory glance, see Evelyne Oliel-Grausz, 'La circulation du personnel rabbinique dans les communautés de la diaspora séfarade au XVIIIe siècle', in Esther Benbassa (ed.), *Transmission et passages en monde juif* (Paris: Publisud, 1997), pp.313–34.

28. See note 4; and Richard D. Barnett, 'The Correspondence of the *Mahamad* of the Spanish and Portuguese Congregation of London during the 17th and 18th Centuries', *Transactions of the Jewish Historical Society of England* XX (1964), 1–50; Simon Schwarzfuchs, 'Le registre de correspondance des Juifs de Lorraine (1783–1791)', *Archives Juives* 27.2 (1994), 51–61; Menache (see note 4), pp.22–9; the issue of early modern correspondence and its social uses has become the focus of numerous publications, not limited anymore to the realm of the '*République des Lettres*': Pierre-Yves Beaurepaire, *La Plume et la Toile: Pouvoirs et réseaux de correspondance dans l'Europe des Lumières* (Arras: Artois Presses Université, Histoire, 2002); historians of the Huguenot diasporas play in this growing historical production a key role; see for instance the forthcoming *Atlas de la communication manuscrite à l'époque moderne*, under the supervision of Hans Bots, Eric-Olivier Lochard and Anthony McKenna.

29. Archives of the London Spanish and Portuguese Synagogue, Minutes of the *Mahamad*, 1678–1723, fo.142, letters to Barbadoes and Jamaica, dated 28 *Kislev* 5451, fo.144, letter to Senhor *Haham* Ruby Abraham Galante in Safed, dated *Roshodes Sebat* 5453.

30. The name of both communities is Shaar Hashamayim. Archives of the London Spanish and Portuguese Synagogue, Minutes of the *Mahamad*, 1776–1788, letters to the Tetuan and Gibraltar *Parnassim*, dated 12 November 1776. For the links between Tetuan, Gibraltar and Livorno, see Daniel J. Schroeter, *The Sultan Jew: Morocco and the Sephardi World* (Stanford, CA: Stanford University Press, 2002), pp.41–3; GAA, 334 95, *Copiador de cartas* 1773–1784, fo.162, 18 September 1776, letter to the Tetuan *Parnassim*.

31. Except for mentions dealing with the commerce of kosher wine, or occasional attempts at tracing the origins of a synagogue ritual holdings, this subject has been ignored by historians, except for Simon Schwarzfuchs, 'De Gênes à Trieste: le commerce millénaire des cédrats', in Pier Cesare Ioly Zorattini, Giacomo Todeschini (ed.), *Il mondo ebraico: Gli ebrei tra Italia nord-*

orientale e Impero asburgico dal Medioevo all'Età contemporanea (Pordenone: Edizioni Studio Tesi, 1991), pp.259–85. For the initial results of our investigation, still in progress, on this issue, see the abovementioned dissertation (note 4), pp.361–89.

32. Archives of the London Spanish and Portuguese Synagogue, Minutes of the *Mahamad*, 1776–1788, 13 elul 5546/6 September 1786, letter to the Mahamad of the Kingston *kehilah* in Jamaica.

33. GAA 946 10, da Costa fund. See Odette Vlessing, *Inventaris van het archief van de Familie da Costa 1616–1822*, Gemeentearchief Amsterdam, 1982/2000.

34. Dubin (see note 1), p.48.

35. Todd Endelman's plea for comparative history is widely quoted, but little enacted: 'Introduction: Comparing Jewish Societies', in idem, *Comparing Jewish Societies*, (Ann Arbor, MI: University of Michigan Press, 1997), pp.1–18; see also Lucette Valensi, 'L'exercice de de la comparaison au plus proche, à distance: le cas des sociétés plurielles', *Annales HSS* (2002), pp.27–30.

Were Merchants More Tolerant? 'Godless Patrons of the Jews' and the Decline of the Sephardi Community in Late Seventeenth-Century Hamburg

KLAUS WEBER

The seventeenth-century Hamburg Sephardi community is of general interest in the investigation of the political interactions between varying social and religious groups in early modern times. The first Jews from the Iberian peninsula arrived in this Hanseatic city around 1590 and throughout the seventeenth century they remained the wealthiest of the religious minorities in the city. During the 1680s and 1690s, economic factors and the rising momentum of intolerance caused the emigration of the majority of these Sephardi merchants, among them the most successful families. Most of them went to Amsterdam, many via Altona, a small Danish port neighbouring Hamburg. This essay will cast some light on the debate between the dominant interest groups which participated in the controversy about the status of the Jews who were established in seventeenth-century Hamburg. The three interest groups referred to here were the Citizenry (*Bürgerschaft*); the Senate, as the Hanseatic government was called; and the Chamber of Commerce, then called the *Commerzdeputation*.

As several authors have shown, in early modern Germany, Protestant communities and governments showed greater anti-Jewish tendencies, more often than did Roman Catholics.[1] But Hamburg is quite a special case, for it was there that an anti-Jewish discourse of orthodox Lutheran preachers collided with a tolerance emanating from the mentality of the cosmopolitan maritime merchants. This essay will explain some of the special conditions that enabled the Hamburg Sephardic Jews to withstand almost 100 years of difficult times and the changes in these conditions that caused an almost complete disintegration of their community. However, it will warn against judging this pronounced anti-Jewish phenomena from the perspective of twentieth-century German anti-semitism.[2] The treatment of other religious minorities such as Calvinists and Roman Catholics by the Lutheran preachers in early modern Hamburg may help us to assess these self-same Lutheran positions within the context of the epoch.

The decline of Hamburg's Portuguese Jewish trading community has already been treated by various authors. When dealing with any kind of Jewish matters related to German history, it is difficult to avoid the Nazi period, and this is true even in the context of a micro-study concerning such a distant topic as the history of seventeenth-century Hamburg. Even a very brief survey of the principal literature cannot omit *Sephardim an der unteren Elbe*, which for decades has been the only monograph to treat the early modern history of the Iberian Jews in the port cities on the lower Elbe river. Its author, Hermann Kellenbenz, published it as the thesis for his *Habilitation* in 1958.[3] Thereafter, he was to become one of the most respected German scholars in economic history. In the German context, his particular interest in early modern maritime trade and his frequent publications on this subject made him a unique figure. Yet the study had very particular antecedents. Though published in the late 1950s, the work was already finished in 1944, and these circumstances merit a closer examination. Helmut Heiber, who did consider these facts,[4] suggests that Kellenbenz altered considerable stretches of the manuscript after the end of the war. This may explain why the book lacks any consideration of religious and cultural aspects, and why even political matters are hardly touched upon in the text. Several works by German historians of his generation (and even of some of their junior scholars) show the same approach. It is also striking that the first work on the Jewish presence in Hamburg to integrate thoroughly these aspects was only published in 1985, in England: Joachim Whaley's comparative study on religious tolerance in early modern Hamburg, which is a very complex and illuminating investigation of all religious minorities present in the city. A German edition appeared in 1992.[5] Whaley's work is a useful complement to Jutta Braden's most detailed investigation on policy towards the Jews in Hamburg.[6] Only this recently published work has superseded Kellenbenz's peculiar domination of this field of study. While he offered a mere account of the facts on the rise and decline of the Sephardim, Braden describes and analyses meticulously the attitudes of Hamburg clergy and Citizenry toward both the Sephardi and Ashkenazi minorities and the interactions between policy makers and economic and religious interest groups.

It is also worth mentioning that special aspects of Hamburg's Jewish history have been treated in a collection of articles edited in 1991 by Arno Herzig and Saskia Rohde and published on the occasion of an important exhibition on Hamburg Jewish history organised by the *Museum für Hamburgische Geschichte* in 1991.[7] The museum itself has published a detailed and richly annotated catalogue.[8] The exhibition objects depicted there testify to the material and cultural riches of the Sephardic community. A full bibliographical survey, which cannot be offered here, is provided in Jutta Braden's study.

After giving a chronology of the development and decline of Hamburg's seventeenth-century Iberian Jewish community and of the general debates treating this topic within the Christian corporations of that city, this essay will provide some source-based information about the debate between the *Bürgerschaft*, the Senate and the *Commerzdeputation*, which will illustrate their respective positions on the subject of the Jews.

Chronology

Ever since the commencement of the Reformation in the 1520s, the Hanseatic city of Hamburg has always been devotedly Lutheran. During the first decade of the Reformation, lay institutions were founded for the administration of the town's four parishes and of their social welfare institutions. The parish members elected their own representatives to negotiate the interests of the citizens with the town's Senate, thus forming the first assemblies of the *Bürgerschaft*. Political representation of the Citizenry and the organisation of social welfare were thoroughly interwoven with the religious identity of these city burgers.[9] As a result, the Citizenry may be regarded as the political representation of the parishes, and it always maintained a very decidedly orthodox form of Lutheranism.

In Hamburg, religious conflicts arose mainly with the immigration of Dutch Calvinists during the uprising of the Netherlands against Philip II and thereafter, in the 1590s, with the arrival of new Christians from the Iberian peninsula. The first of these Sephardi Jews, most of them from Portugal, and a small number of Spanish Jews, did not profess their native religion but claimed to be Catholic Christians. It was only after 1610, when their community had been recognised by the Senate and when the impact of their commercial and financial power had been acknowledged and appreciated by the Hanseatic merchants, that this group showed overtly that they maintained their Hebraic beliefs and religious practices. Yet, by 1603 and 1604, the Citizenry, dominated by the guilds and middle-class merchants, sent its first complaints to the Senate, demanding that those Portuguese who where Jews should be expelled.[10] Throughout the century, the citizens' claims were backed by fierce anti-Jewish texts and sermons of a number of pastors. Indeed, the more the diversity of the city's social and economic foundations grew, the more Protestant orthodoxy in Hamburg became hermetic.

But the Senate, consisting of a merchant elite, did not accept the citizens' confessional rigour. In recognition of the stimulating economic activities of the 'Portuguese nation', the senators always maintained a position that vowed to defend the Sephardic community against the intolerant claims of the *Bürgerschaft*. In spite of the attacks from the Citizenry and Lutheran clergy, the

Jewish community grew steadily: in 1610, approximately 100 Iberian Jews were resident in Hamburg, in 1648 there were at least 100 families, and in 1663 the community numbered about 600 persons. The 1660s saw the peak decade of this community's demographic and economic strength. In 1692 there were only 200 persons left, and in 1730 no more than about 50 families remained.[11]

From the beginning, the argument of the Senate suggested that the presence of such a rich community advanced many types of new commercial advantage, so once the Jews had arrived and become established the town could not afford to expel them. Indeed, due to the connections which they maintained to the Iberian peninsula, the importation of raw sugar, wine, oil, tobacco and all sorts of spices was very much stimulated by their presence. In the late 1590s, Jews like Ximenes and Manuel Alvares participated in the direct Hamburg–Brazil trade. The first Hamburg sugar refineries – an industry which in the eighteenth century was to become Hamburg's principal branch – were created by Portuguese Jews before 1610.[12] They received the raw sugar from their brethren established in Brazil, Surinam, Barbados and other places in the New World. We may suggest that in the course of the century they also became increasingly involved with the expanding export trade of central European manufactured goods into the Atlantic basin. Dutch Curaçao for example, where an important Sephardi community was established, served as a major base for smuggling such commodities into the Spanish American mainland. One of its major items was linen, which constituted the bulk of Hamburg's exports.[13]

In 1616 Hamburg Jews participated in the founding of the famous Hamburg Bank, and in the very first year of its existence, some 4.5 per cent of the bank's turnover was the responsibility of Sephardic merchants.[14] The number of Jewish bank accounts in Hamburg rose, while their number in Amsterdam fell.[15] Even more important was their impact on the bill exchange. In this Elbe river port, the presence of Calvinist immigrants from the Netherlands and that of the Iberian Jews had furthered the adaptation of modern financial techniques by local merchants, and the Iberian traders with their access to Spanish American silver helped to transform the city into one of the financial capitals of northern Europe. In its continuous disputes with the Citizenry, the Senate always argued that an exodus of the Portuguese nation would ruin Hamburg's trade with letters of change and its far reaching commerce in general, thus reducing it into an insignificant town – at times the senators exaggerated this point, prophesying that it would be reduced even to a village.[16]

The argument of the Senate was facilitated by the fact that until the beginning of the seventeenth century, hardly any Ashkenazi Jews lived in the town. German-speaking Jews arrived in Hamburg only in the course of the Thirty Years' War, many of them as refugees from the devastations of the eastern German lands. Some of this community found employment in the tobacco factories run by their Portuguese fellow-believers or as servants in their houses.[17] Until the 1680s, the Portuguese nation remained the more numerous of both Jewish communities, and without any doubt it was the one that gathered the riches of all trade.

An early attempt by the Citizenry and clergy to rid themselves of the Jews culminated in 1647. Young people especially menaced Jews by throwing stones and even pulling knives on them. When interrogated on this violation of public order they justified their behaviour with the demands of the pastors to 'abolish' the Jews and to get this 'vermin out of town'. The Senate finally had to accept the citizens' demand for the expulsion of the Ashkenazim, hoping that this would deflect the pressure exercised on the economically much more relevant Portuguese community.[18] Indeed, the Sephardic community was further tolerated, whereas the German Jews were expelled in 1649. Only some of them were allowed to stay as 'servants of the [Portuguese] nation'.[19]

Among the Christian inhabitants, the opulence of the wealthiest among the Portuguese Jews often caused envy and repugnance, not only among the poor, but also among the wealthy. Still, according to taxation sources, the wealth of the richest Sephardim never exceeded that of the city's Christian elite.[20] Nevertheless, in reproachful tones the pastors mentioned in their pleas the expense lavished on banquets, for example with regard to weddings:

> They eat from silver plates and serve a huge number of dishes and confectionery, and finally they drive in such carriages as only persons of high rank should use, and with such carriages they even employ a precursor on horseback ... Their synagogues are adorned with precious silver lamps, worth some one thousand ricksdalers, and within [the synagogues] they cause big howling, bawling, grunting, and therein they blow tubas and horns.[21]

Of course, the privilege to build synagogues was one of the crucial subjects in the discussions about the Jewish community. In the 1650s, the Texeira family, who had arrived from Amsterdam only in 1644 but soon was to become the wealthiest of all families in Hamburg, made several attempts to purchase real estate for this purpose. In 1652, the Texeiras bought two pieces of land. As the Senate could neither persuade the *Bürgerschaft* nor the pastors that even Jews should have their own place of worship, the land was resold and the Sephardim kept on with their practice of using semi-official praying houses and private houses for worship.[22]

Toward the end of the century, constitutional changes in the Hanseatic city fostered the power of the Citizenry and the political influence of the guilds. Under these circumstances the clergy launched another anti-Jewish campaign in the 1690s, backing up the citizens' demands for extra taxes on the Jewish inhabitants. As one of the few printed examples of harsh anti-Jewish preaching, the Hamburg pastor Johann Friedrich Mayers's sermon of 19 August 1692 should be mentioned. The preacher used the stereotypical accusations against the Jews: reviling the blood of Christ and obduracy in face of the Christian messiah. The whole sermon focused on the praying houses of the German and Portuguese Jews, demanding that the Senate should decree the immediate and categorical suppression of what were described as 'Satan's schools'. Otherwise, the Senate itself would be guilty of idolatry for tolerating this practice.[23] In 1697, the Senate's secretary, Julius Hinrich Schaffshausen, criticised the pastor Johann Lange (St Petri's parish) for having greatly over-emphasised Luther's anti-Jewish pronouncements. The clergyman, of course, knew better, and it was easy for him to prove that Luther, in his work *On the Jews and their Lies* (1543), had demanded that synagogues be burnt down. In any case, the Senate banned and confiscated some of Lange's pamphlets, which quoted such statements of the reformer.[24] There is no doubt that these campaigns were deeply imbued with Martin Luther's own polemics. In 1644, for example, the senior at the parish of St Petri, Johannes Müller (already mentioned above, see note 21), published *Judaismus oder Judentum, das ist ausführlicher Bericht von des jüdischen Volkes Unglauben, Blindheit und Verstockung* (Judaism or Jewry, that is a Detailed Report about the Infidelity, Blindness and Obduracy of the Jewish People). His dogmatic principles were developed out of Luther's anti-Jewish writings, and he recommended a complete subjugation of these 'enemies of Christ'.[25] The noises of the 1697 debates, with Luther's anti-Jewish writing being applied and the burning of synagogues considered, echoed even in the foreign press. The *Amsterdam Courante* assumed that the Hanseatic clergy backed the Citizenry in order to have their own demands for restrictions on the Jewish communities accomplished.[26]

However, some of the preachers did not join in the propaganda that most of their colleagues launched from their pulpits, notably pastor Johannes Volckmar (St Katharinen) and pastor Johann Winckler (St Michaelis). They did so because they accepted that the legal status of the Jewish communities should be respected. Pastor Johann Heinrich Horb called for toleration of the Calvinist and Catholic minorities alike.

As mentioned above, the 1660s saw the peak period of Portuguese activities on the Elbe river. In the following years internal and external factors caused a demographic and economic decline. This section will conclude with a brief summary of these factors.

External Factors

In the first place, the downfall of Spain at the end of the Thirty Years' War, fostered by the subsequent defeat in the war with France (1659), was a serious blow to the Sephardic commercial networks with the Hispanic World.

Second, during the 1620s and 1630s, the Spanish embargo of the Netherlands had favoured the neutral Hanseatic city of Hamburg and caused an emigration of probably one quarter of the Amsterdam Sephardic community to the port on the Elbe. After the end of the war, the Amsterdam community recovered fairly quickly, and what then became the 'golden age of Dutch Jewry' seriously affected the community in Hamburg[27] In the 1670s, about 2,500 Jews lived in Amsterdam, while the Hamburg community never exceeded 600 persons. Nonetheless, Hamburg remained the second biggest of the Jewish merchant communities in northern Europe.[28]

There is a third factor, that, as far as I can see, has not yet been considered, but it may be even more important: Between the 1630s and the 1650s, the French consolidated their previously unstable foothold in the Caribbean, taking the island of Martinique from the Dutch and Guadeloupe from the Spanish. In 1650, they conquered the western part of Hispaniola, which then became Saint Domingue. Immediately thereafter, the conquerors started to convert the islands' fertile soils into plantations, mainly for sugar, tobacco and indigo. These acquisitions were officially confirmed in the Treaty of Rijswijk in 1697, thus assuring the rise of France as the world's primary producer of sugar and indigo, essentially important products for Hamburg's economy. This development coincided with the revocation of the Edict of Nantes in 1685. Among the half-million Huguenots who left France in the following years were some quite wealthy maritime traders from south-western France, some of whom arrived in Hamburg and the nearby Danish port of Altona, where they established a thriving import trade of French colonial goods.[29] This new competition accelerated the decline of the Jewish community, and as Colbert's *Code noir* – new laws for the French Caribbean slaving and plantation societies – strictly forbade Jews in French colonies,[30] their co-religionist business partners in the New World could not even shift their networks from declining Brazil to the rising French Caribbean empire. Just as the Jews in the seventeenth century had done, the Huguenots became Hamburg's most successful minority in the eighteenth century. And just as the Portuguese nation had exploited its contacts with Brazil and Hispanic America, the Huguenots maintained close links to the Bourbon plantation empire on the Antilles.

Internal Factors

Since the Reformation, Hamburg's political history has been characterised by a continuous struggle between the Senate and the Citizenry, the latter claiming more influence and responsibility in political matters. From about 1666 onwards, in a series of uprisings against corrupt senators and mayors (in 1684 even leading to a temporary detention of a mayor), the Citizenry and the lower classes prevailed. Only in 1712, with an Imperial diplomat as intermediary, was a constitutional compromise finally found, putting an end to the conflicts that sometimes resembled civil war.[31] In the course of this conflict, the weakened Senate could no longer protect the Jews against the religious and political pressure executed by the Citizenry and backed by the pastors, the craft guilds and lower classes. From the 1670s to the 1690s, these interest groups succeeded in imposing an extraordinary taxation on both Jewish communities, thus increasing the economic stress on their merchants. This culminated in an extra contribution of 20,000 Marks demanded from the Sephardim in 1697, and 30,000 demanded from the Ashkenazim. In the following year, Manuel Texeira and his family moved to the more tolerant city of Altona, but soon they left the Elbe for Amsterdam. 'Other wealthy families like the Nunes Henriques, Soares and Bravo followed his example'.[32] By 1700, the Portuguese nation was in fact nothing more than a shadow of its former importance and splendour.

Second, the sheer smallness of Hamburg's Portuguese colony may have caused considerable social stress among its members. In Hamburg, from 1652 to 1681, their own communal authority punished 41 Sephardim with the *herem*, or the equivalent of excommunication or isolation, for slandering members of the community or for disobeying its internal religious and social order. In the same period in Amsterdam, only 29 persons were excommunicated, though the Amsterdam community was about four times larger.[33] This is a hint that the Hamburg community, in demographic terms, had fallen below the 'critical mass' necessary to secure the internal stability of a diaspora community. This may have been exacerbated by the fact that the Portuguese Jews kept themselves distinct from the socially inferior Ashkenazi community. As Yosef Kaplan stated:

> The deep social gap separating Sephardi and Ashkenazi Jews in Western Europe ... was particularly severe in places like Hamburg and London, where the Sephardi communities were smaller and socially more homogeneous.[34]

As elsewhere, this gap also concerned religious practice. In Hamburg, German and Portuguese Jews always maintained separate communities with their own prayer houses. Meanwhile, the German Jews had recovered from the 1649 expulsion. In the 1690s, their number by far exceeded the Portuguese community and during the anti-Jewish campaign of that decade it was they who could best withstand the pressure while most of the Sephardim emigrated.[35]

The Debate between Senate, Citizenry and Chamber of Commerce

What warrants attention is the chronological coincidence of the Huguenots' arrival with the emigration of the Portuguese Jews. It might suggest that under these circumstances, even the Hanseatic maritime merchants could have been affected by the anti-Jewish propaganda, for purchasing colonial goods from Christian foreigners, even if they where Calvinists, was probably better than buying them from Jews. We know that church sermons in early modern Hamburg very often were crammed with commercial matters. The preachers in general maintained very close relations with the merchants' community, and indeed, many second sons of merchants studied theology or law to start careers as pastors or lawyers, just in the same way as the landed gentry traditionally did. Quite a few pastors invested their own money in commercial ventures. Sermons were announced on the stock exchange, and very often they contained details such as:

> the recommendation of good book-keeping, the description of the importance of timber as a good commodity ... the admonition to lean on wholesale trade instead of hawking with sulphur shreds, if one wants to get rich.[36]

Therefore, early research for this essay was directed towards sermons, hoping to find hints for economic arguments that might have been used to convince the merchants. In the city's archives, huge collections of printed sermons have been preserved. But usually, only sermons treating more general subjects or annual festive occasions were printed. Within these collections, very few sermons deal with contemporary political or economic matters of pressing importance.

Other sources had to be examined. The records of the *Commerzdeputation*, which are preserved as a complete series since the seventeenth century, do offer a fairly good insight into the discussions among the maritime merchants. In the proceedings recorded during the 1690s, not a single hint of anti-Jewish argument within the Chamber of Commerce could be traced. This source confirms the description of this subject as given in the existing studies: In this matter, Senate and *Commerzdeputation* stood shoulder to shoulder against the claims of the Citizenry and the pastors. In 1697, when the Citizenry demanded the heavy tax contribution that caused the final collapse of the Sephardic community, both Senate and Chamber agreed to attend the meetings of the *Bürgerschaft* as often and in as large numbers as possible. The protocol of 23 June 1697 mentions 54 names of Chamber members present at the decisive meeting, and mentions others, whose names where unknown to the recorder.[37] But even with these measures, they could not impede the decree.

In her own study, Jutta Braden takes this memorandum of the merchants and the one of the goldsmith's guild, submitted on 11 February 1697, as a striking example for the diametrically opposed positions within the city's economic interest groups. The goldsmiths claimed that the 'unholy intrigues, usury, violations, evil scheming and caballing' of the Jews would damage any professional group of the city, such as retailers and craftsmen. Further, the Jews were accused of dictating the prices of jewels, gold and silver. In short, their presence was judged as 'poison' and 'plague' to the city, and as a cause for its 'complete doom'.[38] The goldsmiths demanded that Jews be banned from any trade – especially in gold and silver – and from running factories. They asked the Citizenry to consider these pleas, and not to allow 'godless patrons of the Jews' to influence their conclusions.[39]

The memorandum the deputies of the Chamber read to the Citizenry in June that year provides some details about the degree of precaution that the merchants believed to be necessary when negotiating this subject. In order to evade the reproach of maintaining too close relations with the Portuguese Jews, the deputies did not argue that the supplementary contribution would cause too much hardship to the Jews (as they overtly did before when discussing the matter with the Senate). At the meetings of the Citizenry, they only stated that the Jews themselves regarded these contributions as too harsh. The point of their argument was that, if the new tax should be levied, the Jews would 'escape' from the city. This passage may even be read as suggesting that such a reaction only corresponded to the malicious nature of this people: the Portuguese Jews had left the city on several occasions before, thus damaging the commerce of Hamburg. The memorandum goes on:

> We do not talk in this way as patrons of the Jews, but as right honourable patriots, foreseeing very well that the Jews [when expelled from Hamburg] will not move across the Alps or the Pyrenean Mountains, but, once they are out of town and have set foot across the border, they will settle in Altona and establish their commerce there, thus causing severe disadvantages to the commerce of this city ...[40]

Obviously, the memorandum depicts the Jews as a danger for the commerce of the city – but while the Citizenry claimed that Jews were dangerous as long as they lived in the city, the Chamber would say they were dangerous only once they had left. And as far as 'the commerce is the soul of a city' (that is how the deputes put it), any menace to commerce would be a menace to the city as a whole.[41]

As has already been noted above, in their own meetings, the members and the deputies of the Chamber of Commerce never used such rhetoric. It seems that the Portuguese Jews were always respected members of the merchant community, including the last decades of the century when anti-Jewish tendencies were growing. The anti-Jewish propaganda of Citizenry, pastors and crafts guilds did not show any impact on this interest group. In the early eighteenth century, when all the wealthier Portuguese had left the city, the deputies even showed signs of a certain paternalist benevolence in their approach to the few Sephardic Jews who remained. In the 1730s for example, the Chamber of Commerce defended the privileges of the Portuguese tobacco brokers. When the number of brokers admitted to the stock exchange was to be raised, they demanded a proportional increase in the number of Christians and Portuguese Jews.[42]

Conclusion

From the beginning of the Sephardic immigration to Hamburg, the mercantile interests of the maritime traders caused them to choose a decisively tolerant position, defending them against Lutheran orthodoxy and economic envy of the Citizenry, which represented mainly retailers, craftsmen and the lower classes. Due to the constitutional circumstances in late seventeenth-century Hamburg, circumstances that encouraged these dominant factions of the Citizenry, the religious climate turned severely anti-Jewish.

Beside this aspect, we must keep in mind that the religious element was not the only factor that caused the decline and almost complete dissolution of the Portuguese nation. The crisis of the Spanish Empire and the shift of important trade routes to northern competitors such as France and the Netherlands contributed significantly to the decline of the Sephardic community on the Elbe. The growing community in Amsterdam was also important in attracting many of the Hamburg Sephardim, regardless of the disadvantageous political and religious circumstances in the Hanseatic city.

Neither the rising anti-Jewish propaganda nor the growing importance of other merchant minorities in Hamburg, like the Huguenots, affected the pro-Jewish position of maritime merchants and the Senate. To shift their political support from the Jewish to the Huguenot community would have contradicted any commercial reasoning, for it would be only advantageous to the autochthonous merchants if there were several foreign communities importing goods to their market. Consequently, they did not change their attitudes towards the Jewish minority – or at least towards the Portuguese Jews, whose economic importance was prevalent. The line separating the groups debating the status of the Sephardim was so clearly drawn that the question asked in the title of this contribution can be answered: Yes, merchants were more tolerant – most probably not out of an attitude that considered non-Christian immigrants as equals in terms of modern civil rights, but out of mercantile rationale. But obviously, this attitude was limited to the very elite among the burgers of the Hanseatic city. Among the middle and lower classes, the wealth that non-Christian maritime merchants gathered caused a climate of envy that probably was more aggressive than it could be in remote places of the German hinterlands. This suggestion may be backed by the fact that the rather poor Ashkenazi community remained intact, when most of the Portuguese left the city in the late 1690s.[43]

To conclude, was Lutheran Hamburg a place where anti-Jewish sentiment was significantly aggressive? Considering the attitude of the Lutheran pastors towards the Calvinist and Roman Catholic minorities living in Hamburg, this does not seem to be the case, even if the aggressive tone of the sermons seems to be foreshadowing the developments of twentieth-century Germany, its aggressive anti-semitism in particular. Yet, many of the seventeenth-century sermons read to the audience in the Lutheran churches do mention the three heresies present in the city: Papism, Calvinism and the Judaic religion. All three of them were accused of abominations and idolatry.[44] On several occasions, when their religious practice did not appear as discreet as it was expected to be, pastors encouraged young people and members of the lower class to attack members of the non-Lutheran minorities. Twice during such riots, the Catholic chapel permitted by the Senate was completely destroyed, in 1667 and in 1719. On several occasions before, the clergy had demanded the closure of this place of worship. From 1652, when the chapel was run by the French resident in town, they repeatedly requested all services be held in French. This would have excluded the poorer German Catholics. In his close account of the conflict, Joachim Whaley wrote:

> Another chapel was opened in the house of ex-Queen Christina of Sweden, who was based in Hamburg while ordering her financial affairs after her conversion to Catholicism in 1655 ... Queen Christina soon became embroiled in conflicts with the Lutheran clergy who knew that she had attempted to gain widespread support for religious freedom for the Catholics. They also suspected her for having converted several prominent citizens, among them Peter Lambeck who later became the Imperial Librarian in Vienna after his flight from Hamburg in 1662. Matters came to a head in 1667, when the Queen gave a splendid feast to celebrate the election of Pope Clement IX. Free wine was given to the populace, her house was illuminated with an inscription which read *Clemens IX Pont. Max. Vivat*, and *Te Deums* were sung in her chapel. Several Lutheran preachers mingled with the crowd and the result was a violent attack on the chapel which was promptly destroyed while the Queen fled the city in fear of her life.[45]

After 1700, the Imperial embassy was to become protector of the Catholic minority, and a chapel was run within the embassy's house. Early in 1719, works to enlarge this chapel caused protests by the Lutheran clergy. On this occasion, the senior pastor of the parish of St Jacob, Erdmann Neumeister, exclaimed: 'Yet again, I say that Carthage, both of the popes and of the

Calvinists, must be destroyed'. On Sunday 10 September, a day of fierce sermons, this chapel, too, and the embassy itself were completely demolished.[46]

No such destructive aggression is known to have happened to the Jewish houses of prayer, though most of these places were not even officially recognised by the Senate. It must be noted that both Jewish communities in Hamburg never dared to arrange such exalted feasts as Christina did. With the time and the place given, it is not surprising that any public *Vivat* for a newly elected pope was regarded as a severe provocation, and that it produced this violent reaction. There is yet another point that may have stirred up religious sentiments even more. On the occasion of her last visit to Hamburg, Christina was lodged at the house that Manuel Texeira kept in the 'Kraienkamp' street. Whilst still reigning as Queen of Sweden, she appointed this Jewish financier as her ambassador in Hamburg,[47] and she always maintained personal relations with the Hamburg Sephardim.[48] Probably, it was this conjuncture of a converted, formerly Lutheran sovereign with the wealth and splendour of a Jewish magnate that triggered most of the aggression of the clergy and the crowds. Some reports say that the former Queen escaped through a backdoor of the guesthouse only with Texeira's help.[49]

It seems that the religious troubles that plagued the Jewish minority in this epoch must be regarded as part of the tensions that troubled early modern Europe in general. At the same time, we find that the cosmopolitan atmosphere of maritime port cities in fact did favour religious tolerance, at least among the maritime traders, even during the most severe periods of religious trouble. The eighteenth century was much less marked by such violent conflicts, but 'a true watershed in the History of Hamburg' was to come only in 1785, when the Senate and the *Bürgerschaft* launched a new law, granting legal toleration to minorities, though the Lutheran 'position ... of the established church remained unchanged' even under this law.[50]

With regards to rhetoric, the Jews were more severely attacked than the Catholic and the Calvinist communities, but it seems that in terms of physical aggression, in seventeenth- and early eighteenth-century Hamburg, the Catholics suffered most. One of the reasons for the survival of the Christian minorities was their backing by powerful nations acting as protectors: France and the Empire as protectors of the Roman Catholics, the Netherlands protecting the Calvinist Protestants. The Jews, deprived of any such backing, were exposed to political pressure more than any other minority, and this must have been one of the crucial points contributing to the emigration of the Sephardim at the end of the century.

NOTES

1. See for Europe, and Germany generally, Jonathan Israel, *European Jewry in the Age of Mercantilism (1550–1750)* (Oxford: Clarendon, 1998), pp.72–5. For Germany, see Wanda Kampmann, *Deutsche und Juden: Die Geschichte der Juden in Deutschland vom Mittelalter bis zum Beginn des Ersten Weltkrieges* (Frankfurt: Fischer, 1994), p.88. For Hamburg, see Jutta Braden, *Hamburger Judenpolitik im Zeitalter lutherischer Orthodoxie 1590–1710*, Hamburger Beiträge zur Geschichte der deutschen Juden, vol.23 (Hamburg: Christians, 2001), p.18. On the non-existence of Jewish–Lutheran relations (which developed to a certain extent with the other Christian confessions) in the sixteenth and seventeenth centuries, see Jerome Friedman, 'New Christian Religious Alternatives', in Raymond A. Waddington and Arthur H. Williamson (eds.), *The Expulsion of the Jews: 1492 and After* (New York and London: Garland Publishers, 1994), pp.19–40 (at 30).
2. In this text I take the phrase 'anti-Jewish' to represent a conscious opposition within Christian society to Jews, particularly because of their adherence to a perceived antiquated, out-dated religion. 'Anti-semitism', on the other hand, is taken in its broadly understood context to represent the racially founded opposition to Jews as members of an ethnic community.
3. Hermann Kellenbenz, *Sephardim an der unteren Elbe: ihre wirtschaftliche und politische Bedeutung vom Ende des 16. bis zum Beginn des 18. Jahrhunderts*, Vierteljahrschrift für Sozial- und Wirtschaftsgeschichte, Beiheft 40 (Wiesbaden: Steiner, 1958).
4. For details, see Helmut Heiber, *Walter Frank und sein Reichsinstitut für die Geschichte des neuen Deutschlands*, Quellen und Darstellung zur Zeitgeschichte, vol.13 (Stuttgart: Deutsche Verlags-Anstalt, 1966), pp.452–7, 1189. What strikes one most about Kellenbenz's book is the cold, if not icy, distance with which the author regarded his subject. In itself, this is not the worst attitude that a historian may exhibit, but still it seemed strange, even more so as neither the foreword nor any other passage of the book mentions the mass murder more recently committed by the Nazis and their followers. Though it is one of the major and most frequently quoted works on Sephardim in early modern Germany, German scholarly literature hardly gives any hints that Kellenbenz had written his major work as a collaborator in the abuse of historiography for propaganda. When writing it, he was a member of the *Reichsinstitut für die Geschichte des Neuen Deutschland* (The Reich's Institute for the History of the New Germany), directed by Walter Frank, one of the most pronounced anti-semitic historians of that time. The original title of the work was *Das Hamburger Finanzjudentum im 17. Jahrhundert und seine Kreise* (Hamburg's Seventeenth-Century Financial Jewry and its Circles). Kellenbenz had worked in the Munich branch of the *Reichsinstitut* until the very last days of the war. A few weeks before the capitulation of the Third Reich, according to the orders he received from Berlin, he burnt a huge amount of the Institute's documents – at a time when the Red Army was already waging its battle on the German capital. Bernt Engelmann even alludes that Kellenbenz destroyed a lot of the original source material used for his study on the Sephardim, but Engelmann provides no further details to prove this. See Bernt Engelmann, 'Was die meisten nicht wissen, aber wissen sollten', in Sabine Kruse and Bernt Engelmann (eds.), '*Mein Vater war ein portugiesischer Jude ...*' (Göttingen: Steidl, 1992), pp.16–20.
5. Joachim Whaley, *Religious Toleration and Social Change in Hamburg 1529–1819*, Cambridge Studies in Early Modern History (Cambridge: Cambridge University Press, 1985); German edition: *Religiöse Toleranz und sozialer Wandel in Hamburg: 1529–1819*, Arbeiten zur Kirchengeschichte Hamburgs, vol.18 (Hamburg: Wittig, 1992); quotations are taken from the English edition.
6. Braden (see note 1).
7. Arno Herzig and Saskia Rohde (eds.), *Die Juden in Hamburg 1590–1990: Wissenschaftliche Beiträge der Universität Hamburg zur Ausstellung 'Vierhundert Jahre Juden in Hamburg'* (Hamburg: Dölling und Galitz, 1991).
8. Ulrich Bauche (ed.), *Vierhundert Jahre Juden in Hamburg: Eine Ausstellung des Museums für Hamburgische Geschichte vom 8.11.1991 bis 29.3.1992* (Hamburg: Dölling und Galitz, 1991).
9. For a concise description of how Hamburg's constitution and its political and social institutions developed out of the process of reformation, see Whaley (note 5), pp.23–34.
10. Günter Böhm, 'Die Sephardim in Hamburg', in Herzig and Rohde (see note 7), pp.21–40 (at

20–21).
11. Böhm (see note 10), p.25; Whaley (see note 5), pp.79–80.
12. Böhm (see note 10), pp.24–5, 28.
13. Wim Klooster, 'The Jews in Surinam and Curaçao', in Paolo Bernardini and Norman Fiering (eds.), *The Jews and the Expansion of Europe to the West, 1450 to 1800* (New York and Oxford: Berghahn Books, 2001), pp.350–68 (at 357–8).
14. Kellenbenz (see note 3), pp.255–8; Böhm (see note 10), p.27.
15. Israel (see note 1), pp.75–6.
16. Böhm (see note 10), p.26.
17. Yosef Kaplan, *An Alternative Path to Modernity: The Sephardi Diaspora in Western Europe* (Leiden, Boston and Köln: E.J. Brill, 2000), p.173.
18. Braden (see note 1), pp.220–21, see also n.279.
19. Kaplan (see note 17), pp.52–3.
20. Kellenbenz (see note 3).
21. Böhm (see note 10), p.25, cites a 1649 sermon of Johannes Müller, senior pastor at the parish of St Petri: 'Sie speisen auf ihren Hochzeiten aus silbernen Gefäßen und setzen dabei eine große Menge Schüsseln und Confecte auf und endlich fahren sie in solchen Carossen, die nur hohen Standespersonen zustehen, und gebrauchen bei solchen Gelegenheiten noch oben darein vorreuter und ein großes Comitat ... Es werden ihre Synagogen allhie mit silbernen, köstlichen Lampen gezieret, auf etliche 1000 Rthlr. an Werth, darin treiben sie gross Heulen, Plärren, Grunzen, blasen darin die tubas und die Hörner'. On such pleas, see also Braden (note 1), p.222.
22. Whaley (see note 5), pp.77–9.
23. Johann Friedrich Mayers, 'Hamburgische Danck=Predigt / am 19. Augusti 1692 ... gehalten', see library of the Staatsarchiv Hamburg, sign. A 650/8, no.24, pp.18, 24.
24. Braden (see note 1), pp.328–9.
25. Kampmann (see note 1), p.88.
26. Braden (see note 1), p.329.
27. Israel (see note 1), pp.75–6.
28. Kaplan (see note 17), p.168.
29. Commerzbibliothek (Archives of the Hamburg Chamber of Commerce), Protokolle der Commerzdeputation, sign. S/599, vol.D (1691–1693), pp.160–61. In 1692, the deputies of the *Commerzdeputation* (the precursor of today's Chamber of Commerce) do mention the growing trade with France and recently arrived French merchants, who were also engaged in Danish and Hanseatic shipping.
30. Silvia Marzagalli, 'Atlantic Trade and Sephardim Merchants in Eighteenth-Century France: The Case of Bordeaux', in Bernardini and Fiering (see note 13), pp.268–86 (at 274).
31. Whaley (see note 5), pp.34, 38. The new constitution lasted until 1860.
32. Braden (see note 1), pp.301, 322–5.
33. Kaplan (see note 17), pp.176–7.
34. Ibid., p.63.
35. From the 1650s to the 1690s, the Ashkenazi community grew from only 15 to 300 families; Braden (see note 1), p.303.
36. Ernst Baasch, *Der Einfluß des Handels auf das Geistesleben Hamburgs* (Hamburg, 1909), p.10. The citation was taken from Heinrich Laufenberg, *Hamburg und sein Proletariat im 18. Jahrhundert: Eine wirtschaftshistorische Vorstudie zur Geschichte der modernen Arbeiterbewegung* (Hamburg, 1919), p.22: 'bei der ... Empfehlung einer guten Buchhaltung und Schilderung des Wertes, den das Holz für den Handel besitze, angefangen bis zur Mahnung, Großhandel zu treiben und sich der Hökerei mit Schwefelspänen zu enthalten, wenn man reich werden wolle'. The author also mentions the anti-Jewish tendencies of many sermons.
37. Commerzbibliothek, Protokolle der Commerzdeputation, sign. S/599, vol.F (1697–1700), fol.4.
38. For anti-Jewish motives in the pleas of retailers, carpenters and goldsmiths see Braden (note 1), pp.314–15, 331–34; quotations taken from p.332.
39. Braden (see note 1), p.334.
40. Commerzbibliothek, Protokolle der Commerzdeputation, sign. S/599, vol.F (1697–1700), fol.6: 'Es will das Ansehen gewinnen, ob wolten die hiesigen Jüdischen Kaufleute, wegen ihrem Vorgeben nach einige harte Conditiones, so ihnen anitzo angemahnet würden, aus dieser Stadt

entweichen: da uns diese Entweichung vermuthlich geschehen solte, würde dieselbe gewisslich mit großem Abbruch hiesiger gantzen Kauffmanschaft verbunden seÿn. Nicht reden wir solches als Juden Patronen, sondern als ehrliche Patrioten, die wohl sehen, daß die Juden nicht über die Alpes oder das Pireneische Gebirge hinüber ziehen, sondern sobald sie aus dieser Stadt sind, ihren Fuß alsoforth wieder auff diese Grentzen niederlassen, zu Altona ihr Commercium anfangen, und daselbsten eine große Handlung, zum großen Nachtheil dieser Stadt stabiliren werden, woselbsten sie sonder Zweifel der Zollfreÿheit und anderer Privilegien mehr genießen werden. Mit was vor Schaden der hiesigen Handlung solches wird verbunden seÿn, siehet ein jeder leichtlich ein, der nur derselben in etwas kundig ist'.

41. Commerzbibliothek, Protokolle der Commerzdeputation, sign. S/599, vol.F (1697–1700), fol.5.
42. Commerzbibliothek, Protokolle der Commerzdeputation, sign. S/599, vol.Y (1735–1739), fols.65, 217. On this occasion, the Christian merchants defended the privileges of the Sephardim against Ashkenazi newcomers on the stock exchange, arguing that such interlopers would not only ruin the established Portuguese, but also the Christian brokers. Until 1737 the Sephardi Abraham de Castro was responsible for the fixing of prices of 'Brasil-Toback'; after his death the Chamber named Jacob de Leon to do this job, having decided that de Castro's brother Jacob was not sufficiently qualified.
43. Most of the German Jews were small shopkeepers, doing modest trade with textiles and colonial goods. In 1730 about 600 Jewish taxpayers lived in Hamburg, only 27 of them Sephardim. In 1732, there existed 'no less than fourteen unofficial synagogues … together with forty-one schools which taught Hebrew and the Talmud', and they were predominantly Ashkenazim. Whaley (see note 5), pp.80, 90, 92. A survey of the early modern history of the Hamburg Ashkenazim is provided by Günter Marwedel, 'Die aschkenasischen Juden im Raum Hamburg (bis 1780)', in: Herzig and Rohde (see note 7), pp.41–60.
44. The orthodox pastors harshly attacked even the Lutheran deviation of Pietism. Whaley (see note 5), pp.42, 45.
45. Ibid., pp.52–6.
46. On this occasion, the citizens did not get away with it. The Hanseatic City of Hamburg could avoid a military occupation by Imperial troops, but an Imperial Commission sentenced it for the heavy fine of 400,000 guilders and the replacement of the embassy building, for not having prevented this breaching of the agreements on religious peace that had been concluded in Germany after the ending of the Thirty Years' War. A legation to the Court in Vienna in 1721 succeeded in decreasing the fine to 200,000 guilders, but still it took the city decades to pay the costs of reconstruction of the embassy and the chapel. Even then, this outcome did not affect very much the attitudes of the Lutheran clergy. For details see Whaley (note 5), pp. 58–63, quotation p.59.
47. Bauche (see note 8), p.162.
48. For example, Benedict Castro (alias Baruch Nehemias), son of the famous medical doctor Rodrigo (Ruy) de Castro, had been her personal physician. Both were established in Hamburg. See Wilfried Schleiner, 'The Contribution of the Exiled Portuguese Jews in Renaissance Medical Ethics', in: Waddington and Williamson (see note 1), pp.147–59 (at 148–9, 154). See also Böhm (see note 10), p.21.
49. Bauche (see note 8), p.162.
50. Whaley (see note 5), pp.164–9.

Identity, Space and Intercultural Contact in the Urban Entrepôt: The Sephardic Bounding of Community in Early Modern Amsterdam and London

ADAM SUTCLIFFE

Port cities are places of diversity. In these zones of vigorous commercial interchange, people of different cultural and social backgrounds have typically encountered each other more frequently and more intensely than in inland cities of similar size. It is out of the routinisation of these contacts that cultures of cosmopolitanism – a feature associated both with port cities and with Jews – have been able to emerge. In Trieste, as Lois Dubin has shown, the 'equalities and privileges' extended to the Jewish community must be understood in terms of an explicit Habsburg policy to attract a diversity of foreign merchants to the free port. Similar privileges to those extended to the Jews were also granted to Greek and Serbian Orthodox, Calvinist, Lutheran, Armenian Uniate and Turkish merchant communities, all of which jostled alongside each other in the vibrant commercial atmosphere of the port city.[1] Such intense economic interaction, in Trieste and elsewhere, inevitably gives rise to a significant measure of social and cultural exchange as well. Different ethnic groups in trading and port cities exist in a complex relationship with each other, as both rivals and collaborators, inhabiting worlds that in some respects closely overlap each other, and in others are sharply demarcated. How, in the case of early modern port Jews, can we analyse the cultural impact of the dynamics of intercultural interaction in these entrepôt settlements?[2]

The cosmopolitan energy of port cities and of major metropolises is an inherently unstable cultural phenomenon. A city that is cosmopolitan – at least in the sense I will here make use of this notoriously slippery concept – is one that hosts a diversity of cultures and religions, and thrusts these contrasting life worlds into everyday contact with each other.[3] However, the cosmopolitan worldliness that these contacts make possible inevitably also to some extent engenders a new standardisation. As these diverse city-dwellers grow more familiar with each other, not only do they frequently adopt some of each other's customs, but they also to some degree forge a common culture. This communality is rooted not only in the practicalities of communication and of shared space: it is also a product of cosmopolitan self-consciousness itself. As city-dwellers become cosmopolitans, they adopt a common identity as urbane and sophisticated. This cross-culturally shared identity is, though, quietly corrosive of the very cultural differences that make cosmopolitanism both possible and necessary in the first place.

This dilemma was perhaps first experienced with significant collective intensity by the Sephardic elites of seventeenth- and eighteenth-century Amsterdam and London. It was in these thriving commercial entrepôts that the cosmopolitan embrace of diversity first began to crystallise as a defining characteristic of modern city life. A widespread cultural acceptance of Jews, and the rise of non-Jewish interest in them, was both symbolically and materially central in this cultural shift. For the Sephardim this environment of economic dynamism and relative social and political openness was extremely enticing. However, it also posed problems. The primary goal of the religious and lay leadership of these communities was to reinforce loosely normative structures and practices of Jewish communal life. In doing so, they sought to assert the cultural boundaries of the Sephardic sphere, and to regulate intellectual and social contacts with the world outside. However, the cosmopolitan conditions that enabled these communities to gain acceptance and to prosper also insistently challenged and threatened to undermine these boundaries of cultural separateness. Urban cosmopolitanism, then, simultaneously transformed, celebrated and threatened the collective identity of these Sephardic Jewish communities.

While the broad pattern of Sephardic social transformation in early modern Amsterdam and in London was very similar, there were also significant points of difference. A comparison between these two cities at their highest points of economic exuberance, therefore, can reveal a great deal about the dynamics of Jewish acculturation in dynamic port environments.[4] Amsterdam was the pre-eminent port city of the seventeenth century, where the Sephardim of the city reached their greatest prosperity and visibility in the decades of economic boom that followed the end of the Eighty and Thirty Years' Wars in 1647.[5] The affluence and self-confidence of this community was visibly sealed by the opening of Amsterdam's vast and grand new Sephardic synagogue in 1675. London's Jewish community, semi-formally established in the 1650s, was in the seventeenth century strongly oriented for guidance and sustenance towards its mother settlement in Amsterdam. However, after the Glorious Revolution, as London increasingly eclipsed Amsterdam as the leading world entrepôt, so London's Sephardic community also grew in size and confidence. The challenges to community integrity posed by the posed by the pressures of cosmopolitanism were, in their underlying nature, very similar in these two cities. However, the intensification of assimilatory trends in the eighteenth century, and also the sheer size and spatial disaggregation of London, led to a considerably more dramatic erosion of Sephardic collective cohesion in this latter entrepôt.

Amsterdam

Amsterdam in the seventeenth century was the mercantile hub of international commerce. The population of the city approximately quadrupled over the course of the century, from about 50,000 to over 200,000: a growth rate that both reflected and fuelled Amsterdam's dominance as the key entrepôt of the increasingly integrated global economy.[6] During the first two decades of the century migrants from outside the newly constituted Dutch Republic predominantly arrived from the Southern Netherlands. After the outbreak of the Thirty Years' War, however, Germany emerged as the leading source of immigrants to Amsterdam, while the Revocation of the Edict of Nantes in 1685 led to an influx of more than 5,000 Huguenots into the city.[7] A small but not insignificant number of migrants also arrived from England, as did, of course, both Sephardic and Ashkenazic Jews, who each numbered about 3,000 in the city by 1700.[8]

Migrants were attracted to Amsterdam not only by the abundant economic opportunities, and high wages, that the city offered, but also by its unique atmosphere of urban energy, diversity, fluidity and toleration. Everyday life in this bustling setting enabled and even necessitated an unprecedented degree of interaction across multiple boundaries of cultural difference. Other early modern cities – most conspicuously, perhaps, Venice – had been host to notably diverse populations, but in seventeenth-century Amsterdam Flemish, English and German migrants, sailors often from Germany or Norway, Huguenots, Mennonites, Quakers, Catholics, Sephardic and Ashkenazic Jews, and blacks from Suriname and other colonial outposts mingled with striking ease among and alongside the native Dutch.[9] This unique environment was not only extremely conducive to commerce – it was also, for most of the city's inhabitants and visitors, alluringly exciting.

Amsterdam at its heyday was, in a sense, the first truly cosmopolitan city. The presence of large numbers of people from a wide range of other places stamped the flavour of the city, and the energy of its economic and social life, more profoundly than anywhere else in seventeenth-century Europe. In the words of the most recent synoptic historian of the city, Geert Mak, by the 1630s 'Amsterdam had … acquired the dynamics of a city of outsiders'.[10] The commercial vigour and maritime transience of the city created a sense of urban anonymity, and thus of freedom. 'Everyone is so preoccupied with his own profit', wrote René Descartes around 1635, 'that I could live here for all my life without ever being noticed by anyone'.[11]

However, despite this pragmatic indifference to the private habits of others, Amsterdam was also a place where it was almost impossible to be blind to the multifarious and in some respects nefarious aspects of life in the urban maelstrom. The rituals of prostitution, for example, were inescapably visible to all who had business in the central areas of the city surrounding the docks. As long as certain boundaries of discretion were not too flagrantly transgressed, the sex trade, then as now, was largely tolerated.[12] Similarly, the presence of a range of national, ethnic and religious groups in the city was a reality reinforced on a daily basis by myriad visual encounters and routine transactions along Amsterdam's narrow canalside walkways and bridges. The cosmopolitan culture of the city was characterised not simply by a tolerant acceptance of this diversity, but also by a pattern of urban living that necessitated a high degree of awareness of and contact with alien cultures and lifestyles.

The Sephardic community of the city was a particularly significant and conspicuous fragment of this urban mosaic. The detailed, respectful and elaborate manner in which Jewish customs, buildings and monuments were represented by Dutch artists – most famously exemplified by the meticulous depictions by Emmanuel de Witte and Romeyn de Hooge of the grandiose Sephardic synagogue – reflected the confidence with which Amsterdam's elite incorporated the presence of this prosperous, respectable, but still somewhat exotic community into their image of their city as a haven of cosmopolitan civility.[13] Lived experience at this cultural interface is difficult to penetrate; however, there is much to suggest that the Amsterdam Sephardim were readily accepted, without drama but with a distinct measure of curiosity and pride, as an important element in the cultural mosaic that lent the city its distinctiveness.

A source that offers an intriguing window into this relationship is the coverage of the Sephardic community in the first true guidebook to the city: Filip von Zesen's *Beschreibung der Stadt Amsterdam* (Description of the City of Amsterdam), published in 1664. Zesen's guide may well be the first detailed, tourist-oriented guide to any European city. Its structure and tone is strikingly similar to that of a modern Baedeker or Fodor. Like these guides, Zesen's *Amsterdam* was written by an informed non-native, for use by his compatriots: though he had lived in the city for about 30 years by the time that he wrote his guide, by origins Zesen was, like his readers, German. His volume opens with an extensive historical overview, and then leads us off on a walking tour of the highlights of the city, with abundant commentary on Amsterdam's most significant churches, civic institutions and curiosities.

Almost four pages of this 400-page text are devoted to the exploration of the Sephardic community. He introduces the Sephardic neighbourhood along the Breestraat undramatically, noting that the Jews had arrived there several decades earlier, in order to escape persecution in Iberia.[14] He carefully describes their synagogue – the 'Grosse Juden-Kirche' – constructed from two houses, and thus with two entrances. He explains why visitors will notice a hand-pump and towel outside the synagogue: this is so that congregants can wash their hands before services. He then gives a detailed description of the interior, clearly assuming that his readers will not hesitate to enter. He explains that the balcony is for women, and that the wooden ark contains the books of Moses, in their elaborately embroidered cover. He also provides a brief account of Shabbat customs.[15] For the curious tourist a visit to the Sephardic neighbourhood was simultaneously architecturally and ethnographically interesting. Zesen anticipates a broad curiosity on the part of his readers not only in the built infrastructure but also in the basic history and traditions of the Sephardim. He does not, however, inflect his descriptions with a tone of exoticism or of distance: the community is presented, rather, as one among many distinctive neighbourhoods, which together make up Amsterdam's compelling cosmopolitan mix.

Zesen also provides a brief account of the nearby neighbourhood of 'Flöhenburg' (Vlooienburg), which he identifies as predominantly inhabited by Polish and German Jews. However, he has much less to say about this community, which he clearly regards of less interest, lacking the prosperity and status of the Sephardim, and perhaps also because Ashkenazic Jewish mores would have been more familiar to his German-language readership. Indeed, the most intriguing sightseeing tip Zesen offers for this part of the city relates to its most prominent Sephardic resident. Here was the home of the famous Rabbi Jacob Jehuda Leon, who in the 1640s had constructed a meticulously detailed model of Solomon's Temple, which had attracted widespread attention not only in Holland, but also in England, when it was briefly in display in London. The model is now housed, Zesen tells his readers, in the rabbi's home. Visiting procedures are not quite made clear, but the guide's users are implicitly invited to call on Rabbi Leon, with the expectation that he will offer them a guided viewing of his model. Leon's model was perhaps the earliest example of an initiative that, while in part an intellectual and religious exercise, was also an explicit tourist attraction, capitalising on Protestant interest in Judaica. Zesen's guide shows the endurance of this interest, and its incorporation into the cosmopolitan tourist trail of 1660s Amsterdam.[16]

What, though, of the Sephardic experience of these cross-cultural encounters? While the unprecedented security and acceptance the Sephardim experienced in Amsterdam were, of course, deeply cherished, the ease of contact with non-Jews in the city was also regarded by the community authorities as both precarious and in some respects dangerous. The research of Yosef Kaplan has highlighted the continual arduousness of attempts by the patrician *parnassim* to impose disciplinary norms on the community, particularly through the unusually extensive use of the *herem* (ban).[17] A perusal of the disciplinary pronouncements recorded in the community *livros de escamoth* (regulation books) for the seventeenth century presents a suggestive picture of the concerns of the community leadership, and reflects the numerous but interrelated fronts on which they struggled to assert the integrity and cultural boundedness of Sephardic life. Numerous rulings indicate the eagerness of the *Mahamad* (council of elders) to discourage forms of intercultural contact that it regarded as dangerously intimate: activities such as entering Christian churches (whether during services or simply to listen to the organ), passing on Jewish religious texts to non-Jews, purchasing bread products from non-Jewish bakeries, and purchasing meat from the Ashkenazic or even non-Jewish butchers, were all forcefully condemned.[18] Theological disputations with Christians, several of which took place during the seventeenth century, were regarded as particularly alarming: in 1677 the *Mahamad* forbade such debates, on the grounds that the risked arousing 'the hatred of the gentiles among whom we dwell'.[19]

The regulation of public social interaction with non-Jews was also an abiding concern of the *parnassim*. In 1655 the *Mahamad* pronounced against members of the community gathering with non-Jews on the 'Lions' Bridge', on both Saturdays and Sundays. This behaviour, the ruling warned, could provoke scandals that would 'damage our nation'.[20] Thirty years later the *herem* was declared for those guilty of 'insolence' in the taverns or in the streets of the city. Such rowdy miscreants, it was implied, endangered the security of the whole community, which, the edict reminded, was only present in Amsterdam thanks to 'the benevolence of the very noble and magnificent magistrates of this city'.[21] The fact that these pronouncements were considered necessary, but only rather vaguely specified the transgressions they sought to discourage, corroborates the general impression that by the later seventeenth century social contact between Jews and non-Jews was a routine occurrence. The authorities sought to discourage all overly intimate or high-spirited conviviality with non-Jews. Their overriding practical concern, however, was with the public reputation of the community. Elite social life, mostly taking place in private homes, was thus largely ignored by the *Mahamad*. Younger and poorer Sephardim, who were more likely to gather in taverns or on the streets, were more closely scrutinised.[22]

The erosion of the boundaries that demarcated Jewish space and communal life was, however, an inexorable process. The raw mercantile energy of Amsterdam brought people together, generating a social familiarity that increasingly transcended cultural differences. This was precisely what Sir William Temple, an English diplomat, celebrated in his *Observations Upon the United Provinces of the Netherlands* (1673):

I believe the force of Commerce, Alliances and Acquaintance ... [in Holland] may contribute much to make conversation, and all the offices of common life, so easy, among so different Opinions, of which so many several persons are often in every man's eye; ... no man checks or takes offence at Faces, or Customs, or Ceremonies, he sees every day ...[23]

For Temple, in Holland these differences have become so familiar that they are seen by all as virtual irrelevances. Rather than provoking shock or conflict, they provide mere 'entertainment and variety', serving as the conversational basis for temperate exchanges pursued 'without interest or anger'.[24] The United Provinces, and Amsterdam in particular, were for Temple a beacon of the future, in which the intolerance of difference, still prevalent elsewhere, had been eroded through the gentle impact of everyday contact.

Insofar as Temple was right, however, he also ignored a concomitant problem, of which the Amsterdam rabbinate and *parnassim* were keenly aware. Once Sephardic cultural differences had come to be seen almost as merely decorative, what was to sustain them – and particularly those religious observances, such as the laws of *kashrut*, that were to some extent designed precisely to impede easy and intimate intercultural contact? In the first half of the eighteenth century, as the Dutch economy sank into recession and the Amsterdam Sephardic community declined both demographically and economically, these assimilationist trends among the Sephardic elite only intensified. By the middle of the eighteenth century the richest Sephardim were markedly less willing than their forefathers had been to take on membership of the *Mahamad* or other leadership roles in a community that was now afflicted by considerable poverty.[25] Increasingly remote from collective Jewish life, the Sephardic elite, many of whom were still immensely wealthy, aspired above all to emulate the lifestyle of their non-Jewish economic peers. A vignette of their success in this respect is provided in the diary of Moses Cassuto, a Florentine Jew who visited Amsterdam on business between 1741 and 1743, and who vividly recounts his visit to the country estate of David de Pinto at Overton, two hours from Amsterdam. Profoundly impressed by de Pinto's gracious hospitality in his gardens sumptuously landscaped with tree-lined avenues, grottoes, pools and floral arrangements, Cassuto also proudly notes that this same ground had been trodden by such notable previous guests as the Grand Duke of Tuscany and the Electress of the Palatinate.[26] The acceptance that such visits indicated was, it seems, for the Amsterdam Sephardic elite the highest mark of social success.

London

These processes of elite Jewish acculturation, accompanied by a increasingly carefree approach to religious observance, reached their fullest extent in the city that in the eighteenth century took over from Amsterdam the mantle of the world's primary port: London. From the time of its foundation the Sephardic community of London was subject to the same underlying pressures as those experienced in Amsterdam, but to an intensified degree. This initially very small settlement, in cultural and theological terms until at least 1700 essentially an outpost from Amsterdam, was from the outset powerfully shaped by the longstanding crypto-Jewish background of its membership, and by the commercial dynamism and flexibility of London.[27] A significant proportion of the Portuguese *Nação* ('Nation') of London did not affiliate with the synagogue, or did so only sporadically. Nonetheless, and despite the attempt of the rabbinical leadership to discourage the social acceptance of those on the margins of the community, these 'semi-Jews', Yosef Kaplan has shown, continued to constitute an important element within the Sephardic world.[28] 'Semi-Jews' were also present in Amsterdam in significant numbers, but they seem to have been proportionately a good deal more numerous in London, where their presence both reflected and heightened the blurring of the boundaries of Sephardic Jewish identity in this booming, bustling metropolis.

The London Sephardim were also, almost from the moment of the resettlement, markedly concerned to protect their respectability by distancing themselves from any associations with poverty, and in particular by discouraging Ashkenazic immigration. While the Amsterdam Sephardim showed no less disdain for their Ashkenazic neighbours, the co-existence of the two communities, with their disparity in wealth, was almost from the early decades of the seventeenth century an accepted reality. In London, however, the Sephardic community first attempted to stem the arrival of poor Ashkenazim in 1669. Ten years later, in 1679, an order of the community proclaimed that any mendicant Ashkenazim should be given no more than five shillings from the *sedaca* funds, and that the community *gabbai* should arrange for their transport on the first available boat to Rotterdam or Amsterdam.[29] After the establishment of a separate Ashkenazic community of worship in the 1690s, the arrival of poor Sephardim in London continued to trouble the community, particularly in response to the renewed vigour of the Inquisition on the Iberian peninsula in the 1720s and 1730s. The London Sephardim responded to this with repeated attempts to discourage immigration, limit poor relief and promote onward migration of the poor to the Americas.[30]

The London census lists of 1695 indicate a Jewish population of about 600 Sephardim and 250 Ashkenazim: far fewer than the numbers in Amsterdam at this time.[31] The Jewish community was at this stage also heavily concentrated. Six hundred and eighty-one of these Jews were recorded by the census as residing in six of London's 110 parishes, while 264 Jews lived in the St James

Duke Place parish alone, where both the Sephardic and the Ashkenazic houses worship were located, and where Jews numbered over 25 per cent of residents.[32] However, the rising prosperity of the Anglo-Jewish elite was already eroding the traditional cohesiveness of the Sephardic *kehillah*. By the early eighteenth century several of the most successful Anglo-Jewish financiers and traders were largely assimilated into English gentry society, retaining only loose ties with traditional Judaism. Most significantly, elite families such as the Mendes da Costas and the Salvadors were quick to imitate their non-Jewish commercial peers in buying elegant country estates, in Surrey or Hertfordshire, where, largely isolated from most other Jews, they acquired social respectability and essentially mingled as equals with their Anglican neighbours.[33] This spatial distancing, so crucial in the establishment of English class hierarchies, was also a key centripetal force in Sephardic community life. The relative density and smallness of Amsterdam to some extent counterbalanced the erosion of community boundaries. In London, however, the lure of rusticity and the ease of class segregation enabled the richest Sephardim to assimilate into the gentile mainstream much more rapidly and intensively.

The establishment of country residences was, at the beginning of the eighteenth century, a powerfully seductive fashion among London's newly wealthy merchants, bankers and brokers, who flocked to establish weekend retreats in the villages of Middlesex and Surrey. The richest Jews were part of this trend almost at its outset. Already before the end of the seventeenth century the financier and military contractor Solomon de Medina had established a residence in Richmond, where in November 1699 he hosted to dinner no less a personage than King William III.[34] Conveniently connected to London by regular boat service on the Thames, Richmond was the most fashionable of the satellite centres of gentry conviviality in the eighteenth-century, and probably also the most significant location of early Jewish entry into English elite social circles. As Rachel Daiches-Dubens has aptly noted, Richmond was for London's Jewish plutocrats 'a handy side-entrance into English society'.[35] Solomon de Medina was joined, around 1710, by Moses Hart, who was a leading figure in the establishment of London's first Ashkenazic synagogue, the Great Synagogue, while later arrivals included the Franks family, which established itself across the river in Isleworth.[36]

While Richmond and neighbouring communities to the south-west of London were particularly popular because of their prestige, there was no real clustering of Jewish country homes, which over the first half of the eighteenth century scattered in almost all directions. Joseph Salvador, the financier, inherited in 1736 his grandfather's estate in Tooting, which he greatly extended in 1752;[37] another branch of his Rodrigues family settled further south in Epsom, while to the north and north-west there were the Mendes da Costas at Highgate, the Capadose and Pereira families in Stanmore, Joseph d'Almieda at

Watford, and the da Costas in Totteridge.[38] This dispersion also affected some Ashkenazic Jews who were employed as staff in these homes. The earliest account book of the Great Synagogue, from 1718, lists one servant and a cook of the Rodrigues family in Epsom. Such servants were excluded from full membership of the synagogue, and were also explicitly forbidden by regulation to attend services in their livery.[39]

These retreats were primarily used, at least by heads of households, essentially as weekend and summer homes. It was essential for Jews active in commerce and finance also to maintain a city residence, from where to conduct business: these homes were generally in or near London's Jewish heartland, at the eastern end of the city, often above their counting houses around Bishopsgate or Broad Street.[40] The establishment of a country residence did not, therefore, automatically imply severance from the Bevis Marks synagogal community, of which these individuals typically regarded themselves as fully fledged and prominent members. However, geographical separation inevitably to some degree distanced them from community life. When, in the late spring of 1755, Rabbi Aluzay, a fund-raising emissary from the community of Hebron in Palestine, arrived in London after an arduous journey, he was disappointed to find that all the worthies of the community had left the city, in order to 'visit their gardens'.[41]

In choosing to centre their social life at a distance from their fellow Jews, surrounded not by the wider community, or even by each other, but by non-Jewish economic peers, these members of the Anglo-Jewish elite were essentially declaring a new social allegiance. Their eager rush into suburban rusticity both reflected their desire to integrate themselves into English high society, and also undoubtedly accelerated this process. Jewish religious observance, to which these relatively isolated locations were scarcely conducive, became increasingly erratic. London's Sephardic elite became, in general, not totally heedless of the laws of Sabbath observance and of *kashrut*, but considerably inconsistent in their interpretations of them. As Todd Endelman has observed, the religious laxity of Jews of eighteenth-century England was, at least outside the New World, without parallel.[42] Moses Cassuto of Florence, who visited London in 1741 before progressing to Amsterdam, was struck by the high status and geographic dispersion of the city's Sephardic Jewish population. He noted that the London Jews 'do not become excited in matters of religion',[43] and observed that they were so comfortable among non-Jews that they even entrusted their children to them:

> The Jews have Protestants in their employ as maid-servants, waiters, servants, and coachmen, even as wet-nurses, and entrust to them without any trouble their own little children to be brought up, the suspicion that they might baptise them never occurring to them … So

without concern they send their little girls to Protestant women teachers, and little boys to Protestant teachers, to acquire manners and good qualities and learning.[44]

This practice, as Cassuto himself discerns, revealed not only the high degree of mutual trust between Jewish employers and Protestant employees, but also a belief within the Anglo-Jewish elite that it was from non-Jews that their children could best acquire a suitably English patina of refinement.

A particularly interesting insight into both the laxity and the internal tensions of the Sephardic community in London in the mid-eighteenth century is offered by Meyer Schomberg's *Emunat Omen* (The True Faith) (1746). Schomberg was the most prominent Ashkenazic doctor in London in this period: born in Fetzberg in Germany in 1690, he studied medicine at the University of Giessen before coming to London around 1720, soon after which he was admitted into membership of the Royal College of Physicians.[45] In the 1740s he and his family severed their ties with the Jewish community, and the tone of *Emunat Omen* reflects both Schomberg's transition towards a deistic view of the world and his anger towards London's Portuguese Jewish elite, against whom this polemic is directed.[46] His charges against this caste could scarcely be more damning:

> These hypocrites maliciously break all Ten Commandments. All they do is only for show ... They are entirely devoted to multiplying riches and property, silver and gold in abundance, and to collecting it in their treasure-houses in order to display a rich store of those securities of mighty London's treasure-house called bank-notes.[47]

They defile the Sabbath, he claims, not only by eating non-kosher food and drinking wine and liquor 'in the company of strange women', but also by remaining preoccupied with the concerns of business and profit.[48] Their erotic dalliances with non-Jewish women seems to disturb Schomberg with particular intensity: 'Not only do they lie with women, daughters of the gentiles ... without shame, but they also live and dwell and lodge with them in intimate embrace, and reject the *kasher* daughters of Israel who are our own flesh and blood ...'.[49] Rivalry between (Sephardic) Jewish families, each feeling themselves to be of superior lineage and pedigree, has, Schomberg asserts, turned them away from each other:

> For this reason they do not wish to mix with one another and to intermarry among themselves. They set up divisions between themselves as if they did not come from one stem and root. On the contrary they turn their eyes to the daughters of the land, and raise their eyes to women of their own choice, whom the Lord has not chosen.[50]

Schomberg regards the Sephardic elite as succumbing to a particularly extreme and hypocritical form of assimilation, ironically fuelled by their own distinctively Sephardic sense of familial blood pride.[51] Schomberg's own sense of attachment to the Jewish community was also rapidly eroding in the 1740s, but he saw his own disaffection as intellectually honest, ethically lofty and ethnically unapologetic, in contrast to the greed and hypocrisy of the Sephardic social climbers. While accusing the Jewish financial elite of proudly boasting that they never defile the Sabbath by riding in a carriage, while deliberately walking home from synagogue via 'Exchange Alley', in order to check the latest securities prices,[52] Schomberg frankly admits that he at times violates this commandment, but in a different spirit:

> It is true that sometimes I have been called on the Holy Day of Rest to visit some patient at a distance. Now this city that I dwell in is London, a great city of God's in which it is impossible for a human being, be he mighty as a lion or swift as a hart, to cover on foot the whole great area even in a whole day ... It is even more difficult outside the city. Therefore I am forced to take a carriage. I consider that assuredly if I tired and wearied myself I would have lost the rest that the honoured and revered God has commanded me to observe.[53]

It is interesting that both for Schomberg and for the Sephardim he attacks the immense size and diffuse spatial organisation of London was a significant factor in a drift away from traditional Jewish religious observance and from strong communal identification. For the moneyed elite able to purchase entry into the country-house culture of Richmond, Highgate and the other villages and proto-suburbs surrounding London, the geographical dispersal necessitated by the cult of rusticity among England's newly affluent intensified the centripetal impact of Jewish upward mobility. Schomberg, an Ashkenazic professional, did not actively participate in or desire this dispersal. However, many of his clients did – and so his life, too, was transformed by the sprawl of the city and its periphery.

Economics, Space and Cultural Identity

The trend towards assimilation among the Sephardic elite in London in the eighteenth century in many respects simply furthered a trend already clearly in evidence in late seventeenth-century Amsterdam. However, particular aspects of the social configuration and cultural preferences of London high society intensified the softening of Sephardic identity. Most conspicuously, the phenomenon of the country house was not nearly as pronounced in the Dutch Republic. The lure of rusticity was less intense in Holland's strongly civic-oriented culture; and, even if it had been, very few in the Sephardic community, stagnating both economically and demographically in the eighteenth century, were in a position to take part. While intercultural social contacts certainly grew more frequent and in the coffee houses, Masonic lodges and private homes of eighteenth-century Amsterdam, specifically Sephardic institutions such as Hebrew literary societies also endured, and in general the process of Sephardic assimilation was much less pronounced than in London.[54]

Differences in place of the Sephardim in the economic life of the two cities is also significant in this regard. The Portuguese Jews of Amsterdam were in the seventeenth century heavily concentrated in a relatively narrow range of commercial activities. On the Amsterdam stock exchange, although most officially licensed brokers were Calvinists, by the 1670s Sephardic Jewish *accionistas* (share dealers) dominated day-to-day dealings.[55] This domination is reflected in Joseph Penso de la Vega's *Confusion de Confusiones* (1688), a guide to the hidden workings of the stock exchange, written without any specific Jewish content but in an intensely Iberian cultural idiom that would have been mystifying to all but a Sephardic readership: the performative composure of stock speculators, for example, is compared to that of a *toreador*.[56] In London, in contrast, the financial concentration of Jews was capped by their rival City merchants. In 1697 the number of licensed Jewish brokers at the Royal Exchange was set at 12, out of a total of 124. Three attempts to increase this number, in the 1720s and 1730s, failed, and the cap remained in force until 1830.[57] There was debate over this policy of limitation: in 1714 John Toland eloquently argued for the elimination of such constraints.[58] However, as the controversy of the Jew Bill in 1753 highlighted, the anxieties and prejudices that lay behind them were deeply rooted in England.[59] While the disadvantages of these restrictions for Jews are self-evident, it is also true that they intensified the degree to which those Jews working in the financial sector did so in close interaction with non-Jews. This made them subject to heightened assimilatory pressures and temptations.

The urban configuration of intercultural contact was, then, significantly different in these two cities during their respective economic heydays. In a certain sense it might be argued that Amsterdam, despite its smaller size, at its peak attained a cosmopolitan energy never quite matched by London. The Sephardim of Amsterdam, while intimately woven into the economic weft of the city, never came close to losing their sharp distinctiveness: they remained geographically and economically highly concentrated, and retained an intensely proud sense of their Iberian identity, reflected in their language use and in their patterns of cultural consumption.[60] In the eighteenth century, Jews in Amsterdam, London and elsewhere drifted towards an increasingly assimilated and secular lifestyle.[61] However, nowhere was this trend more pronounced than in London – and the specific character of elite social life in this city was in large measure the reason for this. While in seventeenth-century Amsterdam a multiplicity of ethnic groups jostled together within relatively limited urban confines, in the much vaster expanse of London Jews tended either to be somewhat isolated or highly assimilated. For the Sephardic community (and later for the Ashkenazic community too), the choice was essentially between living in the East End, in an intensively Jewish environment, and in close proximity to other recent immigrant groups, but distant not only geographically but also economically and culturally from the burgeoning West End districts of Georgian London – or moving west, or outward to the rustic suburbs, thus asserting Jewish comfort and security in English society, but to a large degree also assimilation into it.

There is an inescapable internal strain in the lure of urban cosmopolitanism that still today animates many new arrivals in the great cities of the world. This tension can clearly be discerned among the Sephardim of early modern Amsterdam and London, and also in later Ashkenazic semi-assimilated cultural elites in Berlin and elsewhere. The desire to be distinctive, and therefore also to some extent separate, strained insistently against the contrary desire to take full advantage of the cosmopolitan possibilities offered in these unprecedentedly interactive urban environments. The Sephardic elites of Amsterdam and London in the decades around 1700 showed little sign of inner torment over this issue: the pleasures of social acceptance were extremely seductive, and seemed to be majestically compatible with a refashioned, hybrid sense of Jewish identity. However, this new configuration of Jewishness, while exhilarating, was also fragile. The historical experience of these communities precociously highlighted the paradox that remains today an abiding characteristic of modern city life. While the excitement of cosmopolitan urban energy is largely derived from the contacts between people of different cultural backgrounds, these contacts inevitably threatened to erode those very differences, and thus also the possibility of cosmopolitanism itself.

NOTES

1. Lois Dubin, *The Port Jews of Habsburg Trieste: Absolutist Politics and Enlightenment Culture* (Stanford, CA: Stanford University Press, 1999), p.201; idem, 'Between Toleration and "Equalities": Jewish Status and Community in Pre-Revolutionary Europe', *Simon Dubnow Institute Yearbook* I (2002) 219–34 (at 221–6).
2. For a comparative investigation of this issue in the nineteenth and early twentieth centuries, see Maria Vassilikou, 'Greeks and Jews in Salonika and Odessa: Inter-ethnic Relations in Cosmopolitan Port Cities', in David Cesarani (ed.), *Port Jews: Jewish Communities in Cosmopolitan Maritime Trading Centres, 1550–1950* (London: Frank Cass, 2002), pp.155–72.
3. On the concept of cosmopolitanism, see Timothy Brennan, *At Home in the World: Cosmopolitanism Now* (Cambridge, MA: Harvard University Press, 1997); Bruce Robbins, 'What's Left of Cosmopolitanism?', *Radical Philosophy* 116 (November–December 2002), 30–37.
4. On methodologies of comparison in Jewish history, see Todd M. Endelman (ed.), *Comparing Jewish Societies* (Ann Arbor, MI: University of Michigan Press, 1997).

5. Jonathan Israel, 'The Republic of the United Netherlands until about 1750: Demography and Economic Activity', in J.C.H. Blom, R.G. Fuks-Mansfeld and I. Schöffer (eds.), *The History of the Jews in the Netherlands* (Oxford: Littman, 2002), pp.85–116 (at 90–91).

6. Leonardo Benevolo, *The European City* (Oxford: Blackwell, 1993), p.135. On the economic significance of Amsterdam, see Jonathan Israel, *Dutch Primacy in World Trade, 1585–1740* (Oxford: Oxford University Press, 1989).

7. Jonathan Israel, *The Dutch Republic: Its Rise, Greatness and Fall* (Oxford: Oxford University Press, 1995), pp.328–31, 629.

8. Ibid., p.330; Jonathan Israel, *European Jewry in the Age of Mercantilism, 1550–1750*, 3rd edn. (London: Littman, 1998), p.198.

9. On the black presence in Amsterdam, see Alison Blakely, *Blacks in the Dutch World: The Evolution of Racial Imagery in a Modern Society* (Bloomington, IN: Indiana University Press, 1993), esp. pp.225–7.

10. Geert Mak, *Amsterdam* (Cambridge: Harvard University Press, 2000), p.100.

11. Quotation in ibid.

12. Lotte van de Pol, *Het Amsterdams hoerdom: Prostitutie in de zeventiende en achtiende eeuw* (Amsterdam: Wereldbibliotheek, 1996), pp.94–5.

13. See Richard I. Cohen, *Jewish Icons: Art and Society in Modern Europe* (Berkeley, CA and Los Angeles: University of California Press, 1998), pp.34–43; Simon Schama, 'A Different Jerusalem: The Jews in Rembrandt's Amsterdam', in Susan W. Morgenstein and Ruth E. Levine (eds.), *The Jews in the Age of Rembrandt* (Rockville, MD: Judaic Museum, 1981), pp.3–17.

14. Christian Gellinek (ed.), *Europas Erster Baedeker: Filip von Zesens Amsterdam 1664* (New York: Peter Lang, 1988 [1664]), p.191.

15. Ibid., p.192.

16. Ibid., p.198. See also A.K. Offenburg, 'Jacob Jehuda Leon (1602–1675) and his model of the Temple', in J. van den Berg and Ernestine G.E. van der Wall (eds.), *Jewish–Christian Relations in the Seventeenth Century: Studies and Documents* (Dordrecht: Kluwer, 1988), pp.95–115.

17. Yosef Kaplan, 'The Social Functions of the Herem', in idem, *An Alternative Path to Modernity* (Leiden: E.J. Brill, 2000), pp.108–42.

18. *Compendio de escamoth* (1728), Gemeentelijke Archiefdienst Amsterdam, Archieven der Portugees-Israelitische Gemeente te Amsterdam, vol.XXII, pp.27, 77, 199 and passim.

19. Yosef Kaplan, 'The Jews in the Republic until about 1750: Religious, Cultural and Social Life', in Blom, Fuks-Mansfeld and Schöffer (see note 5), pp.157–8.

20. *Compendio de escamoth*, p.60.

21. Ibid., pp.60–61.

22. This class distinction in the social policing of the community is excellently explored in Yosef Kaplan, 'The Threat of Eros in Eighteenth-Century Sephardi Amsterdam', in Kaplan (see note 17), pp.280–300.

23. Sir William Temple, *Observations Upon the United Provinces of the Netherlands* (Farnborough: Gregg, 1971 [1673]), pp.183–4.

24. Ibid., p.182.

25. See Israel (note 5), pp.113–15.

26. Richard Barnett, 'The Travels of Moses Cassuto', in John M. Shaftesley (ed.), *Remember the Days* (London: Jewish Historical Society of England, 1966), pp.73–121 (at 111–12).

27. See Todd M. Endelman, *Radical Assimilation in English Jewish History 1656–1945* (Bloomington, IN: Indiana University Press, 1990), pp.24–5.

28. Yosef Kaplan, 'The Jewish Profile of the Spanish-Portuguese Community of London during the Seventeenth Century', in Kaplan (see note 17), pp.155–67; Matt Goldish, 'Jews, Christians and Conversos: Rabbi Solomon Aailion's Struggles in the Portuguese Community of London', *Journal of Jewish Studies* XLV (1994), 227–57.

29. Lionel D. Barnett (ed.), *Bevis Marks Records* (Oxford: Oxford University Press, 1940), vol.I, p.31; David S. Katz, *The Jews in the History of England 1485–1850* (Oxford: Oxford University Press, 1994), pp.181–2.

30. Todd M. Endelman, *The Jews of Georgian England, 1714–1830* (Philadelphia: Jewish Publication Society of America, 1979), pp.167–9.

31. Katz (see note 29), p.184.

32. Ibid.

33. See Endelman (note 27), pp.11–19.

34. Rachel Daiches-Dubens, 'Eighteenth Century Anglo-Jewry in and around Richmond, Surrey', *Transactions of the Jewish Historical Society of England* 18 (1958), 143–168 (at 144).
35. Ibid.
36. Ibid., pp.145–53. See also Hilda F. Finberg, 'Jewish Residents in Eighteenth-Century Twickenham', *Transactions of the Jewish Historical Society of England* 16 (1952), 129–35.
37. Maurice Woolf, 'Joseph Salvador 1716–1786', *Transactions of the Jewish Historical Society of England* 21 (1968), 104–37 (at 104, 108).
38. Vivian D. Lipman, 'The Rise of Jewish Suburbia', *Transactions of the Jewish Historical Society of England* 21 (1968) 78–103 (at 79–80); Cecil Roth, *The Rise of Provincial Jewry* (London: Jewish Monthly, 1950), p.16.
39. Roth (see note 38), p.16; Harold Pollins, *Economic History of the Jews in England* (London: Littman, 1982), pp.67–8.
40. Endelman (see note 30), pp.127–8.
41. R.D. Barnett, 'Anglo-Jewry in the Eighteenth Century', in V.P. Lipman (ed.), *Three Centuries of Anglo-Jewish History* (London: Jewish Historical Society of England, 1961), pp.45–68 (at 56).
42. Endelman (see note 30), p.132.
43. Barnett (see note 26), p.103.
44. Ibid.
45. Edgar R. Samuel, 'Dr. Meyer Schomberg's Attack on the Jews of London, 1746', *Transactions of the Jewish Historical Society of England* 22 (1961), 83–100 (at 86).
46. On Schomberg's opinions in a wider context of heterodox thought in eighteenth-century Anglo-Jewry, see David Ruderman, *Jewish Enlightenment in an English Key: Anglo-Jewry's Construction of Modern Jewish Thought* (Princeton, NJ: Princeton University Press, 2000), p.128.
47. Meyer Schomberg, *Emunat Omen*, trans. Harold Levy, *Transactions of the Jewish Historical Society of England* 22 (1961), 101–11 (at 102).
48. Ibid.
49. Ibid., p.103.
50. Ibid.
51. The intensity of Schomberg's attacks on the London Sephardim were undoubtedly intensified by his own professional and personal disputes with members of the community, and particularly with the rival physician Jacob de Castro Sarmento, whose election as a Fellow of the Royal Society Schomberg had, in 1729, unsuccessfully attempted to block. See Ruderman (note 46), pp. 186–7; Matt Goldish, 'Newtonian, Converso and Deist: The Lives of Jacob (Henrique) de Castro Sarmento', *Science in Context* 10 (1997), 651–75.
52. Schomberg (see note 47), p.102.
53. Ibid., p.105.
54. See R.G. Fuks-Mansfeld, 'Enlightenment and Emancipation from c.1750 to 1814', in Blom, Fuks-Mansfeld and Schöffer (see note 5), pp.164–191 (at 167–71).
55. Jonathan Israel, 'The Amsterdam Stock Exchange and the English Revolution on 1688', *Tijdschrift voor Geschiedenis* 103 (1990), 412–40 (at 416–17). See also Daniel M. Swetschinski, *Reluctant Cosmopolitans: The Portuguese Jews of Seventeenth-Century Amsterdam* (London: Littman, 2000), pp.102–64.
56. Josef Penso de la Vega, *Confusion de Confusiones*, ed. and trans. Herman Kellenbenz (Cambridge, MA: Harvard Graduate School of Business Administration, 1957), esp. p.54.
57. Endelman (see note 30), p.22.
58. John Toland, *Reasons for Naturalizing the Jews in Great Britain and Ireland* (London, 1714).
59. On the 'Jew Bill' controversy, see Thomas W. Perry, *Public Opinion, Propaganda and Politics in Eighteenth-Century England: A Study of the Jew Bill of 1753* (Cambridge MA: Harvard University Press, 1962); Justin Champion, 'Toleration and Citizenship in Enlightenment England: John Toland and the Naturalization of the Jews, 1714–1753', in Ole Peter Grell and Roy Porter (eds.), *Toleration in Enlightenment Europe* (Cambridge: Cambridge University Press, 2000), pp.133–56 (at 136–9).
60. See Miriam Bodian, *Hebrews of the Portuguese Nation: Conversos and Community in Early Modern Amsterdam* (Bloomington, IN: Indiana University Press, 1997), pp.76–95.
61. See Israel (note 8), pp.254–7; Chimen Abramsky, 'The Crisis of Authority Within European Jewry in the Eighteenth Century', in Siegfried Stein and Raphael Loewe (eds.), *Studies in Jewish Religious and Intellectual History* (University, AL: University of Alabama Press, 1979), pp.13–28.

Trading Globally, Speaking Locally: Curaçao's Sephardim in the Making of a Caribbean Creole

LINDA M. RUPERT

'*My diamanty no laga dy skirbimy tudu kico my ta puntrabo – awe nuchy mi ta warda rospondy*' ('My diamond, do not fail to write me everything I am asking you. Tonight I await an answer'). So Abraham de David de Costa Andrade Jr. wrote to Sarah de Isaac Pardo y Vaz Farro in 1775.[1] This fragment from an impassioned love letter between two Sephardic Jews living in Curaçao is the earliest known document written in Papiamentu, a vibrant creole language that today is spoken by approximately 200,000 people of all ethnicities and social classes on the Dutch Caribbean islands of Curaçao, Aruba and Bonaire.[2] Unlike most other Caribbean creoles, Papiamentu is not exclusively the vernacular of the lower-class black majority. Since the eighteenth century it has been a powerful communications vehicle that cuts across social class, race and ethnicity, gaining 'a greater degree of respect and universality of use in all social settings than any other Creole in the Caribbean'.[3] Moreover, of the world's over 200 documented pidgin and creole languages, Papiamentu is one of only six with an extensive written literary production.[4] For over 200 years Curaçao's Sephardim have had a key role in the language's development.

Why did two Sephardic Jews on a small Dutch Caribbean island in the late eighteenth century chose an incipient creole language in which to communicate their most intimate feelings?[5] How were Sephardic merchant families involved in the genesis and diffusion of the Caribbean's most successful creole – a language genre that usually is associated with the transatlantic slave trade, plantation society and people of African descent? I suggest that we must seek answers to these questions in the specific conditions of Curaçao's port city of Willemstad, and in the social and economic relations among its inhabitants during the eighteenth century, when Papiamentu was evolving as a language. I am concerned not with the linguistic aspects of the language's birth and development, but rather with the historical context that facilitated its consolidation as a *lingua franca* both across the divides of social class, race and ethnicity, and also within the Sephardic community. At the very time they were participating in far-flung trade networks around the Atlantic world, I suggest, Curaçao's Sephardim also were helping to forge a strong inter-ethnic colonial identity in the port city of Willemstad, one that is clearly expressed in the rise and consolidation of Papiamentu. By analysing the role of the Sephardim in the emergence of Papiamentu and the language's role in local identity formation, I hope to contribute a different angle to the discussions of the social type of the port Jew, bringing in questions of local identity formation and the process of creolisation in the colonial Atlantic world.

Curaçao's Sephardim in the Making of a Caribbean Port City

Throughout the eighteenth century Curaçao was home to the largest and most prosperous Sephardic Jewish settlement in the Americas.[6] The earliest permanent Sephardic immigrants arrived from Amsterdam in the early 1650s, responding to offers of free land by the Dutch West India Company.[7] Finding the land unsuitable for agriculture, they, like most of the island's other free white inhabitants, soon turned to trade. Throughout the eighteenth century, Curaçao's Sephardim established themselves in the island's local, regional and international commercial circuits.[8]

A small, arid island under the administrative control of the Amsterdam Chamber of the Dutch West India Company, Curaçao did not fit the Caribbean plantation paradigm. Following the Peace of Westphalia in 1648, the Company transformed the island from a struggling military outpost of a few hundred inhabitants into a thriving commercial entrepôt and trans-shipment centre. In 1675 the Dutch West India Company declared the island a free port, the Caribbean's first, a full hundred years before open trade became common in the region. Rather than producing cash crops for international markets, the Company used Curaçao's natural deepwater harbour as a home base from which to conduct a vigorous, largely contraband trade with Spanish, English and French colonies throughout the Americas.[9] As the eighteenth century progressed, independent merchants assumed an increasingly important role in regional trade, alongside the Dutch West India Company. With no large-scale agriculture producing for export, Curaçao had no landed gentry or planter class. Instead, the island's most powerful denizens were urban merchants, who depended entirely on the trans-shipment trade.

The port city of Willemstad was Curaçao's only urban settlement, and the hub of its economy. As early as 1707, 80 per cent of the island's taxpayers lived in town. By 1789, 55 per cent of the island's total population lived in Willemstad – 11,543 out of 20,988 people. Sephardic Jews, numbering 1,023, made up almost a quarter of the port's entire white population. People of African descent were another key urban ethnic group. The 2,617 free coloureds comprised over a third of the town's total free population, white and black. Forty-two per cent of all the island's slaves lived in Willemstad rather than in the countryside.[10] These included house slaves, artisans, craftsmen and seafarers, many of whom laboured for wages and enjoyed a fair amount of autonomy in their daily lives. Many slaves eventually purchased their freedom and entered the ranks of Willemstad's growing free black and mulatto population. Black women worked in small-scale commercial ventures while many men fled to nearby Venezuela and Colombia, often escaping on the numerous craft that departed daily to trade with the South American mainland.[11]

Willemstad's diverse socio-economic, ethnic and racial groups lived and worked in close proximity, crossing paths in the crowded streets of the port, along its harbour front, and in the many commercial establishments that lined its streets and alleyways – bars, brothels, warehouses and shops. The docks along St Anna Bay, the deep, narrow channel that cut through the centre of Willemstad, were the port's centralised trans-shipment centre. Frigates, brigantines and snows owned by the Dutch West India Company departed regularly to cross the Atlantic, carrying tobacco, cacao, hides, coffee, indigo, sugar, precious metals and dyewood to ready markets in Europe.[12]

Independent male merchants of various nationalities sailed smaller craft around the Caribbean and its littorals, conducting a significant percentage of regional trade. Wim Klooster argues that these small-scale merchants played a more important role in Curaçao's commerce than hitherto has been realised.[13] Unlike the elite Dutch West India Company functionaries, the island's small-scale merchants often went to sea along with their crews, spending weeks at a time calling at ports around the Caribbean and the Americas. At sea, in regional ports and at home in Willemstad, male merchants and the seafarers who sailed for and with them interacted in ways that have yet to be documented adequately. Meanwhile, women of diverse ethnicities anchored the homeport of Willemstad, undertaking multiple, small-scale economic transactions with each other and crossing paths in their social and cultural lives.[14]

Curaçao's Sephardim took on an increasingly important role in the island's regional trade as the eighteenth century progressed.[15] As early as 1652 some of them already had their own seacraft; by 1726 Curaçao's Sephardim owned over 200 vessels and controlled most of the island's regional navigation.[16] Drawing on a tight-knit, interconnected network of family members and associates around the Atlantic basin who were deeply involved in commerce, Curaçao's Sephardim traded regularly with close to two dozen ports in North and South America, the Gulf coast of Mexico, and the Caribbean islands.[17] This was not without its perils; Jews caught trading illegally with the Spanish colonies risked the tortures of the Inquisition or imprisonment in Spain.[18] It is important to note that, although by the mid-nineteenth century Curaçao's Sephardim emerged as a *bona fide* elite, throughout much of the eighteenth century they still were very much an up-and-coming merchant group. For example, in the early decades of the eighteenth century, three-quarters of the island's Sephardim were assessed in the lowest two of seven tax brackets (and none in the top three tiers), while between 1719 and 1765 between 70 and 80 per cent paid third class family tax – the lowest level.[19]

Alongside the merchants, scores of seafarers of a variety of ethnicities and races inhabited the port city of Willemstad. These included both itinerant sailors from different European countries and their American colonies, and a relatively stable core group of local seamen, especially free blacks, mulattos and slaves. By 1741 two-thirds of Curaçao's sailors were of African descent.[20] Some slaves were freed (either temporarily or permanently) specifically to go to sea; others forged manumission petitions, stowed away on merchant vessels or posed as freemen.[21] In port and at sea, members of Curaçao's two diaspora groups, people of African and Sephardic descent, were in close contact with each other via the maritime economy.

Willemstad's population was both highly cosmopolitan and highly stratified. A somewhat oversimplified but useful categorisation of the eighteenth century demographics of Willemstad divides the island's population along three parallel religious and ethnic lines, with the Dutch Protestant elite at the top, up-and-coming Jewish merchants in the middle, and the island's black and mulatto Catholic majority at the bottom.[22] Initially, this religious and ethnic division also had a linguistic component. The island's elite spoke Dutch, Sephardic merchants Portuguese and Spanish, and the black majority a variety of African languages, as well as four related dialects of another creole, Guene.[23] In the course of the eighteenth century however, this linguistic division was superseded, as increasing numbers of locals of all strata began to communicate in Papiamentu (although the elite Dutch continued to maintain their language). As different as the island's two diaspora groups were, they soon shared a common tongue. How did this happen?

Port Jews, Papiamentu and the Formation of a Local Curaçaoan Identity

While there is debate about whether Papiamentu is a Portuguese- or a Spanish-based creole, leading linguists from both camps agree that it was established in Curaçao by the late seventeenth century.[24] According to the proto-Portuguese theory (which I find the most compelling), all Caribbean creole languages had common origins in several Portuguese-based pidgins that developed in the slave camps on the west coast of Africa and in the Atlantic islands, perhaps as early as the sixteenth century.[25] Enslaved Africans, who had grown up already speaking these budding Afro-Portuguese tongues, carried them across the Atlantic to the Americas, where they developed into a variety of different creoles, including Papiamentu and Guene in Curaçao.[26] By the early nineteenth century Papiamentu had become the island vernacular, successfully edging out Portuguese, Spanish, Guene and Dutch.[27] Although Portuguese remained an important language for several generations among Curaçao's multilingual Sephardim, by the early nineteenth century Papiamentu clearly was their language of choice for daily communication, not only with other local groups, but also with each other.[28] As the 1775 letter demonstrates, by the last quarter of the eighteenth century, Curaçao's Sephardim had embraced Papiamentu sufficiently that it was an option for even the most intimate written communication.

The earliest recorded uses of Papiamentu occur, not surprisingly, in the oral culture of Afro-Curaçaoans. These include work, harvest and protest music, folktales and poetry.[29] There are numerous references in the writings of temporary residents and travellers in the eighteenth and early nineteenth centuries that provide a glimpse into the language's ongoing development. One of the earliest is that of Father Alexius Schabel, a Bohemian Jesuit, who observed in a 1704 diary entry that 'the Negroes of Curaçao speak broken Spanish'.[30] The earliest known mention of Papiamentu as a completely separate tongue is in a 1732 letter from another priest, Father Caysedo.[31] Dutch visitors, in particular, were often very deprecating in their remarks, complaining that locally born children spoke an unintelligible language among themselves.[32] Papiamentu was the language of mediation in the island's largest slave uprising in 1795, while the rebellious slaves communicated secretly among themselves in Guene.[33]

There is limited but firm evidence of written Papiamentu beginning in the early eighteenth century: a smattering of words in official Dutch deeds and in fragments of a 1713 Dutch diary; the names of at least eight seacraft that were owned by Sephardic merchants between 1701 and 1793; and the 1775 letter.[34] Numerous written records survive from the nineteenth century, especially following the introduction of the printing press, which stimulated literary production in Papiamentu.[35]

Frank Martinus, a leading proponent of the proto-Portuguese theory, suggests that the role of the Sephardim in the transatlantic slave trade, and Sephardic enclaves on the West African coast and in the Cape Verde islands, are possible explanations for the development of Papiamentu and other proto-Portuguese Atlantic creoles.[36] I am somewhat cautious about this, especially given subsequent research by Eli Faber and Saul Friedman that debunks the myth of a disproportionate Jewish role in the transatlantic slave trade.[37] However, Martinus's contention that there was a significant Sephardic presence on the Atlantic coast of Africa and in the Cape Verde islands does merit further consideration, and it certainly would bear directly on discussions of port Jews in the early modern Atlantic world, as well as on studies of the processes of creolisation and colonial identity formation.[38] (I return to this point in more detail in the final section below.)

Regardless of its origins and early development, how did Papiamentu successfully emerge as the island's primary language, transcending barriers of race, ethnicity and social class in a way that no other Caribbean creole has achieved for a sustained period of time? Hoetink has suggested that the existence of two, rather than one, upper strata in Curaçao – the Dutch and the Sephardic Jews, each speaking a different, mutually unintelligible language, and largely separated from each other socially – led to the adoption of the creole spoken by the lower class as the island's common *lingua franca*.[39] However, he does not elaborate the specific ways in which this occurred, and he ignores the presence of Guene, which, as we have noted, was spoken by the black majority. It is also important to remember that Curaçao's Sephardim did not emerge as an elite until the nineteenth century, well after Papiamentu's entrenchment.

What specific kinds of contact occurred across social class and ethnicity in the port city of Willemstad that helped consolidate Papiamentu? One possibility is the role of the black nanny or nursemaid (often a slave, but sometimes a free black woman), who suckled and brought up the master's children, often alongside her own, thus providing ample opportunity for cultural and linguistic exchange between children of different races and social classes, as well as the opportunity to transmit her own language to white children.[40] However, although this was clearly an important sphere of contact, it was a widespread practice throughout slave societies of the Americas, and there is no reason to think that there was any peculiarity of its style in Curaçao that would broaden Papiamentu's sphere in comparison to that of other creole languages. Moreover, black nannies in Curaçao equally might have been expected to transmit Guene as Papiamentu. Frank Martinus and May Henriques both point to the role of women in developing Papiamentu, because immigrant women frequently did not learn the dominant language as easily as men did.[41] Others have suggested that communication among children on the streets and alleyways of Willemstad spurred the development of the new language.[42] (Recall that several eighteenth-century observers complained that local children were speaking a corrupt new language.) Again, although both of these are vital spheres of contact, they are common processes and so would not account for Papiamentu's unusual success.

Rather unique in the case of Curaçao, I suggest, is the intersection of the lives of urban blacks (enslaved and free) and up-and-coming Sephardic merchants across the relatively porous boundaries between race, social class and ethnicity in the cosmopolitan port city of eighteenth-century Willemstad.[43] Men, women and children of different ethnicities and social classes were in close contact as they went about the business of the port. The kinds of experiences that black seafarers and Sephardic merchants shared in their numerous voyages around the region parallel the conditions leading to the development of the proto-creole languages known as sailors' or trade jargons.[44]

Women of African and Sephardic descent had numerous opportunities for close contact as they tended to homes and businesses while their menfolk were at sea. The Sephardim had a key role in propagating Papiamentu. As up-and-coming merchants, not yet an established elite, and in regular, close contact with seafarers and dockworkers of African descent, they were uniquely positioned to stimulate Papiamentu's development and legitimate its use as an interethnic communications medium in a way that Afro-Curaçaoans were unable, and the Dutch-speaking elite was unwilling.

As Gert Oostindie has pointed out, precisely because Papiamentu became the *lingua franca* of all the island's different races and social classes, it was more than a communications vehicle. Throughout the nineteenth and twentieth centuries Papiamentu emerged as a central way of affirming a unique local identity, even when Curaçao has never become fully independent from the Netherlands. Unlike race and colour, which in Curaçao, as throughout the Caribbean, have been arenas of contention, negotiation and conflict, Papiamentu has served as a powerful unifying force throughout the island society, across ethnicity and social class.[45] As anthropologist Alan Benjamin has noted, Papiamentu also has become a fundamental component of identity construction within the Sephardic community of present day Curaçao.[46] Moreover, Sephardim have played a disproportionate role in the development and maintenance of Papiamentu as a vigorous, living language, both within their own community and in the wider society, throughout the twentieth century and up to the present.[47] This is particularly striking given the fact that their numbers have dwindled to only 350, out of a total current island population of approximately 150,000.[48]

Creolisation, Colonial Identity and the Port Jew in the Atlantic World

Documenting the contribution of Curaçao's Sephardim to the consolidation of Papiamentu puts us smack in the middle of an intense wider debate about creolisation throughout the Caribbean and the Americas. While creolisation has often been seen as a process that occurred among white elites, recent work has begun to rediscover the major contributions that the black majority made to local identity formation in the slave societies and ports of the colonial Americas.[49] Ira Berlin and others have argued persuasively that the creolisation process began on the eastern shores of the southern Atlantic, on the west coast of Africa and on nearby islands, well before the establishment of creole American societies.[50] The high degree of interracial and intercultural contact that occurred in the Cape Verde islands and in Portuguese trade depots along the coast of West Africa in the fifteenth and sixteenth centuries birthed not only Atlantic creole languages, but also a wide range of hybrid cultural expressions.[51] If Frank Martinus is correct that there was a significant

Sephardic presence in Cape Verde and on the Atlantic coast of Africa from the earliest days of the transatlantic slave trade, then the Sephardic diaspora may well have played a vital role in this wider Atlantic creolisation process from its earliest years.[52] Martinus's description of close, ongoing contacts between Sephardic enclaves in western Africa and throughout the Caribbean, and of their role in trade and as cultural brokers, certainly fits our image of the early modern port Jew. We might consider the extent to which members of the Sephardic diaspora – the earliest port Jews of the Atlantic – participated in the centuries-long creolisation of the Atlantic world, from tentative beginnings on the western shores of Africa to the consolidation of the vibrant ports along the eastern coasts of the Americas and around the Caribbean Sea and its littorals.

Clearly, the specific conditions of the port city of Willemstad and its inhabitants created unusual conditions for the development of Papiamentu, and the island's Sephardic enclave played an unusually prominent role in the local economy and society. Nevertheless, the case of Curaçao raises some broader issues about the insertion of port Jews into local societies of the early modern Atlantic world, and the role of the Sephardic diaspora in the process of identity formation and creolisation in colonial societies. Judaica scholarship has documented amply the internal dynamics and cohesive identity of early modern Atlantic Sephardic enclaves and, increasingly, their insertion in global trade networks.[53] But the case of Curaçao shows that Sephardim also were key players in the internal social and cultural dynamics of an Atlantic colony, and had a major role in developing a unique local identity. Surely similar processes played out in other colonial ports that had Sephardic enclaves, albeit in markedly different ways according to the specific conditions of each port city, local society and the corresponding imperial power.

To what extent does the social type of the port Jew allow for such local processes? Or is it more concerned with wider processes of globalisation and intra-ethnic identity formation that transcend locality? What kinds of alliances did port Jews form with other local groups (especially enslaved and free men and women of African descent), and how did this contribute to the formation of local, regional and in some cases ultimately national identity in colonial ports? Is there is an identifiable *colonial* port Jew prototype? Or does port trump colony? How did the Jews of other colonial Atlantic port cities – such as Charlestown, Newport, New York, Bridgetown, Port Royal – tie into the specifically colonial aspects of their ports' identities, including the complex race relations that were such a key feature of all American and Caribbean ports in this period? These questions point to a new direction that we could take the study of port Jews. This also would involve exploring in much more detail both the decidedly ambivalent situation of port Jews *vis-à-vis* race and ethnicity, and their complex interactions with local merchant elites who were more closely tied to imperial European powers.[54] Finally, I think we must analyse more precisely the geopolitical positioning of each specific port *vis-à-vis* empires (and, later, nation states), and the corresponding effect on social relations within each port. Whether a given port was at the heart of an empire (or nation state), a colonial hub, or somewhere in the interstices matters greatly, not only to the internal dynamics of Jewish communities, but, more vitally, to the (often changing) role these diaspora groups could and would play in local and regional dynamics and social relations of specific ports.

While Willemstad's Sephardim may have been unique in their role in the genesis of a new creole language, the papers presented at these two conferences make it clear that all port Jews were intimately involved in eminently local and regional processes at the same time that they were connected to wider world commercial circuits and ethnic networks.[55] The specifics of their insertion in local societies, and how this affects our understanding of the port Jew prototype, merits further consideration. Ultimately, not just Curaçao's Sephardim, but all port Jews, traded globally but also communicated locally.

NOTES

I am grateful to the Center for International Studies, Oceans Connect, the Center for Latin American and Caribbean Studies, and the Graduate School of Duke University for funding summer research in the Netherlands and Curaçao which contributed to this essay. I would like to thank Martin Bernal, Wim Klooster and Richenel Ansano for their comments on earlier drafts. I regret that I have not been able to incorporate all their suggestions. Lively discussions at the Port Jews conference held in Cape Town, South Africa in January 2003 helped me hone my analysis.

1. For a transcription of the surviving one-page fragment of the letter, an English translation and linguistic analysis, see Efraim Frank Martinus, *The Kiss of a Slave: Papiamentu's West-African Connections* (Ph.D. dissertation, University of Amsterdam, 1996), pp.9–10. For analysis of the letter in the context of the development of Papiamentu, see Richard Wood, 'New Light on the Origins of Papiamentu: An Eighteenth-Century Letter', *Neophilologus* 56 (1972), 18–29. The attribution of the author and recipient of the unsigned letter is by Eva Martha Eckkrammer, 'The Standardisation of Papiamentu: New Trends, Problems, and Perspectives', *Bulletin suisse de linguistique appliquée* 69.1 (1999), 61 n.2. There is a photograph of the letter in Isaac and Suzanne Emmanuel, *A History of the Jews of the Netherlands Antilles* (Cincinnati: American Jewish Archives, 1970), plate 78, following p.256. The original has disappeared from the archives.

2. Papiamentu also is spoken by a fluctuating Antillean diaspora group in the Netherlands of at least 70,000, and by increasing numbers of people on the Dutch-owned, English-speaking islands of St Maarten, Saba and St Eustatius. See J.C. Birmingham, Jr., 'Lexical Decreolization in Papiamentu', *Kristòf* IV.2 (1977?), 49; and Eva Martha Eckkrammer (note 1), p.59.

3. Richard E. Wood, 'The Hispanization of a Creole Language: Papiamentu', *Hispania* 55.4 (December 1972), 857; See also John E. Reinecke, 'Trade Jargons and Creole Dialects as Marginal Languages', *Social Forces* 17.1 (1938), 117; and Richard E. Wood, *Papiamentu: Dutch Contributions* (Ph.D. dissertation, Indiana University, 1970), pp.15–21.

4. Derek Bickerton, 'Pidgin and Creole Studies', *Annual Review of Anthropology* 5 (1976), 169. For analysis of the development of Papiamentu literature, see especially Aart Broek, *The Rise of a Caribbean Island's Literature: The Case of Curaçao and its Writing in Papiamentu* (Ph.D. dissertation, Free University of Amsterdam, 1990).

5. There are different conventions regarding the capitalisation of the word creole. I use lowercase

except when it is the name of a specific language or proto-language, such as Spanish Creole.
6. Emmanuel and Emmanuel (see note 1), p.7.
7. The first group of ten families arrived in 1651, a larger group of 70 families in 1659. See Emmanuel and Emmanuel (note 1), pp.38–48. For the 12-point agreement between the Company and the first group of Sephardic settlers, see 'Freedoms and Exemptions granted and Awarded by the Directors of the West India Company …', 22 February 1652, reproduced in C. T. Gehring and J. A. Schiltkamp (eds.), *New Netherlands Documents Volume XVII: Curaçao Papers 1640–1665, Interlaken* (New York: Heart of the Lakes Publishing, 1987), Nos. 11–12, pp.49–51.
8. Wim Klooster, 'The Jews in Suriname and Curaçao', in Paolo Bernardini and Norman Fiering (eds.), *The Jews and the Expansion of Europe to the West, 1450–1800* (New York and Oxford: Berghahn Books, 2001), pp.350–68. João de Yllan, who brought the first small group of Sephardic settlers from Amsterdam to Curaçao in 1651, probably conducted the earliest independent commerce between Curaçao and mainland North America. He began exporting horses and timber to New Netherlands as early as 1652. Governor L. Rodenburch to Amsterdam Directors, 2 April 1654, in Gehring and Schiltkamp (see note 7), No. 14, pp.55–61.
9. See especially Wim Klooster, *Illicit Riches: Dutch Trade in the Caribbean 1648–1795* (Leiden, The Netherlands: KITLV Press, 1998); Ramón Aizpurua Aguirre, *Curaçao y la costa de Caracas: Introducción al estudio del contrabando de la provincia de Venezuela en tiempos de la Compañía Guipuzcoana, 1730–1788* (Caracas: Biblioteca de la Academia Nacional de la Historia, Fuentes para la Historia Colonial de Venezuela No.222, 1993); Celestino Andrés Arauz Monfante, *El contrabando Holandés en el Caribe durante la primera mitad del siglo XVIII*, vols.I and II (Caracas: Biblioteca de la Academia Nacional de la Historia, Fuentes para la Historia Colonial de Venezuela Nos.168 and 169, 1984).
10. National Archives of the Netherlands, The Hague (formerly Algemeen Rijksarchief; hereafter NAN), Nieuwe West Indische Compagnie (NWIC) 1176, 9 August 1790, pp.430–47. According to Johannes Postma, during the heyday of the Dutch West India Company's involvement in the transatlantic slave trade, 1658–1729, 72 per cent of the slaves transported by the Company were landed at Curaçao. See Johannes Menne Postma, *The Dutch in the Atlantic Slave Trade, 1600–1815* (Cambridge: Cambridge University Press, 1990), Table 2.6, p.54, and Table 9.6, p.223. For an overview of the role of Curaçao in the Dutch slave trade, see Cornelis Goslinga, *The Dutch in the Caribbean and in the Guyanas: 1680–1791* (The Netherlands: van Gorcum, 1985), pp.244–50. Far more enslaved Africans passed through Curaçao then actually remained on the island. The transients were held temporarily in an area just north of Willemstad to recuperate from the Middle Passage before being sold to the plantations of the Spanish, English and French colonies. See Wim Klooster, 'Slavenvaart op Spaanse kusten: De Nederlandse met Spaans Amerika, 1648–1701', *Tijdschrift voor zeegeschiedenis* 16.2 (1997), 121–40.
11. See, among others, Resolution of DWIC Directors, 26 May 1644, in Gehring and Schiltkamp (see note 7), No. 8c, p. 39; Curaçao Governor to Company Directors, 11 June 1657, in ibid., No. 27, p.98.
12. See Klooster (note 9), esp. pp.173–98, and the Appendices.
13. See Klooster (note 9), p.200.
14. It must be stressed, however, that the character of all these interactions remained fundamentally unequal in a slave society such as Curaçao, and that Sephardim were slaveholders.
15. The most complete documentation of this process of transformation remains Emmanuel and Emmanuel (see note 1).
16. Emmanuel and Emmanuel (see note 1), p.681. Appendix 3 (pp.681–746) provides comprehensive lists of Sephardic ship-owners and captains from the 1680s. Volume One contains several photos of Sephardic tombstones in Curaçao that were decorated with maritime vessels.
17. For the expanse of this trade, see, among others, the essays in Bernardini and Fiering (note 9). Emmanuel and Emmanuel (see note 1), provide a comprehensive list of dates, places and people involved in this trade in Appendix 16, pp.822–40. Also see Isaac S. Emmanuel, *Precious Stones of the Jews of Curaçao* (New York: Block Publishing Company, 1957), pp.261–339; Arauz Monfante (note 9); Aizpurua Aguirre (note 9); and Wim Klooster, 'Contraband Trade by Curaçao's Jews with Countries of Idolatry, 1660–1800', *Studia Rosenthaliana* 31.1–2 (1997), 58–73.
18. NAN Oud Archief Curaçao (OAC), 820.11, 6 January 1749; Governor Hart of St Christopher to Mr Popple, 30 November 1726, in Cecil Headlam (ed.), *Calendar of State Papers, Colonial Series,*

America and West Indies, Preserved in the Public Records Office (London: His Majesty's Stationary Office, 1934–36), No.306, pp.179–80. Also see Klooster (note 17).

19. Klooster (see note 17), p.68; NAN NWIC 1166.83, 'Leijste van de familien', 2 June 1775; Emmanuel and Emmanuel (see note 1), Appendix 8, pp.763–8. Simply having enough income to be taxed, however, meant that they had achieved a certain economic status.

20. Klooster (see note 9), p.68. By comparison, one-third of the sailors involved in the trade between the Caribbean and North America in the 1770s were of African descent, while blacks comprised 20 per cent of United States seafarers in the early nineteenth century. See Herbert C. Bell, 'The West India Trade Before the American Revolution', *American Historical Review* 22.2 (January 1917), 280; and Jeffrey W. Bolster, *Black Jacks: African American Seamen in the Age of Sail* (Cambridge, MA: Harvard University Press, 1997), p.2.

21. Klooster (see note 9), pp.68–9. Curaçao manumission petitions frequently refer explicitly to seafaring. See To van der Lee's compilation of all known manumission letters filed on the island between 1722 and 1863, *Curaçaose Vrijbrieven 1722–1863* (The Hague: Algemeen Rijksarchief, 1998). In the decade between 1750 and 1759, I found that five per cent of all petitions specifically mentioned seafaring as the reason for manumission.

22. See H. Hoetink, *Het patroon van de oude Curaçaose samenleving* (Amsterdam: S. Emmering, 1987). One problem with this model is that it does not allow for the ethnic and linguistic diversity of small-scale merchants and itinerant seafarers who passed through the cosmopolitan port of Willemstad.

23. See Frank Martinus, 'The Value of Guene for Folklore and Culture', in Edwin N. Ayubi (ed.), *Papers of the Third Seminar on Latin-American and Caribbean Folklore* (Willemstad, Curaçao: Archaeological-Anthropological Institute of the Netherlands Antilles, 1996), pp.181–93; and Martinus (note 1), chs.9 and 10.

24. The different theories of Papiamentu's origins and development parallel the wider debates about creole languages. The central question is whether creole languages are descended from a single common proto-Afro-Portuguese *lingua franca* (the monogenetic theory), or germinated independently from different European languages in the Americas (the polygenetic theory). For a general introduction that is accessible to the non-specialist, see Bickerton (note 4). For a brief description of five different theories of Papiamentu's origins, see Martinus (note 1), pp.12–17. For the Spanish Creole origin hypothesis, see, among others, Dan Munteneau, *El Papiamentu, Lengua Criolla Hispánica* (Madrid: Editorial Gredos, 1996); and Wood, 'The Hispanization of a Creole Language' (note 3). Martinus (see note 1) is perhaps the most complete analysis of Papiamentu to date, amassing impressive evidence for the proto-Afro-Portuguese theory. See also Tomás Navarro, 'Observaciones Sobre el Papiamento', *Nueva Revista de Filología Hispánica* 7 (1953), 183–9; and H.L.A. van Wijk, 'Orígenes y Evolución del Papiamentu', *Neophilologus* 48 (1958), 169–82. For a rebuttal to Martinus, see Antoine Maduro, *Kaboberdiano i Papiamentu* (Curaçao: Maduro & Curiel's Bank, 1987). A book-length description of Papiamentu written for the general public in English is Gary C. Fouse, *The Story of Papiamentu: A Study in Slavery and Language* (Lanham, MD: University Press of America, 2002).

25. Birmingham (see note 2), p.49. Martinus (see note 1), p.1, argues that Papiamentu began to develop as early as 1640.

26. See Martinus (note 1), pp.119–45 and 267.

27. Ibid., p.11.

28. Curaçao's Sephardim conducted worship, kept synagogue records and often wrote their epitaphs in Portuguese, as well as using it in their international trade dealings. See Emmanuel and Emmanuel (note 1), p.482. The Emmanuels reproduce photographs of a variety of documents in Portuguese throughout their two-volume work. For the emergence of Papiamentu among the Sephardim, see May Henriques, *Ta Asina? O ta Asana? Abla, uzu, i kustumber sefardí* (Curaçao: self-published, 1988), p.xii. According to Henriques, many local Sephardic women were fluent in both Portuguese and Papiamentu, but never learned Dutch. Many of the island's Sephardim also spoke Spanish, due, no doubt, to close trade ties with the neighbouring Spanish colonies. Interestingly, when the local Sephardic community split in the 1860s, the younger group formed a congregation that worshipped and kept its minutes in Spanish. Multiple language use has continued to thrive both in the wider society of Curaçao and among the Sephardic enclave up to the present. Anthropologist Alan Benjamin suggests that this multilingualism reflects a

multinational identification on the part of many of Curaçao's Sephardim, many of whom might equally be portrayed as Jewish, Curaçaoan, Cuban, Caribbean and Sephardi. See Alan Benjamin, *Jews of the Dutch Caribbean: Exploring Ethnic Identity on Curaçao* (London and New York: Routledge, 2002), pp.150–51.

29. See, among others, Sidney Joubert, 'Literatura Neerlandoantillana', *Kristòf* 3.2 (April 1976), 75–6.

30. Alexius Schabel, 'Dagboek-Fragment van Pater Michael Alexius Schabel Societatis Jesu Missionaris op het eiland Curaçao loopend van 21 October 1707 tot 4 Februari 1708', Central Historical Archives of the Netherlands Antilles. For an English-language reference, see Wood, 'New Light on the Origins of Papiamentu' (note 3), p.18. Some proponents of the Spanish-based theory have used this as supporting evidence, although it is not at all clear whether Schabel, a German-speaker who kept his diary in Latin, would have been able to distinguish between Spanish and Portuguese variants.

31. Cited in J. Hartog, *Curaçao: From Colonial Dependence to Autonomy* (Aruba: De Wit, 1968), p.157.

32. Broek (see note 4), p.26.

33. Guene died out by the mid-twentieth century, surviving only in songs, proverbs and other bits of oral tradition. The most extensive published collection of Guene material was compiled by Paul Brenneker and Elis Juliana between the 1950s and 1970s, and appears throughout the ten-volume collection, Paul Brenneker, *Sambumbu: Volkskunde van Curaçao, Aruba, en Bonaire* (Curaçao: Van Dorp, 1969–75). Over 1,400 items contributed by 267 elderly Afro-Curaçaoan informants are on audio recordings known as the *Zikinzá* collection. For analysis of the richness of this material, see Martinus (note 1), esp. pp.17–18, and chs.9 and 10, pp.193–263. Rene Rosalia, Richenel Ansano, Eric La Croes and others have compiled largely unpublished collections of Guene material from original research among elderly informants, most of them now deceased.

34. Martinus (see note 1), pp.3, 8–11. The vessels are listed in Emmanuel and Emmanuel (see note 1), pp.682–723. See Martinus (note 1), p.146, for detailed linguistic analysis of eight of these vessel names. Joubert (see note 29), p.75, also mentions a 1775 transcription of a dialogue between two black women (he does not specify enslaved or free) in Papiamentu, but I have not yet found a more complete reference to this.

35. Hartog (see note 31), p.227. For description and analysis of early nineteenth century written works in Papiamentu, see Wood, 'New Light on the Origins of Papiamentu' (note 3), esp. p.21; and Hartog (note 31), pp.302–3. The earliest studies of Papiamentu I have found are Alfred Sintiago, *Gramatica Corticoe de Idioma Papiamentoe* (Curaçao: Imprenta A.Bethencourt é Hijos, 1898); W.M. Hoyer, *Papiamentoe i su Manera de Skirbié* (Curaçao: Imprenta A. Bethencourt é Hijos, 1918); and Rodolfo Lenz, *El Papiamento. La Lengua Criolla de Curazao. La Gramática más Sencilla* (Santiago de Chile: Balcells, 1928). For discussion of nineteenth-century references to the language, often disparaging, see van Wijk (note 24), p.169.

36. Martinus (see note 1), pp.119–45. It is likely that many of the Sephardim that Martinus refers to here were either *conversos* or *marranos*. There are several other theories that postulate a major role for the Sephardim in the creation of Papiamentu: that the language has roots either in the Portuguese spoken by the Sephardim of the diaspora or in the Spanish-influenced Ladino that they spoke, or that it took root in the first Sephardic community of the Americas in Recife, Brazil, whose residents (both Sephardic and African) then transported it to Curaçao in the second half of the seventeenth century. See Martinus (note 1), p.103. None of these arguments is convincing. There is no evidence that Curaçao's Sephardim widely spoke Ladino, for example, or that Sephardim fleeing Brazil either took their slaves with them or came directly to Curaçao. Indeed, the Dutch West India Company did not allow the Jews of Curaçao to buy slaves either for their private use or for sale until 1674, two decades after the first permanent Sephardic settlers arrived. See Emmanuel and Emmanuel (note 1), p.75.

37. Eli Faber, *Jews, Slaves and the Slave Trade. Setting the Record Straight* (New York: New York University Press, 1998); and Saul Friedman, *Jews and the American Slave Trade* (New Brunswick, NJ and London: Transaction Publications, 1998).

38. For one primary reference to Sephardim on the Atlantic shores of Africa, see Boleslao Lewin, *La Inquisición en México: Impresionantes relatos del siglo XVII* (Puebla: Editorial José M. Cajica Jr., 1967), pp.19–23. I am grateful to Wim Klooster for sharing this reference with me. There is still much research and theoretical work to be done in this area, including addressing the question to

what extent small groups of *conversos* and *marranos* can be considered as either Sephardim or port Jews.

39. Hoetink (see note 22). For a summary of his argument in English, see Sidney Mintz, 'The Sociohistorical Background to Pidginization and Creolization', in D. Hymes (ed.), *Pidginization and Creolization of Languages* (Cambridge: Cambridge University Press, 1971), pp.481–96.

40. Eckkrammer (see note 1), p.61; Frank Martinus, 'The Victory of the Concubines and the Nannies', in Kathleen M. Balutansky and Marie-Agnès Sourieau (eds.), *Caribbean Creolization: Reflections on the Cultural Dynamics of Language, Literature, and Identity* (Florida: University Press of Florida, 1998), p.114; Reinecke (see note 3), p.115.

41. Martinus (see note 1), p.103; Henriques (see note 28).

42. The role of children in developing and propagating creole languages is a well-established linguistic phenomenon. For Papiamentu, see Martinus (note 40); Martinus (note 1) pp.128–30; and Derek Bickerton, 'An Afro-Creole Origin for Eena Meena Mina Mo', *American Speech* 57.3 (Autumn 1982), 225–8.

43. For an initial exploration of this idea, see Linda M. Rupert, 'Curaçao: ¿entrepôt neerlandés o puerto caribeño?', in Instituto Mora (ed.), *El golfo-caribe y sus puertos, siglos XVIII y XIX* (Instituto Mora, Mexico City: forthcoming 2006); and Rupert, 'Rethinking Curaçao's Commercial History: Some Initial Notes on the Role of Black Seafarers and Jewish Merchants in the Early Modern Period', *Lanternu: Journal of the Central Historical Archives of the Netherlands Antilles* 20 (September 2001), 5–21.

44. See Reinecke (note 3).

45. See Gert Oostindie, 'Ethnicity, nationalism and the exodus: the Dutch Caribbean predicament', in idem (ed.), *Ethnicity in the Caribbean: Essays in Honor of Harry Hoetink* (London: Macmillan Caribbean, 1996), pp.222–4. In recent decades, the role of Papiamentu in society – especially in local education – has been the focus of an impassioned debate in Curaçao. A rich advocacy literature has developed, stressing the importance of teaching children in their native language rather than in Dutch, and its vital role in nation-building projects. For a good representation of this debate in English, see Enrique Muller, 'Papiamentu and the Search for a Better Community', *Kristòf* VI.1 (1979?), 25–33.

46. Benjamin (see note 28), pp.82–6. Benjamin has a good summary of some of the present-day struggles for promoting Papiamentu in the wider context of defining local identity, both throughout Curaçaoan society and within the local Jewish community.

47. May Henriques (see note 28) analyses the particular Sephardic usage of close to 1,500 Papiamentu words and expressions. She examines both the role of the Sephardim in maintaining Papiamentu, and the unique ways that they continue to deploy the language in their own circles. Henriques identifies Papiamentu words of Hebrew, Spanish, Portuguese, French, Ladino and Guene origins that have particular meanings in the Sephardic community. For analysis of the linguistic richness of her work, see Martinus (note 1), pp.102–6. Emmanuel and Emmanuel (note 1), pp.482–3, identified nine Papiamentu phrases that were clearly of Hebrew origin, and three words that resemble Ladino. It is also worth noting that Aruban linguists have documented hundreds of words that appear to have their roots in the language of the islands' original native population, the Caquetíos. See G. van Buurt and S.M. Joubert. *Stemmen uit het Verleden: Indiaanse woorden in het Papiamentu* (Alphen aan den Rijn: Van Buurt Boek Produkties, 1997).

48. Charles Gomes Casseres, 'Papiamentu, The Language of Curaçao and its Sephardim', unpublished manuscript, 1997, no pagination (I am grateful to the author for sharing this essay with me). With easy migration to and from the Netherlands, Curaçao's population fluctuates between 140,000 and 170,000 depending on the state of the economy in both places.

49. Arguably, this may be a return to the historical roots of the term creole, which, according to the early Peruvian chronicler Garcilaso de la Vega, was first used by enslaved people of African descent to distinguish those who were born in the Americas; cited in Martinus (see note 1), p.198. Groundbreaking contributions to the discussion of creolisation include Sidney W. Mintz and Richard Price, T*he Birth of African-American Culture: An Anthropological Perspective* (Boston: Beacon Press, 1976); John Thornton, *Africa and Africans in the Making of the Atlantic World, 1400–1800*, 2nd edn. (Cambridge: Cambridge University Press, 1998); and Judith Carney, *Black Rice: The African Origins of Rice Cultivation in the Americas* (Cambridge, MA and London: Harvard University Press, 2001). For an overview of theories of creolisation, see the introduction by

David Buisseret in David Buisseret and Steven G. Reinhardt (eds.), *Creolization in the Americas* (College Station, TX: Texas A&M University Press, 2000), pp.3–17; and Carney, *Black Rice*, pp.1–8. See also Stuart B. Schwartz, 'The Formation of a Colonial Identity in Brazil', in Nicholas Canny and Anthony Pagden (eds.), *Colonial Identity in the Atlantic World, 1500–1800* (Princeton, NJ: Princeton University Press, 1987), pp.15–50.

50. Ira Berlin, 'From Creole to African: Atlantic Creoles and the Origins of African-American Society in Mainland North America', *William and Mary Quarterly*, 3rd Series, 53.2 (April 1996), 251–88.

51. See Martinus (note 1), pp.119–45; and Berlin (note 50).

52. See Martinus (note 1), esp. pp.142–5; see also note 37 above.

53. For the former, see Miriam Bodian, *Hebrews of the Portuguese Nation: Conversos and Community in Early Modern Amsterdam* (Indiana: Indiana University Press, 1997); and Daniel Swetschinski, *Reluctant Cosmopolitans: The Portuguese Jews of Seventeenth Century Amsterdam* (London and Portland, OR: Littman Library of Jewish Civilisation, 2000). For the latter, see especially Bernardini and Fiering (note 9); and David Cesarani (ed.), *Port Jews: Jewish Communities in Cosmopolitan Maritime Trading Centres, 1550–1950* (London and Portland, OR: Frank Cass, 2002); and the essays in this volume.

54. For the former, see Jonathan Schorsch, 'Portmanteau Jews: Sephardim and Race in the Early Modern Atlantic World', in Cesarani (see note 53), pp.59–74. For the latter, see Stephen Alexander Fortune, *Merchants and Jews: The Struggle for British West Indian Commerce, 1650–1750* (Gainesville, FL: University Presses of Florida, 1984).

55. In addition to the works in this volume, see also Cesarani (note 53).

Ethnicity, Identity and 'Race': The Port Jews of Nineteenth-Century Charleston

GEMMA ROMAIN

Introduction

This essay explores the ethnicity and identity of the Jews of antebellum Charleston with specific reference to their status as 'port Jews' or as potential 'cosmopolitans' and how this identity impinged upon their interaction with non-Jews. Charlestonian Jews have been perceived as the pre-eminent American community of the antebellum period, composed of the most educated, refined and prosperous individuals, who were accepted politically and socially into the fabric of white middle-class society. Likewise the Jewish community has been characterised as embracing Charlestonian culture in its entirety, fighting in wars, being 'loyal' to the nation, the state and the city and holding excellent relations with white Charlestonians.[1]

The mythologies within this description will be scrutinised as will the question of whether the particularities of Charleston's economy and society were reasons for this apparent cultural harmony. I argue that the characteristics of the Charleston Jewish community in the antebellum period stem from a mixture of the internal dynamics of the community and from Charleston's location as an eastern seaport linking the Atlantic world to Europe, its symbolic and cultural position as the cosmopolitan capital of southern society, and the fact of its dependence on plantation slavery and on the horrific trade, exploitation and enslavement of African-Americans.

Within this essay I look at how Jews in Charleston negotiated their identities, how non-Jews viewed Jews, and how Jewish life in Charleston has been represented or neglected in wider historiographical debates. I also utilise some specific primary and published materials: mainly wills, diaries and genealogical material. An analysis of aspects of the ethnicity of the community can serve to expand the model of the port Jew, coined by Lois Dubin and conceptualised by David Sorkin.[2]

I am particularly interested in questions concerning the ethnicity of antebellum Charleston Jews and their relations with both the white and black populations. It is my contention that the history of the Charleston Jew has been romanticised and been subject to 'forgetting' due to its problematic place within the conventional narrative of modern Jewish history. I will argue that the ethnicity of Charleston's Jews is multiple and includes a strong diasporic identity formulated through the Jewish mercantile past with a corresponding 'loyal' and sometimes passionate local identity.[3]

The Port Jew: Definitions

Sorkin's definition of the port Jew represented a new way of looking at the beginnings of modern Jewry. Sorkin argued that although the *maskil* (the exponent of the *haskalah*, or the Jewish Enlightenment) and the 'court Jew' were undoubtedly representations of Jewish modernity, a third way in which the Jews gained rights and acculturated transpired through the lives of the 'port Jew'. Those were 'merchant Jews of sephardi or, to a lesser extent, Italian extraction who settled in the port cities of the Mediterranean, the Atlantic seaboard and the New World'.[4] The ports where Jews settled were cities and towns built upon the importance of commerce and pragmatism and as a result mercantile Jews often gained privileges and rights that Jews elsewhere did not have.[5]

It is my opinion that a port Jewish identity cannot be seen in purely mercantile terms – the port Jewish society was one surrounded by the merchant Jews but also the Jewish community in general, including Jews who worked in related industries and Jews who were associated with mercantile Jews. Additionally, not all port Jews were wealthy or necessarily religiously lax. The particular dynamics of each individual port needs to be considered. In terms of the example of the Charlestonian port Jew, the process of acculturation needs to be addressed not only in terms of customs and interaction with the non-Jewish world but also of ethnicity.

Historiographical Explorations

There have been a series of marginalities and historical amnesia within the historiography pertinent to Charleston Jewry. The grand narrative of Jewish modernity is a Eurocentric and Ashkenazified narrative of Jews 'entering' the modern world, developing a Jewish Enlightenment or *haskalah* and eventually achieving emancipation. Modern Sephardi history was traditionally characterised as an anomaly and a romantic but insignificant factor in Jews gaining rights and becoming acculturated. When Sephardi history was described it was done so in nostalgic terms focusing on what were considered important, 'noble' great men. Yet a more inclusive and de-romanticised Sephardi history is essential in any understanding of how Jews came to modernity. Much of current scholarship into Sephardi history, particularly transnational history, is increasingly complex and nuanced.

Traditional historiography separated the American-Jewish experience in the form of three stages, using ethnicity as the index of categorisation: first the Sephardi era, secondly the German, and lastly the eastern European. The early era of the Sephardim has been romanticised to a large degree. Sephardi settlers were seen as noble, adventurous, acculturated and respected by their Christian neighbours. Early American-Jewish historiography was also notable in another respect – by its claim that when Jews landed on the shores of America they had entered the Promised Land – a land free from anti-semitism.[6]

Considering Charleston's place in the early American-Jewish experience, the historiography of the community has been surprisingly slow to develop.[7] There are various explanations for this absence. Compared to the large-scale migrations of the late nineteenth century, the southern Jewish community was seen as comparatively unimportant in the American-Jewish narrative. Additionally, southern Jewry's 'loyalty' to the 'customs' of the South, particularly to slavery, was an embarrassment. Lastly, Charleston's community was seen as only important in its heyday of the late eighteenth and early nineteenth century – particularly when describing the Sephardi period of American history. Thereafter as the conventions of the three-stage historiography deemed the early nineteenth century the era of the German Jew, no major attention was given to the progression in time of the earlier communities.

In the early part of the twentieth century, the main historical attention on individual antebellum southern Jewish communities came from local historians, genealogists and commemorative community publications. In a similar vein to early historical works, community publications have stressed the tolerance of America and particularly of the South, the way in which the community excelled financially and socially, and how the community fitted in with all aspects of southern life, including slavery (a subject I explore later in the essay).[8]

In recent decades there has been a new school of historians assessing the community in different ways.[9] The Southern Jewish Historical Society has done much to promote diverse histories of southern Jews, as has the recent work of Dale Rosengarten and Harlan Greene of the Jewish Heritage Collection at the College of Charleston.[10] An important development in Charlestonian historiography was James William Hagy's 1993 publication, which provided documentation of the history of the Jewish community in the colonial and antebellum periods. Hagy was the first historian to write a book-length general history of the community without turning to the 'great man' brand of history.

Jews in both the Caribbean and Charleston have been under scrutiny recently as a result of the views of some academics such as Tony Martin and in particular an anti-semitic publication by the Nation of Islam arguing that the Jews were responsible for the transatlantic slave trade. As a result of this publication there has been a resurgence of interest in the communities in these areas.[11] The detestable opinions expressed in publications such as the Nation of Islam's does not mean that the history of Jews in the South and Jewish attitudes towards slavery should as a result be ignored or seen as unimportant in the overall construction of a southern Jewish identity. Although perhaps not the case now, many historians had previously approached the subject of black–Jewish relations in pre-civil war society in a somewhat apologetic manner and also had not focused attention on the voices and experiences of the enslaved person.[12]

Most of the literature on black–Jewish everyday relations in the United States has focused on the interaction between the groups in the North, between Jews who migrated to America at the turn of the nineteenth century and African-Americans who lived in New York and who had migrated from the South to the North.[13] Many more historians looking at the Jews of the South are now exploring relations between blacks and Jews instead of always solely focusing on white Christian and Jewish relations. Additionally, a few of these historians now examine how both communities viewed one another rather than purely on how Jews viewed blacks.[14] The focus on issues of ethnicity and race, as carried out by Schorsch with regard to the colonial Caribbean, serves to reveal the complexities of the port Jew model and suggests that Jews partly 'entered modernity' in the Atlantic world as a result of fitting into or desiring to fit into the emerging notions of whiteness.

I now analyse general themes within the experiences of the Charleston Jewish community, identifying some of the ways in which Jews in Charleston interacted with others and how they created and shaped their ethnicity. Although the Charleston Jewish community in this period was increasingly diverse, general themes regarding ethnicity can be ascertained. The examples given in this essay highlight that whilst Jews were largely accepted into Charleston society, at times of crisis they were deemed inferior and traditional anti-semitic stereotypes emerged within the public arena. Nevertheless, Jews in Charleston were active agents and did not have their identity determined or involve themselves in Charleston life through fear of persecution.[15]

The Port of Charleston

Charleston was a pinnacle of the British colonial and mercantile world and continued to exert economic importance until the 1820s. The port town first came into existence in 1670 as Charles Town and from the start had a 'liberal' constitution based on Lockean principles, where there was freedom of religion to 'dissenters'. Charles Town became a mercantile trading centre attracting a multitude of different nationalities to its shores, including French Huguenots, Dutch, English, Scottish and Sephardi Jews.[16] From the 1730s Charles Town's economy began to grow, exporting goods from the hinterland and the low country, first deerskins and later rice and indigo and eventually sea island cotton, the latter which developed in the post-revolutionary era of Charleston.[17] Charleston's economy was established upon the African slave trade and plantation slavery. Charleston maintained a society based on a system of strict racialised and aristocratic principles – the right to vote was given to white, male property owners. The federal census in 1790 showed that Charleston Country had a population of 11,801 whites and 34,846 blacks. The ratio within the city was 8,831 African-Americans to 8,089 whites.[18]

Jewish Life in Charleston

There were Jews in Charleston from the beginning of the colony's establishment, although the community did not properly emerge until the mid-eighteenth century. Jews settling in Charleston were from a multitude of countries and as they were involved or connected with the mercantile trade a large number of them were from London and the Caribbean, as well as Germany and Poland.[19] By the late eighteenth century Ashkenazi Jews outnumbered Sephardim. By 1820 Charleston had the biggest Jewish population in the whole of the country – 800, with New York in second place.[20] Charleston's Jewish community also became notable for creating the first American reform movement, as well as for its prominent Jewish figures such as the statesman Judah P. Benjamin.

One of the most important aspects of Jewish ethnicity in Charleston was their diasporic identity. They belonged to a larger migratory movement and were part of what can be described as a port Jewish diaspora. A large proportion of them were Sephardi Jews whose ancestors were *conversos* who had to flee Spanish and Portuguese expulsions. These Jews settled in various ports around the world as they were given more freedom and often equality in these areas. Whole families would often migrate and would usually maintain links with family members and associates from the areas they had left and other port areas. Jews who came to Charleston retained links with Jews in the Caribbean, Europe, the southern hinterland and other port cities such as New Orleans, New York and Philadelphia. While settling in the ports, these Jews would often move from one port to another and would have resided in several ports during a lifetime. Although this cultural fluidity was not as great in nineteenth-century Charleston, it was still certainly a feature of this port Jewish experience. The Cohen-D'Azevedo family represent one of the many families exhibiting this diasporic network during the nineteenth century. The *Haham* Moses Cohen-D'Azevedo was born in Holland in 1720 and died in London in 1784. His children and grandchildren lived in, among other places, London, Charleston, Philadelphia, St Kitts, Barbados, Martinique and Surinam.[21]

During the antebellum period Jews found employment in all sectors of society. However, Jews were still primarily involved in mercantile trade or in merchant related employment such as storekeeping.[22] As Jacob Rader Marcus observed, the new Jewish merchants had much in common with the earlier mercantile Jews, selling at retail and wholesale, and occasionally carrying out imports and exports. The main change was that now they focused on domestic trade.[23] Jewish women played an important role in the economy, often working as shopkeepers. Many women in this period became sole traders – and thus if they were married their husbands had no right to interfere with their business practices and no right to take any of their profits. Previous to James Hagy's work, most analyses of Charlestonian Jewish women centred on those who extolled 'feminine virtue' such as Penina Moise and subsequently women's roles in the economy have been ignored.[24]

Charleston's Jewish community was supplemented throughout the nineteenth century with Jews from Germany and later from eastern Europe. There appears to have been less antipathy between the German and Sephardi Jews than that which occurred between the established Jewish community and East European Jews. The early Ashkenazi settlers 'intermarried' with Sephardim and joined the Sephardi-oriented synagogue, Kahal Kadosh Beth Elohim.[25] Unlike the Sephardi synagogues in the 'mother country' communities of London and Amsterdam, there existed no *ascamot* disqualifying Ashkenazim from joining in with the communal and religious life of the Sephardi Jews.[26]

Antebellum Jews also maintained transnational religious networks and these diasporic links were a crucial factor in the shaping of their ethnicity. These networks were formed between Jews living in Charleston and Jews living in other specifically maritime, or port Jewish, societies. Trustees of the Coming Street cemetery, the oldest Jewish cemetery in Charleston, included Jews from Charleston, London, Jamaica, Barbados, New York, Newport and Savannah.[27] Most significantly, the community often appealed to London for its ministers. For example, in 1805 the leaders of the London Sephardi synagogue Bevis Marks sent Benjamin, the son of *Haham* Moses Cohen-D'Azevedo to Charleston to become the new minister of Beth Elohim. However, the congregation were not happy with their new minister and sent him back to London.[28]

This cosmopolitanism did not conflict with the protocols of Charleston society. Unlike previous historiographical assumptions of the South as a uniform, homogeneous society, Charleston was, at least up to the early nineteenth century, very much influenced by intellectual and cultural trends in other parts of the world, and because of her position as a port, different ideas and people were always reshaping Charleston society – the different ideas, however, were not often liberal. Charleston was ethnically diverse throughout the colonial and antebellum periods. The ethnic diversity of societies set up in Charleston to help the poor exemplify this. According to George C. Rogers, pre-revolutionary Charles Town was hospitable to all who were 'enterprising'.[29] This obviously only applied to the white inhabitants of the city. Charleston's Jewish community was not therefore alone in establishing societies designed specifically to aid its own members.

The cosmopolitanism of the port meant that Jews from diverse backgrounds were accepted into society so long as they fitted into the strict racial hierarchy of the city. Cosmopolitanism relied on strict religious principle. Judaism was generally seen in a much more favourable light than in many parts of the world, partly through the Charlestonian belief in the centrality of religion to morality, whatever the religion might be. Thus religious Jews were generally accepted more than secular Jews, who were frowned upon. The religious environment of Charleston contributed in part to a port Jewish identity that was far from being religiously lax. The synagogue served to integrate Jews into the community and achieve social respectability. Nevertheless, we must not ignore the experiences of Jews who were not particularly religious, but who have been marginalised in historiography.

Although most Jews did not generally socialise with non-Jews, there appears to have been some evidence of mutual respect and cooperation between Jews and white non-Jews. For example, in 1847 the Hebrew Benevolent Society held a benefit ball to raise funds. The Saint Andrews Society donated its hall for use and many non-Jews attended the ball.[30]

Jewish/Non-Jewish Relations

It has been presumed that as Jews were involved in trade and storekeeping, the planter elites wholeheartedly accepted them; they performed the function of the middleman and carried out the activities the planters thought were below them.[31] Apart from the problems of the middleman theory, it is also circumspect to conclude that cordial relations existed as a result of Jews carrying out trade and financial occupations.[32] As Gregory Allen Grebb has argued, 'planter antagonism had an ethnic component', that when talking about merchants 'the label "Jew" came to be used with almost the same meaning and opprobrium as that of "Yankee"'. Grebb found little evidence of anti-semitism among planters, but argued that they almost certainly looked down upon those engaged in trade.[33]

Anti-semitic views expressed about Jews in the economy mainly occurred from visitors to Charleston. For example, in their diary one New England visitor commented when visiting King Street:

I've not a nod & a smile for every blackguard that comes in with a four
pence in his hand. I would think my own Father an accomplish'd knave
if he had been any time, & made money in the dry goods line in *King St.*
They are all jews or worse than jews—*Yankees*—for a Yankee can jew a
jew directly.[34]

This use of the word 'jew' as a verb denoting shady practice became common
currency in the antebellum period.

John C. Calhoun (who was a Senator from South Carolina and also a Vice
President of the United States) expressed similar opinions, claiming that the
Jews were 'notoriously a race of brokers, bankers, and merchants'.[35] However,
in general the term merchant signified prestige and power. Many Jewish
shopkeepers would call themselves merchants because it enabled them to get
onto a higher rung on the social ladder. Wealthy shipping merchants achieved
considerable power within Charleston society and this included Jewish
merchants and businessmen. An examination of Jewish marriage notices
appearing in the Charleston newspapers reveals that with one exception the
groom's occupation is only mentioned when he was a merchant.[36]

The Jewish economist and newspaper editor Jacob N. Cardozo recollected
on good relations between planters and merchants. In his reminiscences of
Charleston, published in 1866 he argued 'there was a geniality in this
intercourse that rendered it highly attractive – the mercantile and planting
classes were on the best terms … The Sea Island and Rice planter were often
found at the table of the merchant, and this hospitality was reciprocated'.[37] As
with all memories there is probably an element of romanticism at play in this
recollection. However, the 'great' merchants gained status and entered
Charleston's elite society. Although it certainly was the case that merchants
were in the main not part of the 'highest' echelons of Charleston society,
perhaps we should be far more analytical in our assumptions that trade was
always neglected or frowned upon in the antebellum period.

Apart from the economic sphere, how can we define the level of interaction
between the communities? The remaining part of this essay focuses on some
of the ways in which Jews and non-Jews interacted with each other and how
this interaction affected the way in which they constructed their identity.
Ethnicity is not just reactive – in other words it is not solely to do with being
either accepted or rejected by the dominant society. It is, as Werner Sollors
argues, about consent and descent.[38] The ethnic group themselves are active
agents in the construction of their identity, including their racialised identity.

It is fair to say that most Jews in antebellum Charleston saw themselves as
white and that likewise they were treated in the main as white citizens, at least
in the public sphere. Their ethnicity was composed of various nationalities but
was, in a similar vein to the Jews of Savannah, generally solidified through a

middle-class identity.[39] The 'higher' echelons of Charleston society were characterised by family lineage and genealogy – wealth was not the indicator of social standing, instead how long a person's family had lived in Charleston and whether they had prominent individuals in their lineage was the mainstay.[40] Jews who had 'noble' ancestors would join societies such as the Daughters of the American Revolution, and as Sephardim were (or at least were recognised as) the earliest settlers some Ashkenazi Jews changed their names to Sephardi names, usually those names of prominent families.[41] This last point is particularly interesting, as many theorists have believed it was generally Ashkenazi Jews who were considered white, but here we have a case of the Ashkenazim trying to be Sephardim in order to be more accepted within a society with its social structure based upon longevity.

How can one define whiteness as a concept specifically useful when speaking of an antebellum society? Can one adopt the theories of post-colonial and ethnicity scholars to talk of hybridity and fluidity in a society where the racial categories employed were designed specifically not to foster the blurring of boundaries? The concept of whiteness is still being debated by theorists and has only been analysed recently by those concerned with ethnicity, primarily by Richard Dyer. Dyer states that 'as long as race is something only applied to non-white peoples, as long as white people are not racially seen and named, they/we function as a human norm. Other people are raced, we are just people'.[42] The literature concerning Jews and ethnicity has mainly examined the way in which Jews were constructed as black in the nineteenth century and how they 'became' white in the mid-twentieth century. In terms of American historiography, less attempts have been made to examine how and if Jews became white in the early and antebellum periods. It is my view that 'whiteness' has multiple meanings, concerns power relations and has often been defined as Anglo-Saxon.

Although Jews in Charleston were accepted as equal to white non-Jews, their racial identity was not fixed in the public imagination. They were designated as white in the political arena, but general attitudes were more ambivalent on how white Jews really were. As Rogoff argues 'Jews were accepted as white, but their precise racial place was not fixed'.[43] However, in the antebellum period any views about Jews and their 'indeterminate' racial place did not negatively impinge on the Jews' lives in any overt way.[44] In terms of racial identity, theories of natural law were growing in prominence. In the nineteenth century racial theorists discussed Jews because they were seen as a pure and undiluted race, which could act as a test case to see how and why physical features changed or remained over time and place. For example, in 1850 the racial theorist Josiah Nott gave a lecture in Charleston in which he referred to the Jews and how their physical features always remained the same even if their skin colour was variable.[45] Race theories were not popular with everyone at that time, but they certainly had currency in a region whose fabric of society relied on the belief in the difference of races.[46]

So far in my research I have uncovered more opinions of non-Jews than Jews concerning views about Jewish identity. However, my initial examination of the Jewish diaries from the Jewish Heritage collection at the College of Charleston indicate that many Jews in this specific locale do not see themselves as particularly different from white non-Jews. I have begun an examination of a series of diaries written by a Charlestonian Jew, David Henry Mordecai, who was the son of the prominent Jewish merchant, businessman, politician and slaveowner Moses Cohen Mordecai.[47] David Henry Mordecai was born in 1833 and died in 1859, when he was only 26 years old. He spent the last few years of his life travelling through Europe and when he was increasingly ill he went to, among other places, the Middle East. In his diaries he often referred to his internal thoughts and emotions, particularly about his depression as a result of his illness. He also talked about various Jewish and non-Jewish friends in Charleston. However he did not often refer to his Jewish identity in any explicit way. He described visits to churches in England and Germany but made only brief mention of the Jewish community in Germany. Near the end of his life he visited Palestine. This was the first time that he documented his feelings about his Jewish identity in any explicit way, when he wrote: 'this then is the land of my forefathers'. However he did document his reaction to seeing some of the Jews who lived in Jerusalem who were in his mind inferior and worlds apart from his own sense of Jewishness. He saw them as living in 'poverty, squalor and what is worse, abject superstition'. When in Palestine he visited the Wailing Wall and wrote in his diary:

> this afternoon I walked to see the temple wall to see the wailing of the Jews ... the loud weeping and wailing – the kissing of the stones [a ceremony which they probably borrowed from the similar one in the church of the sepulchre] ... rather tend to disgust the spectator. It is not the picture, which the mind imagines of the 'daughters of Zion' weeping and refusing to be comforted.[48]

Although it is difficult to assess how everyday non-Jewish Charlestonians viewed Jews, in terms of the private sphere, people sometimes referred to Jews in their diaries. Most of these diaries were written during the Civil War, when there had been an increase in anti-semitism particularly in the North but also in the South, where Jews were stereotyped as exploiting the bad economic situation. The Charlestonian Emma Holmes mentions Jews solely in a hostile and anti-semitic manner. Her diary is conspicuous by its apparent honesty – throughout the diary she makes unpleasant remarks about a whole range of acquaintances. During the war she made reference to her dislike of Jews and alluded to her view of underhand Jewish economic activities. She mentioned

Jews two more times in her diary – both thoughts concerned her views on miscegenation and she obviously distinguished Jews from black people in her use of the term. On 9 July 1864 she recorded 'having for fellow passengers in the omnibus, two Jewish youths & their two Negro female servants, one a respectable old "mauma" but the other girl with whom they seemed on the most familiar & intimate terms ... I thought *miscegenation* had already commenced – disgusting'. And again on 15 August 1865 she recorded:

> two of the Brownfields' former negroes have married Yankees – one a light colored mustee had property left her by some white man whose mistress she had been. She says she passed herself off for a Spaniard, & Mercier Green violated the sanctity of Grace Church by performing the ceremony. The other, a man, went north & married a Jewess – the idea is too revolting.[49]

Other white people acknowledged what they viewed as Jews' racial difference but viewed their racial characteristics on a par with their own. In her wartime diary, Mary Chesnut made frequent reference to her Jewish friends, whom she termed beautiful Jewesses, and singled out their Jewishness as something to praise. She wrote 'the beautiful Jewess, Rachel Lyons, was here to-day. She flattered Paul Hayne audaciously, and he threw back the ball'.[50] She saw Jewishness as a distinct racial identity and within her diary also wrote of the beauty of the 'typical' Anglo-Saxon. She stated,

> To-day I saw the Rowena to this Rebecca, when Mrs. Edward Barnwell called. She is the purest type of Anglo-Saxon – exquisitely beautiful, cold, quiet, calm, lady-like, fair as a lily, with the blackest and longest eyelashes, and her eyes so light in color some one said 'they were the hue of cologne and water'.[51]

Intermarriage between Jews and non-Jewish whites did occur in Charleston and in the early years this seems to have happened often, in comparison to later in the period. Robert Rosen has documented an interesting occurrence of a relationship between a Jew and a non-Jew within 'high society'. The poet Henry Timrod became fixated upon Rachel Lyons, someone who he claimed was 'rapidly conquering [his] old prejudices against the Hebrew'. Although he was apparently concerned about having a close relationship with a Jewish woman he still wrote a poem about her and had it published in the *Charleston Daily Courier* and in other southern newspapers.[52] Timrod's poem indicates that Jews were seen as exotic and alien – he sees her as having the lids of Eastern eyes and being the noblest woman of her race. Although these relationships were not hidden, the Jewish community may have been opposed to them. The Jewish community might have publicly accepted intermarriage, but it was certainly not something that was generally welcomed.

Jews in Charleston were largly in favour of transatlantic and plantation slavery. According to Hagy, in 1830, 87 per cent of the white households and 83 per cent of Jewish households had slaves.[53]

Some Jews in Charleston mentioned enslaved persons in their wills and thus these documents are an important source in assessing the way in which Jews accepted slavery. Hagy has calculated that 'at least 58 slaves belonging to Jews changed hands between 1761 and 1823', either 'as gifts, as bequests in wills, or when estates were settled'.[54] Enslaved people were talked about as property and were mentioned in the same context as talking about household belongings. For example, in Israel Joseph's 1798 will he gave his wife, Mariam Joseph, money, jewellery, household objects and also the use and benefit 'of my Negro Wench Molly, her Child and future Issue for and during the term of her natural life'.[55]

Some well-known Jews, such as Jacob Cardozo, publicly defended slavery. In his *Reminiscences* he expressed the belief that,

> there was a species of patriarchal relation in the mode of life when surrounded by his household slaves, in that reciprocity of protection and obedience that exists between master and servant, when the child of the former becomes the playmate and companion of the latter, mingling their pastimes, and when sickness and old age required that attention which are due to imbecility and infirmity.[56]

It is hard to reach any conclusion on the other interactions between blacks and Jews in the antebellum period. As many Jews were shopkeepers, day-to-day interaction occurred between blacks and Jews when enslaved persons purchased goods from Jewish owned stores. When Jews occasionally sold their goods to blacks on Sundays there was anti-semitism directed at the community. Jews were reminded that they were in a 'Christian land' and should respect the Lord's Day.

In terms of religion there was little interaction. In Beth Elohim's 1820 constitution, proselytes who were 'people of color' were barred from becoming members. There is evidence of one black person who was allowed to attend the synagogue and was 'well respected' by members of Beth Elohim, Billy Simmons. Simmons was a black Jew who was well known in Charleston and is the only black Jew documented in the antebellum South.[57] Simmons was accepted within white Charlestonian society in general as he was seen as an 'exceptional' black person, thus his acceptance would not disrupt the racial status quo.

One antebellum Jew, David Brandon, wrote about his friendship with a black person. Brandon's 1831 will stated:

> I recommend my faithful Servant and friend Juellit or Julien free negro, to my Dear Rachel and W.C. Lambert my friend & request them to take him under their protection to treat him as well as they would do me and to give him Such portion of my Cloths as they will think ~~necessary~~ useful to him and never to forsake him being the best friend I ever had.[58]

Bertram Korn used wills of this nature as evidence that some antebellum southern Jews were sensitive to black people, although this example is quite unusual, when compared to other wills.[59]

Another main interaction on a personal level occurred between Jewish men and black women. Similar to the Caribbean, southerners often had black 'concubines'. This practice was common and common knowledge but was not talked of in 'polite' company. Often enslaved women were raped and abused by men. It was in the latter part of the nineteenth century when slavery as an institution was being challenged that 'racial mixing' was fiercely contested. Sometimes blacks and whites would cohabit in the form of a marriage.

It is difficult to explore this subject in any thorough way due to the often hidden nature of 'interracial' relationships in the antebellum South. There is evidence of black and Jewish relationships in antebellum Charleston. Often wills give clues as to these relations. However, these wills never explicitly declare relationships of this kind. For example, in his will Samuel Jones gave much of his personal belongings to 'his Negro woman' Jenny and her son Emanuel. The first person he referred to in his will was Jenny, he left her the majority of his property and referred to Jenny and Emanuel more than any other people in his will. It is likely that Samuel Jones and Jenny were involved in a relationship and that Emanuel was Samuel's son.[60] His will states:

> If I should not emancipate My Negro Woman Jenny, and her Son Emanuel during My life time, it is my desire that my Executors Do, emancipate My Negro Woman Jenny, and her Son Emanuel, and give to Jenny My Bed Sheets, Bedstead, Blankets, Tables, Pots, Plates, Chairs, Looking Glass, allowing to Nanny, such part of them as she may stand in need of and also to Benjamin … To My Negro Woman Jenny two hundred Dollars To My Mullatto Woman Nanny One hundred and fifty Dollars … My Lot up King Street, which is let on Leases, I leave to Nanny and Jenny, during their lives, the income of the same, after the Taxes are Paid, to Jenny I leave of the income of the Leases One hundred Dollars Pr. Year to be paid to her Quarterly To my Mulatto Woman Nanny Ben, Nathan, David, and Emanuel I leave three hundred Dollars, to be equally divided amongst them, and to be Paid Quarterly If in case of the Death of Either Jenny or Nanny their respective incomes to be divided equally amongst their Children … And it is my further

desire not to drive Jenny and her Children out of my House in King Street, untill they have time to Procure a Place for their abode ...[61]

Another interesting case of black–Jewish interaction in the antebellum period concerns the Cardozo family. As previously mentioned, either Jacob Nunez Cardozo or Isaac Cardozo – although probably the latter – and Lydia Williams, a woman of African and Native American heritage, had a relationship and had three sons – Henry, Francis Lewis (the famous black Reconstruction leader), and Thomas. As with most interracial relationships in this period, the actual record of their relationship and the history and personal identity from the perspective of Lydia Williams are obscured. Earl Lewis has argued that Isaac was involved in the lives of his partner and sons until his death in 1855.[62] These stories have been referred to in historiography but more work needs to be carried out on them.

Conclusion

To conclude, within this essay I have attempted to demonstrate some of the ways in which Jews in Charleston shaped their ethnic identity. Jewish identity in Charleston was very much constructed as a result of the port Jewish diaspora – religious, family and economic ties between Charleston Jews and communities in places such as London, Germany and the Caribbean were still strong in the antebellum period. In conjunction with this diasporic identity, Charlestonian Jews also held a strong local identity. They principally identified with the emerging notions of whiteness and held as part of their identity the 'norms' of antebellum Charleston – respect for ancestry and genealogy, 'southern loyalty' and an acceptance of slavery. Similarly, Jews were for the most part accepted into white society. However, despite its religious cosmopolitanism Charlestonian society was certainly not immune from anti-semitism and Jews were, at least in the private sphere, often singled out as racially different.

NOTES

I additionally presented a paper, which was a version of this essay, at a conference entitled, 'Seascapes, Littoral Cultures and Trans-Oceanic Exchanges', Library of Congress, Washington, DC, 13–15 February 2003, organised by the American Historical Association and the Library of Congress. The American Historical Association has published an earlier version of this article, as part of their 'Seascapes' Conference Proceedings online publication; see Gemma Romain, 'The Jews of Nineteenth Century Charleston: Ethnicity in a Port City', *The History Cooperative: Conference Proceedings, Seascapes, Littoral Cultures, and Trans-Oceanic Exchanges*, http://www.historycooperative.org/proceedings/ seascapes/romain.html (© 2003 American Historical Association, compiled by Debbie Ann Doyle and Brandon Schneider, format by Chris Hale). I would like to thank the British Academy for providing me with funding in order to carry out research for this project and also the American Jewish Archives for providing a visiting Fellowship for a subsequent visit to the archives. I also wish to thank the staff at the American Jewish Archives and the Jewish Heritage Collection at the College of

Charleston for the help given to me during my research visits to both archives. Additionally I am grateful to David Cesarani, Julie Gammon, Tony Kushner, Elisa Lawson and Gavin Schaffer for their useful comments on earlier drafts of this essay. Within this essay I refer to those people of African descent who were 'slaves' as 'enslaved persons', indicating that their 'slave' status was forced upon them and was not their own personal identity. I use the word 'black' to mean a person of African descent.

1. For example, the historian of Charleston Jewry, James Hagy, maintains 'they adopted the way of life of other white southerners. Some grew rich and powerful. All deeply appreciated the economic, social, and political opportunities offered to them. Again and again, they referred to their home as "the Happy Land"; it was their New Jerusalem, New Palestine – the Promised Land'. James William Hagy, *This Happy Land: The Jews of Colonial and Antebellum Charleston* (Tuscaloosa, AL: University of Alabama Press, 1993).

2. The port Jew concept was first coined by Lois Dubin. See Lois Dubin, *The Port Jews of Habsburg Trieste: Absolutist Politics and Enlightenment Culture* (Stanford, CA: Stanford University Press, 1999). David Sorkin formed the concept of the port Jew, which I focus on in this study. See David Sorkin, 'The Port Jew: Notes Towards a Social Type', *Journal of Jewish Studies* 1.1 (Spring 1999), 87–97. A collection of articles arising from the AHRB Parkes Centre 2001 symposium on 'Port Jews' has recently been published. See David Cesarani (ed.), *Port Jews: Jewish Communities in Cosmopolitan Maritime Trading Centres, 1550–1950* (London and Portland, OR: Frank Cass, 2002).

3. Question I explore in the project are: How far is the Charleston Jewish identity constructed upon their experiences of living in a port and of their early history and community structures being based upon Sephardim? Did Charleston's Jews receive toleration from the Christian majority and how far can their identity be explained as a result of the particular milieu of the port, especially the southern port? How far did Jews participate in the life of Charleston society and was the way in which they participated or the way in which they reacted to certain events due to the particularities of Charleston as a port?

4. Sorkin (see note 2), p.88.

5. Sorkin, ibid., defines the port Jew in five points: the importance of migration and commerce; the valuation of commerce – that Jews were given rights due to their commercial utility; their different legal status – unlike other Jews the port Jew was not part of an autonomous community, therefore their path to equality was not challenged by their different political status; their different experience of Judaism – coming from former *converso* heritage they had to rediscover Judaism and did not have to develop a *haskalah* as they were already integrated within the non-Jewish world; and lastly also springing from their *converso* background, they could be neglectful of Jewish law but still maintain their Jewish identity.

6. The great American Jewish historian Jacob Rader Marcus was one of the few to document anti-semitism in America and previous to Leonard Dinnerstein's 1994 *Antisemitism in America* there existed no book-length survey on the subject. Increasingly historians are coming to deconstruct the myth of America as the Promised Land and focus on instances of anti-semitism in America, including the colonial and antebellum periods. See, Leonard Dinnerstein, *Antisemitism in America* (New York: Oxford University Press, 1994).

7. Before 1993 there was only one full book-length study of the community, by Charles Reznikoff and Uriah Z. Engelman in 1950, and one analysis of the Jewish community in South Carolina, by Barnet Elzas in 1905. See Charles Reznikoff, with the collaboration of Uriah Z. Engelman, *The Jews of Charleston: A History of an American Jewish Community* (Philadelphia, PA: Jewish Publication Society of America, 1950); and Barnet Abraham Elzas, *The Jews of South Carolina: From the Earliest Times to the Present Day* (Philadelphia, PA: J.B. Lippincott, 1905). Elzas also produced several booklets and articles on 'notable' Charlestonian Jews such as the British born indigo merchant Moses Lindo, and he also carried out detailed surveys on cemetery gravestone engravings, marriage and death notices. See Barnet Abraham Elzas, *Moses Lindo: A Sketch of the Most Prominent Jew in Charleston in Provincial Days* (Charleston, SC: Daggett Printing Co., 1903); idem, *The Jews of South Carolina: A Review of the Article "Charleston" in Col. 3, of the Jewish Encyclopaedia* (Charleston, SC: Daggett Printing Co., 1903); idem, *The Jews of South Carolina: A Survey of the Records at Present Existing in Charleston* (Charleston, SC: Daggett Printing Co., 1903); idem, *The New Jewish Cemetery of K.K. Beth Elohim at Charleston, SC* (Charleston, SC: Elzas, 1910); and idem, *Jewish Marriage Notices*

from the Newspaper Press of Charleston, S.C., 1775–1906 (New York: Bloch Publishing Company, 1917). Elzas's work exemplifies the drive of earlier southern Jewish historiography towards romanticism and southern 'loyalty'. He viewed South Carolinian history as from the beginning 'one long tale of glorious achievement'; Elzas, *The Jews of South Carolina: From the Earliest Times to the Present Day*, p.166.

8. For example, the publication celebrating *One Hundred Years: Accomplishments of Southern Jewry* argued that 'the Jewish race is like a strange, drab plant that can live interminably in rocky, barren ground, resisting all of nature's destructive forces, but given friendly conditions, a tolerant atmosphere and a slight degree of rooted security, it will put forth dazzling blossoms and magnificent fruits. Such was the case of these early South Carolina Jews, transplanted from all corners of a hostile world to the compassionate soil of America'. *One Hundred Years: Accomplishments of Southern Jewry* (Atlanta, GA: Southern Newspaper Enterprises, c.1934), p.13.

9. See Leonard Dinnerstein and Mary Dale Palsson (eds.), *Jews in the South* (Baton Rouge, LA: Louisiana State University Press, 1973); Nathan N. Kaganoff and Melvin I. Urofsky, *Turn to the South: Essays on Southern Jewry* (Charlottesville, VA: University Press of Virginia, 1979); and Samuel Proctor and Louis Schmier (eds.), *Jews of the South: Selected Essays from the Southern Jewish Historical Society* (Macon, GA: Mercer University Press, 1984).

10. There has recently been a travelling exhibition on the Jews of South Carolina called *A Portion of the People: Three Hundred Years of Southern Jewish Life*, and also an accompanying publication. See Dale Rosengarten and Theodore Rosengarten (eds.), with a preface by Eli N. Evans, *A Portion of the People: Three Hundred Years of Southern Jewish Life* (Columbia, SC: University of South Carolina Press in association with McKissick Museum, 2002).

11. Publications refuting the Nation of Islam pronouncements include Eli Faber, Jews, *Slaves, and the Slave Trade: Setting the Record Straight* (New York and London: New York University Press, 1998); and Saul S. Friedman, *Jews and the American Slave Trade* (New Brunswick, NJ and London: Transaction, 1998).

12. Jonathan Schorsch is right to argue that too much historiography on the subject results in defensive comparisons that remove 'historical agency from the Jews in question and, together with the continual resorting to quantification, shirks the crucial and [to his mind] far more interesting matter of actual relations between Jews and blacks'. Jonathan Schorsch, 'American Jewish Historians, Colonial Jews and Blacks, and the Limits of Wissenschaft: A Critical Review', *Jewish Social Studies* 6.2 (2000), 102–32 (at 117). In my view Jonathan Schorsch's work is exceptional and most certainly the best literature on this subject. See also Schorsch's article in the first port Jews publication, 'Portmanteau Jews: Sephardim and Race in the Early Modern Atlantic World', in Cesarani (see note 2), pp.59–74.

13. For example, Emily Miller Buddick, *Blacks and Jews in Literary Conversation* (Cambridge: Cambridge University Press, 1999); Murray Friedman, *What Went Wrong? The Creation and Collapse of the Black–Jewish Alliance* (New York: Free Press, 1994); Seth Forman, *Blacks in the Jewish Mind: A Crisis of Liberalism* (New York: New York University Press, 1998); and Joseph R. Washington, Jr. (ed.), *Jews in Black Perspectives: A Dialogue* (Rutherford, NJ: Fairleigh Dickinson University Press, 1984).

14. There have also been some studies focusing on black–Jewish relations in the Reconstruction era, including the as yet unpublished thesis by Mordechay Lior, comparing the Jewish economist Jacob Nunez Cardozo and the prominent black reconstructionist Francis Lewis Cardozo, who was the son of either Jacob or Isaac Cardozo, both pro-slavery Charlestonians. Mordechay Lior, *Jacob Nunez Cardozo and Francis Lewis Cardozo: Jews and Blacks in 19th Century South Carolina* (unpublished Ph.D. dissertation, University of Haifa, 1992). See also Louis Schmier, '"For Him the 'Schwartzers' Couldn't Do Enough": A Jewish Peddler and His Black Customers Look at Each Other', *American Jewish History* LXXIII.1 (September 1983), 39–55; and Earl Lewis, 'The Need to Remember: Three Phases in Black and Jewish Educational Relations', in Jack Salzman and Cornel West (ed.), *Struggles in the Promised Land: Toward a History of Black–Jewish Relations in the United States* (New York and Oxford: Oxford University Press, 1997).

15. My understanding of ethnicity is influenced by post-colonial and cultural theorists such as Paul Gilroy and Stuart Hall, who stress the fluidity and hybridity of identity. See Paul Gilroy, *The Black Atlantic: Modernity and Double Consciousness* (London: Verso, 1993); and Stuart Hall, 'New Ethnicities', in David Morley and Kuan-Hsing Chen (eds.), *Stuart Hall: Critical Dialogues in Cultural Studies* (London and New York: Routledge, 1996).

16. Robert Rosen, *A Short History of Charleston* (Columbia, SC: University of South Carolina Press, 1982, 1992, 1997).

17. George C. Rogers, Jr., *Charleston in the Age of the Pinckneys* (Norman, OK: University of Oklahoma Press, 1969).

18. Walter J. Fraser, Jr., *Charleston! Charleston! The History of a Southern City* (Columbia, SC: University of South Carolina, 1989), p.178.

19. According to the thorough research carried out by Hagy, of 3,083 Jews believed to have lived in Charleston before the Civil War, the place of birth for 1,517 has been recorded. Most Jews (869) were born in South Carolina; 548 were listed as being born in Charleston. Jews from across the Atlantic came predominantly from Germany and England, although 17 per cent were from Poland – thus from the start they were not all Sephardi Jews even if they were port Jews. Hagy (see note 1), pp.11–12.

20. Ibid., pp.15–16.

21. Malcolm H. Stern, *First American Jewish Families: 600 Genealogies: 1654–1988* (Baltimore, MD: Ottenheimer, 1991), p.51.

22. Of the Jews listed in the 1790 City directory (which would not include the poor), 50 per cent were shopkeepers, eight per cent vendue masters, eight per cent brokers and six per cent merchants. Hagy (see note 1), pp.190–91, reports that these proportions remained the same until the 1820s.

23. Jacob Rader Marcus, *United States Jewry, 1776–1985*, Vol.I (Detroit: Wayne State University Press, 1989), pp.147–8.

24. James W. Hagy, 'Not Subject to his Control: Jewish Women as Free Traders in South Carolina, 1766–1827', American Jewish Archives, Histories file. Studies of Jewish women during this period of American history are rapidly increasing within American Jewish historiography. For example, see Pamela S. Nadell and Jonathan D. Sarna (eds.), *Women and American Judaism: Historical Perspectives* (Hanover and London: Brandeis University Press/University Press of New England, 2001).

25. There is evidence that the early community had two synagogues – one German and one Portuguese. Elzas was aware that two groups might have existed but thought it 'improbable' because he knew of no discord between Portuguese and German Jews before 1800. See Solomon Breibart, 'Two Jewish Congregations in Charleston, S.C. before 1791: A New Conclusion', *American Jewish History* LXIX.3 (March 1980), 360–63.

26. Alan D. Corré, 'The Sephardim of the United States of America', in Richard Barnet and Waller Schwab (eds.), *The Western Sephardim: The Sephardi Heritage*, Vol.II (Northants: Gibraltar Books, 1989), pp.389–430 (at 394–5).

27. Barnet Elzas, *The Old Jewish Cemeteries at Charleston* (Charleston, SC: Daggett Printing Co., 1903), p.3.

28. Corré (see note 26), p.401.

29. For example, societies established in the colonial period include The St Andrew's Society (1729), the St George's Society (1733), The German Friendly Society (1766), the Friendly Sons of St Patrick (1744), and the Hebrew Orphan Society (1791). Rogers (see note 17), p.5.

30. Hagy (see note 1), p.44.

31. Barbara Mann has argued that 'a unique situation had evolved in Charleston. The planters, being neither inclined towards nor talented in any commercial or financial calling, had allowed the functions of the economic sector to devolve upon its middle stratum of Jews. This was particularly true as it touched on international (or intra-national) contact with the abhorred capitalists'. Barbara Mann, *Jews in a Place Called Charles Town* (unpublished Senior Thesis, University of Toledo, 1982), American Jewish Archives, pp.50–51.

32. For an analysis of the middleman theory and its problems, see Walter Zenner, 'Middlemen Minorities', in John Hutchinson and Anthony D. Smith (eds.), *Ethnicity* (Oxford: Oxford University Press, 1996), pp.179–86.

33. Gregory Allen Grebb, *Charleston, South Carolina, Merchants, 1815–1860: Urban Leadership in the Antebellum South* (Ph.D. dissertation, University of California, San Diego, UMI Dissertation Information Service, 1978), p.8.

34. W. Thacher Diary, 14 July 1816–31 December 1818, entry of 25 October 1818, as cited in ibid.

35. Leonard Rogoff, 'Is the Jew White? The Racial Place of the Southern Jew', *American Jewish History* 85.3 (1997), 195–230 (at 201).

36. Elzas, *Jewish Marriage Notices from the Newspaper Press of Charleston* (see note 7).

37. J.N. Cardozo, *Reminiscences of Charleston* (Charleston, SC: Joseph Walker, 1866), p.9.

38. See Werner Sollors, *Beyond Ethnicity: Consent and Descent in American Culture* (New York and Oxford: Oxford University Press, 1986); and Mark I. Greenberg, *Creating Ethnic, Class, and Southern Identity in Nineteenth Century America: The Jews of Savannah, Georgia, 1830–1880* (Ph.D. dissertation, University of Florida, 1997).

39. Greenberg (see note 38).

40. Don Doyle, 'Leadership and Decline in Postwar Charleston, 1865–1910', in Walter J. Fraser and Winfred B. Moore (eds.), *From the Old South to the New: Essays on the Transitional South* (Westport, CT: Greenwood Press, 1981), pp.96–7.

41. Conversation with Dale Rosengarten, September 2002.

42. Richard Dyer, *White* (London: Routledge, 1997), p.1.

43. Rogoff (see note 35), p.195.

44. Ibid., p.201.

45. Ibid., p.200.

46. For an analysis of the way in which Jews were posited as racially black during the nineteenth century, see Sander Gilman, *The Jew's Body* (New York and London: Routledge, 1991).

47. I would like to express my sincere thanks to Harlan Greene for bringing these diaries to my attention.

48. Diaries of David Henry Mordecai (1833–59), Jewish Heritage Collection, College of Charleston, T.J. Tobias Papers: Mordecai Family, Mss 1029.

49. John F. Marszalek (ed. with an introduction and notes), *The Diary of Miss Emma Holmes, 1861–1866* (Baton Rouge, LA and London: Louisiana State University Press, 1979), pp.359–60 and 466.

50. Isabella D. Martin and Myrta Lockett Avary (eds.), *A Diary from Dixie, as written by Mary Boykin Chesnut, Wife of James Chesnut, Jr., United States Senator from South Carolina, 1859–1861, and Afterward an Aide to Jefferson Davis and a Brigadier-General in the Confederate Army* (New York: D. Appleton and Company, 1905), p.208. This work is an electronic version of the diary and is the property of the University of North Carolina at Chapel Hill.

51. Ibid.

52. Robert N. Rosen, *The Jewish Confederates* (Columbia, SC: University of South Carolina Press, 2000), pp.237–8.

53. Hagy (see note 1), p.92.

54. Hagy (see note 1), pp.98–9.

55. Will of Israel Joseph, American Jewish Archives, Wills file.

56. Cardozo (see note 37), p.8.

57. Ralph Melnick, 'Billy Simons: The Black Jew of Charleston', *American Jewish Archives* XXXII.1 (April 1980), 3–8.

58. Will of D. Brandon, American Jewish Archives, Wills file.

59. Bertram W. Korn, 'Jews and Negro Slavery in the Old South, 1789–1865', in Abraham J. Karp (ed.), *The Jewish Experience in America: Selected Studies from the Publications of the American Jewish Historical Society* (Waltham, MA: American Jewish Historical Society, 1969), p.187.

60. James Hagy also believes that Samuel Jones and Jenny may have been in a relationship. See, Hagy (note 1), p.100.

61. Will of Samuel Jones, American Jewish Archives, Wills file.

62. Lewis (see note 14), pp.236–7. I wish to pursue this subject further in my work and focus particularly on how people of African descent (enslaved persons and 'free persons of colour') themselves recollected on their interactions with Jews.

The Jews of Bristol and Liverpool, 1750–1850: Port Jewish Communities in the Shadow of Slavery

DAVID CESARANI

The Ambiguities of Commercialism and Cosmopolitanism

In 1850, the Jewish communities of London, Liverpool and Bristol were amongst the oldest, largest and best developed in England. London with a Jewish population of 20–25,000 far outstripped the rest and comprised around two-thirds of the entire Jewish population of the British Isles. Liverpool followed with 1,500 and Bristol with about 300 Jews. Even though these provincial Jewish communities were small in number, Liverpool was the second in the kingdom. Birmingham was home to no more than 1,000 Jews and Manchester, though gaining fast, still lagged behind its Merseyside rival. Bristol was the largest surviving port Jewish community of those founded in the mid-eighteenth century.[1]

The period during which these three cities attracted increasing numbers of Jewish settlers, the 'long eighteenth century', was a stretch of unprecedented economic growth and prosperity. Although London Jewry dates back to the mid-1650s, it expanded rapidly between the 1700s and the 1800s, while the Jewish communities of Bristol and Liverpool only come into formal existence in this phase of urban and commercial dynamism. Much of the wealth that fuelled the growth of these cities and offered opportunities for Jewish migrants was generated from the transatlantic slave trade. Between 1698 and 1807, British merchants employed 11,000 ships from British ports to carry 3 million slaves from Africa to the West Indies and North America. Britain was the dominant force during this phase of the 'triangular trade' and merchants and ship-owners in London, Bristol and Liverpool controlled it. The direct and indirect profits from slavery, in the words of James Walvin, 'recast the face of eighteenth century Britain'.[2]

Until recently, however, the role of the transatlantic slave trade in the growth and development of these British port cities has been treated in a brusque, apologetic vein or almost completely ignored. To quote Walvin again, from a book published only quite recently,

Historians of the slave trade tend to be specialists in colonial/ maritime/ American issues. Historians of Britain on the other hand have tended to view slavery as a distinct, colonial or American phenomenon and therefore of only tangential interest to Britain itself ... historians primarily interested in the *domestic* history of Britain have yet to incorporate slavery into the history of Britain in the seventeenth and eighteenth centuries.[3]

Apart from Walvin's pioneering work and two exhibitions in Bristol and Liverpool, only Madge Dresser has addressed this glaring omission. Her study of Bristol – *Slavery Obscured: The Social History of the Slave Trade in an English Provincial Port* (2001) – is a model of how the history of the slave trade can and must be integrated into domestic social and cultural history.[4]

In view of the late development of such research it is hardly surprising that historians of the Jews in Britain have hardly dwelt upon the interconnections between the slave trade and Jewish settlement or commercial enterprise. Anglo-Jewish historiography was poorly developed until the 1980s and is still extremely patchy.[5] Since the corps of professional historians of Britain failed to engage with the issue of slavery, there was little chance that Jewish historians, many of them antiquarians, apologists and amateurs, would do so within their own field of interest. Indeed, the only modern history of the Jews in Liverpool was published by a sociologist over 20 years ago while the Bristol story was told in 1997 by an amateur local historian. Slavery is not mentioned even once in either case.[6]

I am not making this point in order to open a new front in the unpleasant controversy about the alleged extent of Jewish participation in the slave trade. In fact, as we will see, what information does exist about the relation of Jews in Bristol and Liverpool to the slave trade bears out the findings of Seymour Drescher and others who have worked on the better-documented case of London. The available evidence shows that Jews were a marginal element at worst and at best had no part in it at all.[7]

Rather, I am interested in the wider impact which the transatlantic slave trade, and the closely associated commerce with the West Indies and North America, had on the development of Bristol and Liverpool and how this, in turn, exerted an influence on the evolution of their Jewish populations. For, although Jews arrived too late and had nowhere near enough capital to invest directly in slave ships before the slave trade was abolished in 1807, they were enmeshed in the local economy which was indubitably driven by the 'triangular trade'. Indeed, anything else would have been impossible. Writing about Bristol, Dresser gives some idea of the dimensions of the commercial and manufacturing web woven by slavery:

as processors of slave-produced commodities, as supplier of goods to West African slave traders, as purveyors of both slaves and goods to the plantations, and as planters and planters agents, Britain's merchant community derived wealth from the slave colonies. Some of this wealth was recycled into the city's infrastructure in the form of new housing, infrastructure and public buildings.[8]

The same was true of Liverpool. F.E. Hyde, an economic historian of the city, errs on the apologetic side concerning its place in the odious trade but even he acknowledges that 'Indirectly, however, it was a source of profit to the town and to the hinterland of Liverpool in as much as it needed supplies of cheap goods to maintain it, and was a ready source for the supply of food such as sugar and raw materials such as cotton'. The slave trade 'stimulated a commercial mechanism which embraced the exchange of any variety of products which could be brought and sold at a profit'. He concludes that 'there can be no doubt that the commercial advantages accruing to Liverpool from the slave trade were inherently bound up with the port's growing prosperity'.[9]

In other words, the slave trade touched everyone in business in Bristol and Liverpool, no matter how high or low they were in the pecking order. It indirectly touched the life of every inhabitant who benefited from the gentrification and improvement of their city, a process that was heavily financed by the proceeds of the slave trade and the plantations. The slave trade had a huge multiplier effect on the local economy. It lifted everyone up and enriched their lives in all things – as direct income from modest investments, remuneration from employment, profits from exchange, the sweetened tea they drank, the cotton shirts they wore, the plays they enjoyed in theatres funded by entrepreneurs drawn to boom towns, the pipes they smoked and the books they read in libraries paid for by philanthropists made wealthy by slaves.

Jews were no exception to this rule and the rest of this essay will explore how the history of the Jews in two port cities needs reconfiguring to take account of this fact. However, this research is not intended as a contribution to the vast corpus of work on slavery and its ramifications. I want to use the issue of slavery and its legacy in two port cities to reappraise the concepts of the port Jew and port Jewry.

Both Lois Dubin and David Sorkin have drawn our attention to the relatively benign conditions which Jews experienced in certain port cities in the eighteenth century thanks to the doctrines of mercantilism and utility. Sorkin defines port cities as 'cities, polities or colonies that were built upon and valued commerce'. Jews were allowed to settle in these centres of mercantilism, notably London, Amsterdam, Bordeaux and Trieste, to form communities, to worship openly and to engage in business because 'the wealth they could generate convinced rulers to act on considerations of *raison d'état* rather than religion'. Ultimately, port cities afforded Jews a degree of 'civic inclusion' that segued into emancipation and enabled port Jews to achieve civic equality with much less friction than was the case elsewhere.[10]

Lois Dubin, who provided much of the inspiration for this instrumental view of cosmopolitan maritime trading centres, made a case study of Trieste. She deduced that:

> Jewish merchants were invited or welcomed because of their presumed commercial expertise which was deemed of prime value to the port city. They were seen to have demonstrated their economic and social utility both in the past and present. Commerce and culture fused as secular virtue, as their behaviour, morals and culture were seen as all of a piece with their utility. Proving their utility and virtue meant continuing along a path they were already on; they did not have to prove them for the first time.

Having achieved this the way towards the attainment of civic equality was smoothed.[11]

But how representative were London, Amsterdam, Bordeaux and Trieste? Was commerce really a source of sympathy for immigrating Jews? Did the doctrine of utility always warm the hearts of rulers and merchants in port cities when confronted by the presence of Jews? In a previous paper on London, I tried to show that mercantile interests could militate against the settlement of Jews perceived as a source of competition. The port Jews of seventeenth and eighteenth century London were marginalised by the established mercantile elite (which was only continuing a practice they used against all foreigners and perceived aliens) and forced to resist repeated attempts to have them ejected or placed under a discriminatory regimen. These efforts were only rebuffed thanks to patronage from the court. London Jews benefited from being both court Jews and port Jews, and British monarchs intervened time and again to protect them against attacks by vested interests in the City of London.[12]

In this contribution I hope to illustrate that a similar antagonism was at work in Bristol. Although eighteenth-century Bristol had a very strong commercial ethos and was a boom town, it was decidedly unfriendly to Jews. So where does this leave the concept of the port Jew, even if we restrict the social type to the eighteenth century, the very period preferred by David Sorkin? Liverpool was no less in the grip of a commercial spirit and was, in addition, a far more diverse and cosmopolitan city than Bristol. It sucked in vast numbers of Welsh, Irish (both Catholics and Protestants) and Scots before a Jew ever set foot in the place. This is important to note because many historians and commentators have treated cosmopolitanism as one ingredient of the tolerance which Jews enjoyed in port cities.[13] Yet Liverpool became one of the most sectarian cities in the British Isles, with residential districts and occupations – not to mention politics – rigidly segregated by religion, ethnicity and nationality.[14]

Using the case of Bristol, I will suggest that, while some port cities offered Jews a specific route to modernity others did not and we may need to think harder about why some rather than others acted in a benign fashion on the development of Jewish society. Taking Liverpool next I will elaborate the notion that cosmopolitanism could take many forms, not all of which afforded comfort or security to Jews. I have to confess that when I embarked on the port Jews research project in 2000 I assumed that cosmopolitan societies were automatically favourable to Jews. Now I am not so sure.

Bristol

The port of Bristol, which dates back to 1171, was in the vanguard of maritime exploration from England in the fifteenth century. Although the first ship to trade between Bristol and West Africa sailed in 1552, transatlantic traffic did not develop on a large scale until the capture of Jamaica in 1655. A few privateers may have taken part in the slave trade from the 1660s, but Bristol merchants were largely reduced to protesting about the monopoly of the Royal African Company. Lobbying against the monopoly position of London was led by the Society of Merchant Venturers, the corporate body of Bristol merchants which had controlled the port and regulated trade since the mid-sixteenth century. It was rewarded with success in 1698 when the Africa trade was opened to all who could afford the capital outlay and pay a tax of ten per cent to the Royal African Company.[15]

This was not an unprecedented opportunity. Ships from Bristol had carried white slaves in medieval times and, more recently, had transported convicted Irish 'rebels' and indentured servants to the Americas. Bristol also supplied manufactured goods to the plantations in the West Indies that employed slave labour and imported their produce. However, nothing matched the scale or the value of the transatlantic slave trade. In 1700, there were just five clearances by ships bound for African coasts from Bristol. Between 1740 and 1760, the number of departures averaged 24 per year. This was more than London and far more than other European ports involved in slavery. From 1733 to 1743, Bristol was England's 'premier slaving port'.[16] It is estimated that between 1698 and 1807, when the slave trade was abolished, Bristol ships making 2,008 voyages transported 486,059 Africans into slavery, of whom approximately 90,000 died en route or soon after arrival. The number of large merchants who dominated the trade may have been small, amounting to no more than 20, but it encompassed a far broader circle of Bristol's business community. When the Company of Merchants was set up to oversee the trade in place of the Royal

African Company the number of freemen of Bristol who joined it numbered
157 in 1753 and 237 in 1755, as compared to 147 Londoners and 89 from
Liverpool.[17]

The eighteenth century was Bristol's 'golden era'. Between 1700 and 1801
the city's population trebled from 20,000 to 64,000. It was a boom town and
slavery, alongside the related trade in sugar, rum and tobacco, made it tick.
Slavery animated ship-owners, merchants, captains and crews; shareholders
and officers of the merchant societies, municipal post-holders; carters, porters
and pilots; manufacturers and importers of trade goods. The slavers required
textile products from India and the west country, glassware manufactured in
the city's many glassworks, umbrellas, hats, beads, utensils, iron and copper
rods, guns, cutlasses and knives, for trading with the Africans who supplied the
slaves. The Africa-bound ships needed copper bottoms, and provided endless
work for sail makers, producers of navigation instruments, chandlers, coopers,
apothecaries and food suppliers. When in port the ships and crews needed the
services of laundry women, cleaners and warehousemen. The city developed
large-scale industries for processing the raw materials purchased from the
plantations with the proceeds from the sale of slaves, notably sugar, tobacco,
cocoa, cotton and ginger.[18]

This intense, fervent commercial activity lent Bristol and Bristolians a
curious reputation. According to the poet Alexander Pope, it was 'a very
unpleasant place and no civilized company in it'. Another versifier, Thomas
Chatterton, deemed its inhabitants 'Lovers of mammon, worshipers of trick'.
Daniel Defoe, who paid the city numerous visits, observed that its inhabitants
had 'narrow minds' and were 'rough gentlemen'. In 1742 he remarked that
'Their souls are engrossed by lucre, and are very expert in affairs of
merchandise; but as to politeness, it is a thing banished from their republic as
a contagious distemper'.[19] The similarity between these ascribed characteristics
and the negative stereotype of the vulgar, avaricious, cunning Jew is
remarkable.[20] And, indeed, the parallel was drawn explicitly by contemporaries.
The writer Samuel Curwen recorded that 'This city is remarkable for sharp
dealings; there runs a proverb: "one Jew is equal to two Genoese, and one
Bristolian to two Jews"'.[21]

Yet despite these alleged affinities, or perhaps because of them, the
mercantile class of Bristol was less than welcoming to Jews. A shared
commercial acumen and a predilection to value a man for his uses or what he
was worth seemed to have no ameliorating effect. Thomas Cox, writing in 1731,
noted that Bristolians were 'remarkably insolent to Strangers', which he
explained was 'because become rich by Trade, as (to use their own phrase) to
care for no Body, but whom they can gain by'. Defoe had noted ten years earlier
that the city may have been alive with the spirit of trade and manufacture but it
excluded anyone who was not a Freeman from enjoying a part in this activity.[22]

The mercantile elite gave practical expression to its dislike of aliens in general and Jews in particular. In November 1753, the Society of Merchant Venturers petitioned Parliament for the repeal of the Act for the Naturalization of the Jews passed earlier that year. There was much correspondence about the Act in the local press, most of it hostile, and the city corporation added its authoritative voice to the campaign for repeal. The xenophobic and anti-Jewish nay-sayers did not go unchallenged, though. One of the most eloquent arguments for the Naturalization Act came from the pen of Dr Josiah Tucker, a Bristol man. He made the classic mercantilist case for allowing foreign-born Jews to become naturalised:

> As to the Bill itself, it only empowers rich Foreigners to purchase lands, and to carry on a free and extensive commerce, by importing all sorts of Merchandise and raw materials, allowed by Law to be imported, for the Employment of our own People, and then Exporting the Surplus of the Produce, Labour, and manufactures of our own Country, upon cheaper and better Terms than is done at present. This is all the Hurt, that such a Bill can do; for this is the meaning of that odious word Naturalization.[23]

Notwithstanding this concise statement of the mercantilist position and the encomium to utility, Tucker remained in a minority and his views attracted opprobrium. According to Cecil Roth, 'he was attacked in the streets of Bristol by an angry crowd which, disappointed at seeing him escape, comforted themselves by burning him in effigy'. Those of Tucker's persuasion were in a minority around the nation, too, and the Act was removed from the statute book as a consequence of the widespread outcry it aroused. The repeal was celebrated very publicly and noisily in Bristol on 20 December 1753.[24] Nor did the voters of Bristol forget the issue in the General Election the following year. Robert Nugent had voted for the Act when he was MP for the city, but now as a parliamentary candidate he was held to account. Horace Walpole recorded that 'The great cry against Nugent at Bristol was for having voted for the Jew Bill: one old woman said, "What, must we be represented by a Jew and an Irishman?"' Walpole was highly amused that Nugent offered to drop his breeches to prove that he was indeed an Irishman but not a Jew.[25]

This legendary unfriendliness to foreign-born competitors and more specifically to Jews could manifest itself in other, more petty and vicious ways. In 1757 Moses Cohen, a trader in gold and silver ware, was prosecuted by the Bristol city council for trading without being a 'free burgess' of the city. Harold Pollins deduces from this case that for many years after they first reached the city, Jews were prevented from operating shops and were obliged to remain itinerant traders.[26]

The local campaign against slavery made matters worse for the tiny Jewish community. Madge Dresser has noted that negative images of the Jew were frequently invoked in the rhetoric associated with the campaign. 'Both Jews and blacks were invoked as figures of fun in popular political discourse, as in a 1784 spoof playbill against the Tory candidate of the day' which dubbed him 'the artful Jew candidate' and referred to 'Shylock the Jew', 'the whole negro' and 'Gaby Short Cock'. Both sides in the contest over slavery made frequent reference to circumcision, castration and crucifixion in their polemics. In 1791, after the election of two abolitionist MPs, the Bristol Royal Theatre produced a play called 'John Bull, the Jew, [and] the English Sea Captain'.[27]

Indeed, while historians of the anti-slavery movement have remarked that it was rooted in Protestant non-conformity,[28] few have considered that by routinely and repetitively declaring slavery intolerable to the Christian conscience in a Christian country, the anti-slavery lobby cultivated the impression that England was the domain of Christians alone. In this sense, and less inadvertently through the harnessing anti-Jewish stereotypes to the anti-abolition cause, the debate over slavery reinforced negative perceptions of the Jews.

There is evidence that this hostility towards Jews was maintained into the 1830s and co-mingled with arguments over the abolition of slavery in the British West Indies. In the course of General Election campaign of 1830, Robert Claxton, a West India merchant and parliamentary candidate, alleged that his opponent, the abolitionist Edward Protheroe, had been nominated by the 'Jew Sir Manasse Lopes'. Claxton asked rhetorically: 'Is he really the son of the person the Quakers pretend he is? Or is he some CIRCUMCISED pencil or orange boy from Change Alley; and this by one of the most impudent sects in existence thrust on the People of Bristol, is the son of Protheroe?' Lopes was actually a Jamaican-born Jewish convert to Anglicanism, who settled in the west country and purchased land and political influence, becoming a baronet in 1802 and an MP in 1806. It is not clear whether he was or was not backing Protheroe. But Claxton jested, 'I think the Quaker women ought to sit in Committee and examine if he really is an Israelite indeed – and the cry from mouth to mouth ought to run – Is he Circumcised?'[29]

That Jewish identity could be invoked as a negative quality to besmirch a political opponent suggests that Jews in Bristol were seen in less than a glowing light. Just as significant is the evidence that abusing them was considered well within the bounds of acceptable political discourse. The restrictions on Jewish economic activity and the intermittent abuse which Jews faced may go some way towards explaining why the Jewish community of Bristol remained small despite the enormous opportunities which the booming city afforded immigrants. This may also help to explain the failure of a Portuguese *converso* community in the mid-sixteenth century. A case held before the Inquisition between 1557 and 1558 brought to light a community of Portuguese Jews that was present in the city under the leadership of a physician Hector Nunes for at least a decade from 1545 to 1555. This community engaged semi-covertly in collective acts of Jewish worship and communicated with other *conversos* in London. Yet although it had a significant role in the extensive trade between Bristol and the Iberian peninsular, this community of around 60 persons (not much smaller than the one that emerged in London a century later) faded away.[30]

Jewish settlement in modern Bristol was initiated by peddlers who reached the city from London and ports on the south coast in the 1740s. A synagogue was established in 1751 and a burial ground was purchased at around the same time. The first synagogue was in an old alehouse, but in 1786 the heads of the community were able to afford a significant move upwards to the Weavers Hall, the vacated premises of a Bristol guild. A contemporary observer recorded that the building was refitted in a 'neat, expensive manner' and spectators were impressed by the rich decoration. It was, said a visitor, 'one of the handsomest places of worship in Bristol'.[31]

This observation is heavily freighted with meanings. It indicates that within a relatively short period of time the Jews had established themselves and that at least a section of the community had accumulated considerable surplus capital. This more than hints that Bristol's Jews benefited from the general conditions of prosperity that were buoyed up by the proceeds of the triangular trade. And just as the city was trying to shrug off its vulgar, rough image so were they. Between 1650 and 1770, Bristol experienced an urban renaissance. New port facilities were constructed, terraces of elegant town houses were built, most notably Queen Square, and smart suburbs laid out in Clifton and other sites. At the same time as planters from the West Indies and Africa merchants purchased town houses and country estates, the city's streets were paved and it was provided with new assembly rooms, a theatre and a spa.[32]

Not wishing to be left out or to appear unworthy of their physical surroundings and social milieu, Bristol's Jews sought to demonstrate their virtue and display their newly gained wealth by creating a place of worship that was decorous, ornate and dignified. But where did their wealth come from? We know little about the first wave of settlers, but using what data we do have and extrapolating backwards from the early decades of the nineteenth century it appears that they were employed in the luxury and fancy goods trades. These were the staple occupations of Jewish entrepreneurs who made the transition from peddling to keeping a shop. Some examples from those known to be economically active between the 1780s and 1850s will give an idea of the general economic and social profile. Samuel Isaacs traded in diamonds and silver plate; Joseph Rothschild was a watch- and clockmaker as well as a dealer in jewellery, plate, pipes and fancy goods; Samuel Solomon sold hats and furs; David Hyman ran an 'outfitters emporium'. A few, like Joseph Alexander, were directly connected with the shipping industry. His son Joseph became a ships' broker and his sons followed him in their turn. Lazarus Jacobs and his son Isaac Jacobs were prominent in Bristol's glass making industry. Isaac became glassmaker to George III. Montague Durlacher and Levy Levy marketed glass products. Only the wine merchants John and Joseph Abraham, the ship brokers Abraham and William Wolf Alexander, and Jacobs *pere et fils* came near the apex of mercantile society.[33]

Aside from this tiny elite, few of the Jewish artisans and traders would have had the wherewithal to invest in slave ships even if they or their forebears had been economically active before 1807. But all depended upon a vibrant consumer culture and a buoyant market amongst the urban bourgeoisie and the landed class. Walter Minchinton comments that 'Rum, slaves, tobacco, and sugar were the main ingredients of Bristol's prosperity in the eighteenth century',[34] and a part of this wealth flowed into the businesses run by the city's Jews which was, in turn, invested in their own civic building – the synagogue. It is noteworthy that the first recorded marriage solemnised in the new synagogue in 1786 was between Mr Israel Cohen of Virginia and a Miss Solomon from Exeter. Ties of kin as well as commerce bound Bristol Jews to the plantations and to slavery.[35]

By the 1830s, Bristol's leading Jews were eager to take a share in municipal governance. This was important not only to signify the wealth, prestige and dignity of the Jewish community; it was also vital to the promotion of business. Trade in and out of the port, as well as within the city, was regulated by the mercantile associations and the municipal council. Dock schemes, canal projects and railways necessitated acts of Parliament. For Jews, too, the advancement of commercial opportunity required access to local and state power. But by now such a gesture of civic inclusion suited a city that wished to put slavery behind it and show a progressive face to the world. Bristol championed the abolition of oaths that prevented Jews taking municipal office. Abraham Alexander was the first Bristol Jew to win election to the council, in 1846, and be permitted to take office under a suitable oath. He represented the dock interest until he retired in 1866. His brother William Wolf Alexander was elected an alderman in 1850 and held office till 1874, taking over representation of the docks from his brother. Both men used their positions to campaign for the wider relief of Jewish disabilities. Joseph Abraham, who sat on the Local Board of Health, served as mayor in 1865.[36]

Bristol's Jews had 'arrived' by the middle of the nineteenth century. It was a small community, but a wealthy one. In 1861 Bristol Jews donated £800 for the relief of distress in Palestine, a princely sum in those days. Yet while the community absorbed some East European immigrants from the 1860s onwards, it never exceeded 2,000.[37] This stagnation to some extent reflects the story of the city and the port. From the 1750s Liverpool supplanted Bristol in the slave trade and though the city continued to prosper it only managed this by diversification. It was not conveniently situated for mass emigration and never developed a significant passenger handling capacity. Bristol missed out on the revenue produced by the mass migration from eastern Europe to the United States and the flow of Jews associated with it. The efflorescence of Bristol Jewry was thus located primarily in the nexus of the transatlantic slave trade. Slavery needs to be written into the history of Bristol Jews just as the peculiar antipathies of Bristol's Christian population must be heeded as a qualification of the assumption that port Jews enjoyed tolerance because of the local prevalence of a mercantile spirit.

Liverpool

Liverpool, by contrast with Bristol, continued to expand throughout the nineteenth century and sucked in immigrants, Jews amongst them. The basis for this growth was the port. Although it received a royal charter in 1207 Liverpool was a backwater until the end of the seventeenth century. It conducted some trade with the Iberian peninsular but mostly it handled traffic to and from Ireland. The transportation of convicts to the West Indies and the importation of sugar and tobacco on a small scale created an interest in breaking the monopoly of the Royal African Company in the 1690s and laid the basis for entry into the slave trade after 1709. Within ten years Liverpool was a major player and by 1740 it had outstripped Bristol. In 1720–29 it cleared 96 ships for West Africa, 231 in 1730–39, 322 in 1740–49, and 521 in 1750–59, reaching a first peak of 725 in 1760–69 before war disrupted traffic to the Americas. Between 1790 and 1799 Liverpool dispatched 1,011 slave ships, falling slightly to 876 in the last years of the trade. By this time Liverpool was responsible for 75 per cent of all British slave ships and was the 'most important slave trading port in the world'.[38]

Slavery may not have generated huge profits directly, but it had a multiplier effect on the whole region. While ships were chartered and outfitted by a small core of regular Africa merchants, hundreds more were involved via ship building and outfitting; banking, broking and insurance; the production and supply of trade goods to be exchanged for slaves; and the processing of slave-produced foodstuffs and raw materials. A host of small manufacturers, craftsmen and traders serviced the sea captains, seafarers, merchants and professionals who served them.[39]

The docks and the city now entered a long period of tumultuous growth. From 1715 onwards a series of dock improvements were set in motion and a new Custom House built to handle the increased volume of trade. The city, which had 28 paved streets in 1700, boasted 222 in 1750. In the following century the population soared from 4,000 in 1680 to 34,400 in 1773, to 53,853 in 1790, and 77,600 in 1801, reaching 223,000 in 1841. It attracted immigrants from its immediate hinterland, Ireland, Wales and Scotland. Thanks to the influx of wealth and entrepreneurship the city acquired elegant terraced squares and suburbs, and was provided with a new Town Hall, a concert hall and music rooms.[40]

Jews first reached Liverpool in the 1740s. The earliest arrivals were itinerant traders operating independently or as the agents of shops in older established Jewish centres. By the 1750s a few had accumulated enough capital to purchase shops themselves. Many clustered around the Customs House and supplied goods to the numerous seamen. By the 1770s this community numbered around 100 and comprised mainly jewellers, watchmakers, drapers, slop merchants, pawnbrokers and spectacle makers, plus the still ubiquitous peddlers. The latter group existed on the margins of both Jewish and gentile society, teetering on the edge of poverty and often resorting to crime in order to survive. Liverpool-based Jews were caught up in well-publicised crime stories in 1771, 1775 and 1776.[41]

Yet, for the upper strata of settlers who had gained a foothold in property and settled trade, the last decades of slavery were good years. In 1775, after about ten years of making do in a room in a house in Cumberland Street, the synagogue moved to more commodious accommodation in Turton Court. In 1789 it was relocated to a further improved location in Frederick Street. Finally, in 1808 a purpose built synagogue was opened in Seel Street on land donated by the Corporation at the request of prominent Jewish merchants and businessmen. It was completed at a cost of £2,224, an enormous sum, most of which was borne by just 35 families. A visitor to the synagogue in 1825 observed that it served 'an opulent and rather numerous body'.[42]

Liverpool's Jews benefited from the city's curious local economy. For Liverpool was not an industrial city: its prosperity was founded on the port and commercial distribution. It lived and died by commercial acumen. A visitor in 1795 remarked on 'this large, irregular, busy, opulent, corrupted town, where so many men and so many women use so many ways and means of gaining and spending so much money'. It was also a magnet for immigrants which gave it a highly cosmopolitan aspect. One observer dubbed the city 'the Marseilles of England'. Like Marseilles it had a vast population of recent immigrants, unskilled labourers who flocked to the docks and warehouses for employment. Hundreds of thousands of Irish and tens of thousands of Welsh poured into Liverpool during the same period as the relatively tiny Jewish immigration prior to 1860. However, these groups did not mix. Housing, employment and education were informally segregated according to class, religion and nationality.[43]

Jewish merchants, professionals, traders and shopkeepers found a ready market for their skills and services in this booming metropolis. They also observed the rules of sectarianism. The Jewish community clustered in Edge

Hill around the synagogues of the Old and the New Hebrew Congregations, founded in Hope Place in 1838–39 after a secession from Seel Street. The community was extremely cautious about its public image. According to Nicolas Kokosalkis, 'In Liverpool decorum in public worship became almost an obsession with the officers of the Old Hebrew Congregation throughout the nineteenth century'. Three years after they opened Seel Street, the elite of the community founded a Jewish Philanthropic Society to deal with the Jewish poor – a constant problem given city's magnetic power. The communal leadership took care to invite Liverpool's civic leaders to the annual fundraising dinner for the Society and so advertise their determination not to allow the Jewish poor to become a burden on the wider society. In 1841 they founded a school for the Jewish poor and five years later launched the Hebrew Mendicity Society, an unsuccessful attempt to deal with the increasing number of mendicants turning up at the doors of their synagogues.[44]

The increasing volume of Jewish transmigrants reaching Liverpool from east coast ports, notably Hull and Grimsby, followed inexorably from the completion of the rail network linking the two coasts in the mid-1840s. It was accentuated by the contemporaneous intensification of competition for transatlantic passenger traffic which began the cyclical downward pressure on the cost of fares to America. Liverpool differed from Bristol in its capacity to handle passenger traffic and from the 1850s the shipping lines developed this business as a way to smooth out fluctuations in trade.[45] The inception of mass migration westward through Liverpool marks the beginning of the final chapter of the relationship between the port and its Jews, but there is not space here for a detailed account of this huge and complex subject. I want only to close with some remarks on the character of Liverpool and Bristol and the long-term impact of the slave trade on their overall development and the genesis of their Jewish population.

Conclusion

Both Bristol and Liverpool had tenuous links with Spain and Portugal in the sixteenth and seventeenth centuries, but only Bristol acquired a *converso* population. It never took root and in both ports the Jewish population that did eventually establish itself was made up predominantly of Ashkenazim from Poland and the German lands. Both ports experienced explosive growth in the eighteenth century on the strength of the slave trade, either directly or through trade with the West Indies and North America. In London Jews were able to invest in the companies that conducted the transatlantic slave trade from the 1660s onwards,[46] but Jews arrived too late in Bristol and Liverpool to take an immediate part in it. However, their presence in both cities cannot be explained without taking cognisance of slavery. Jews were attracted to Bristol and Liverpool because of the economic opportunities offered by these booming mercantile centres. The slave trade required, stimulated and maintained a huge range of commercial activity and occupations. The products of the trade, if not the profits, touched all aspects of life in the two cities. As James Walvin writes, 'The fruits of slave labour had been inserted into every conceivable cranny of British domestic life by the end of the eighteenth century'.[47]

Jews drank sweetened tea and smoked pipes. They supplied glass beads to slave traders and chronometers to seafarers. They provisioned ships at the quayside. A few chartered ships and insured them, and acted as brokers for those returning from the plantations with cargos. Even after the abolition of slavery, for 30 years ships from Bristol and Liverpool carried trade to and from the British Caribbean where slavery persisted till 1838, and the United States where it was not terminated until 1865. Jews had business connections and ties of kin with both these regions of slavery. And yet in the historiography of the Jews in these two cities there is absolutely no mention of slavery.

Ironically, the cool reception the Jews enjoyed in Bristol, especially, and to a lesser extent in Liverpool, ensured that they were locked out of the dark heart of the slave-based economy. Prejudice and exclusivity ensured that apart for some rare individuals they were peripheral to the odious trade. Indeed, by a curious inversion of the normal assumptions about the doctrine of utility as a thing favourable to Jewish settlement, the very mercantile spirit of Bristol seems to have worked to their initial disadvantage. Nor was the cosmopolitanism fostered in an age of mass migration necessarily beneficial to them. In Liverpool immigration created a highly segmented and sectarian urban landscape that was regularly disfigured by confessional violence, including intermittent assaults on the Jewish community.

Ports are incontrovertibly a motor of economic growth and port cities do offer distinctive opportunities for those with entrepreneurial flair. But the modality of their expansion and the kind of openings they provide cannot be easily generalised. The concepts of the port Jew and port Jewry are immensely valuable research devices, but we need to pay more heed to the ports themselves, their history, economy and social structure if we are to understand exactly where and how Jews fit in. It may be that those ports that developed with the slave trade are a sub species that require consideration in their own right, as do the Jews who flourished in the shadow of slavery.

NOTES

1. Geoffrey Alderman, *Modern British Jewry* (Oxford: Clarendon Press, 1992), pp.3–23. For comparisons and context, see also Cecil Roth, *The Rise of Provincial Jewry* (London: Jewish Monthly, 1950).
2. James Walvin, *Britain's Slave Empire* (Stroud: Tempus, 2000), pp.26–7.

3. Ibid., p.8.

4. Madge Dresser, *Slavery Obscured: The Social History of the Slave Trade in an English Provincial Port* (London; Continuum, 2001).

5. Tony Kushner (ed.), *Jewish Heritage in British History: Englishness and Jewishness* (London: Frank Cass, 1992); and editor's introduction to David Cesarani (ed.), *The Making of Modern Anglo-Jewry* (Oxford: Blackwell, 1990).

6. N. Kokosalkis, *Ethnic Identity and Religion: Tradition and Change in Liverpool Jewry* (Washington: University Presses of America, 1982); Judith Samuel, *Jews in Bristol: The History of the Jewish Community in Bristol from the Middle Ages to the Present Day* (Bristol: Redcliffe, 1997).

7. Seymour Drescher, 'Jews and New Christians in the Atlantic Slave Trade', in Paolo Bernadini and Norman Fiering (eds.), *The Jews and the Expansion of Europe to the West* (London: Berghahn, 2001), pp.439–70. In general, see Saul Friedman, *Jews and the American Slave Trade* (New Brunswick, NJ: Transaction Books, 1998); and Eli Faber, *Jews, Slaves and the Slave Trade: Setting the Record Straight* (New York: New York University Press, 2000).

8. Dresser (see note 4), p.97.

9. F.E. Hyde, *Liverpool and the Mersey: An Economic History of a Port, 1700–1970* (Newton Abbot: David Charles, 1971), pp.32–3.

10. David Sorkin, 'The Port Jew: Notes Toward a Social Type', *Journal of Jewish Studies* 50.1 (Spring 1999), 88, 90; idem, 'Port Jews and the Three Regions of Emancipation', in David Cesarani (ed.), *Port Jews: Jewish Communities in Cosmopolitan Maritime Trading Centres, 1550–1950* (London: Frank Cass, 2002), pp.37–8.

11. Lois Dubin, 'Researching Port Jews and Port Jewries: Trieste and Beyond', in Cesarani (see note 10), p.52.

12. David Cesarani, 'The Forgotten Port Jews on London: Court Jews Who Were Also Port Jews', in Cesarani (see note 10), pp.111–24.

13. See for example, Maria Vassilikou, 'Greeks and Jews in Salonika and Odessa: Inter-ethnic Relations in Cosmopolitan Port Cities', in Cesarani (see note 10), pp.155–72.

14. P.J. Waller, *Democracy and Sectarianism: A Political and Social History of Liverpool 1868–1939* (Liverpool: Liverpool University Press, 1981).

15. James Bird, *The Major Seaports of the United Kingdom* (London: Hutchinson, 1963), pp.181–205; Sir David J. Owen, *The Ports of the United Kingdom* (London: Allman and Sons, 1939), pp.129–32; W.E. Minchinton (ed.), *Politics and the Port of Bristol in the Eighteenth Century: The Petitions of the Society of Merchant Venturers, 1698–1803* (Bristol: Bristol Record Society, 1963), p.xii.

16. David Richardson, *Bristol, Africa and the Eighteenth Century Slave Trade to America*, vol.1, *The Years of Expansion 1698–1729* (Bristol: Bristol Record Society, 1986), and vol.2, *The Years of Ascendency 1730–1745* (Bristol: Bristol Record Society, 1987). In 1725, Bristol ships carried 16,950 slaves to the West Indies and North America; in 1771, when Bristol's share was declining relative to Liverpool, 8,136.

17. C.M. MacInnes, 'Bristol and the Slave Trade', in Patrick McGrath (ed.), *Bristol in the Eighteenth Century* (Newton Abbot: David Charles, 1972), pp.162–9; Dresser (see note 4), pp.27–8.

18. Dresser (see note 4), pp.19, 30–31, 34.

19. Peter T. Macy, 'Eighteenth Century Views of Bristol and Bristolians', in McGrath (see note 17), pp.29–30.

20. See Frank Felsenstein, *Anti-Semitic Stereotypes: A Paradigm of Otherness in English Popular Culture, 1660–1830* (Baltimore, MD: Johns Hopkins University Press, 1995).

21. Macy (see note 19), p.36.

22. Ibid., pp.18, 30.

23. Minchinton (see note 15); Josiah Tucker, *A Second Letter to a Friend Concerning Naturalization* (London, 1753), cited in Cecil Roth, *A History of the Jews in England* (Oxford: Clarendon Press, 1978), p.250.

24. Minchinton (see note 15), p.80; Felsenstein (see note 20), pp.187–214. Cf. T.W. Perry, *Public Opinion, Propaganda and Politics in Eighteenth Century England: A Study of the Jew Bill of 1753* (Cambridge: Cambridge University Press, 1962); Todd Endelman, *The Jews of Georgian England, 1714–1830* (Philadelphia: Jewish Publication Society of America, 1979), pp.59–64, 88–94; Katz, *The Jews in the History of England* (Oxford: Clarendon Press, 1994), ch.7.

25. Felsenstein (see note 20), pp.146–7.

26. Harold Pollins, *Economic History of the Jews in England* (London: Littman Library of Jewish Civilisation, 1982), p.78.
27. Dresser (see note 4), pp.154–5.
28. David Turley, *The Culture of English Antislavery, 1780–1860* (London: Routledge, 1991), pp.6–11, 17–21.
29. Robert Claxton, *Replication to the Parson*, cited in Dresser (see note 4), pp.212–13.
30. Lucien Wolf, *Essays in Jewish History*, ed. Cecil Roth (London: Jewish Historical Society of England, 1937), pp.84–8.
31. Samuel (see note 6), pp.63, 66–7, 70.
32. Dresser (see note 4), pp.96–108.
33. Samuel (see note 6), pp.45–62; see also Pollins (see note 26), pp.78, 81, 83–4, 101, 107.
34. Walter Minchinton, 'The Port of Bristol in the Eighteenth Century', in McGrath (see note 17), pp.128–9.
35. Samuel (see note 6), p.45. Judith Samuel does not make this connection and asserts rather absurdly that the Virginia in question was 'probably not USA'.
36. Samuel (see note 6), pp.129–34.
37. V.D. Lipman, *Social History of the Jews in England 1850–1950* (London: Watts, 1954), pp.23, 171; Samuel (see note 6), p.118.
38. Bird (see note 15), pp.277–306; Owen (see note 15), pp.61–8; Hyde (see note 9), pp.11–15; Kenneth Morgan, *Slavery, Atlantic Trade and the British Economy, 1660–1800* (Cambridge: Cambridge University Press, 2000), pp.88–9; David Richardson, 'The British Empire and the Atlantic Slave Trade, 1660–1807', in P.J. Marshall (ed.), *The Oxford History of the British Empire*, vol.2, *The Eighteenth Century* (Oxford: Oxford University Press, 1998), pp.446–9.
39. Hyde (see note 9), pp.16–19, 27–29, 31–2; Morgan (see note 38), pp.89–90; Richardson (see note 38), pp.461–3. See also, James Pope-Henessy, *Sins of the Fathers: A Study of the Atlantic Slave Traders 1441–1807* (London: Weidenfeld and Nicolson, 1963), pp.146–7.
40. Hyde (see note 9), pp.43–6.
41. Bill Williams, *The Making of Manchester Jewry 1740–1875* (Manchester: Manchester University Press, 1976), pp.1–12; Kokosalkis (see note 6), p.43.
42. Williams (see note 41), pp.25, 39; Kokosalkis (see note 6), pp.44, 48, 50. For a contemporary account, see Richard Brooke, *Liverpool as it was during the last quarter of the eighteenth century: 1775–1800* (Liverpool: J. Mawdsley and Sons, 1853), pp.60–61.
43. Waller (note 14), pp.1, 7, 15; Howard Channon, *Portrait of Liverpool* (London: Robert Hale, 1970), p.96, remarks on the tradition of sectarianism and inter-communal violence stretching from the 1770s.
44. Williams (see note 41), pp.144–6; Kokosalkis (see note 6), pp.87–8.
45. Hyde (see note 9), pp.110–13; Channon (see note 43), pp.67–8.
46. Drescher (see note 7), pp.451–4; Friedman (see note 7), pp.92–3, 96–8.
47. Walvin (see note 2), p.25.

The 'Jewish Nation' of Livorno:
A Port Jewry on the Road to Emancipation

CARLOTTA FERRARA DEGLI UBERTI

Port and Privileges: The Background to the Jewish Community

For Jews, whether Italian or not, the name of Livorno has long conjured up visions of a sort of happy island, an oasis of peace and tolerance in a world that was by and large decidedly hostile. Livorno's Jewish community – with an overwhelming Sephardic majority – shared its origins with the port and the city itself, and its development was at the same time cause and effect of the port's rising economic fortunes. Underpinning all this were the Letters Patent of 1591–93, known as the *Livornina*, which called upon merchants '*di qualsivoglia Nazione*' ('of any Nation whatsoever'),[1] to populate the city of Pisa and the lands of Livorno and thus, with their trades, to bring prosperity to them. Indeed, Livorno rapidly acquired city status, and in 1675 was declared a free port.

As for the term 'nation' and its derivatives, such as the adjective 'national', in this context it had a very different sense from the connotation we now attribute to it, which is more a matter of nineteenth-century type national and nationalistic ideologies and the creation of the modern nation state. During the *ancien régime* the term referred to a group of people within a state system differentiated by various possible characteristics, which might be religious creed, special juridical status, language, foreign citizenship or ethnic origins. Attribution of the term 'nation' in no way implied something alien to the social body, but rather offered legitimisation through inclusion in a hierarchical, structurally non-homogeneous social-normative system. Thus 'Jewish nation' and 'Jewish community' may be taken as synonymous in this period, as were the adjectives 'national' and 'community'. It was only in the course of the nineteenth century that the term 'Jewish nation' fell into disuse on account of the new connotations with which the term 'nation' was then being invested.

The clauses of the *Livornina* make it quite clear that the invitation was aimed in the first place at the Jews, since constant reference is made to the administrative autonomy represented by the *Massari* – the heads of the Jewish community – and to the place of worship, indicated as the 'Synagogue'; moreover, the difference in treatment as compared with the other Jews of the

Grand Duchy, and in particular the Florentine and Sienese communities, is explicitly sanctioned.[2]

The privileges were originally intended for the earlier settled Jewish community of Pisa, while the Jews settling in Livorno were to depend on the *Massari* of Pisa. As early as 1597, however, the Jewish Nation of Livorno adopted the status of an independent body, autonomous in its internal organisation and relations with the government of the Grand Duchy, taking as a basis the Letters Patent guaranteeing freedom from persecution by the Inquisition, the right to profess their own religion and, for those who had been forced to convert, to re-embrace Judaism, the possibility to acquire real estate without any limitations, and tax amenities for trading activities connected with the port, which also enjoyed the protection of the government and consuls of the Grand Duchy.

The Jewish community and the city alike grew at a remarkably brisk pace, and continued to do so through the eighteenth century, considered the 'Golden Age' for both. By the end of the century the Jewish Nation numbered about 5,000. The role played by the Jews in the city's society was much in evidence, to be seen in their physical occupation of the urban area, with shops, villas and, above all, the synagogue, rising in the immediate vicinity of the Cathedral. Neither Livorno nor indeed Pisa ever knew the institutionalised ghetto, although in practice the Jewish community was concentrated around the Temple. Apparently this was an impressive pile showing considerable architectural qualities, worthy to represent such an important part of the population,[3] but it has, alas, since been destroyed, and the present building hardly does justice to its former glory.

On the basis of articles 31 and 35 of the Letters Patent the Jews of Livorno enjoyed a privilege marking them out from the members of the other nations, investing their relations with the authorities of the Grand Duchy and the city with very special status. The heads of the Jewish nation were empowered to deliberate upon the applications for admission to the nation – and thus enjoyment of the privileges – sumbitted by the newcomers (immigration was a source of lifeblood for the port and the Jewish community itself). Known as *ballottazione*, this procedure automatically entailed Tuscan naturalisation. As the Florentine authorities pointed out very clearly to the Governor of Livorno in 1774,

> It is indeed noteworthy that the Jewish Nation, unlike the other [foreign nations], represents in Livorno a body politic, governed with its own laws and virtually separate jurisdiction. The reason for the aforementioned difference lies in the fact that *the Jewish Nation is regarded in Livorno as a subject nation* [that is, the Jews are regarded as Tuscan nationals], which is not the case with the others.[4] (emphasis added)

The members of the other nations – French, British, Dutch and so on – continued to look back to the countries they came from, remaining subjects of France, Great Britain and so forth despite their long-established residence in Livorno. The Jews, however, had no state and for the most part descended from refugees expelled from Spain and Portugal in the late fifteenth century, which gave rise to the so-called Sephardic diaspora. This must have been a consideration underlying the special procedure of *ballottazione* at the time of the Letters Patent.[5]

In addition a substantial juridical independence, mentioned in the passage cited above, was achieved, which further extended the already considerable autonomy of the Jewish community. Cases between Jews and Jews, whether civil or penal, could be tried by the *Massari* on the basis of the Judaic law (*Din Torà*) without any interference by the state authorities; in cases between Jews and gentiles, on the other hand, a special judge – necessarily a lay figure with a degree in law (the Governor of Livorno was designated for the role) – was called upon to guarantee objectivity, according to the legislator's intention. Such a degree of independence in so very delicate a field represented, to my knowledge, a unique case in the normative jurisdiction of Jewish communities in the modern age.

An important point to bear in mind here is that the privileges granted by Ferdinando I de' Medici were not merely for the benefit of individual, wealthy Jews but sanctioned the recognition of a community in its own right: a substantially independent administrative structure took shape with ample legislative and judicial autonomy. Moreover, these privileges were not to be enjoyed at the cost of any tax, and their renewal – originally scheduled every 25 years – actually went through quite automatically. Thus from the very beginnings of the history of Livorno's Jewish community the collective aspect assumed decisive importance. Indeed, in the case of Livorno the collective category of *port Jewry* clearly applies, underlining this particular aspect.[6] For a long time – through the eighteenth century – the nation stood as the institutional reference point for Jews, with a role of administration and guarantee, but also representing the cornerstone of individual and community identity.

Thus it was that the Letters Patent assured full legitimisation of the Jewish community, explicitly asserting its useful role in the city's economic life and activity and indeed associating it with the very birth of the urban site. The special status of the Jews was justified by the cosmopolitan, culturally and socially variegated world surrounding port activities, representing a condition of privilege in inequality where inequality was the norm – the organisational basis of civil society.[7]

Long after the *Livornina*, in 1780, the Jews of Livorno also acquired the right to be represented in the city's magistracy. This was indeed a rare privilege for Jewish communities in the *ancien régime*, and a significant recognition of the important role the Jewish community played in the city's life. This arrangement was part of the general reform of the city's magistracy decreed by Pietro

Leopoldo, and provided for the appointment of a Jewish nation deputy, endowed with the same rights and duties as his colleagues but called upon to represent a separate group in the city's population. It undoubtedly marked a significant step in the direction of increasing integration in the social system, with acquisition of a right generally denied to members of the Jewish communities at the time. In 1845, in a greatly changed cultural and political climate, a new law on the city's magistracy decreed that the names of the Jews satisfying the estate criteria be included in the same 'bag' from which the names of the other citizens were drawn. Thus the Jewish nation lost the certainty of having a representative of its own but, at the individual level, its members gained the same rights as their fellow citizens.

Given the evidence so far assembled, the case of Livorno can be seen as a clear example of integration of the Jewish community in the socio-economic context of the city, sanctioned with full legitimisation on the part of the state institutions, recognising with the privileges granted an important, official place for the Jewish nation in the Tuscan society of the *ancien régime*. Naturally, within the Jewish community there reappeared what we might call – albeit with some anachronism – class differences, showing a marked polarisation between a very well-to-do, well integrated elite increasingly involved in the life of the city, including its cultural sphere, and a mass of poor persons bordering on indigence, dependent on the charitable associations. Our account of the situation here applies above all to the elite.

To sum up this condition I used the formula 'privilege in inequality', but this may sound somewhat ambiguous, evoking concepts of liberty and equality inapplicable to the period we are dealing with here. It is in fact more appropriate to the retrospective view – ours, and indeed that of the Jews of Livorno in the 1840s – than indicative of eighteenth-century political sensibility. To avoid misunderstanding, it might be better to adopt the definition 'civil inclusion' proposed by Lois Dubin to describe the social and normative condition of the Jews of Trieste in the eighteenth century,[8] and coined precisely to exclude anachronistic references.

To Dubin also goes the credit of having coined the category of 'port Jew', prompting new research and opening up fresh paths for studies already under way: here we take her researches as a cue for considering another problem, which has to do with the bases of this integration and the representation and self-representation of the Jewish core. Central to our investigation is the concept of utility, constantly invoked to justify the privileges granted in the modern age to individual Jewish tradesmen or whole Jewish communities, and notably in the case of port cities, which is the world we are exploring here. Livorno was no exception, and I believe that many of the points Dubin makes on the subject in relation to Trieste and the Habsburg legislation can also be applied to the Tuscan port without any substantial qualification. Moreover, considering that the

Medicean privileges date back far earlier than those reserved to Trieste by the Habsburgs, it would certainly prove interesting to analyse how the issue developed from the sixteenth to the eighteenth century, but this is a task that has yet to be embarked upon. Actually, Livorno's *port Jewry* represented a precedent and explicit model for Trieste, and close comparative analysis of the two situations could well lead to some extremely interesting findings.

For the time being, however, let me simply recall two basic points of convergence: the Jews arrived in Livorno because they had been explicitly invited by the government of the Grand Duchy, the invitation being motivated by the conviction that their presence would be of use for the economy of the city and state. The privileges granted with the Letters Patent represented the legal sanction for these premises. The category of 'utility' opened the way for the Jews to be integrated not only in a socio-economic system, but also within a system of values, valid at least in the dynamic, cosmopolitan environment of the port city: 'A wholly secular definition of virtue emerged: to contribute to maritime commerce meant to be useful, which in turn meant to be virtuous'.[9] As time went by, the Jewish nation showed itself to be fully aware of all the implications so far considered, and on these foundations built its own identity.

The concept of economic utility could also be invoked as a rhetorical means of defence in disputes with the government of the Grand Duchy or the city authorities, to be used as a lever to claim independence and negotiate rights. Of the countless examples that might be adduced, we may recall an episode that occurred in the autumn of 1814. A Jew was accused of having sexual intercourse with a Christian woman, and was arrested.[10] The nation promptly stepped in to defend him, denouncing the accusers of slander, and talking of persecution being brought against honest '*Negozianti*' 'tradesmen' (a significant qualification):

> And at a time when the recovery of trade in the port of Livorno attracts Jewish houses from abroad, and especially from the Levant, to enjoy the beneficial effects of the government of V.A.I. e R. [*Vostra Altezza Imperiale e Regia* – 'Your Imperial and Royal Highness'], such harassments could halt it in its course.
>
> We supplicants therefore flatter ourselves to think that A.V.I. e R. [*Altezza Vostra Imperiale e Regia*] will deign to take the matter into consideration, and decree those measures that Your Highness will deem apt in the circumstances without prejudicing the laws, in order that the individuals of the Jewish nation may apply themselves to their trade untroubled and in safety, and *prove useful* to the city and the state as indeed they have done at all times.[11] (emphasis added)

The picture thus hitherto outlined was to undergo profound changes in the course of the nineteenth century, not only, and not so much, in its concrete applications to everyday life, as in the manners in which it was perceived and judged by the Jews, by the rest of the population and by the state institutions. Let me now sketch this very aspect, with a few examples to make the theoretical discourse clearer.

From Civil Inclusion to Emancipation

The process of emancipation – a central issue for authors studying nineteenth-century European Jewry – must in the case of Livorno be reconsidered in the light of the historical, cultural and normative context outlined above.

To begin with, let us take a look at the three main stages in the emancipation of the Tuscan Jews, representing the turning point in the dynamics analysed here and my chronological limit. In February 1848 Leopoldo II granted a charter that, while recognising Catholicism as the state religion, asserted in article two that: 'Whatsoever religion they may practise, the Tuscans are all equal before the law, contribute without distinction to the revenues of the state in proportion to their property, and are all equally eligible for civil and military employment'.[12] This moderately liberal charter remained in force for only four years: four turbulent years that saw a vigorous spate of revolutionary upheavals, eventually driving the Grand Duke to flight. Once peace was restored – thanks in part to the intervention of Austrian troops – the charter was abrogated in May 1852, and the old juridical status of the Jews was reintroduced. For lasting emancipation they had to wait until the unification of Italy was achieved through annexation to Piedmont and extension of the Savoy legislation to the entire territory of Italy. Of particular interest to us here is the Statute of King Charles Albert ('Statuto Albertino') and the law of 19 June 1848, which declared: 'Difference in religion entails no exception to the enjoyment of civil and political rights, and eligibility to civil and military posts'.[13]

If we are to analyse and appreciate the impact that these normative measures had on the life of Livorno we cannot confine our attention to the critical years around 1847–48, although they marked a truly momentous breakthrough, but must take a significantly longer period into account. When considering the transformations taking place in the first half of the nineteenth century we must also bear in mind the earlier developments between the sixteenth and eighteenth centuries, with particular attention to the characteristics we dealt with in the previous section; otherwise, the risk is that we may fail to grasp the sense of claims asserted or waived and modes of self-representation rooted in that more distant time. To pick up the thread, then, let us turn to another defining moment, in the year 1814.

After the revolutionary fervour that came with the French troops in the late eighteenth century, the 1814 restoration saw the status of the Jews – as indeed of the other subjects – once again much as it had been before the Napoleonic occupation. It was in fact the Jewish nation itself that petitioned to have all the old privileges sanctioned by the Letters Patent restored, with the exception of jurisdictional autonomy. The assembly determined to beseech Ferdinando III:

That all the old privileges, and concessions that our nation enjoyed under the beneficent government of Your Imperial and Royal Highness – S.A.I. e R. [*Sua Altezza Imperiale e Regia*] – and Your Highness's august predecessors be maintained, except for those regarding particular civil jurisdiction and police, for which the Jews must depend upon and be subject to the general dispositions of the civil and municipal laws, like all the other citizens of Livorno, while however preserving the ordinances regarding our sacred rites with respect to marriage and divorce, and that which concerns them.[14]

On this as on almost all the other important decisions the community council was not undivided, many and varied opinions being voiced. It was even mooted, for the first time, that full equality with the other subjects might be requested, with the consequent acquisition of new rights but at the same time loss of the old privileges and the end of autonomy for the community. In the end it was the more wary attitude that won the day.

Here we are still in a stage of transition from the idea of a society consisting of intermediate bodies endowed with autonomous juridical status to the triumph of an ideal of equality seeing all distinctions as being in themselves detrimental to the natural rights of man and citizen, whose relations with the state authorities should not be subject to any mediation. Nevertheless, the fact that the idea of full equality was making its way into the arena is significant of a change in mentality under way, evidencing the inroads opened with the revolutionary ideals of 1789 exported by Napoleon's troops.[15] In this case, however, caution also found very sound justification on the grounds of immediate practical considerations, suggesting a certain 'diffidence in taking the first faltering steps on the way to emancipation – admittedly of a conservative, reactionary kind, but not unmotivated if, as we have seen, the "privilege" set at least some Jews above certain groups of Christians'.[16]

As for the decision to forego autonomous jurisdiction, the official reasons adopted were the excessive demands made on the *Massari*, the costs the community had to bear for every case and the fact that Judaic law had by then become anachronistic, inapplicable to civil and commercial proceedings. From then on the Jews would be judged individually by the common law courts, like all other subjects of the Grand Duchy: the figure of the special judge in cases between Jews and Christians disappeared, as did the powers of judgement held by the *Massari*, with the important exception of matrimonial matters.

This did not, however, mean loss of the status as a separate body for the Jewish community. Legislative and organisational autonomy was retained, and with it the right of *ballottazione*, tax concessions for the trade practised by members of the community and exemption from military service (and all related contributions). The condition of a separate body was still perceived by the majority of Livorno's Jewish elite, much as it always had been, to be normal and, on the whole, desirable, affording legitimisation. And yet the indecisiveness and division within the community assembly are evidence of ideas coming into collision, opening up a scenario of generational conflict that was to loom ever larger in the following decades. In general the younger generations seem to have been more responsive to the new cultural and political ferments.[17]

The issue of conscription offers an interesting example of the winds of change then blowing. The crux of the problem can be briefly expressed in a few words. The Jews of Livorno had always been exempt from any type of military service in accordance with article 40 of the Letters Patent of 1593, and far from calling for equal treatment they had always regarded this state of affairs as a privilege. Immediately after the Restoration of 1814 the Jews that had been enlisted under the French occupation were left free to return to their homes on the orders of Governor Francesco Spannocchi Piccolomini, who addressed the chancellor of the Jewish nation, Daniel di [son of] David De Medina, thus: 'it has never been expected that the individuals of your nation should be destined for military service but only for trade, where the members of your nation have always achieved distinction ...'[18]

As from 1820 the Florentine government in search of funds changed policy and sought in various ways to levy a tax on the Jewish community for every Jew deemed fit for military service, thereby flagrantly breaching the conditions of the *Livornina*. The interesting thing about this is the reaction of the Jewish nation. Its representatives did not protest over the violation of privileges, nor about the cost as such; rather they contested the principle according to which the nation was considered a collective body, and thus called upon to answer for individuals. In a document dated 9 June 1820 and addressed to the Grand Duke they pointed out that 'the nation has never formed a separate body but indeed has always been considered like all the other subjects', and added with reference to the abolition of jurisdictional autonomy in 1814:

> But if it is true that when the nation had civil and criminal jurisdiction it had never been considered a separate body in the general affairs, but rather the individuals of the said nation were treated without distinction like all the other classes of the population, all the more should this be so after your Imperial and Royal Highness rendered them equal to all the others, subjecting them to the same laws and courts and having created a representative body solely to control the maintenance of our religion, national education and charity ...'[19]

The distortion of historical facts is perfectly evident in this claim, which seems to me symptomatic of the embarrassment of the community leaders, but also a sign of profound changes in mentality. In comparison with previous texts of a similar nature – memoranda addressed to the state authorities – a difference appears in the ideological references. Implicitly invoked here is an idea of equality closer to our current one, applied here to interpret past events that had been governed by very different parameters. In these old and new forms of pleading there remains as common ground the reference to the division of the population into 'classes'.

In the case of Livorno, two parallel processes contributed to modify the community elite's attitude towards privileges and their own social image. On the one hand, its members entered fully into the ferments of the general cultural and political climate as there gradually emerged a liberal conception of the state institutions and an ever-stronger national ideology with low tolerance of separate bodies. On the other hand, as an international entrepôt Livorno experienced dramatic downgrading in the first half of the nineteenth century, entering an irreversible crisis that became fully evident in the 1830s and 1840s: the city's identification with its sea outlet gradually waned as it turned its attention increasingly to the Tuscan hinterland. David LoRomer makes much of this point in his study on *Merchants and Reform in Livorno, 1814–1868*: the commercial elite gradually left behind it that 'extraterritorial status' that had formerly made its fortune, 'becoming more involved in working for the long-term stability of the urban economy and in strengthening the relationship of the city and the hinterland'.[20]

Various scions of the great families of traders began to look for alternative careers, and this is a phenomenon that would merit further study. Without doubt it must have had to do with the struggle undertaken by individual Jews with the support of the community in order to be able to graduate in civil law. Unlike the territories dominated by the Habsburgs, Tuscany did not admit Jews to degrees in jurisprudence *in utroque iure* (civil and canon law), and a degree in civil law alone was not officially contemplated in university regulations.[21] In practice, therefore, it was impossible for Jews to graduate in jurisprudence, although this flew in the face of article 19 of the *Livornina*. Even if a Jew managed to graduate in civil law in virtue of special, strictly personal provisions, he could only practise law in cases between Jews and Jews, which was not only felt to be unjust and humiliating but also set severe limits on the chances of earning a reasonable living.

The search for new openings in the liberal professions coincided with an unhappy conjuncture for trading activities connected with the port, but in many cases it also reflected a new set of values which held the legal profession to be morally and socially more prestigious. The kudos that came with money and affluence – the apanage of the Jewish tradesmen – no longer ensured social standing, and choice of the profession of lawyer, especially for the new generations, evidenced the need felt by Jews to redefine their social role. A good example of this can be seen in the case of Alessandro Franchetti,[22] whose father, David, petitioned in 1826 that his son might be enabled to graduate in civil law solely for the sake of a 'title of honour, and for the advantages it brings in social repute',[23] even though he would not be able to practise the profession. Thus economic considerations and cultural changes reinforced one another.

In this period of transition change naturally did not follow a smooth, linear course. The attitude of the community leaders was ever wavering between protection of privileges and requests for their retrenchment in the interests of greater juridical equality. For example, in 1836 the governors of the Jewish nation set up a staunch defence of their right to *ballottazione*. This was the year that saw abolition of the safe-conduct guaranteeing on the basis of the Letters Patent to all those who settled in Livorno total impunity for any offence committed before their arrival, and the possibility was aired of abolishing *ballottazione* for the Jewish nation with it. In their memorandum urging conservation of the privilege, which in fact remained in force well into the 1850s, the community leaders once again underscored the point that the chance of becoming Tuscan subjects and enjoying privileges, and above all the protection of the Grand Duchy consuls over their trade, continued to attract wealthy foreigners, and as always the great advantage this spelt for the city's economy was given all due emphasis.

As for the role played by the community institutions, far-reaching change came in the space of 40 years. The nation increasingly confined itself to guaranteeing respect for religious prescriptions, assistance to the needy and education, paying particular attention to the civil and religious instruction of the most indigent, as was common practice for the Jewish institutions of the time. This was a development in part pursued by the leaders themselves, but also in part a matter of sheer necessity: for some time the community government had been noting a fairly high level of absenteeism in its assemblies, together with a progressive slackening in community ties, one reason for this being a shift in the geographical area occupied by the core of the community in the city. For, while a large part of Jewish population remained concentrated in the city centre, in the neighbourhood behind the cathedral traditionally occupied by Jews, many well-to-do families of tradesmen and bankers were moving out into the new suburbs created for the residence of the city bourgeoisie. Thus the community was no longer quite so compact, and even the synagogue, whose majestic proportions reflected the strong Jewish presence in the urban area, now risked losing its centrality.[24]

The line of developments we have traced out here is not always easy to follow stage by stage, but at this point it obliges us to reconsider our previous observations on economic utility as the basis for legitimisation of the Jewish presence, and on the close link between public virtue and utility, both in the common perception of contemporaries and in the collective and individual identity of the Jews of Livorno. The road leading from civil inclusion to emancipation took in on its way a shift in theoretical references regarding public morals and policy, and the sense of community dwindled as individualism gained ground. More than actual changes in the conditions of life, which were far from sweeping in Livorno, it is the conceptual hiatus that needs emphasising: just two decades, between the mid-1820s and the mid-1840s, sufficed for transition to be accomplished from staunch defence of privileges to assertion of principles in the name of justice and equality. Such a change is incomprehensible if we fail to take into account the parallel evolution of the state institutions towards a liberal model based on a new conception of civil society – a process by no means confined to Italy but burgeoning throughout the whole of Europe. In the light of these new, ideal references the privileges of the Jewish nation of Livorno appeared odious, symbolic of a separateness no longer considered 'normal' but downright discriminatory.

So it was that economic utility and commercial success finally lost their function as means to guarantee compatibility with civil values. Indeed, a fairly dim view was now being taken of activities connected with pecuniary transactions, both by public opinion and by a goodly part of the Jewish elite, and above all by the young generations and segments particularly sensitive to the cultural changes under way. In this respect, despite its long history as a dynamic port city Livorno went along with the general trend. A good example of this can be seen in the discussions over the Charity School system – the *Scuole Pie* – often on the agenda of the nation assembly meetings, since instruction for the young, and especially the youth of the lower classes, was deemed of primary importance to the entire community. In 1844, pleading the case for the establishment of an arts and crafts school in line with the pedagogic thought of the time, Sansone Uzielli[25] argued:

> We must not lose sight of the fact that the promotion of arts and crafts amongst us has the all-righteous aim of not throwing all our young poor into the careers of business clerks or small tradesmen – careers growing harder by the day as competition waxes keener, careers full of contest and conflict, and *far less improving for the poor than a craft, or a mechanical skill*.[26] (emphasis added)

Later, in 1847, the draft drawn up by the five communities of Tuscany – Livorno, Pisa, Florence, Pitigliano and Siena – petitioning the Grand Duke for official emancipation asserted the virtuous conduct of the Jews of Tuscany and their integration with the moral values of society, pointing out as a particular claim to merit that 'among us, today, many Israelites [are] no longer engaged in commerce or purely lucrative professions'.[27] The debate on the emancipation of the Jews filling many pages of the periodical press offers a wealth of such examples. Moreover, it is surely significant that in her studies on the events of 1848 in Trieste Tullia Catalan points to a similar trend among the young, often openly contesting the social and moral values of their parents, to eschew commercial activities.[28]

In the light of these considerations one is put in mind of the fundaments of the so-called regeneration theory underlying debate on the emancipation of the Jews in the eighteenth and nineteenth centuries, beginning in France and Germany well before Italy. The debate in Italy came to a head in the course of the 1840s, and thus in a period that saw an exceptionally intense spate of political agitation as the process of national unification got under way.[29] Within the Jewish community of Livorno – at least at the level of official discussions held in the community assembly and in relations with the government authorities – the subject of regeneration was never explicitly raised, even when the general climate of mobilisation in public opinion prevailing in 1847 and the contributions of various intellectuals to the leading press persuaded the governing elite that it was time to start moving, and to call upon the Grand Duke for emancipation. Nevertheless, the impression is that certain aspirations characteristic of regeneration, first and foremost that of weaning the Jews from commercial activities and the corruption they generated, had been absorbed by a large proportion of the community leaders. To state the case in broad terms, we might argue that the Jewish elite of Livorno saw absolutely no need to be regenerated, holding themselves already integrated in the framework of dominant values, but took upon themselves the moralising task of regenerating the most indigent strata of the population, who might otherwise compromise the image of the Jews in the city's society. We must also remember that this was an attitude typical of the ruling groups of the Jewish community in this period.

What is certain, and indeed of fundamental importance, is that the yardstick of morality, able to legitimise integration in the civil society of Livorno in the mid-nineteenth century, had undergone definitive change, no longer invoking peculiarities connected with the particular history of the city and its port. What was now expected was morality in conduct as reflected in typical nineteenth-century bourgeois respectability, and above all love of the homeland, long to remain the ultimate criterion for Jews to judge themselves and to feel themselves judged, until the tragedy of the fascist Race Laws. With full integration at cultural level the Jews of Livorno – and of Tuscany in general – were able to adhere in great numbers to the new tenets of the national ideology which, once the revolutionary upheavals of 1848–49 in Tuscany had ended in debacle, saw the emphasis shifting ever more from local to Italian connotations. The transition implied – not only for Jews – partial abandonment of the manifold, cosmopolitan identity typical of '*livornesità*' and increasing commitment to a clear-cut, unambiguous national identity. As we have seen, in 1847 and 1848 the Jewish community of Livorno for the first time took an explicit stand in favour of full juridical equality, and thus also of total abolition of their privileges. Clearly, in this process the cultural and ideological influences of the times interacted with the changes coming about in the city's economic situation, contributing to the gradual disappearance of the conditions that had for centuries underlain the fine balance between Jewish community, city and port.

Now indissolubly linked with the cause of Italian unity, emancipation unquestionably opened up new opportunities for individual Jews but, together with the abolition of free port status in 1868, it also saw the sun irrevocably set on the once-glorious Jewish nation of Livorno.

NOTES

1. The complete text of the Letters Patent is given in the appendix to Renzo Toaff, *La nazione ebrea a Livorno e a Pisa (1591–1700)* (Florence: Olschki, 1990).
2. Cf. article 5: 'We release you from being any further burdened with registration, arbitrary taxation, capitation taxes, regarding property or person, taxes already in force, and any that may in future be levied by us or by those who come after us, … not wishing that you … be subjected to payments, subservience, laws or statutes, such as the Jews living in Florence and Siena are, or may in the future be, subjected to', Toaff (see note 1), p.421.
3. Michele Luzzati, 'La sinagoga a Livorno: Monumento ebraico monumento pubblico', in Michele Luzzati (ed.), *Le tre sinagoghe* (Livorno: Umberto Allemandi, 1995), pp.9–27.
4. 'Istruzioni segrete al Governatore di Livorno del 26 aprile 1774, art. 8, annesse alla lettera dei 5 luglio detto', cited in Toaff (see note 1), p.47.
5. on *ballottazione*, cf. Jean-Pierre Filippini, 'La ballottazione a Livorno nel Settecento', *Rassegna Mensile di Israel* 49 (1983), 199–224.
6. Lois Dubin, 'Researching Port Jews and Port Jewries: Trieste and Beyond', in David Cesarani (ed.), *Port Jews: Jewish Communities in Cosmopolitan Maritime Trading Centres, 1550–1950* (London and Portland, OR: Frank Cass, 2002), pp.47–58.
7. On this point, cf. Lois Dubin, 'Between Toleration and "Equalities": Jewish Status and Community in Pre-Revolutionary Europe', *Yearbook of the Simon-Dubnow-Institute* 1 (2002), pp.219–34.
8. Cf. Lois Dubin, *The Port Jews of Habsburg Trieste: Absolutist Politics and Enlightenment Culture* (Stanford, CA: Stanford University Press, 1999), pp.198–225. Dubin distinguishes (see ibid., p.223 n.63) between *civil* and *civic inclusion*, referring the latter to the conquest of political participation. In this respect the 1780 disposition could be seen as a first step towards *civic inclusion*, but I believe the matter needs further examination.
9. Ibid., p.199.
10. Such conduct had been outlawed since the Letters Patent of 1593. A recent study by Cristina Galasso shows how in practice the ban could be eluded, thereby rendering the scenario of everyday relations between Jews and gentiles more variegated and dynamic. Cf. Cristina Galasso, *Alle origini di una comunità: Ebree ed ebrei a Livorno nel Seicento* (Firenze: Olschki, 2002).
11. Archivio della Comunità Ebraica di Livorno (henceforth ACEL), Tempo del Concistoro, filza D, no.82.
12. For the text of the statue, see *Assemblee del Risorgimento, III, La Toscana*, vol.I (Rome: Tipografia della Camera dei Deputati, 1911), pp.6–13.
13. For a more detailed picture of the events and the issues raised by the Risorgimento process, see Alfonso Scirocco, *L'Italia del Risorgimento 1800–1871* (Bologna: Il Mulino, 1990); Gilles Pécout, *Naissance de L'Italie contemporaine, 1770–1922* (Paris: Nathan, 1997); Lucy Riall, *The Italian Risorgimento: State, Society and National Unification* (London: Routledge, 1994).
14. ACEL, Tempo del Concistoro, filza D, no.40, 13 May 1814.
15. On the evidence of research carried out to date, the Jews of Livorno do not seem to have given the French troops a particularly warm welcome despite the promises of equality they came with, and despite the fact that public opinion had immediately branded the Jews as Jacobins. Cf. on this aspect Carlo Mangio, 'Tra conservazione e rivoluzione', in Giuseppe Galasso (ed.), *Storia d'Italia*, XIII, 2, *Il Granducato di Toscana. I Lorena dalla Reggenza agli anni rivoluzionari* (Turin: UTET, 1997), pp.425–509; idem, 'La communauté juive de Livourne face à la Revolution française', in Bernhard Blumenkranz and Albert Soboul (eds.), *Les Juifs et la Revolution Française: problèmes et aspirations*

(Toulouse: Privat, 1976), pp.191–209; see also the observations by Jean-Pierre Filippini, 'La nazione ebrea di Livorno', in Corrado Vivanti (ed.), *Storia d'Italia*, XI, 2, *Gli Ebrei in Italia* (Turin: Einaudi, 1997), pp.1045–1066.

16. Michele Luzzati, 'Privilegio e identità nella storia degli ebrei livornesi', *Studi livornesi* 1 (1986), p.38.

17. See in particular Tullia Catalan, 'La "primavera degli ebrei"': Speranze e delusioni di Ebrei italiani del Litorale e del Lombardo Veneto nel 1848–1849', *Zakhor: Rivista di storia degli ebrei d'Italia* 6 (2003), pp.35–66.

18. ACEL, Tempo del Concistoro, filza D, no.51, letter dated 4 May 1814.

19. ACEL, Minute, filza 115, 1820–1825, no.13.

20. David LoRomer, *Merchants and Reform in Livorno, 1814–1868* (Berkeley, CA, Los Angeles and London: University of California Press, 1987), p.15.

21. With a resolution of 5 June 1820 the fairly numerous population of Greek students was enabled to graduate in civil law, but the Jews and other heterodox communities remained excluded from the ordinance. With a Notification of the Grand Duchy Studies Superintendence of 2 June 1841 civil law graduation was introduced for the heterodox communities; see also the Archivio di Stato di Pisa, Università di Pisa, II versamento, sezione A.II.6, no.52. On the evidence of certain documents held in ACEL, Carteggio, filza 58, it appears that inclusion of Jews in this ruling was not automatic, and that heterodox was taken to refer strictly to non-Catholic Christians. What is certain is that before the Tuscan statute of 1848 Jews were not allowed to practise the profession.

22. On the Franchetti family, one of Tuscany's most important Jewish families of bankers and dealers, see the recent study by Mirella Scardozzi, 'Itinerari dell'integrazione: una grande famiglia ebrea tra la fine del Settecento e il primo Novecento', in Paolo Pezzino and Alvaro Tacchini (eds.), *Leopoldo e Alice Franchetti e il loro tempo* (Città di Castello: Petruzzi, 2002), pp.271–320. Alessandro (1809–74) became well-known for his literary interests, and in particular for his studies on Dante.

23. ACEL, Minute, filza 116, 1826–1828, no.63. Franchetti actively sought information on the situation in other states, and had received from some acquaintances copies of two civil law degree certificates awarded by the University of Padua, one to a Christian and one to a Jew, as concrete proof of even-handed treatment.

24. Significantly, the governors of the Jewish nation continued to issue regulations clamping down on the constitution of *Yeshivot*, that is, religious study and prayer groups beyond their direct control, calling upon the faithful – or at least those directly answerable to them, like the masters and pupils of the Charity Schools – to attend daily morning prayers in the Temple.

25. Sansone Uzielli (1797–1857) was an important banker and businessman with vast cultural interests that led him to collaborate on Gian Pietro Vieusseux's 'Antologia' and cultivating contacts with the dynamic, liberal-leaning world of Tuscan evangelism.

26. ACEL, Minute, filza 124, 1844–1845, no.154, 10 September 1844.

27. ACEL, Carteggio, filza 58, Documenti riguardanti la laurea in diritto civile. Emancipazione degli 27. israeliti (loose, unnumbered pages).

28. In particular, see Catalan (see note 17). Particularly striking here is the observation by Angelo Cavalieri that 'our elders were not inclined to believe their sons fit to do justice to academic qualifications … and depending on the living afforded by Trieste, which was all and will largely remain in its trade, … were loath to sap them of their youthful energies' (p.44).

29. Indispensable on this subject is the study by Gadi Luzzatto Voghera, *Il prezzo dell'eguaglianza: Il dibattito sull'emancipazione degli ebrei in Italia (1781–1848)* (Milan: Franco Angeli, 1998). For a well-focused view of the case of Tuscany and Livorno, see Ulrich Wyrwa, 'Die Debatte über die Emanzipation der Juden und die Jüdischen Erfahrungen 1848/1849 in der Toskana', *Quellen und Forschungen* 81 (2001), 397–438; idem, 'Jewish Experiences in the Italian Risorgimento: Political Practice and National Emotions of Florentine and Leghorn Jewry (1849–1860)', *Journal of Modern Italian Studies* 8.1 (2003), 16–35; Carlotta Ferrara degli Uberti, 'La questione dell'emancipazione ebraica nel biennio 1847–1848: note sul caso livornese', *Zakhor: Rivista di storia degli ebrei d'Italia* 6 (2003), 67–91.

The Port Jews of Corfu and the 'Blood Libel' of 1891: A Tale of Many Centuries and of One Event

SAKIS GEKAS

Introduction

The Sorkin-Dubin thesis has provided an alternative framework for conceptualising the Jewish experience in cosmopolitan maritime trading centres by focusing on the exceptional North Atlantic and Triestine Jews during the eighteenth century and their distinct road to emancipation and, thus, modernity.[1] The challenge to those wishing to engage with the debate on 'port Jews' is to investigate the possibilities of extending the concept chronologically (before and after the eighteenth century) and geographically (in ports other than the North Atlantic and western-central Mediterranean). In this essay the port of Corfu during the nineteenth century will be examined with relation to its transition from being the capital of the British-protected Ionian State to a peripheral, but nevertheless important port of the Greek kingdom. The issues discussed are the degree of participation of the Jewish population in the port economy, and the tolerance or intolerance of the Jews as a minority depending on the port's growth or decline. The first issue relates directly with the problem of definition of port Jew/Jews/Jewry, a concept the historiographical value of which Lois Dublin argues 'can be realised only if we broaden the purview to identify and analyse port Jews in other locations'.[2] The approach adopted in this research is a quantitative analysis of the Jews of Corfu who chose to become Greek citizens when the Ionian Islands were ceded to Greece in 1864 after 50 years as a British protectorate. Despite the vigour of existing and ongoing research employing the concept of 'port Jews', analysis of the occupational and social structure of Jews in the port towns, with few exceptions,[3] has been sidestepped precisely due to the identification of port Jews with merchants and commerce in general. The occupational classification of the Jews as part of the occupational classification of the urban population will demonstrate the multi-faceted role of the Jews in the urban commercial economy, against contemporary as well as historiographical accounts, which have depicted Jews as moneychangers and olive oil merchants. These accounts tend to portray Jewish merchants as a single occupational group, dominant of the credit market and olive oil trade, while ignoring the tens of other Jews who were otherwise involved in the port economy.

The source which provided the basis for the occupational classification comes from a significant moment for the history of the Jews and the island of Corfu as a whole: the moment of union of the Ionian Islands with Greece in 1864. This event, the incorporation of Corfu into the Greek nation state had important consequences for the Jews of Corfu. The rights to citizenship they received with the 1864 constitution meant political inclusion. Nevertheless, this did not prevent the rise of anti-semitic feelings based on an aggressive nationalism, which culminated in the riots of 1891, known as the 'blood libel'. The limitations of the Electoral List (and of the occupational classification for that matter) are encapsulated in the fact that it included those Jews only who wished to become Greek citizens, and thus registered.[4] As a consequence, in this essay the occupational classification concerns only the Jews who wished to become Greek citizens. Significantly, the same group examined in the occupational analysis came under attack in the years before the events of 1891 through an anti-semitic discourse, which claimed that the Jews were not worthy of their rights as Greek citizens. Still, this is not to say that only the Greek-Jewish citizens were affected and suffered during the blockade of the ghetto, where the majority of all Jews (Greek citizens or not) resided.

Although there are accounts of the events which led to the displacement of approximately 2,000 Jews,[5] the aim of this essay is not to provide simply another narrative, but instead to identify the relation between the rise of anti-semitism and the decline of the port of Corfu. The assertion that ports, despite being cosmopolitan and dynamic, are not immediately and unconditionally havens for tolerance is of course anything but new,[6] and similarly, the loss of the cosmopolitanism and prosperity of a port cannot be unquestionably considered to have led to anti-semitism. The concept of 'port Jew' with particular reference to the issue of tolerance can be applied and perhaps modified in the light of the interpretations, existing and new ones, of this tragic event. The aim of this essay nevertheless is not simply to add another 'case study' to the ones conducted already, but also to amalgamate Jewish history with Greek history and vice versa, a task long overdue.[7]

The exclusive, intolerant and violent riots of 1891 were the result of a nationalist ideology, which elevated irredentism to the highest national priority: 'the liberation of "unredeemed brothers" suffering under the Ottoman yoke'.[8] In the case of Corfu this doctrine entailed that the most radical nationalist and anti-semitic elements of Corfu society denied Jews equality and rights to citizenship. This essay will first provide a background of the history of the Jews in Corfu, before analysing the occupational structure of Corfu and providing an operational definition for the concept of 'port Jews'. Finally, the events of 1891 are analysed through the prism of contemporary ideology and long-established manifestations of judeophobia in Corfu urban society.

The History of the Jews of Corfu: A Tale of Many Centuries

The Jews of Corfu were not a homogeneous community. They consisted of the Romaniotes or 'Greek Jews', who came to Corfu in the twelfth century from the east,[9] and 'Italian Jews' who came from Apulia, where they had settled after being expelled from Spain at the end of the fifteenth century. From the first years of Jewish settlement in the island of Corfu subsequent authorities (the King of Naples, Anjou, followed in 1386 by the Venetian Republic) issued a number of decrees for the protection of Jews from Christian harassment and persecution, granting also the freedom to religious practice and protecting the Jewish burial grounds from sacrilege.[10] The decrees indicate the problem of persecution faced by the Jewish population of Corfu since their early settlement in the island. Towards the end of the fourteenth century, the Jews were barely tolerated and the constant protection of the authorities had to be employed to enable a decent life in the town of Corfu. In 1386 the aristocracy of Corfu decided to surrender the island and thus to place themselves under the protection of Venice by sending a delegation of six members, among which was David Semo, one of the principals of the Jewish community.[11] Venetian power during the four centuries of domination, however, oscillated. Ostensibly, the Venetian Doge maintained the decrees issued by Anjou, thus safeguarding the position of the Jews against arbitrary harassment and persecution. In practice, the Venetian authorities often yielded to the demands of the local ruling class of Corfu, forcing the Jews to wear distinctive symbols as early as 1406 and forbidding the Jews to own houses, land and serfs outside the Jewish quarter; the Jews not wearing the distinctive mark would be subject to a 300 ducats fine.[12] Around the middle of the sixteenth century, though, the new wave of Apulian Jews arrived on the island. The immigrants brought their own traditions, culture and especially language, which continued to be spoken by the Jews of Corfu at least until the end of the nineteenth century.[13] However, the Romaniotes did not accept Apulian Jews, nor were the latter allowed by the Venetian authorities to found their own community.[14] Romanos provides some information for these first years of the new settlement:

Many Jews subjected themselves to labour and conducted jobs vulgar and degrading, albeit necessary, which the rest of the inhabitants looked down upon. The most eminent of them involved in trade and managed to acquire most of the commercial business of the island, accumulating power and wealth which on many occasions used to the benefit of the town as a whole.[15]

The institutionalisation of difference that was implemented through the restriction of the Jews of Corfu to one residential area, the creation of a ghetto, dates to the seventeenth century. In 1622, a strict edict came as a result of the pressure yielded by the Corfu aristocracy on the Venetian authorities, restricting Jewish settlement in one quarter, from where they were not allowed to leave without a written permit.[16] The decree, a result of an increasing hostility especially targeted against the wealthy Jewish newcomers, was the foundation of the segregation of the majority of the Jewish population until recent times.[17] Still, as Preschel argues, the terms of the segregation and the living conditions of the Jewish population were much better compared to other Venetian towns.[18] Preschel's account emphasises the privileged position of the Jews of Corfu in areas such as occupation (practising law and medicine), organisation of the community and protection from harassment by the Christians. Moreover, the degree of relative autonomy to stage special ceremonies is used as an example to state that the Jews of Corfu were allowed greater freedom than the Jews of Rome.[19] The public ceremonies, religious in principle but always having political and power connotations, have been extensively researched in Corfu and Preschel's argument is corroborated by recent scholarship. Nikiforou's work has demonstrated that by the eighteenth century, when Jews were dominating the town's commerce and olive oil trade in particular, their ceremonies could not be ignored, despite the fact that they were restricted to celebrating inside the walls of the synagogues.[20]

The Republican French, having abolished Venetian sovereignty, ruled Corfu from 1797 until 1799. As in France and elsewhere in Europe, the supporters of the Revolution advocated the emancipation of the Jews everywhere.[21] The abolition of the privileges of the aristocracy and the establishment of a municipal council in Corfu following the model of the French Directory resulted in the participation of two Jews in the council, a development unacceptable to some of the Christian members of the council and part of the Christian population.[22] The failure to implement the organisation of the polity along republican lines cannot be attributed only to anti-semitism of course, but also to the resistance of the old aristocracy in Corfu to abandoning its privileges. The example is representative, though, of the refusal of the majority of the Christian population to allow any involvement of Jewish representatives in institutions of civic governance and political life. Could this refusal by the Christian population to yield civic equality to the Jewish population, or at least their representatives, be considered as another case of 'false emancipation', similar to the promises for political equality given to the Jews of Amsterdam one year earlier, in 1797, and never fulfilled?[23] The striking analogies indicate that it could.

After a period of Russo-Ottoman rule and administration of the islands known as 'Septinsular Republic', and a period of Napoleonic rule (1807–14), during which Corfu commerce suffered from the blockade of the port by the British navy, from 1815 until 1864 the Ionian Islands formed a quasi-independent state under the protection of Great Britain. Corfu was the administrative and commercial capital. For the British it was an important naval and commercial station, where troops were stationed and manufactured goods from Britain were stored for re-export to neighbouring markets. As a result, Corfu became a vibrant commercial port town, attracting merchants from the opposite continent and from England, as well as travellers that gradually became acquainted with the cosmopolitanism of the town and the natural beauty of the island. The prosperity of the port and the beneficial effects for its people during the nineteenth century (the Jews included) certainly warrants the application of the concept and social type of 'port Jew', in an economically expedient environment. Was this actually the case, though? Did the growth of Ionian economy, despite its fluctuations due to bad harvests and external economic conditions (the Crimean war, for example), and growth of the port of Corfu in particular, lead to the advancement of Jewish emancipation, and contribute to greater tolerance being demonstrated by the Christians towards the Jews? And if so, for how long did this tolerance last? The rest of this essay will attempt to answer these questions.

The picture described by contemporaries can shed some light on the condition or, more accurately, on the perception of the condition of Ionian Jewry at the time. Interesting as they are on their own, these accounts can provide varied information on the history of the Jews of Corfu. Contemporary travellers were impressed by the number of Jews in Corfu, as well as by their degree of participation in the economic life of the port. Jervis, writing in 1852, noted that in the occupational structure 'occupying every position from the highest to the lowest are the Jews'.[24]

Albert Mousson, in his travel memoirs from the Ionian Islands, presented a similar picture. In his work Jews are the moneychangers at the port, the tailors and cloth merchants who exploit their monopoly, the usurers who obtain the fortunes of decaying aristocrats, as well as the ones who live in the most impressive houses in town, together with other merchants.[25] Needless to say this is far from being a representative, let alone accurate, account of the

Jewish population and its activities in Corfu during the mid-nineteenth century. It is more likely that he refers to the few Jewish wholesale and olive oil merchants and a few members of the professions who did in fact live outside the Jewish quarter.

Another account provides a different insight into the social reality of the Corfu Jewry. In November 1845 the 'Occident and American Jewish Advocate' published a short report on the Jews of Corfu:

> There are about 2,000 Jews in Corfu. They inhabit a separate quarter of the city, but which is not separated from the rest of the town by a wall, as is the case at Rome, at Ancona, and other towns in Italy. The Jews of Corfu are, generally speaking, slovenly, both in their houses and in their dress, and their ignorance is so great, that numbers among them do not even know the principal events in the history of their nation. Those of a higher class are merchants, and trade chiefly in cloth and linen; the middle class consists of artisans, and for the greater part of tailors. The lower classes are the most numerous; they are dealers in old clothes, porters, and sailors. They are generally speaking, laborious, and have, in the midst of a very poor population, attained to comfortable circumstances, and even riches. The Greeks hate them, and seize every opportunity for injuring and ill-treating them; so that their situation would be very pitiable, if the English did not take them under their protection. Twenty years ago no Jew dared show himself in the streets during the Holy Week; but things have changed since that time.[26]

Hindsight, and the events of 1891, indicate that things had changed only temporarily, if at all. What is interesting though in the above account is the attempt to categorise the Jewish population in terms of class. This in fact is one of the most important issues which leads directly to the question of whether Jews can be considered to have constituted a separate class from the classes dividing the gentile population (in which case the term class would be synonymous with the term community), or whether they can be incorporated into a class analysis of Corfu, and for that matter any urban, society, not separate from the Christian, or other majority population group. Given that religion is usually considered to have been the defining characteristic of Jewish identity, the issue of whether class can be used as an analytical tool for the study of Jewish communities such as the one in Corfu remains to be researched.[27] An initial approach to this issue can be attempted through the occupational classification of the Jews of Corfu, aiming to demonstrate the manifold participation and role of the Jews in the port economy.

Occupational Classification of the Jews of Corfu

In 1865 the population of Corfu was 17,111.[28] Considerable variations in different sources mean that the population of Jews can only approximately be estimated. A census of the town and the surrounding districts in 1853 recorded 2,160 local and 224 foreign Israelites.[29] Non-demographic sources talk of 6,000 Jews in 1856,[30] while Mousson reported that they formed approximately one-sixth of the town's population.[31] Kirkwall, providing a short history of the Jews of Corfu, mentions 1,171 souls in 1760, 2,000 when the French occupied Corfu in 1797 and 6,000 'at present', which was in 1864, when he wrote his historical account of the islands.[32] Contemporary and recent historical accounts present an equally vague picture of Jewish economic activity during the period of British rule. Against these contradictory numbers and accounts an investigation of the role of Jews as a separate religious and ethnic group, and most importantly the extent of their participation in the port economy, is attempted through the examination of a demographic source, the Electoral List of 1865 and the classification of occupations recorded for each individual.[33]

The classification of occupations can have enormous value to economic and social historians. Research conducted in the UK on the census for the period after 1851 has demonstrated that occupational titles can provide information on social and economic status and on the economic structure at the time.[34] However, occupational titles should not be taken at face value, assuming that they represent a social and economic reality. Occupational classification is a very apt way to approach the issue and quantify the port and other occupational activities of the Jewish population, but it must be treated carefully, since to start with occupational titles are value-laden by the collector of the information. They represent an activity at the time of the registration, although limited occupational mobility allows us to infer that the occupational titles are quite representative of an activity that lasted for a considerable period. Despite these limitations the gains are significant. More specific questions can be asked with relation to the occupational structure of the community, issues of social class and the extent of the participation of the Jewish population in the port economy and the idiosyncrasy of this involvement. The source examined was created at a significant moment, that of union of the islands with Greece. The figures do not claim accuracy and it has to be noted here that the low number of the Jews recorded in relation to contemporary accounts that speak, perhaps with doses of hyperbole, of 4,500 to 6,000 Jews could be accounted for by the fact that not all Jews chose to become Greek citizens. For the needs of the collection of the information the town was divided into three districts, a categorisation reflecting older divisions of the town.[35] All the occupations were recorded, coded and then classified

TABLE 1
OCCUPATIONAL CLASSIFICATION OF JEWS IN THE 2ND DISTRICT

Labourers		Employed		Commerce		Professions		Craftsmen		Retail		Proprietors	
Porter	65	Clerk	10	Merchant	210	Teacher	8	Tailor	127	Pedlar	63	Proprietor	7
Olive oil worker	19	Workshop empl.	3	Industrialist	23	Advocate	7	Tinmaker	19	Spiritseller	23		
Water carrier	6			Commercial Agt	1	Physician	5	Tanner	16	Wineseller	11		
Builder	2			Broker	14	Surgeon	1	Soapmaker	13	Grocer	8		
				Public Broker	3			Shoemaker	7	Butcher	6		
				Leather merchant	2			Mattress maker	5	Baker	2		
				Merchant, Tailor	1			Glassware maker	3				
								Coppersmith	2				
								Goldsmith	2				
Total	92		13		268		21		194		113		7

Note: The difference between those under the class 'employed' with 'labourers' is that they were employed on a more permanent basis than the 'labourers'.

Source: Electoral List 1544, Enhoria Diaheirisi [Domestic Administration], Istoriko Arheio Kerkyras [Corfu Records Office].

TABLE 2
OCCUPATIONAL CLASSIFICATION OF TOTAL POPULATION RECORDED AND
PERCENTAGE OF JEWISH OCCUPATIONAL CLASSES IN THE 2ND DISTRICT

Occupational Class	Total	Jews	%
Labourers	110	92	83
Servants, Clerks, employed	145	13	9
Commerce	432	268	62
Professions	106	21	19
Craftsmen	392	194	49
Retail	209	113	54
Other	11	1	9
Proprietors	195	7	3
Total	1,600	709	44

Source: Electoral List 1544, Enhoria Diaheirisi [Domestic Administration], Istoriko
Arheio Kerkyras [Corfu Records Office].

TABLE 3
OCCUPATIONAL CLASSIFICATION OF TOTAL POPULATION RECORDED AND
PERCENTAGES OF TOTAL AND JEWISH OCCUPATIONAL CLASSIFICATION
OF JEWS IN THE 2ND DISTRICT

Occupational Class	1st dist.	2nd dist.	3rd dist.	Total	per cent	Jews	per cent
Labourers	6	110	79	195	6	92	47.0
Servants, employed	120	145	245	510	15	13	2.5
Commerce	87	432	148	667	19	268	40.0
Professions	81	106	108	295	9	21	7.0
Craftsmen	142	392	337	871	24	194	22.0
Retail	51	209	150	410	12	113	27.5
Other	2	11	15	28	1	1	3.5
Proprietors	114	195	180	489	14	7	1.5
Total	603	1,600	1,262	3,465	100	709	20.5

Source: Electoral List 1544, Enhoria Diaheirisi [Domestic Administration], Istoriko
Arheio Kerkyras [Corfu Records Office].

according to classification schemes devised mostly in Britain by researchers of the census. The scheme adopted in this research takes into consideration both activities in the local economy and a certain degree of status that derived from them. A scheme of classification that will use a mixture of criteria might be more suitable for Corfu, in this pre-industrial stage.[36] Without entering into too many details of the classification scheme adopted, the first findings of the research are presented here, focusing on the classification of the Jewish population recorded in the second district, and as a part of the total population recorded.

The occupational classification of the Corfu Jews recorded is presented in Tables 1, 2 and 3. This is a first attempt to quantify the position of the Jewish recorded population in the town's economic structure. The above data provide a first mapping of the occupational distribution in Corfu town among Christians and Jews. Thus merchants, the first group among Jewish occupational titles, constitute 40 per cent of the total number of recorded merchants. Jewish craftsmen, tailors being the overwhelming majority, are 22 per cent of craftsmen in all three districts. Also high, 27.5 per cent, is the percentage of retailers, mainly pedlars but also shopkeepers. The extremely low percentages of proprietors should not surprise since Jews were not allowed to own property, except in the Jewish quarter, and clearly not many of them considered themselves as proprietors. Similarly, the prohibition to practice law under British rule, which had just ended at the time the source was created, explains the equally low percentage of Jews belonging to the professions. The most unexpected finding, though, and the most impressive one is the extremely high percentage of labourers, 47 per cent of the total and 83 per cent in the second district, mainly porters, among the Jews living in the second district. These were dockworkers, working in the transfer of goods from the ships to the custom house, and vice versa when merchandise was being re-exported. This of course is a completely different finding from contemporary accounts and even more recent accounts of nineteenth-century Corfu. These accounts tended to associate Jews with usury, the local bourgeois elite and the owners of capital.[37] The domination of the olive oil trade by Jews often led to accusations of monopoly, or monopsony (in the sense of the Jews being *one* group of buyers-exporters), since they were in a position to buy the produce from the growers in advance for past debts, and then sell it in as profitable terms as possible. Overall, a very high percentage of Jews can be categorised as being related to the port economy, merchants, retailers (mainly pedlars) and dockworkers, that is 67 per cent of the Jews of the second district. The percentage of the total population related to the port economy is only 37 per cent, if not less, since not all retailers (mainly shopkeepers) were directly involved in the port economy.

The findings presented in this essay strengthen the argument for an inclusive view of the Jewish population as part of the town's economy at a crucial moment, that of the union of Corfu with Greece. Corfu Jews from the time of their settlement in Corfu seem to have developed trading activities as well as an interest in the textile manufacture, and during the nineteenth century, many earned their living as labourers in the port, unlike the stereotypical depiction of Jews as involved in money lending, financing and banking,[38] probably one of the most enduring anti-semitic myths.[39]

Most significantly, though, the above data demonstrate the extent and diversity of Jewish participation in the port economy. In this respect, the social type of the 'port Jew' can be extended to include all Jews living in port towns such as Corfu, where most of the occupations were related to the port economy. It is not only merchants who can be included and examined in the light of the 'port Jew' concept, no matter how significant the number of Jewish merchants was. The findings in this research resemble the case of Salonika, where 'Jews were represented at all levels of the town's occupational structure', thus 'transcending' the 'port Jew type of the Sorkin-Dubin model, based as it is on essentially wealthy entrepreneurial elites'.[40]

Nevertheless, in Corfu, as in other ports qualifying for examination, port Jews as merchants were an important stratum. Towards the end of the period of British rule, Jewish merchants were a considerable part of the commercial world of Corfu. In 1860, they constituted 27 per cent of the recorded merchants (52 out of 187), while in 1862, two years before unification with Greece, they appear to be 78 out of 210 (37 per cent).[41] It is important to note here that not everyone could be recorded as a merchant in the list officially constructed by the merchants themselves (criteria devised by them) and the state authorities. This is corroborated by the different numbers in different documents: the number of Jews recorded as merchants in the Electoral List in 1865 (286) and the Jews registered as merchants in the lists of the Chamber of Commerce (78) in 1862.[42]

In 1856 the merchants of the Chamber of Commerce asked and were granted the right to elect their representatives to the Commercial Tribunal, thus administering their own cases of insolvency.[43] Jewish merchants were excluded from election to the Tribunal as assessors since they were not Christians, a necessary rule for eligibility. However, this institutionalised exclusion of the Jewish merchants from the very important commercial mechanism of the Chamber of Commerce, and therefore their exclusion from being elected as assessors to the Tribunal, must have been particularly disturbing to the Jewish merchant elite. In an attempt to redress this injustice, eight Jewish merchants petitioned the central and highest authority of the state, the Lord High Commissioner, requesting to be admitted to appear before the Commercial Courts as assessors.[44] The Jewish merchants argued that while the laws passed by the Senate did not distinguish between Ionian citizens, the decree of the municipal council excluded non-Christians from the post of assessor. The petitioners, established merchants of Corfu, after emphasising the central role of Jews in the town's trade and commercial life, asked for the protection of British power emanating from its liberal spirit which could not allow, as they say, discriminations of this kind in the nineteenth century. Here is a rare piece of evidence of self-perception of the Jewish merchants and a case of promoting their interests collectively and against the rest of the business world of Corfu. This claim for equal representation to the Chamber of Commerce is very similar to the petition of the Jews of Trieste to Vienna to redress their exclusion from the town's *Borsa*. It is impressive that the same arguments were used to persuade the authorities of the injustice towards the Jewish merchants: the general good of commerce and the benefits to derive from the participation of Jews in the regulation of commerce through the institutions established. The argument of the Jews of Trieste was precisely the same as the position of the Jews of Corfu: the essential Jewish contribution to the town's commercial life.[45] The petition of the Corfu Jewish merchants was successful and in 1858 Joseph Courage was elected as a representative of the Chamber in the Tribunal. Interestingly, however, he was forced to resign because of the inability to conduct business in Greek, which by this time was becoming the official language of the courts and administration, excluding those not fluent in Greek.[46]

While the merchants of Corfu, wholesale merchants, grain importers and exporters to neighbouring markets, did promote their interests collectively, Jewish merchants involved in these trading activities were excluded from this collective promotion of interests. This is evident from petitions sent to the Lord High Commissioner by the merchants of Corfu on several issues (more frequent communication with other imports, free trade of grain being the most important). Jewish merchants are absent from this process, effectively a lobbying process. Analysis of the petitions mentioned above shows the exclusion of Jewish merchants, especially the ones involved in the import and re-export of grain, the most lucrative trade by far, by other merchants. The signatures at the end of a number of petitions belong to merchants from Corfu, from Epirus (the opposite mainland), established a few decades earlier in Corfu, and of foreign merchants settled in Corfu as company owners or commercial agents, but not to Jewish merchants. Thus, a polarisation based on religion seems to have been one of the characteristics of the Corfiote business elite around the middle of the nineteenth century. Moreover, petitions from other occupational groups, such as porters, bakers and shopkeepers, did not include their Jewish colleagues, an indication of a similar polarisation outside the narrow group of wholesale merchants.

One extremely lucrative form of economic activity in the port towns of the Ionian Islands during the nineteenth century, especially from the 1850s onwards, was investment in maritime insurance companies. The representative of the first insurance office established in Corfu, a branch of the Austrian-Italian Insurance Company, which was based in Trieste, was Abraham de Castro. The pioneering activity of the Jewish merchant should be attributed to the well-established relations between the Jewish merchants of Corfu and commercial centres in the Adriatic, especially Trieste and Venice. Other Jewish merchants did get involved without being the principal shareholders, though, in the two insurance companies established in Corfu in the early 1850s.[47] Other activities of the principal Jewish merchants included the well-documented olive oil trade with the above-mentioned ports. For example, Yerak & Olivetti, Sabbato Tedesco and Rietti Mordo all exported olive oil from Corfu. Joseph Courage imported coal for the steamships calling at Corfu as well as corn, while Salamon Mordo spread his business between wine and olive oil export and rents from property, which was no different from the practice of many Christian merchants, drawing income from different sources, thus reducing commercial risk.

The characteristics of the Jews of Corfu so far delineated certainly qualify them for inclusion in the 'port Jews' conceptual schema: they were extensively involved in commerce, but also in many other sectors of the port economy, they formed networks with Jews in other ports, such as Venice and Trieste, they achieved a somewhat favourable status on commercial affairs, although by no means in the professions (law and medicine). Other features of the Jews of Corfu, such as the nature of the community, ideology and responses to reforms taking place during the nineteenth century elsewhere in Europe, still remain to be researched, in order to complement the tentative conclusions presented here, primarily concerned with the occupational structure of the Jewish population and the events of 1891. The organisation of the Jewish community and the educational reforms that took place between the 1840s and the 1850s and led to the establishment of a single community school where the Talmud, Greek and Italian languages were taught, are thoroughly discussed in Preschel's work on the Jews of Corfu.[48] On the contrary, in this research the aim is to identify the elements which rendered co-existence between the two religious communities, Christians and Jews, problematic and which ultimately triggered the atrocities of 1891.

From Emancipation to Dislocation

On May 1864 Corfu, together with the rest of the Ionian Islands, was ceded by Great Britain to Greece. The first municipal elections under the new regime, for which the Electoral List previously analysed was devised, took place a year later. The participation of the Jewish population was crucial for the electoral result. From these first elections the Jewish population who chose to become Greek citizens were invited to participate with their vote in the pivotal issues of public life. These were primarily the agricultural question, which dominated the economic, social and political life of the islands and especially Corfu immediately after union with Greece.[49] Two speeches addressed to the Jewish community, one next to the other, were published and circulated in the town in May 1865. One was written by the representatives of the community and future candidates for the municipal council and indicates the political climate of the time, while the second was written by the Christian supporters of the candidates proposed.[50]

The first, signed by the 'representatives of the Israelite community', expressed the devotion of the Israelites to justice, order and the authority of law, their conviction that they live among 'an excellent and generous people' with which they communicate in every aspect of social life, people that 'understand the concept of love, brotherhood and humanity that constitutes the basis of every civil process'. Most significantly they emphasised the duty of the Jewish community to contribute to the public good, the good of the country and national prosperity. These words reflected an acute awareness of the role the Israelites could play in the new circumstances as well their position in the new regime. This demonstrated the support of the Jewish representatives for the candidates proposed in the next speech. The writer of the latter, self-described as 'one of your fellow citizens', praised the civic awareness of the Jewish electors indicated in the first speech. 'One of the most democratic constitutions in the world', as contemporaries noted,[51] with its provisions of universal male suffrage seemed to have emancipated politically the Jews of Corfu who had chosen to be part of the Greek polity.

During the following years the involvement and participation of Jews in public life was indeed significant. They were elected to membership of the municipal council, and they continued to be active in the economic life of the town. The mutual acknowledgement (at least during election periods) by Jews and Christians alike that harmonious symbiosis under the auspices of a supposedly liberal and multi-religious Greek state was the only way forward was demonstrated by the high level of political rhetoric, but also at a more grassroots level. This was the level of intra-working-class relations, where attempts at integration advanced even further. The establishment of the workers' fraternity in Corfu provides an example of cooperation and symbiosis between Christians and Jews. While, however, the initiative for the founding of the fraternity in 1887 could not have been more representative of the different religious elements in Corfiote society (one Orthodox, one Roman Catholic and one Jew put forward the idea), the final charter was amended after pressure from Athens. The revised charter, in contrast to the original charter which aimed at bringing about 'union of the working class in Corfu of any nationality', spoke of the 'union of the Greek working class in Corfu' and of providing 'self-help among Greek workers'. This clause, a product of government intervention, resulted in the exclusion of all non-Greeks, among whom were several Jews who had chosen not to become Greek citizens, despite the fact that they constituted one third of the fraternity's members, thus creating a crisis in the fraternity.[52]

Although a compromise was reached several years later, and perhaps in the light of the events of 1891, the case seems typical of the myopic and exclusive policy and reluctance of the Greek state authorities to acknowledge the multi-religious character of communities such as Corfu. As Psallidas notes,

> the crisis of 1889–90 served as a reminder of the religious and ethnic 'otherness' of non-Greeks in relation to the majority of Corfiot society and occurred at a time when the Greek state was seeking the ideological assimilation of the lower social strata and the propagation of a Greek national consciousness by unreservedly adopting irredentist nationalism.[53]

The schism in the relations between the two communities was apparent by the late 1880s; yet, it must have been extremely hard for the Jewish population to predict the outbreak of anti-semitic fanaticism, which ultimately resulted to the displacement of 2–3,000 people in 1891.[54]

The events of April–May 1891 have been extensively (but not exhaustively) discussed in the works of Dafnis and Preschel. In this essay the events are unfolded as depicted in newspaper articles and other documents published at the time and circulated around the town. A narrative of the events will be followed by an interpretation of the events in the light of the long history of anti-Jewish manifestations in Corfu, the rise and decline of the Corfu port economy in the nineteenth century, and most significantly the priorities and policies of the Greek state during the last quarter of the nineteenth century, fuelled by a surging nationalism.

On 14 April Rubbina Sarda, an eight-year-old girl was found dead in an alley in the Jewish quarter. Her father, Vita Sarda, a tailor, had informed the police from the previous day that his daughter was missing. The girl was found in a sack, with numerous wounds on her hands and head, and a deep injury on the neck that was the fatal wound. Before the police conducted a proper investigation, and after the initial arrest of the father and two other Jews as suspects for the murder, rumours spread all over Corfu town. Initially the Jews accused the Christians of the murder, but when the suspects were released, it was the Christians who became agitated and talked of the girl being a Christian killed by the Jews for sacrifice during Passover.[55] The blood libel of Corfu was developing along the lines of a very old pattern of blood libels.[56]

People gathered in the Jewish quarter, lit a fire and asked for the Jews to be burned right there. When the authorities ordered the police and the army stationed in Corfu town to intervene and surround the quarter, prohibiting all movement in and out of the quarter, most Christians became convinced that the authorities were trying to protect the 'real' murderers and the Jewish community that was providing sanctuary for them. While a few fanatics instigated the initial abuse and riots, the blockade of the Jewish quarter and the enforced closure of all Jewish shops magnified and distorted the situation, as well as leading to the starvation of the Jews enclosed in the ghetto. It is clear from the proclamation by the mayor of Corfu on 18 April that he aimed at ending the riots, asking everyone to remain calm and certifying that the girl was Rubbina Sarda.[57] Many Christians were outraged by the proclamation. They considered it a falsification of the events and an attempt by the municipal authorities to mislead them. Mobs formed and for days, in fact weeks, until mid-May the Jewish quarter was besieged. The Jewish cemetery was completely destroyed: gravestones were overturned and monuments broken.[58] Occasionally Jews trying to obtain food, mainly bread and milk, were beaten, shot, stabbed and as a result forced to starve inside their houses. During all this time the local newspapers covered the events, by and large taking an anti-Jewish viewpoint.[59]

The newspaper reports ranged from openly anti-Jewish to more moderate expressions of embarrassment at the mob rule and the powerlessness or unwillingness of the authorities to respond effectively and stop the atrocities.[60] The general tendency of even the most moderate reports was to attribute the events to irrational and even farcical interpretations. It is also important to note the association of the events in Corfu with one of the worse persecutions in Jewish history, the Russian pogroms. These events dominated the foreign press and although the riots in Corfu were serious enough for *The Times* to report them on a daily basis in mid-May, the events in Russia were far more important. The contemporary association of the two events allows the historian of today to explore these persecutions in a comparative framework of anti-semitic outbursts at the end of the nineteenth century. The events in Corfu attracted considerable international attention in parallel to the simultaneous pogrom of the Jews in Russia, or perhaps because of them. If the Russian Emperor could not be persuaded to end the persecution of the Jews there, the Greek kingdom was far weaker and more susceptible to international pressure. Warships from Athens, as well Britain and France, arrived in Corfu to protect the Jewish population and try to intervene. This development ended the spasmodic reaction of the Greek government in Athens.[61]

Shops finally reopened towards the end of May, although Christians continued to boycott Jewish traders. Two thousand or more Jews were forced to leave Corfu for Italy (mainly Trieste), Salonika and other cities in the

Ottoman Empire.[62] In fact the forced migration continued for months after the events. According to contemporaries, the majority of the migrants were the poorest Jews.[63]

Contemporaries from all sides (Christians – anti-semites and moderates – Jews, the Greek government) gave their own interpretations of the occurrences. For the majority of local papers in Corfu, the events were instigated and provoked by 'dark centres' and people who had to gain from the overall disturbance. They were supposed to have belonged to the opposition to the government of the time. The accusations were so widespread that the Greek minister in London in the above-mentioned letter had to dismiss them as completely unfounded, praising the democratic sentiments of both Prime Minister Delyannis and the opposition leader Trikoupis. According to both contemporary sources and the works of Preschel and Dafnis the causes were predominantly political, with economic and religious overtones. While these explanations have to be taken into account and are based on the interpretations of contemporaries they do not provide a satisfactory analysis of the events and why they took place at that particular moment. These interpretations can be enhanced if placed in the context of the policies and dominant ideology of the day.

The main argument proposed in this essay in an attempt to account for the eruption of violence is that an anti-semitic discourse began to develop in the mid-1880s in Corfu. Mediated through the local press, this discourse was a catalyst for the 1891 events, as it cultivated anti-semitic feelings and vehemently attacked the Jewish population of Corfu. The use of stereotypes was paramount as in most anti-semitic propaganda. However, one of the most fervent arguments in this literature was the construction of the image of Jews as not worthy of the rights granted to them by the Greek state after union in 1864.

In July 1885 the newspaper *The Brave* (subtitled 'our purpose is the liberation of the People from the social and political tyrants') published an article which depicts the anti-semitism cultivated by members of the Christian urban elite who objected to the equal participation of the Jews in economic, social and, since 1864, political life. The article is discussed *in extenso* in order to highlight the aggressive tone of the writer and indicate the reception by the supporters of those ideas. The article shows that a persistent and explicit attack on the Jews, in general, and of the Jewish-Greek citizens in particular, was taking place:

THE NECESSARY RESTRICTIONS OF THE JEWS
We do not deny that we fight the Jews. In fact we consider this an essential part of our mission. We fight them in order to restrict them … We should not permit anymore the Jews having more privileges and rights than the Christians. This is a very important issue and we should

all deal with it. For this reason we call upon the aid of all Greek Christians and especially journalists, in order to reach to a fair result, according to our national interests. And after public opinion in Corfu and the rest of the Greeks is well informed on the necessity of the restriction of an element that erodes the guts of Hellenism like a poisonous worm, we will have the power to demand from our Government the application of the Laws.[64]

The writer is Iakovos Polylas, a politician, writer and literary figure during the second half of the nineteenth century. His role as the main figure in the self-proclaimed war against the Jews is less well known.[65] In the article he attacked the organisation of the Jews as a religious community, and argued that after union with Greece there was no justification for the preservation of the Jewish communal organisation, using the example of Roman Catholics who do not constitute, according to Polylas, a separate community.[66] The argument for the restriction of the supposedly dominant position of Jews in the local economy and society is very similar to the arguments voiced by anti-semites in Germany earlier in the nineteenth century,[67] and in fact in most cases of anti-semitic propaganda. Polylas provided his historical interpretation of the reasons that compelled the Jews through the ages and under the different regimes to maintain their religious organisation. After union with Greece, though, he claims they received rights and privileges that they had never dreamed of:

> This position in which the Jews were elevated by the Greek laws, their new place in the polity safeguards their interests and their several businesses. They should feel grateful towards the Greek nation and they should be interested in the progress and prosperity of the nation, considering that they are Greeks too and boosting that they received a nationality. Instead, they never ceased to be the most malicious enemies of the Greeks. They would sacrifice everything to sell Corfu to a foreign government and separate it from Greece, which they hate implacably. And when in 1870 they saw the possibility of war against Turkey, they were hoping Turkey would suck (as they used to say) Greece, since they only of all nations like Turkey ... And all the rights they can enjoy as Greeks, they have used always to the damage of Corfu and the whole nation fighting systematically the liberal and progressive elements of the country.[68]

Polylas's views in the above extracts demonstrate the construction of anti-semitism based on an aggressive nationalism. From the mid-nineteenth century, irredentism was the dominant ideology and the decisive factor in power politics in Greece. This policy often resulted in extreme populism and, in the case of Corfu, anti-semitic riots. As the example of the workers' fraternity mentioned above shows, it was not just a few local newspapers in Corfu and some dangerous madmen like Polylas who argued for the exclusion, if not worse, of the Jewish population. Intervention often originated from the Greek authorities in Athens that were too busy organising the next military campaign in the north. The further expansion of the Greek state with the acquisition of Epirus and Thessaly (what is today western and central Greece) in 1881 accelerated the appetite for liberating more 'enslaved lands'. Amidst this nationalist fever there was little room for communities with 'ambiguous' national affiliation, the accusation voiced by Polylas, which left those communities susceptible to vilification.

Dafnis quotes at length an interview Polylas gave during the 1891 anti-semitic riots, in which he emphasised that he had warned the Jews of the riots that he had predicted. There is a real point in Dafnis's argument that Polylas coalesced with members of the Corfu business world who were losing out to the Jewish traders.[69] However, Victor de Semo, a physician, ex member of the municipal council of Corfu and one of the principals of the Jewish community in another interview dismissed accusations that a reason for the rage of the people was the position of Jews as the economic elite of Corfu. This dispute cannot be resolved at the moment and the question whether real economic interests could incite such violence is still under examination. Yet Polylas's words point to an explanation different from the conspiracy theory that suggests the merchants of Corfu plotted the extermination of the Jewish merchants. Note the tone of Polylas in the interview he gave during the riots, cited by Dafnis:

> No, I don't consider anti-semitism ridiculous. It is natural feeling; it is the normal reaction of modern societies against the invasion of the Jews. The Jew absorbs and does not give back. They are even worse than leeches, because leeches first suck blood and then they throw up. The people have the wisdom and realise all this very well. Religious reasons, political reasons urged the people to these riots.[70]

The attempt of Polylas to present the anti-semitic riots as a natural and normal response to modernity in order to justify the atrocities of May 1891 indicates the extremity of the discourse produced and employed against the Jews. The nauseating and venomous associations of humans with animals, in which Jews are depicted as worse than animals, indicate that the local anti-semitism was based not only on an aggressive nationalism but also on racism. We also need to consider, as a final point, the importance of the port of Corfu, the site where the events took place, and the extent to which the port economy impacted on the eruption of anti-semitism.

The decline of port activity is bound to have had a considerable impact not only on the business of merchants, but also on other occupational groups whose daily income depended entirely on the port (dockworkers for instance). The transition from the requirements of a colonially oriented economy (under British rule Corfu port served as a depot for grain), to the priorities of the Greek protectionist economy reduced the activity of port; this is not to say, however, that the Corfu town economy stagnated altogether.[71] Nevertheless Semo's rejection of commercial rivalry between Jewish and Christian merchants should not be accepted unquestioningly. As the port of Corfu declined in importance during the last quarter of the nineteenth century, commercial activity diminished to the detriment of all, especially to the merchants involved in the grain trade. Traditionally throughout the nineteenth century these merchants were Christians. The persistence or re-emergence of olive oil as the island's principal export business (which was traditionally in the hands of Jewish merchants), as opposed to the grain trade, and the decline of Corfu as a port for conveying goods to the neighbouring markets, particularly Epirus, was a catalyst for the local economic depression. Contemporaries were aware of the 'real economic crisis in our place, the once affluent Corfu', and of the fact that 'it is impossible that the condition of the poor labourer will become any worse'.[72] The absence of industry that could revive the port-related prosperity of previous decades and the hoarding of existing wealth seem to have been two characteristics of the Corfu economy during the period. Similarly, according to one of the most important Greek economists, A. Andreadis, a Corfiote himself:

> The loss of the trade of Epirus which was once carried through Corfu and which is now, thanks to new steamer lines, carried directly, mainly through the ports of Santi-Quaranta, Parga and Preveza.[73] And secondly the crisis in the wine industry. Corfiote wine was exported to France and Italy; both those markets are now closed owing to the adoption of protective tariffs.[74]

Andreadis related the decline of Corfu to external economic developments, from which Corfu could not emerge unscathed. His letter to *The Times* was a response to a report in which the correspondent emphasised the absence of industry (apart from a few factories) and, with remarkable foresight, predicted the economic take off of the island during the second half of the twentieth century.[75]

It is also important to note that by 1891 most Corfu merchants were involved in local politics, whereas the political class of members of parliament, even one Prime Minister, Theotokis, continued to belong to the land-owning class. Therefore tensions among traders were likely to be expressed in the sphere of politics as well as that of business. The political equality that the British tried to maintain by basing the criteria for the franchise primarily on religion (as well as on income), while providing the business environment for the entrepreneurial Jews to prosper and work in the port economy, could not be sustained under the Greek state despite the granting of citizenship to all, regardless of religion. Unlike France, for example, where Jews and especially the Rothschilds were considered to be undermining the foundations of French society by aiding what anti-semitic press called 'a Semitic invasion',[76] in Corfu, symbiosis was possible and had been achieved, however tenuously, for centuries. After all, Corfu was part of the recently established and still weak and fragile but ambitious Greek kingdom, and a town that had experienced the influence of British rule, with liberal institutions introduced years earlier than anywhere else in Greece. Corfu town was also characterised by a well-established bourgeoisie that by the 1890s had asserted its hegemony over the decaying 'nobility'. Yet none of this seemed to matter in 1891.

Conclusion

The old established presence of Jews in Corfu town and the changes in their status under the different regimes through the ages makes the history of this community quite exceptional. The Jewish presence and role in the port economy was always vibrant and despite the limitations in the ownership of property, or perhaps because of them, Jewish merchants had managed since the Venetian years to dominate the olive oil trade. During the period of British rule, they expanded their business opportunities without becoming the dominant business elite, as contemporaries often asserted. To contest such claims, and in an attempt to expand the concept of 'port Jews', this investigation of the Jewish occupational structure has demonstrated the very significant participation of the Jewish population in the port economy, not only in its commercial sector but also and to a greater degree in the port's vital labour force, such as porters. Tailors and pedlars were the two more common occupations of the Jews of Corfu in the mid-nineteenth century. The prosperity of Corfu as the commercial centre of the Ionian State, under British protection from 1815 to 1864, provided a safe environment and business opportunities for entrepreneurial Jews. However, this participation in the port's economy did not take place in a climate of cooperation with the rest of the commercial world and business rivalry can be discerned during the period of British rule. Both during this period and also during the period of Venetian rule, Corfu as a peripheral maritime centre did form an environment that advanced the position of Jews in comparison with other places in Europe. For this reason, perhaps, it continued to attract Jews from places where they had been persecuted. The union of the Ionian Islands with Greece in 1864 meant the inclusion of Jews in the Greek polity with equal rights. This was an opportunity that some of the Jews of Corfu embraced, especially since they formed a very substantial part of the population and were already an organic element of the business world. Yet, instead of this becoming an opportunity for the further advancement of the Jewish population and greater integration, anti-semitism assumed more organised forms than the popular superstition expressed in judeophobic manifestations during the Holy Week. The decline of the port of Corfu, due to external economic developments, towards the end of the century coincided with the rise of Greek nationalism. The late nineteenth century was for Greece, as for the rest of Europe, the period during which anti-semitism acquired its modern characteristics. In Greece and in Corfu in particular, this resulted in the first persecution of Jews in 1891 and the displacement of more than half of the Jewish population. When the port lost its cosmopolitanism to an excluding Greek state and to a society intolerant of its multi-religious environment, things for the Jews of Corfu could only get worse. The port of Corfu and its historical development through the transition from a cosmopolitan port during the first half of the nineteenth century to a peripheral one towards the end of the century was decisive for the history of the port Jews of Corfu. Amidst these changes Jews tried to adapt and exploit the opportunities offered first due to the economic development and later due to their equal rights of citizenship. However, when combined, the forces of nationalism and anti-semitism impeded any process of integration between Christians and Jews and a great opportunity of acculturation was irreparably lost.

NOTES

1. David Sorkin, 'The Port Jew: Notes Towards a Social Type', *Journal of Jewish Studies* 50.1 (1999), 87–97; Lois Dubin, *The Port Jews of Hapsburg Trieste: Absolutist Politics and Enlightenment Culture* (Stanford, CA: Stanford University Press, 1999).
2. Lois Dubin, 'Researching Port Jews and Port Jewries', in David Cesarani (ed.), *Port Jews: Jewish Communities in Cosmopolitan Maritime Trading Centres, 1550–1950* (London: Frank Cass 2002) p.48.
3. Paul Demont, 'The Social Structure of the Jewish Community of Salonika at the End of the Nineteenth Century', *South-Eastern Europe* 5.2 (1979); A.D. Meyers, 'Ethnic Distinctions and Wealth among Colonial Jamaican Merchants, 1685–1716', *Social Science History* 22.1 (1998), pp.47–81; and especially Mark Levene, 'Port Jewry of Salonika: Between Neo-colonialism and Nation-state', in Cesarani (see note 2), p.127.
4. According to Psallidas, these were the minority, although the justification is rather inchoate. Psallidas categorises Jews together with the Roman Catholics since both were considered to be foreigners: 'In the aftermath of the Ionian Islands' cession to Greece in 1864, most of them had not acquired Greek citizenship for a number of (mainly subjective) reasons'; Gregoris Psallidas, 'Social Solidarity on the Periphery of the Greek Kingdom: The Case of the Workers' Fraternity of Corfu', in Philipp Carabott (ed.), *Greek Society in the Making, 1863–1913* (London: Ashgate, 1997), p.24.
5. These accounts are P.L. Preschel, *The Jews of Corfu* (unpublished Ph.D. thesis, New York University, 1984); Kostas Dafnis, *Oi Israelites tis Kerkyras* [The Israelites of Corfu] (Corfu: n.p.,

1978); I. Romanos, 'H Evraiki Koinotis tis Kerkiras' [The Jewish Community of Corfu], in K. Dafnis (ed.), *Ioannou Roamanou Istorika Erga* (Corfu: n.p., 1957).

6. David Cesarani, 'Port Jews: Concepts, Cases and Questions', in Cesarani (see note 2), p.6.

7. It is characteristic that in the two more recent 'histories' of Modern Greece, references to Jews in Greece occupy a few lines only, mentioned in passim. These are the recently revised and widely acclaimed history of R. Clogg, *A Concise History of Greece* (Cambridge: Cambridge University Press, 2002); and T.H. Gallant, *Modern Greece* (London: Arnold, 2001).

8. George Andreopoulos, 'State and Irredentism: Some Reflections on the Case of Greece', *Historical Journal* 24.4 (1981), 949–59. As Andreopoulos rightly remarks, irredentism was an organic element of the policies of both political parties in the last quarter of the nineteenth century, despite the usually differentiated 'modernising' Trikoupis and 'populist' Deliyiannis.

9. Preschel (see note 5), p.14; Romanos (see note 5), p.387. They both cite the Jewish traveller Benjamin de Tudela and his visit to the island in 1147.

10. Ioannis Romanos, 'H Evraiki Koinotis tis Kerkiras' [The Jewish Community of Corfu], in Dafnis, *Ioannou Roamanou Istorika Erga* (see note 5), p.390. The destruction and sacrilege of burial grounds should be kept in mind as a recurring manifestation of anti-semitism.

11. It is interesting to note here that two of the major historians of Corfu and the Ionian islands, and perhaps the founders of the Ionian historiographical tradition, Marmora and Rodostamo, concealed the presence of Semo to the delegation, for their own anti-semitic reasons, according to Romanos (see note 5), p.391.

12. Proclamations such as the above led to delegations of the principals of the Jewish community to Venice, who only two years later in 1408 managed to secure the ownership of land up to a certain sum of money, purchase of bread, food and vegetables from the market and penalties for harming or insulting Jews.

13. Cecil Roth, *The History of the Jews of Italy* (Philadelphia, PA: Jewish Publication Society of America, 1946), p.287.

14. Preschel (see note 5), p.22. It should be noted that many Jews from Spain passed first through Naples, from where they were expelled by the French in the first half of the sixteenth century. The two communities of the town, Romaniotes and Spanish-Apulian, have a long history of friction. The Romaniotes felt threatened by the newcomers and asked for the protection of their position in the town from the Doge in Venice. The two communities came to peace and reconciliation by 1664, when they were given equal status by the Venetian authorities.

15. Romanos (see note 5), p.393.

16. Until the fifteenth century the town was confined to the ancient fortress on the citadel. Population rise led to the expansion of the town boundaries outside the fortress, where the majority of the Jews begun to settle. The dispersion of Jewish houses among the Christian population, argues Romanos, 'scandalised' the Christians and the long process of achieving a segregation decree from the Venetian rulers began; ibid., p.400.

17. Preschel (see note 5), p.25.

18. Since the sixteenth century there is evidence on the active role of several Jewish inhabitants in commerce and banking. This was the basic argument to prevent an expulsion in 1572, phrased in a petition to the Doge, following the decision of the Senate to expel the Jews of Venice. The demand was heard and the Jews of Corfu were exempted; ibid., p.33.

19. Ibid., p.46.

20. Aliki Nikiforou, *Dimosies Teletes stin Kerkira kata tin periodo tis Venetikis Kyriarxias* [Public Ceremonies in Corfu during the Period of Venetian Rule] (Athens: Themelio, 1999), p.137.

21. Dan Cohn-Sherbok, *Anti-semitism: A History* (Stroud: Sutton, 2002), p.182.

22. Viscount Kirkwall, *Four Years in the Ionian Islands*, vol.1 (London 1864), pp.46–7.

23. David Sorkin, 'Port Jews and the Three Regions of Emancipation', in Cesarani (see note 2), p.35.

24. Henry Jervis White, *History of the Island of Corfu* (London, 1852), p.261.

25. Albert Mousson, *Ein Besuch auf Korfu und Cefalonien im September 1858* (Greek translation) (Athens: Istoritis, 1995), pp.55, 56, 62, 63 and 70.

26. http://www.jewish-history.com/Occident/volume3/nov1845/news.html#Corfu.

27. Research on social stratification and the role of Jews in a port economy through the examination of probate inventories has been conducted in another setting and for an earlier period; Meyers (see note 3).

28. Michalis Chouliarakis, *Geografiki, Dioikitiki kai Plithismiaki Ekseliksis tis Ellados, 1821–1971* [Geographical, Administrative and Population Development of Greece] (Athens: EKKE, 1973), vol.A, part I, p.163.

29. Census 1853, Executive Police Documents, 1719, 1/91, Istoriko Arxeio Kerkyras [Corfu Historical Archive] (hereafter IAK).

30. Typaldos Pretenteris, *Peri tis en Kerkira choleras kata to 1855* [On the Corfu Cholera of 1855] (Corfu: Corfu Printing Office, 1856), p.8.

31. Mousson (see note 25), p.56

32. Kirkwall (see note 22), p.52.

33. The occupational classification of the Jews of Corfu is part of the research on the urban social classes in Corfu under British rule. The source quantified and examined for this purpose is the 1865 Electoral List, devised for the registration of all voters above 21 after the union of the islands with Greece. According to the constitution of 1864, universal male franchise was introduced and all the electors had to be registered. The list, to be found in the Corfu Historical Archive, contains surname, name, patronymic, age and occupation. 3,465 persons are registered, far less of course than the male population of Corfu at the time.

34. For the use of occupations in historical research, see Robert J. Morris, 'Qualitative to Quantitative By Way of Coding and Nominal Record Linkage: The Search for the British Middle Class', *History and Computing* 11.1–2 (1999), 9–30; Matthew Woolard, 'The Classification of Occupations in the 1881 Census of England and Wales', *History and Computing* 10.1–3 (1998), 17–36; D.R. Mills and K. Schurer, 'Employment and Occupations', in Dennis Mills and Kevin Schurer (eds.), *Local Communities in the Victorian Census Enumerators Books* (Leigh-on-Sea, Essex: Progressive Printing, 1996); Robert J. Morris, 'Occupational Coding: Principles and Examples', *Historical Social Research* 15 (1991), 3–29.

35. The second district is the one of primary interest. In this district, near the port of the town, belongs the Jewish quarter, one of the most populated districts of the town during the nineteenth century. Of those recorded in the second district (1,600), 709 or 45 per cent were Jews. Only 39 Jewish names were recorded in the first district out of 603, or 6.5 per cent and none in the third. These numbers show the concentration of the Jewish population in the second district, basically the Jewish quarter and the areas on the western part of the town. For those reasons the Jewish occupations appearing in the second district *only* have been classified.

36. Dennis and Joan Mills, 'Occupation and Social Stratification revisited', *Urban History Yearbook* (Leicester: Leicester University Press, 1989), p.64.

37. See for instance the account of post-union Corfu written by the MP Romeos in 1867; cited in G. Chytiris, *Corfu in the Mid-Nineteenth Century* (Corfu: Etaireia Kerkiraikon Spoudon, 1988), p.57.

38. Cecil Roth, 'The Economic History of the Jews', *Economic History Review* 14.1 (1961), pp.131–5.

39. G. Moore, 'Socio-Economic Aspects of Anti-semitism in Ireland, 1880–1905', *Economic and Social Review* 12.3 (1981), pp.187–201.

40. Mark Levene (see note 3), p.128.

41. Ionian Islands Government Gazette (hereafter IIGG), No.491, 15–27 October 1860, and No.598, 1–13 September 1862.

42. Pedlars, for example, would not have been recorded since merchants were required to keep books properly, otherwise they were liable to insolvency and fraudulent bankruptcy if their business failed.

43. Petition 149, Register of Petitions 1856, CO 136/1050, National Archives (formerly Public Record Office), London (hereafter NA).

44. Petition 400, 8 December 1857, CO 136/857, NA.

45. Dubin (see note 1), p.34.

46. IIGG, No.338, 15–27 February 1858.

47. IIGG, No.44, 18–30 October 1852, and 3–15 March 1851.

48. Preschel (see note 5), pp.61–70.

49. This issue involved the disappearance of feudal relations of property which had been abolished in paper but not in practice during the period of British rule, and continued to subject the peasants-sharecroppers to perpetual indebtedness to landlords and merchants.

50. Political speech to the Jewish Community, Dafnis Documents, 14, IAK.

51. Christos Hadziiossif, 'Class Structure and Class Antagonism in Late Nineteenth-Century Greece', in Carabott (see note 4), p.4.

52. Psallidas (see note 4), pp.19–33.

53. Ibid., p.30.

54. Dafnis, *The Israelites of Corfu* (see note 5), p.29.

55. Ibid., p.18–20.

56. Jacob Barnai, 'Blood Libels in the Ottoman Empire of the Fifteenth to Nineteenth Centuries', in Shmuel Almog (ed.), *Antisemitism Through the Ages* (Oxford: Pergamon Press, 1988), pp.189–94.

57. Dafnis, *The Israelites of Corfu* (see note 5), p.21.

58. Preschel (see note 5), p.91.

59. 3706, Documents on the murder of Rubbina Sarda, Rading Society, Corfu.

60. 3732, Documents on the murder of Rubbina Sarda, Rading Society, Corfu.

61. The international dimensions of the issue went to such extremes that the Greek Minister in London was compelled to write to *The Times*, on 26 May. There is a considerable attempt to play down the events in Corfu as 'less than eight years ago we stood aghast at the horrors of Tisza-Eszlar in Hungary, before which the occurrences at Corfu pale into insignificance'. He then goes on to attribute the anti-semitic riots to an old established tradition during the years of Venetian rule 'that is not wholly extinct', and praised his government that 'took from the very outset the most stringent measures for the repression of the disorders'. He cites at the end the expression of gratitude by members of the Israelites community towards the Greek authorities for the handling of the situation, which reads more like a statement of appreciation for the fact that matters did not get any worse for the Jews of Corfu. *The Times*, 26 May 1891, p.13, c.b.

62. I would like here to thank Tulia Catalan for the very useful information she provided me with on the settlement of approximately 1,000 Jews in Trieste. They subsequently formed the core of the Jewish Triestine community.

63. 3741, Documents on the murder of Rubbina Sarda, Rading Society, Corfu.

64. Newspaper *Tolmiros*, No.18, 15 July 1885.

65. Dafnis, however, makes extensive use of an interview he gave during the events, revealing his vitriolic views against the Jewish population as a whole; Dafnis (see note 5), pp.23–4.

66. However, this was not true anyway, because Roman Catholics in Corfu, as well as in other Greek towns, maintained their religious autonomy after the establishment of the Greek state.

67. Jacob Katz, *From Prejudice to Destruction* (Cambridge, MA: Harvard University Press, 1980), p.94.

68. Newspaper *Tolmiros* (see note 65).

69. Dafnis (see note 5), p.23.

70. Ibid., p.24.

71. The number of light manufacture industry from the 1860s and 1870s onwards as well as the small working class under formation at the time, as a result of this extremely limited industrialisation, and the increase of the population of Corfu town indicate that the decline took place over a number of decades. Here, though, the emphasis is primarily on commercial activities associated with the port's exporting business. For the embryonic Corfu industry, see Christina Agriantoni, *Oi Aparxes tis Ekviomixanisis stin Ellada ton 19o aiona* [The Beginnings of Industrialisation in Greece in the Nineteenth Century] (Athens: Emporiki Trapeza tis Ellados, 1986), pp.120, 126–7, 138, 149 and passim.

72. Newspaper *Epoptis*, No.616, 16 May 1888.

73. Ports in the opposite mainland.

74. *The Times*, 9 September 1905, p.13, c.b.

75. 'No productive industry exists in Corfu. In the circumstances the inhabitants have based all their hopes on the possibility of attracting foreign tourists. Some foreigners recently begun to build a game house, but the works have been stopped in consequence of the discouraging attitude of the Greek Government. Negotiations are now going on between the Austrian agent and some foreign capitalists who are disposed to buy the palace built at Gastouri by the late Empress Elizabeth and transform it into a sanatorium'; *The Times*, 23 August 1905, p.10, c.f.

76. David Vital, *A People Apart: The Jews in Europe 1789–1939* (New York: Oxford University Press, 1999), p.317.

The Port Jews of Libau, 1880–1914

NICHOLAS J. EVANS

Within the field of Jewish historiography there are many studies of life in nineteenth century Russia, the journey west undertaken by hundreds of thousands of Jews during the reign of the last two Tsars of Imperial Russia, and the eventual settlement of Ashkenazi Jews in western Europe and the Atlantic basin.[1] Yet despite the scale and depth of these assessments little attention has been paid to the contribution of Libau (the modern day port of Liepāja) in the development of a distinctive port Jewish community in the Russian Baltic. In Libau Jewish merchants worked alongside their non-Jewish counterparts. The port itself was a major entrepôt for emigrants fleeing the ordeals of life 'in the Pale'. Yet despite anti-semitic pressures, Libau's Ashkenazi Jewish community had, by the time of the 1897 census, grown to become the second largest port Jewish community in the Baltic region and the town's great synagogue would dominate the skyline as much as the Russian Orthodox Church. The Jewish presence in this Baltic port was thus real and visible, sizeable and influential.

This essay aims to explore how a study of Jewish merchants operating in Libau and other Baltic ports can contribute to the evolution of the port Jewish concept.[2] Did the port Jew 'concept' apply to collective economic influence as much as the concentration of great wealth in the hands of a few port-based 'court Jews'? Could the fluidity of a port's mercantile community further port Jewish influence beyond the maritime region in which it was situated? Can the concept of port Jewry be applied to a port whose Jewish residents were predominantly of working-class or mercantile status? Having outlined the problems faced by Libau's Jewish community under the control of Imperial Russia, attention will then be afforded to the scale and patterns of Jewish emigration from the port and the ramifications that this 'trade' would have upon port Jewish identity in those western ports to where so many Ashkenazi Jews were destined between 1881 and the outbreak of the First World War in 1914. Were the gains made by port Jews in important centres of Jewish settlement in the West undermined by the arrival of their poorer co-religionists from smaller Baltic communities epitomised by Libau? Did anti-Jewish sentiment in Europe and America in the opening decade of the twentieth century owe its origins to their poorer co-religionists that had arrived directly from a port under Imperial Russia's control?

The Rights of the Jews in Courland within the Russian Empire

When the partition of the kingdom of Poland began in 1772, Imperial Russia found herself in control of the largest concentration of Jews in Europe. Though most lived in what became defined as the Pale of Settlement, the westward expansion of Russia meant that, by the time of Nicholas II's accession, there were sizeable Jewish communities in Russia's vibrant maritime centres at St Petersburg, Riga, Jacobstadt and Libau. Each port lay within a different province of Imperial Russia and commercial rivalry between them was rife. Each had an active Jewish mercantile community and as debate raged as to the rights to be given to Jews living in both urban and rural areas throughout Russia, so the influence that Jews exercised in maritime life was similarly questioned. Though life in the Pale was growing increasingly intolerable, the economic strength that port Jewish commerce represented in other parts of Russia was so important that Jews who worked in Riga were granted greater freedom of mobility to trade there so that other rival ports, where they were less constrained, would not disturb the predominance of Russia's second largest port. As Herman Rosenthal (in *The Jewish Encyclopaedia*) noted, regarding the notion in the eighteenth century that Friedrichstadt (a port within the state of Courland) could eclipse the larger port of Riga if economic freedoms were not granted to Jewish merchants who traded in the port:

> The edict of Empress Elisabeth (1742) expelling the Jews from Russia interfered considerably with this business [of moving goods such as flax, grain, lumber and other Russian goods to merchants based in Riga]. The Council of Riga, fearing that the Jewish merchants might direct their trade to Windau, Libau and Königsberg, petitioned the Senate in the matter, and, pending the resolution of the Senate, the vice-governor of Livonia stopped the Jewish traders in Friedrichstadt.[3]

These privileges not only increased the economic opportunities available to Jewish merchants working within Livonia and Courland, but they also helped Riga's Jewish population to grow from just over 500 in 1824 to 21,963 by 1897 to the detriment of ports such as Friedrichstadt (whose Jewish population was only 3,800 at the time of the 1897 census). Even though many Jews were expelled from St Petersburg, Riga and Libau in the early 1890s, Riga's role as the main port Jewish community in the Baltic continued to grow as one of Russia's largest ports expanded throughout the nineteenth century, helped by the rights awarded to her Jewish merchants in the mid-eighteenth century.

Though the rights of Jews in neighbouring Courland would vary enormously in the eighteenth and nineteenth centuries, the communal and economic strength of the port Jews working in the port of Libau continued to grow as the port expanded.[4] Situated in the eastern Baltic between Riga and

Danzig, it lay within the province of Courland and came under the administrative control of Mitau, the provincial capital.[5] Though Courland bordered the northern extremities of the Pale of Settlement, and despite being under the rule of Russia since 1795, those living within the duchy retained more religious and economic freedom than their less fortunate co-religionists living in neighbouring Kovno. As Simon Dubnov noted regarding the rights of those living in this region:

> The brief reign of Paul I (1796–1801) added nothing of moment to the Russian legislation concerning the Jews. The law imposing a double tax was confirmed, and also the other restrictions were left in force. The newly acquired Government of Courland, on the outskirts of the Empire, increased the area of Jewish settlement. In this Duchy, which was annexed in 1795, there were several thousand Jewish inhabitants, who had been 'tolerated' as foreigners, after the German pattern, and had only partly succeeded in forming a communal organization. The question now arose as to the best way of collecting the taxes from the itinerant chapmen who formed the bulk of the Jewish population, and were enrolled neither among the rural nor the urban estates, and were not even affiliated with Jewish communities. The Russian Government solved this question in 1799, by placing the Jews of Courland in the same position as their coreligionists in the other western Governments, and by granting them the right of enrolling themselves among the mercantile or burgher estates, as well as establishing their own *Kahals*. In this case fiscal considerations were responsible for the organization of the Jewish masses in the dominion of the German barons.[6]

Though they suffered discrimination because of their faith, the Jews of Courland were still free to participate in the commerce of the land, because of their commercial acumen and because of the revenues generated through the taxes imposed upon them.[7] Under successive Imperial Russian edicts, they faced increased threats to the rights they had enjoyed under the protection of the nobility prior to 1795. But such incursions upon their rights were often challenged, not by the Dukes of Courland, but by their noble subordinates who recognised the important contribution that Jewish merchants made to Baltic commerce, and their own revenues, as the port developed.

The Development of Libau's Port Jewish Community

The port of Libau, unlike the neighbouring ports of Riga and St Petersburg, did not 'close' each winter when the ice closed much of the Baltic to navigation.[8] This geographic factor was one of the main reasons why investment in the port's development took place during the period 1880 to

1914. Investment transformed the port from that described by Brian Hoyle as a primitive port/city into that of an expanding port/city.[9] The maritime opportunities that the locality presented to the port's merchants were significantly boosted in 1880 with the opening of the railway link from Romny (near Poltava in modern-day Ukraine) to Libau. The line ran through some of the most populous areas of the Pale including Gomel, Minsk and Vilna. Commercially it connected the Baltic port of Libau with urban districts in the Pale of Settlement, the agrarian regions of Russia and the important railway line that carried freight between Kiev and Moscow. By 1880 the port was equipped with an integrated transport system that rivalled its neighbouring Baltic ports. It was connected with urban and agricultural regions, which produced commodities that could be exported. The port Jews situated in this expanding maritime centre were free to take advantage of the opportunities with which Hoyle notes expanding port cities of the time were presented.

> In the expanding port cities of the nineteenth century, rapid commercial and industrial development induced major changes in traditional port-city inter-relationships. Old harbours were overcrowded, new quays and basins were constructed ... and port growth was paralleled by industrial and urban expansion.[10]

As the port grew, so its Jewish presence was maintained as economic opportunities made the port a magnet for internal economic migrants and merchants living in the Pale.[11] The Jewish community of Libau, though between 43 and 47 per cent smaller in size (in 1881 and 1897) than that of the neighbouring port of Riga, grew rapidly throughout the nineteenth century. It rose, according to Dov Levin, from 19 in 1795, to 1,218 in 1850, 1,700 in 1863, 6,651 in 1881, 9,454 in 1897, 10,398 in 1911 and 7,163 in 1915. The Jewish population of Courland expanded from 9,000 in 1835 to 49,102 in 1897.[12] As the port expanded after 1880, the Jewish merchants and their gentile neighbours would profit equally. Some Jews grew wealthy, many prosperous, and even the poorest were educated.

The Jews living or working in Libau during the period in question may not have been as free and enlightened as some of their predecessors. They did not champion or sponsor *haskalah* (enlightenment). But their status as subjects was, at least after 1893, stable. They were free to trade and achieved a degree of cultural assimilation with their gentile neighbours that distinguished them from their Yiddish-speaking co-religionists in the Pale. An emigrant who lived at the nearby town of Talsen recalled his own middle-class Jewish upbringing in Courland:

> We did not know a word of Russian, we spoke German because it had once belonged to Germany, my mother went to a German school, we all

spoke German ... [the] middle class[es] went to German schools, to my mother we spoke in German, not in Yiddish.[13]

But though this German influence was stronger in Courland than in other Baltic port Jewish communities, its educational institutions in Libau still included a government school for Jews, a Jewish general school for girls and a Talmud Torah. Prior to 1893 the port even had its own Rabbinical School that was influential throughout the Ashkenazi world.

Despite the continued emigration of so many of its Jews and the forced movement of part of its community in 1892, the natural fecundity of the Jews of Libau ensured that the port retained its status as the second largest port Jewish community in the Baltic in the 1897 census.[14] The Jewish community thus reflected the city's physical presence in the Baltic and mirrored that of other port Jewish communities of the period. The Jews of Courland, and Libau in particular, thus embodied the processes and identity formation that Louis Dubin and David Sorkin have associated with the Sephardi port Jews of Trieste. The Jews of Libau may not have been patronised by monarchs in the way that those of Trieste, London or Amsterdam were, but they certainly gained economic freedoms from the successive absolutist monarchs and their ducal lieutenants who governed the duchy.[15] Though they lost their rabbinical school under edicts of Tsar Alexander III (in 1893), it has to be remembered that the port had no such institutions for much of the time before Russia partitioned the Kingdom of Poland.[16]

Libau's contribution towards Jewish culture – namely the constant cycle of foreign-born rabbis and other influential men from the port who subsequently settled in other port cities – offers an example of the port's own form of religious enlightenment. Though not as visionary nor as enlightened as contemporaries writing in other more influential port cities, such as Hamburg or Trieste, Courland was noted by some nineteenth-century historians as enjoying close rabbinical links to those such as the Mendelssohns and Mordecai Aaron Ginzburg (1796–1846), described by Simon Dubnov as one of the founders of Neo-Hebraic literary style who lived 'for some time' in Courland.[17] Though many of the most influential rabbis would be forced to leave Libau following the Regulations on Passports issued in 1890, which permitted only Jews whose families were registered in the census of 13 April 1835 to remain in the port, the influence they exacted upon Jewish identity in the West would spread as these Ashkenazi Jews established new centres of scholarship in the West.[18] In this way, Dubin's theory that port Jews created opportunities for Jewish culture to develop was as applicable to the Ashkenazi Jews of Baltic Russia as it was to those of the Adriatic. But as with the Jews of Trieste, the Jews of Libau were only presented with such opportunity and 'freedom' because of the contribution they made to Baltic maritime commerce.

The Economic Contribution of Baltic Jewry

As with port Jews in other western cities, the granting of certain freedoms and rights was mirrored by the ability of governing regimes to tax Jews heavily. Jews were also denied many of the rights of their gentile colleagues, such as the right for their children to play on the Libau sands. Many recently arrived Jews were expelled from Libau in 1893. Despite all this, the contribution that Jews made to Baltic trade was both valued and encouraged. Foreign agents vying for a share of Russia's exported commodities of ponies, butter, eggs, timber, grain and third-class emigrants saw in the Jews of Libau the means to control and profit from the export of the Imperial Russia's agrarian produce. As the port reached what Hoyle styled the second stage in the evolution of port city inter-relationships, so its port Jewish population expanded to ever-greater heights. By the time of the visit of Major William Evans-Gordon, the MP for Stepney in London in 1902, the Jewish merchants controlled a large proportion of the export trade of perishable commodities.

> The commercial harbour is convenient, and is being much improved. A very large export trade is carried on from here in the produce of the country – grain, wood, eggs, etc. – and this is entirely in the hands of Jewish merchants.[19]

The influence of these port Jews was not just confined to their locality. Whether based in Libau, Riga or even St Petersburg, the Port Jews of the Baltic often had smaller offices, branches or sub-agents based in other Baltic or North Sea ports. Whether they remained or departed Russia's Baltic ports in the wake of the anti-semitic measures introduced during the early 1890s, the networks that they had established would continue to develop in Russia's northern ports, and those port cities to which they had emigrated.

Nathan Schapiro, who ran a business that exported Russian ponies to the coalfields of northern England and to the London Omnibus Company, typified the port Jew of the period.[20] Schapiro emigrated to England with his family in 1866, and settled in Doncaster, a town situated on the edge of the Yorkshire coalfields, around 1876. Though living in Britain he had relatives in the ports of Riga and Hamburg, commercial associates in Hull and a business based in Doncaster. He, his port Jewish relatives and the network of horse dealers that they knew throughout Russia then arranged for ponies to be transported from the Russian interior to the port city interface, where the Wilson Line of Hull (who provided the scheduled steamships needed to export livestock, emigrants and perishable produce between the Baltic ports of St Petersburg, Riga, Libau, Windau, Stettin and Copenhagen) then transported these goods to the British ports of Hull and London. From these British ports, the ponies were then transported to the coalfield or transport depot – with all the profit from the export being retained by the Jewish merchant. The links established between Jewish merchants who exported ponies, horses, eggs, grain and butter, and the company that conveyed the goods was imperative to the long-term success of both agent and ship-owner alike. Business associations in this sphere often passed from generation to generation. When Schapiro died he wished to be buried 'back home'. Yet his children and grandchildren continued to live in the western cities where they had established themselves.

Through serving as brokers, the Jews of Libau, like the Schapiros at Riga, gained an important niche in an expanding export market. Throughout the period between 1880 and 1914, as exports of horses, butter and timber grew, so the contribution they made to port-based commerce expanded – at the same time as their rights as citizens declined.[21] As Table 1 demonstrates, the import of timber, horses and what Gordon Jackson referred to as the 'breakfast trades' were as important to Britain as the products imported from the British Empire.[22]

TABLE 1
THE SCALE OF SPECIFIC IMPORTS TO BRITISH PORTS
FROM RUSSIAN BALTIC PORTS, 1894–1905[23]

Year	Number of Aliens	Number of Horses	Tons of Grain	Number of Eggs	Loads of Timber
1894	4,706	3,653	11,900,832	1,367,559	1,989,455
1895	3,595	2,427	12,841,040	2,215,280	1,935,445
1896	3,353	3,198	11,926,500	2,403,779	2,156,717
1897	5,805	5,662	10,087,880	3,132,333	2,304,977
1898	2,749	5,413	6,758,020(*)	3,645,903	2,174,552
1899	4,453	7,198	5,046,900(*)	4,318,601	2,220,327
1900	8,185	11,779	12,091,970	4,024,712	2,365,645
1901	7,562	10,754	13,365,540	4,492,110	2,390,957
1902	12,479	11,430	8,696,915	5,338,757	2,581,616
1903	11,391	12,801	9,172,644	6,802,773	2,795,353
1904	13,951	2,811	9,655,680	7,032,906	2,855,286
1905	15,086	2,535	11,179,933	7,621,793	2,885,044
Total	93,315	79,661	122,723,854	52,396,506	28,655,374

Source: British Parliamentary Papers (BPP), *Annual Statements of Trade and Navigation* (1894–1905); and BPP, *Statistical Tables Relating to Emigration and Immigration from and into the United Kingdom* (1894–1905).

Notes: The quantity of goods imported included all emanating from Russia's northern ports. 'Horses' included ponies. The term 'Grain' included wheat, barley, oats, rye and buckwheat. 'Timber' included only wood that was hewn, sawn or split, and staves of all dimensions. The rate of aliens arriving in Britain only included those emanating from the port of Libau. Few were ever recorded as leaving from Windau, Riga or St Petersburg. (*) Decreases affected by crop failures.

TABLE 2
THE VALUE OF SPECIFIC IMPORTS TO BRITISH PORTS
FROM RUSSIAN BALTIC PORTS (IN POUNDS STERLING), 1894–1905

Year	Horses	Grain	Eggs	Timber	Percentage of Total Imports from the Russian Baltic
1894	34,686	3,055,053	383,039	3,912,140	61
1895	27,104	3,058,735	596,652	3,665,595	56
1896	33,445	2,985,778	629,101	4,339,444	59
1897	54,589	3,140,300	812,297	4,961,092	59
1898	54,544	2,410,847(*)	966,129	4,714,087	59
1899	73,067	1,382,676(*)	1,183,031	5,030,744	58
1900	116,056	3,245,187	1,109,553	6,143,194	65
1901	107,445	3,848,668	1,207,474	5,520,757	64
1902	114,842	2,797,414	1,509,699	6,086,720	62
1903	134,554	2,461,109	1,866,421	6,512,322	59
1904	29,399(**)	2,956,266	2,042,520	6,221,289	64
1905	27,599(**)	3,228,765	2,425,809	6,297,899	61
Total	807,330	34,570,798	14,731,725	63,405,283	61

Source: BPP, *Annual Statements of Trade and Navigation* (1894–1905).

Notes: The value of goods imported included all emanating from Russia's northern ports. 'Horses' included ponies. The term 'Grain' included wheat, barley, oats, rye and buckwheat. 'Timber' included only wood that was hewn, sawn or split, and staves of all dimensions. (*) Decreases affected by crop failures. (**) Decrease affected by Russo-Japanese War.

The important role that the Jews of the Russian Baltic ports played in this trade cannot be overestimated. As Table 2 indicates, the percentage (in value) of the exported products known to be almost entirely in the hands of Jewish merchants represented between 56 and 65 per cent of all imports arriving into Britain from Russia's northern ports, totalling between three and five million pounds each year. The role they played was visible both on the dockside in Libau and through the official correspondence of the British and US governments.[24] Such figures do not even include goods exported to other trading nations such as Denmark, Germany and France.

Though the trade controlled by Libau's Jewish merchants was less than that at the nearby port of Riga, Libau's role as a conduit of emigrants – Finns, Slavs, Russians, Poles and Jews – inflated her importance beyond that of neighbouring Riga and other Baltic port Jewish communities. Because of the emergence of the port as an outlet for mass migration in the early 1890s, Libau's resident Jewish community acquired importance and developed an identity independently of the role it played in the export of agrarian produce. This 'market' in the movement of humans transformed Libau into one of the world's leading centres for westward migration, providing Libau's Jewish merchants with the opportunity to profit from a trade that was 'open' to them.

The Emigrant Business and the Role of Jewry

As in port cities in Germany, Britain, the United States and South Africa, the Jews of Libau profited from the business of emigration by acting as emigration agents, money exchangers and hoteliers. The so-called emigrant hotels that they ran in Libau varied in size and standard as they did in Hamburg, Hull, London, New York and Cape Town.[25] Though they welcomed gentiles as well as members of their own faith, as with the export of timber, horses and the 'breakfast trades', those who operated the hotels saturated a business opportunity that arose with the expansion of the maritime centre in which they lived. Emigration grew to become an important aspect of Baltic commerce. As Libau developed throughout the 1890s and 1900s as a centre for outward migration from Russia, so her Jews were increasingly important as facilitators of this trade.[26] As the United States Immigration Commission reported in 1910:

> All of the boarding houses [for emigration] visited were kept by Hebrews, but in no instance were the guests confined to any one race, and Poles, Hebrews, and Lithuanians were dwelling in apparent harmony under one roof, and in many instances in the same room.[27]

As the Jewish community grew in Libau, links with family, friends and business acquaintances in the Pale and through other maritime centres in which Jews had settled led to the expansion of exports through the Baltic ports of Libau, Riga and Windau.

The emigrant market had emerged by the mid-1890s as an important source of revenue for Jews situated in the ports of embarkation in Hamburg, Bremen, Liverpool and Southampton, as much as it was for those receiving immigrants in Hull, London, Cape Town or New York (to name but a few). Each of these ports saw large numbers of migrants passing through their transport systems and yet they also served as magnets to other Jews living in *shtetl* throughout the Russian interior. In order to reach such emigration centres the migrants travelled on the same transport routes as the commodities that were being exported to maritime entrepôts in the Baltic, Humber, Thames, Solent or Mersey. As demand to leave the Pale intensified after the Kishinev Pogrom, one trade – the emigrant trade – would grow the most. As the agent for the Wilson Line based in Riga messaged his Hull-based employers in 1904:

> It will also interest you to hear that just now a Mr. Freydberg of the firm of Karlsberg, Spiro and Co., Libau, who ship all their emigrants from Libau by the Forende steamers called and wanted to arrange with us to take emigrants by our weekly boat to Libau, and he also asked if we would take emigrants by our London Boats, as he was unable to deal with the whole lot of them in Libau.[28]

TABLE 3
THE NUMBER AND STATUS OF ALIENS ARRIVING IN BRITAIN FROM LIBAU, 1894–1905

Year of Arrival	Number of Aliens not described as en route to another country*	Number of Aliens described as en route to another country	Total number of Aliens recorded as arriving from Libau
1893	225	204	429
1894	671	4,035	4,706
1895	628	2,967	3,595
1896	1,787	1,566	3,353
1897	4,409	1,396	5,805
1898	2,013	736	2,749
1899	3,122	1,331	4,453
1900	5,226	2,959	8,185
1901	5,743	1,819	7,562
1902	6,941	5,538	12,479
1903	6,580	4,811	11,391
1904	7,656	6,295	13,951
1905	8,646	6,440	15,086
Total	53,647	40,097	93,744

Source: BPP, *Statistical Tables Relating to Emigration and Immigration from and into the United Kingdom* (1894–1905).

Notes: (*) Includes alien seamen. Many of those not described as en route to another destination subsequently re-migrated to America, Canada or South Africa within a short time of their arrival. Prior to 1906 the statistical returns made to Parliament failed to distinguish between the number of immigrants and transmigrants arriving via London.

The large number of Russian and Polish emigrants leaving through the port of Libau continued to grow at an alarming rate. Only when Libau was unable to facilitate all of the Jews that desired to emigrate would 'surplus' Jewish emigrants be sent through Riga (or to a lesser extent via the Finnish port of Hangö). As Table 3 demonstrates, Libau had emerged as an important source of continental embarkation to Britain by 1894. By 1904, as reported in British Parliamentary Papers, it was the second most important source of alien migrants to Britain.[29]

It was of no surprise that so many chose to emigrate via the port of Libau. The rail link that had opened between it and Romny in 1880 also linked the port with Kovno – the *gubernia* that exported more Jews to South Africa than any other region of the Pale – and other important sources of western immigrant origin. The opportunity to leave had now reached all those in the northern half of the Pale and the districts surrounding Libau. Jewish merchants gained from the improvements made to Russia's transport system as much as those wishing to leave. Though the journey could be lengthy (as the trains carried cargo and passengers) it did not include the crossing of an international border that necessitated interaction with border officials nor overland travel through alien lands. The Jews leaving via Libau were spared such encounters, as they did not have to converse in a language other than their native tongue. Jews situated in this Baltic port provided their food and lodgings in a port just 110 miles from Kovno. Though a passport was often required, the gendarmes policing access to the port were as open to bribery as those policing the German and Austrian land borders. Emigration through Libau similarly did not entail as rigorous a medical inspection as had been in place since 1895 on the German border and at German ports as officials representing western governments rarely policed access to the vessels moored in Libau's Winter Harbour and the Russian Imperial Government did not regulate the standards according to which emigrants were transported.

The Threat Libau Posed to Other Port Jewish Communities

Trade brought prosperity and entrepreneurial opportunities to the Jewish merchants operating in or from Baltic ports such as Libau. Though some prospered most of their co-religionists still lived in poor conditions. As with other port Jewish communities the expansion of the community reduced the growth in overall prosperity that buoyant trading conditions offered. In 1903 a British official visiting the Jews of Libau described them as being:

> Very similar to those … at St. Petersburg and Riga. There is a great deal of poverty among[st them], but the houses of the poor appeared excellent to one accustomed to the horrors of the East End [of London]. There is plenty of space and air, and rents are low.[30]

Life for many of those Jews living in Libau was thus very simple. Population increase, from 6,651 in 1881 to 10,398 in 1911, negated any real improvement that they had made in their standard of living. Often those who could leave did so. Even the poor living conditions in western ports where Jewish emigrants settled offered seemingly greater opportunity than the brutality of Imperial Russia and the comparative opportunities provided in Baltic port cities such as Libau. Yet conditions in the new areas of settlement were harsh. Some merchants like Hyman Schapiro's father may have returned home 'to die in their native homeland', while the poor immigrant in the East End of London often yearned for the simple life they had once enjoyed 'in their homeland'.[31] Such commentary on the repercussions of settling in a western port was also noted by those opposed to 'Russia's poor' settling in Britain's imperial capital. As newspapers such as the *Daily Mail* and the *Pall Mall Gazette* ran commentaries championing alien restriction, immigrants arriving in Britain from Libau provided scientific justification for their cause when vessels inspected by the Medical Officers of Health for the Port of London and Hull and Goole Port Sanitary Authorities were deemed unhygienic.[32]

The business of emigration via the port of Libau had grown significantly by the beginning of the twentieth century. Such was the demand that vessels unsuited to conveying passengers were increasingly chartered by foreign companies to meet the pressure for passage westward via a Baltic port, principally Libau. After a three to five day journey to Britain, these unsuitable conditions, chiefly the lack of necessary sanitary facilities, turned the ethnically diverse range of immigrants into a sanitation threat to Britain's port-based populations. Though diseases such as typhus, small pox and diarrhoea were as prevalent in urban Britain as they were in maritime centres, instances of pestilence in Hull, Grimsby, London and Southampton were increasingly blamed on the newly arrived alien. Though conditions could, and were, improved upon for inward-bound merchant ships, the association of the health threat with ethnic identity was to become automatic as far as the anti-semite was concerned.

Dr H. Williams (Port Medical Officer of Health for the Port of London Sanitary Authority) described those arriving from Libau in the evidence that he presented to the Royal Commission in 1903.

> Their clothing was dirty, and the smell was almost unbearable; it was such a smell that you would not like to travel in the same 'bus with these people; it was a peculiar smell – a smell that I have never been able quite to find anything to compare with; the nearest approach to a comparison is the smell of an acetylene lamp which has been blown out. It somewhat resembles that.[33]

The commencement of direct steamship services by the Russian American Line and the Russian Volunteer Fleet (both in 1906) between Libau and New York did not improve matters because the checks in place at Libau were far from adequate.[34] Though every steerage emigrant who embarked for the United States was supposed to undergo a medical inspection at the port of embarkation, as the US Immigration Commission lamented in its report in 1911:

> The American consular agent at Libau had practically no part in the examination of emigrants at the time of the committee's visit. At the examination witnessed by this official was represented at the dock by a clerk who could speak no English, and who mechanically placed the consular seal on every inspection card presented to him without even looking at the person to whom the card had been issued. The committee did not see the consular agent, but was informed that like his clerk, he could not speak English. It was stated that he never attended the embarkation of emigrants, and in fact only signed the ship's bill of health when it was sent to his house or office.[35]

Although the agents of the Russian American Line were penalised by the company for sending to Libau persons who are afflicted with certain diseases, such as typhus, small pox, scarlet fever and trachoma, the providers of direct services continued to send unsuitable immigrants on the transatlantic crossing. Between 1 September 1906 and 10 May 1908 of those emigrants sent by the Russian Volunteer Fleet from Libau a total of 654 emigrants were rejected.[36]

Even when their economic status and not just their physical condition was taken into account, during events like the Boer War, those emerging from the port of Libau were perceived by the receiving governments as a real threat. In the Boer conflict, the Prime Minister of South Africa intervened in the issue of alien immigration by limiting the arrival of those 'via Libau and London' to those of a more desirable class. In the debate over the issuance of passports and or permits to enter the Cape Colony, the Cape Government insisted that 'no difficulty should be placed in the way of the immigration into the Colony of a certain class viz:- British working men, clerks and shepherds, for whom there is great demand'.[37] It was evidently not the British immigrants that the Cape feared. Permits, introduced under the extension of martial law to the ports in September 1901, were to be used to limit 'that very considerable number of Foreigners, especially Polish Jews, [who] are applying for permit[s] to proceed to South Africa [via Libau]'.[38] Sir Henry H. Settle, the General Officer Commanding Cape Town, wrote to the British High Commissioner:

> Relating to the issue of permits at Libau to indigent Russian subjects and to state that indigent foreigners are beginning to arrive in large numbers. As these persons have permits they must be permitted to land but it would appear most desirable to prohibit the issue of permits to foreigners until all prisoners of war have been repatriated. If you concur, I would suggest that representations be made to the Imperial Government on the subject.[39]

The enforcement of the 1905 Aliens Act in Britain from January 1906 onwards reduced the inflow of poor Jewish immigrants to Britain via the port Jewish community at Libau. But, as the US Immigration Commission acknowledged, what ceased to be a problem for London and Hull continued to be an issue for the United States and Britain's Dominions. Despite protestations to the contrary by steamship operators Libau continued to defy the attempts of western governments to regulate the westward flow of Russia's poor.[40]

The passing of the 1906 British Merchant Shipping Act may have finally limited the ability of foreign merchant fleets to convey emigrants in diabolical conditions, but the damage had already been done. The business of emigration via the Baltic port, a business entirely in the hands of Jewish operators, had been used by anti-alien campaigners in Britain to introduce anti-alien, often perceived as anti-Jewish, legislation. The earnest desire by port Jews in Libau to profit had effectively removed from them the long-term opportunity to profit from the movement of their co-religionists. Libau's port Jewish community was not solely to blame. Its merchants had merely acted as they had always done, by maximising the opportunity for entrepreneurial gain in the short term before moving onward to other port Jewish communities in the West in the longer term. The difference with the trade in human cargo was that this aspect of the port Jews' business had declined significantly due to the failure of Jewish agents to curtail the inhumane aspect of the mass migration of people.

Conclusion

Though commented upon extensively in medical, commercial and parliamentary correspondence of the time, Libau's place in Jewish historiography has been largely consigned to oblivion because of the fluidity of her port Jewish community and the overshadowing influence that the larger port Jewish community of Riga would have upon written recollections of the Jews of the Baltic.

Yet Libau was of first-rank importance as an entrepôt for the export of goods such as timber, grain, eggs and butter that arose because of the expansion of the transport system within and without Imperial Russia. Though Jews were forcibly moved from some of Russia's Baltic ports throughout the eighteenth and nineteenth centuries, the freedoms enjoyed by the Baltic Jews of Courland continued to be allowed to Jews in Libau and Riga because their activities were so economically advantageous to an industrialising Russia. Jews within the Pale, in Libau itself and at her harbour profited from the movement of such goods. As the need to leave Russia intensified in the wake of the Kishinev pogrom and the deterioration of life in the Pale, Danish and British shipping lines that had for decades shipped commodities such as timber, eggs and ponies (brokered by Jewish agents) began to export Jews as a staple commodity. The availability of shipping from a port within the Russian Empire enabled many Jews from Libau, the Baltic and within the Pale itself to evade the intensive medical inspections that had been introduced along the Russian border with Germany in the wake of the 1892 cholera epidemic at Hamburg. Though Libau provided a nearby port through which so many could emigrate, or work their passage to the West, the dire state in which so many passengers were transported posed both a visible and invisible threat to Jews that had already travelled to British and other western port cities. The barely established Jews faced a threat to those freedoms and rights which port Jews had previously gained because of the fear of disease carried by those newly arriving from the Baltic – and the port of Libau in particular.

Whether the mercantile status of Jews in Libau equates with the position enjoyed by Lois Dubin's port Jews of Trieste is debateable. Neither is it clear whether the port of Libau enjoyed an equivalent status to the semi-autonomous ports of Trieste or Odessa. But though Riga retained a larger Jewish community than Libau, and although it could be said that it had a greater influence upon Jewish enlightenment than the latter port, the Jews of Libau undoubtedly held a unique position in commercial affairs within and without absolutist Russia during the end of the nineteenth and beginning of the twentieth century. Libau's importance in the forging of a distinctive port Jewish identity, I would argue, is thus far greater than other Baltic ports because she acted as an exporter of Jews and not just because of her communal size or economic strength.

ACKNOWLEDGEMENTS

I would like to thank Marian Smith, Andre Brannan and Michaela Barnard for their assistance whilst researching this essay, and Professor Aubrey Newman, Debbie Beavis and Dr Angela McCarthy for advice regarding earlier drafts. Research for this essay was undertaken at the Maritime Historical Studies Centre, University of Hull and the AHRB Centre for Irish and Scottish Studies, University of Aberdeen. Financial support was provided by the National Maritime Museum, Greenwich, the Faculty of Arts and Social Sciences, University of Hull and the Maritime Historical Studies Centre, University of Hull.

NOTES

1. Foremost in these studies are Irving Howe, *World of Our Fathers* (New York: Simon and Schuster, 1976); Lloyd Gartner, *The Jewish Immigrant in England, 1870–1914* (London: Vallentine Mitchell, 2000); and Ronald Sanders, *Shores of Refuge: A Hundred Years of Jewish Emigration* (New York: Henry Holt, 1988). Each has described the mechanics, motives and patterns of movement evident between 1870 and 1914. Edited works resulting from conferences arranged under the auspices of the Jewish Historical Society of England offer important insights into the migration westward of East European Jewry. See (for example) Aubrey Newman, *Migration and Settlement* (London: Jewish Historical Society of England, 1970); and Aubrey Newman and Stephen Massil (eds.), *Patterns of Migration, 1850–1914* (London: Jewish Historical Society of England, 1996). Recent studies that have examined the westward emigration, movement and settlement of East European Jewry include John Klier, *Imperial Russia's Jewish Question, 1855–1881* (Cambridge: Cambridge University Press, 1995); Rainer Liedtke, *Jewish Welfare in Hamburg and Manchester, c.1850–1914* (Oxford: Oxford University Press, 1998); Tony Kushner and Katherine Knox (eds.), *Refugees in an Age of Genocide: Global, National, and Local Perspectives during the Twentieth Century* (London: Frank Cass, 1999); and Anne Kershen, *Uniting the Tailors: Trade Unionism among the Tailoring Workers of London and Leeds, 1870–1939* (Ilford: Frank Cass, 1995).

2. The conceptual base for the 'port Jew' stereotype has evolved significantly since it was first defined by Lois Dubin and David Sorkin. See Lois Dubin, *The Port Jews of Habsburg Trieste* (Stanford, CA: Stanford University Press, 1999); and David Sorkin, 'The Port Jew: Notes Toward a Social Type', *Journal of Jewish Studies* 50.1 (Spring 1999), 87–97. For recent discussion, see David Cesarani (ed.), *Port Jews: Jewish Communities in Cosmopolitan Maritime Trading Centres, 1550–1950* (London: Frank Cass, 2002). In this latter volume, David Cesarani highlighted the need to examine the port Jews of Riga – for which I hope this essay has offered some contextual insight – and Tony Kushner urged the wider application of non-elite Ashkenazim beyond the eighteenth century, for which the port of Libau (as one source of 'the phenomena of transmigration') will hopefully serve as an important example.

3. I. Singer (ed.), *The Jewish Encyclopaedia* (New York and London: Funk & Wagnall's, 1901–06), vol. 4, p.312.
4. The port was founded in 1625.
5. *The Jewish Encyclopaedia* (see note 3), vol.4, p.621.
6. Simon Dubnov, *History of the Jews in Russia and Poland: From the Earliest Times until the Present Day* (Philadelphia, PA: Jewish Publication Society of America, 1918), vol.1, p.321.
7. An example of the discrimination that the Jews of Courland experienced can be seen in the provincial capital, Mitau. According to *The Jewish Encyclopedia* (see note 3), vol.4, p.312, the Jews of Mitau could only live in 'the so-called Jewish street (known as "Doblen'sche Strasse") as protected Jews ("Schutzjuden")'.
8. For a history of the development of the town and port of Libau, see *Geschichte der Stadt Libau von Alexander Wegner* (Hannover and Döhren: Verlag Harro v. Hirshheydt, 1970). Libau's role as an emigrant port was briefly discussed in Vlad Sosnikov, 'Libau: A Gateway for Emigration From the Russian Empire', *Avotaynu* XV.1 (Spring 1999), 20. Other references are made in *The Jewish Encyclopaedia* (see note 3); and Dubnov (see note 6).
9. Brian Hoyle, 'Fields of Tension: Development Dynamics at the Port–City Interface', in Cesarani (see note 2), p.17.
10. Ibid., p.18.
11. *The Jewish Encyclopaedia* (see note 3), vol.4, p.312, notes that most of the Jews living in Courland were believed to have originated either by sea from Prussia and North Germany or (as described by Brutzkus) from the neighbouring countries of Lithuania and Poland.
12. Dov Levin (ed.), *Pinkas ha-kehilot; entsiklopediya shel ha-yishuvim le-min hivsasdam ve-ad le-aher shoat milthemet ha-olam ha-sheniya: Latvia and Estonia* (Jerusalem: Yad Vashem, 1988), pp.170, 180–86. Data for the size of Libau's Jewish population varies according to which source is used. Libau's total population in 1897 was 64,505 according to *The Jewish Encyclopaedia* (see note 3), vol.4, p.311. Its Jewish community was stated as 9,700 (or 15 per cent of the port city's population). Of these 3,225 were described as artisans (of whom 1,309 were masters) and 117 were day labourers. The Jewish population of Courland similarly expanded during the nineteenth century from 9,000 in 1835 to 49,102 in 1897.
13. BC 949: Kaplan Centre Interviews, Transcript of an interview between Eve Horwitz and Dr Maurice Immerman, p.5, September 1990. Immerman lived in Talsen, Courland before emigrating with his parents and siblings to South Africa (via Libau) in 1906.
14. Libau was the second largest port Jewish settlement within the Baltic region by the time of the 1897 Russian census. According to *The Jewish Encyclopaedia* (see note 3), vol.4, p.311, in 1897 Riga had 21,963 Jews, Libau 10,860, Friedrichstadt 3,800 and Windau 1,350.
15. Courland retained a relative degree of autonomy, unlike the Polish Jews living in the Russian Pale of Settlement. Such territorial 'independence' enabled successive Imperial rulers to grant freedoms to Jews living in this region and for its Jews to retain certain economic privileges unlike those living in neighbouring Baltic ports such as Danzig, Riga or St Petersburg.
16. The port gained its first synagogue in 1708.
17. Dubnov (see note 6), vol.2, p.133. The links between Libau and the Mendelssohns were the direct result of the friendship between Aaron Horwitz, rabbi of Hasenpot (in Courland) and later of Berlin as cited in *The Jewish Encyclopaedia* (see note 3), vol.4, p.315.
18. Philip Klein, a former rabbi of Libau, emigrated to New York and was described by *The Jewish Encyclopaedia* (see note 3), vol.7, p.522, as rabbi of the 'Hungarian congregation Oheb Zedek, perhaps the most important position among the East Side congregations of New York'. Other port Jews who were educated in Libau (before later emigrating to the West) include Joseph Jacobs, Professor of Hebrew and rabbi of Liverpool (*Jewish Chronicle*, 31 December 1881); John Paley, American journalist and editor of *Jüdisches Tageblatt* and *Jüdische Gazetten* (*American Jewish Yearbook*, 5665 [Philadelphia, PA: Jewish Publication Society of America, 1904–05]); and Baltimore rabbi Schepsel Schaffer (*American Jewish Yearbook*, 5665). Perhaps the most renowned emigrant from this period, who left one port for another, was the artist Mark Rothko (born Marcus Rothkowitz), who was born in Libau before emigrating on 5 August 1913 onboard the SS *Czar*. Diane Waldman, *Mark Rothko* (London: Thames and Hudson, 1997), pp.18–19.
19. Evidence of Major William Evans-Gordon to the *Royal Commission on Alien Immigration, Minutes of Evidence* (London, 1903), vol.II, p.455, M.13349.

20. I would like to thank Dr Charles Freeman for information on his great grandfather's business and family history. Details of Schapiro's business featured in his obituary, entitled 'Death of Mr. H. Schapiro. Well-known Importer of Pit Ponies', *Doncaster Chronicle*, 6 May 1921, p.12. An example of the role of Jewish timber merchants providing ports such as Libau with timber for export is provided by Simon Schama, *Landscape and Memory* (London: Harper Collins, 1995), pp.27–9.

21. In 1891, 1892 and 1903 (following the rise of political agitation that followed the Kishinev pogrom), Imperial Russia reduced the rights of relatively free Jews of Libau, just as she had in Riga and St Petersburg.

22. Gordon Jackson, 'Sea Trade', in R.J. Morris, *Atlas of Industrializing Britain* (London: Methuen, 1986), p.102.

23. Though non-Jewish merchants and ship-owners undoubtedly contributed towards the growth of trade in these imported commodities, the dominant influence of the Jewish merchants was noted by political commentators of the time. For an example, see William Evans-Gordon, *The Alien Immigrant* (London and New York: William Heinemann and Chas. Scribner's Sons, 1903), p.98.

24. An image of a port Jewish merchant working in Libau is provided in Evans-Gordon (see note 23), p.105. The Jew illustrated in 'From Other Lands', *Hull Daily Mail*, 16 February 1910, p.4, was most probably one that has just arrived on board a ship from Libau and whose dress shows that those leaving via the Baltic port were not always poor.

25. For a description of arrival at a lodging house in Libau, see the report on emigration via Libau made for the Jewish Colonisation Association by Mr Janovski in 1906: Central Jewish Archives, Jerusalem, ICA, Mr Janovski's Report on his journey of Inspection (October–November [1906]). Similar buildings in British ports were frequently criticised by Urban and Port Medical Officers of Health. See, for example, the Annual Reports of the Medical Officer of Health for the Hull and Goole Port Sanitary Authority, Hull City Archives; the Annual Reports by the Medical Officer of Health to Port of London Sanitary Authority, Corporation of London Record Office; and the Annual Reports by the Medical Officer of Health to the London Metropolitan Sanitary Authority, London Metropolitan Archives. For an analysis of the medical 'threat' of immigration, see Krista Maglen, *Intercepting Infection: Quarantine, the Port Sanitary Authority and Immigration in Late Nineteenth Century Britain* (Ph.D. thesis, University of Glasgow, 2001). Some of the findings of Maglen's work have recently been included in '"The First Line of Defence": British Quarantine and the Port Sanitary Authorities in the Nineteenth Century', *Social History of Medicine* 15.3 (2002), 413–28.

26. The importance of Libau as Russia's premier emigrant port continued until the outbreak of the First World War. *The Times*, 14 March 1914, p.7, in an article on the detrimental effects that Russian legislation may have upon British shipping, noted that 'Libau is the chief Russian port of departure, but many of the emigrants, instead of going directly by the Russian Transatlantic line, proceed by steamer to England and there take passage by one of the English Transatlantic lines'.

27. 'Emigration Conditions in Europe – Libau', in 'The Immigration Commission – Emigration Conditions in Europe', in *Senate Documents* (Washington, DC: US Government, 1910–11), vol.12, pp.104–5.

28. Hull University Archives and Special Collections, DEW/4/31a, letter from Helmsing and Grimm to Thomas Wilson Sons and Co., 27 April 1904. Later correspondence in this collection shows how Freydberg was a Jew. Though he was normally a very able agent for both DFDS (referred to here as Forende) and later Thomas Wilson, Sons & Co., during negotiations for the implementation of the 1910 Russian Emigration Law his ability to represent the foreign shipping lines was ruled impossible because he was both German and Jewish.

29. Hamburg was the most important source for inward Russian and Polish migration to Britain during this period.

30. *Royal Commission on Alien Immigration* (see note 19), vol.II, p.455, M.13349.

31. George Sims, 'Sweated London', in idem (ed.), *Living London: its work and its play, its humour and its pathos, its sights and its scenes* (London: Cassell, c.1902), vol.1, pp.49–55.

32. For an example of the poor state of migrant-carrying vessels arriving in Britain via the Thames and Humber (respectively), see the arrival of the SS *George* on 12 November 1896, Corporation

of London Record Office, CSPR 27.6, p.16; and the SS *Yrsa* on 7 October 1898, Hull City Archives, WHG 1/30, p.79.

33. *Royal Commission on Alien Immigration* (see note 19), vol. II, p.206, M.6116.
34. N.R.P. Bonsor, *North Atlantic Seaway* (St Brelade, Cambridge: Brookside Publications, 1979), vol.III, pp.1346–1357.
35. 'The Immigration Commission – Emigration Conditions in Europe', in *Senate Documents* (see note 27), p.104.
36. Ibid., p.105. Details of the inspection of emigrants leaving for America appears in the *Annual Report of the Commissioner General of Immigration to the Secretary of Labour for the fiscal year ended June 30 1913* (Washington, DC: US Government, 1914), pp.511–12.
37. Cape Archives, PMO 84, Archives of the Prime Minister's Office, Cape Colony, 6 June 1902, No.314.
38. Telegram sent by the Secretary of State, London to the High Commissioner in Johannesburg, Cape Archives, PMO 85, Archives of the Prime Minister's Office, Cape Colony, 19 June 1902, No.4.
39. Cited in Milton Shain, *Jewry and Cape Society* (Cape Town: Historical Publication Society, 1983), p.24.
40. 'The Immigration Commission – Emigration Conditions in Europe', in *Senate Documents* (see note 27), p.104.

Jewish and Catholic Irish Relations: The Glasgow Waterfront c.1880–1914

WILLIAM KENEFICK

Introduction

Glasgow and its hinterland lay at a great centre of industrial production and commerce, and it was these attributes that attracted migrants to the city and the west of Scotland generally. The Jews fleeing the pogroms or working to realise their dreams of making it to America may have disembarked, for the greater part, at Edinburgh's Leith docks on Scotland's east coast, but thereafter made their way to Glasgow: the industrial powerhouse of the Scottish economy. Glasgow also linked Scotland to the rest of the world, and the transmigration west not only provided a means of migration abroad, but accommodation and work. Indeed, many Jews, like a host of other immigrants, were to remain in Glasgow: they did not leave immediately from the quays of the Broomielaw to the United States and '*die goldene medine*' – that 'Golden Land'.[1] Many of these Jews, although a minority, were to make Scotland and Glasgow their home.

Glasgow had an already established Jewish community, but the new arrivals were quite different, not least because they were generally poor (although not bereft of skill). They spoke Yiddish and came from the Pale of Jewish settlement in eastern Europe. They settled in the Gorbals because it was close to the 'railways and shipping of the Clyde and because housing was relatively cheap'.[2] The Irish also settled in this area for the same reason. There were many employment opportunities opening up at Glasgow's rapidly expanding port, and the Irish were engaged as seamen and porters, but mainly general quay labourers and dockers.[3] The Irish and Jews, like many of Scotland's immigrant community, would face considerable discrimination and stereotyping particularly in the workplace: accused by the trade unions, as most immigrant communities were, of undercutting Scottish workers' wages, and acting as strike breakers; and derided by employers, and the wider host community, as political radicals and trade union hotheads. Clearly, there was an inherent contradiction here, but once convinced of the need for unionisation, the Jews and the Irish could bring great militancy and strength to Scotland's trade unions.[4] In time Scotland's new immigrants would became part of the Scottish trade union movement, and with Glasgow functioning as Britain's 'second city of empire' this placed them not only at the very heart of the trade union movement in Scotland, but also Britain.[5]

Investigating Irish and Jewish Relations at Glasgow c.1880–1914

The work and approach adopted by Maria Vassilikou in her treatment of Greek and Jewish relations in Salonika and Odessa, stresses that historians tend to look too fondly through the lens of ethnic conflict and communal violence, rather than positive inter-ethnic relations that stress shared values and similarities. John D. Klier adopts a similar approach, but emphasises developments in the ideology of Zionism, Jewish varieties of socialism, a modern Jewish press, and the modern Jewish stage (all of which existed at Glasgow): noting the 'novelty and innovation' which marked the Jewish contribution to their new societies. Such methodological approaches can readily be extended to the study of the Jewish community in Scotland, and in particular the working class Jews of the Gorbals. It is clear, however, in terms of Scottish historiography that apart from a few notable exceptions – Scottish historians of Jewish history who stress the need to build a genuine 'Jewish history from below' – the contribution of the Scottish-Jewish working class in Scotland has been largely overlooked.

As Vassilikou suggests of the Greeks and Jews of Salonika and Odessa, a similar approach can be adopted to the investigation of Jewish and Irish relations in Glasgow. For example, the manner in which they shared the same social space, in this instance the Gorbals area on the southside of Glasgow, and how both the Jews and the Catholic Irish 'looked for paths of existence', which would guarantee 'their group survival and favour their upwards social mobility'. Importantly, Vassilikou adds:

> Their choices were far from homogenous, but were rather conditioned upon their economic background, social position and ideological legacy. The immediate outcome of this inter-communal fragmentation took the form of social behaviour which cut across their ethnic distinctiveness.[6]

This essay will show that this is what occurred in Glasgow. It was the seeming lack of tension between the Jews and Scots generally, and the Glasgow community and the Irish Catholics in particular, that drives this current research. There was widespread anti-semitism all over Europe from the late 1870s onward, and there had been considerable Catholic intolerance of Jews in Ireland in the early twentieth century. But there is quite literally no evidence to suggest similar patterns of behaviour in Scotland, or in Glasgow, where the great majority of Jews settled. This is also an important period in both Jewish and Irish political history, and for the Irish it was made manifest in the growing demands for Irish Home Rule and Land Reform, which was gathering pace from 1878 onward. Indeed, if Zionism can be argued to have provided a force for unity within the Jewish diaspora before 1914, then the question of Irish Home Rule and Land Reform was no less important in the Irish diasporic context. It is here that we see an important ideological factor at work within both communities.

Between the late eighteenth century and 1914 the physical growth of Glasgow was phenomenal. Glasgow's population not only expanded rapidly, but by the twentieth century Glasgow's labour force also underwent a significant shift in composition. By 1911 those engaged in textiles had fallen from 37.56 per cent to 16.86 per cent. The engineering and metal industries by then accounted for around 16 per cent of the workforce, and there was also a steady growth in employment associated with the food, drink and tobacco industries, as well as the furniture industries.[7] There was also a marked, if less spectacular, decline in those employed as general labourers, but this was compensated for by increased numbers engaged in the timber yards, shipyards, foundries, on the tramways, and most notably in the rapid expansion in waterfront work.[8]

The new wave of Jewish immigrants seldom sought work at the docks, and like the Irish they did not compete directly with Scottish labour. The Jews coming to Glasgow were involved in peddling and hawking (perhaps as high as ten per cent by 1906), the tailoring and furniture trade (tailoring was first noted as a Jewish trade in the city in the early 1870s), and finally tobacco.[9] Clearly, for the Jews of the Pale there was a tradition of going into this kind of work and in particular the tobacco trade. Indeed, Jews from eastern Europe were often wrongly portrayed as poor rural peasants, for they 'possessed skills developed in the urban economy of Europe which they were able to utilize when they settled in Glasgow'.[10]

The Jews did not need to enter into competition with the Irish or the Lithuanians 'for menial work in the docks, mines and steel mills'.[11] In relation to tailoring and furniture making, the southside Jews were renowned for 'their organisation in small sweated workshops, with appalling conditions'. Indeed, it was this factor, perhaps more than any other, which created a high degree of stereotypical anti-semitism in Glasgow. Allied to accusation by the Scottish Tailors' Union that these Jews undercut Scottish workers' wages, the sweated trades came under the ever-watchful eye of the powerful and influential Glasgow Trades and Labour Council.[12] There is another inherent contradiction here. The *Lancet*, reporting in 1888, suggested that 'one of the most distinctive features of the sweating system in Glasgow is the exceptionally large proportion of Scotch and Irish sweaters'. Such evidence, however, went largely unnoticed. Sweating was simply seen as 'a Jewish Problem'.[13]

As for Glasgow's port, economic expansion was to have a significant effect on the operational and employment structure of the port, leading as it did to an increase in traffic and a greater diversity of cargo, particularly from the 1880s onward. Indeed, according to one Glasgow ship-owner: 'Glasgow became a very cosmopolitan sort of place' and its port came to handle 'more different kinds of trade ... more different lines of ships ... more different classes of vessels discharging and loading ... than at any other port ... anywhere!'[14] It was the Catholic Irish who came to dominate waterfront work, although given its casual status and low wages it was never likely to enrich them or their families. As Vassilikou suggested of the immigrant Jews of Salonika and Odessa, access to waterfront work would certainly 'guarantee their group survival', but in the case of the Irish at Glasgow it would not necessarily 'favour their upwards social mobility'.

Jewish Settlement in Glasgow and the Gorbals

Jewish immigration into Scotland was never large-scale, but it was concentrated within the west of Scotland and Glasgow in particular. Some 6,500 Jews (over six per cent of the British total) had settled in Glasgow by 1901.[15] They were concentrated in the Gorbals area on the south side of the river Clyde, and by 1903 there were about 4,000 Jews – mainly Polish and Russian Jews – living there.[16] By 1914 (although accurate estimates are difficult), there may have been some 10,000 Jews living in Glasgow,[17] and perhaps as many as 12,000 before the onset of the First World War.[18] Some time before the Irish had begun to establish themselves in great numbers in this same area of the southside – with a large contingent drawn from County Donegal – because it was near to the docks, wharves and harbours of Glasgow.[19] By the late nineteenth century, for example, over 60 per cent of the Glasgow dock labour force was Irish, and largely Catholic,[20] and they would have been a common sight as they sought twice-daily employment along the waterfront.

Before the 1870s, the Jewish population in Scotland was remarkably small by English standards, but by 1858 the first purpose-built synagogue had been erected in Glasgow within the very centre of the city. Between then and 1879 the Jewish community in Glasgow grew from around 200 to around 700.[21] They lived mainly in the west of the city where they built and consecrated the new Garnethill synagogue in 1879. This became the main place of worship for the 'Glasgow Hebrew Congregation', and Garnethill became known as the 'Cathedral Synagogue of Scotland',[22] servicing the needs of a Glasgow Jewish community then numbering 1,000 people.[23] By 1883, according to the *Jewish Chronicle*, reporting on a meeting of the 'Second Hebrew Congregation' held in the Gorbals that year, there were around 1,200 Jews in Glasgow at that point.[24] By 1891 the Jewish population had increased overall to 2,000, and more than 800 were living and working in the Gorbals.[25] Clearly, this was a sustainable community, for in 1887 a southside branch of the Glasgow Hebrew Congregation was inaugurated, and by 1898 was fully autonomous. Both congregations on the south and north sides of the Clyde by then formed the 'United Synagogue of Glasgow'. One year later, in 1899, a site was purchased to build a new synagogue on South Portland Street in the Gorbals. It was consecrated in 1901 and later became known as the 'Great Synagogue'.[26] Jewish immigration into Glasgow was thus increasingly concentrated in the Gorbals,[27] and by 1903 some 4,000 Jews lived and worked there[28] (between 6,000 and 7,000 Jews lived in Glasgow as a whole[29]). The Gorbals Jews thereafter roughly accounted for around two-thirds of the total Glasgow Jewish population prior to 1914, and if we accept that there was between 10,000 and 12,000 Jews living in Glasgow by 1914, then the Jewish community living in the Gorbals perhaps numbered somewhere between 6,500 and 8,000.[30]

There are other ways in which to plot a growth pattern when there is little or no reliable statistical data available. Kenneth Collins noted that the first Gorbals-based Glasgow Hebrew Sick Society was operational as early as 1878, and ten years later there was a free loan Hebrew Benevolent Society founded in the Gorbals.[31] In November 1883 Mr Michael Simon, honorary secretary of the Glasgow Hebrew Congregation, was elected to the Third Ward of Glasgow Town Council, by a large majority of 400 votes (indeed, he did so against a 'No Jews and No Jesuits' Protestant Clergyman candidate – clearly adversely linking both the Jewish and Irish communities). The *Jewish Chronicle* was proud to report 'that this was the first time that a Jew had been elected to any municipal position in Scotland'.[32] Thus, as Henry Maitles points out, evidenced by the fact they had a councillor, this relatively small Jewish community 'had political awareness and clout', when the Irish community in Glasgow 'numbering many thousands more' had none.[33]

At the time of fresh attack on the Jews in Russia, in September 1902 a public dinner was held for Mr Michael Simons – by then retired from council – convened in the name of the 'citizens of Glasgow'. This indicated the esteem in which he was held in civil circles and by the Glasgow public generally. Within six months – and now a Justice of the Peace – he was elected President of the Committee of Fine Arts, which was a body composed of the leading and most influential citizens of Glasgow. In November 1905 Simons was created a deputy Lieutenant of the County of the City of Glasgow, presented with his robes of office and declared 'a Magistrate of the City'. This was the highest public honour ever awarded a Jew in Scotland, and it was a great source of pride to the Jewish community.[34]

Although a northside and progressive west end Jew, Simons's presence on Glasgow Council undoubtedly helped the developing Jewish community flourish in the Gorbals, while at the same time working positively to develop Jewish acculturation and assimilation within Glasgow society generally. As the numbers of Jews increased during the 1880s, Glasgow Corporation responded by providing English-language evening classes, built a *mikva* (ritual bath) in the new Gorbals bath house in 1886,[35] and in 1901 built another *mikva* near the 'Great Synagogue' in South Portland Street.[36] The good work continued thereafter when Mr Frank Israel Cohen took his seat on Glasgow Town Council in January 1903 – representing the northside, largely working-class Springburn Ward. Cohen portrayed himself as the 'workman's friend' in order to win the seat, and it was perhaps for these reasons 'that he ousted the popular favourite'. He promised to support temperance principles, schemes for better housing, lighting and better administration of wages. With the recent retirement of Michael Simons, Cohen was the only Jewish councillor in Scotland at that juncture. He was a part of a family tobacco business – operating in Buchanan Street – and one of the leading businesses of that type in Scotland.[37]

Lower down the social scale and a good few years before, in 1890, the Jewish Tailors Union was founded in Glasgow, and in 1891 the Jewish Working Men's Club was founded. By the end of the nineteenth century, therefore, the Jewish community in Glasgow was increasingly recognised as an integral part of the life of the city.[38] This conforms well with Klier's thesis; there was clearly a growing confidence manifested by the Gorbals Jews, and we do find 'novelty and innovation' in the Jewish contribution to the burgeoning Gorbals community. For example, there was the formation of the Jewish Lad's Brigade in May 1903, founded by a group from the southside, entirely unaided by any other organisation.[39] The following month the Jewish Workers' Co-operative Society was formed. All their goods were obtained from the Scottish Wholesale Society,[40] and in so doing the Gorbals Jews were embracing mainstream Scottish working-class values and culture.

But what of the Irish? It is clear they had a relationship with the Jews and that this is evident from the *Lancet* report in 1888, but this is more clearly seen in later report in the *Glasgow Evening News*, 11 October 1902. It was a leading article describing 'A Glasgow Ghetto', and was presented for the delectation of the Glasgow reading public as a 'News Special':

> In the Gorbals district, between main and Crown Streets, lies the chief habitat of the struggling Jew … in the Poorer Districts of the Gorbals where Jew and Gentile live cheek by jowl – a district where the sweater draws on his chief source of labour, where the sewing machine purrs in

its feverish haste to keep starvation from the door from Monday morning till Saturday night ...

Along the waterfront, and facing the Clyde Adelphi Street and its environments ... Jews congregate in little groups, chattering with unrestrained freedom in a foreign tongue ...

And the loafer – well, he is strongly represented at the street corners. But he is seldom a Jew – They Never Idle Their Time. Once I did see a Jew laden with pictures on a kerbstone waiting patiently for his Gentile assistant, who had gone inside a public house for a refreshment, leaving his load of pictures outside in care of his master. A striking instance of genial camaraderie between master and servant.

To the casual visitor it is surprising the number of Jewish signs, painted in brilliant yellow, that predominate in the district ... An eating-house that caters to slender purses; a baker's with prominent Hebraic characters, and a host of other dealers amongst which Hibernian names appear above the lintel of the doorway, disputing with the Jew the exclusive right to barter and sell in this Ghetto of commerce.

Like the *Lancet* report of 1888, this illustrates well that the Irish and the Jews (and the 'Scotch'!) lived and worked together, and if there had been 'ethnic conflict and communal violence' one could be certain that the Glasgow press corps would have swooped on it in an instance. Perhaps there was need for conflict in so far as both the Jews and the Irish were too eagerly involved in the daily struggle for survival. Maybe it was a question of acceptance, for as Ralph Glasser suggested, and in spite of some occasional name-calling, the Irish Catholics of the Gorbals had a better relationship with the Jews than they had with the 'indigenous Protestant' population.[41]

Jewish and Irish Politics and the Quiet Art of Peaceful Coexistence

The growth and interest in Zionism is another major theme which permeates this research, and here both Ben Braber and Henry Maitles make a valuable contribution in charting the rise of Zionism in Scotland.[42] A Glasgow Branch of the *Chovevie Zion* – the community for the Colonising of Palestine by Jewish People – was set up in Glasgow in April 1891, enrolling 250 on the first evening. Several others were formed before 1914, including the *B'nei Zion, B'nosh Zion, Dorshie Zion*, the socialist *Poalie Zion*, several Zionist Friendly Societies, and there were also the Daughters of Zion.[43] Yet despite the knowledge that such groups and branches existed, they have received scant attention in Jewish and Scottish historiography – although the work of Braber and Maitles helps to plug this gap. Likewise, the unskilled Catholic Irish workers suffered similarly, being largely excluded from what tended to be institutional, organisational, skilled and Protestant trade union histories.[44]

Interest in Zionism was also apparent within the non-Jewish community of Glasgow. In February 1902, for example, the *Daily Record and Mail* published a 'Review of Zionism: Its Inception and Progress'. This was a full and authoritative account that plotted the modern developments of Zionism from 1881, and that this was a direct result 'of the popular ebullition of temper in Russia demonstrated by anti-Jewish riots ... turned by Ignatieff in his "May Laws" into official persecution'. From then, went the report, Zionism – Regeneration of Israel – 'spread throughout the Jewish World', and from 1896, due to the work Dr Herzl, 'became a force to be reckoned with'.[45]

One of the most popular Zionist groups was *Dorshie Zion* (the literal translation of which is 'a union of many in one Jewish interest').[46] Formed in July 1903, with a membership of 200, they stated they were in no way 'antagonistic to existing Zionist societies' and that they simply wished to 'further the cause of Zionism among the masses generally, and to enlist the sympathy and support of those who still abstain from taking any interest in the movement'. By 1904 they could command regular audiences of 1,000, and the *Jewish Chronicle* was to report: 'Never in the history of Glasgow Zionism had there been such large gatherings as at the attendances of lectures under the auspices of this society'.[47] One report in 1905 noted that 'delegates from several societies and Christian visitors attended regularly'. In the aftermath of Dr Herzl's death, the southside Glasgow Zionists opened their New Zionist Reading Room and Hall – *Beth Herzl*.

The Gorbals Jews were clearly different from the older well-established and relatively 'patrician' Jewish community of the west end. The west end Jews were 'prepared to help their co-religionists', but they also wanted to ensure that 'they should not bear an undue burden of the costs involved'. Henry Maitles argued that this was evidence of a class divide, and noted one example where,

> Chaim Bermant, describing the typical attitude of West End Glasgow Jews towards South-siders, claimed that the West End Jews 'had nothing against the South side, as such, but he did not want his daughter to marry one and if she did, she was considered as having married out of her class'.[48]

Maitles also points to the debates surrounding the restrictions of aliens in 1903, where this class perspective was again in evidence when certain Jews put forward arguments – 'mainly economic and social reasons' – in favour of restricting immigration. This was clearly seen with the Glasgow Jewish Board of Guardians in relation to several cases of Jews being repatriated to Russia and other countries in Europe. They argued that they did this 'only when the applicants themselves desired it and the Board were of the opinion that such procedure was absolutely necessary'.

But for Maitles, however, there were two major problems with this position. First, having made 'the hazardous journey from the Pale to escape repression', why would anyone want to return with 'virtually nothing'? Therefore, considerable pressure must have been put on the applicants in these instances of repatriation. Secondly, that such action simply gave the anti-semitic, anti-immigration lobby a green light to continue with their propaganda, noting that one campaigner in Glasgow argued that if the Jews themselves could return their own people 'why should the British not use legislation to stop immigrants coming in the first place?'[49] Indeed, the Glasgow Jewish Literary Society debated the topic 'Alien Immigration Should be Restricted', and while the overwhelming majority were against the motion, Maitles saw in this clear evidence that 'feelings in the community were not uniform'. Importantly, it showed 'that many Jews opposed the attitudes of the established community and their attempts to halt immigration'.[50] The Aliens Act became law on 11 August 1905, and was argued to have an immediate effect. Indeed, as Maitles points out, Kenneth Collins, in his book *Aspects of Scottish Jewry* (1987), clearly bought into the idea that Glasgow (and Britain as a whole) was about to be flooded by alien immigrant Jews, and that this influx was only brought under control 'after the passage of the Aliens Act'. For Maitles, this illustrates all to clearly that Collins believed the argument that many more immigrants would have come to Glasgow had it not been for the passing of the Aliens Act, and thus Collins, as did the west end Jews at the time of the passing of the act, were buying into the 'spurious and manipulative statistical Tory arguments' of that period.[51] Maitles is perhaps being a little too harsh on Collins, but in perusing the debates and arguments on the issue of the Aliens Act at this time his general conclusions are in the main quite valid.

The Catholic Irish: A Race Apart?

By the mid-nineteenth century there were already around 'one-quarter of a million Irish-born people in Scotland', and this movement was to continue 'on a significant scale' right through to the 1920s.[52] The Irish settled in many areas in Scotland, but, like the Jews, a significant number gravitated towards Glasgow. In 1881, the Irish-born living in England represented 2.2 per cent of the total population, while in Scotland the figure was 5.9 per cent. In Glasgow, however, the Irish-born accounted for 13.1 per cent of the total population of that area, and even by 1911 – when the Irish-born represented only 3.7 per cent of Scottish totals – 7.1 per cent of Glasgow's population was Irish-born.[53] This takes little account of course of second- and third-generation Irish who were argued to be 'often more Irish than their Irish forebears'.[54] During the nineteenth and early twentieth century, when the Irish Catholics and their descendents in Scotland were taken together, they represented approximately 'fifteen per cent the population'.[55]

The Irish brought with them a particular political philosophy and the spectre of Irish nationalism was to cast a long shadow over British politics. By the 1870s, in combination with a widespread and vigorous campaign on the 'Irish Land issue', which argued for greater tenants' rights in Ireland, this movement had hardened into the growing desire for Irish Home Rule. In Scotland this not only threatened the political hegemony of the Liberal Party, as well as the rights of the landlord class, it went much further: the 'Irish Problem' posed a threat to the Union and the Empire, and to free trade, and for Protestant west Scotland, with its strong links with Ulster and the Orange Order, 'Home Rule' meant 'Rome Rule'.[56]

The Scots not only saw themselves as a different people with a different religion, they also viewed themselves as peaceful and law-abiding citizens, loyal to the Crown, the Union and the Empire. The Irish were not simply a race apart but 'a nation in waiting', and this would have serious implications for the Protestant minority landlord class, and their role and status in rural Ireland.[57] It also served to create considerable tensions between the host community, particularly the employing class, and the immigrant Irish in the west of Scotland and Glasgow. The agrarian disturbances that were to take place between 1878 and 1882, and which were widely reported in the Glasgow press, led directly to the prejudicial treatment of the Irish in Glasgow and this seriously affected livelihoods and employment.[58]

When the first reports of the 'Jewish Problem in Russia' began to filter down through the columns of the Glasgow press in the early 1880s, alongside reports of the rise of anti-semitic movements in Germany and 'Roumania', more column inches were given over to Ireland, and the 'Irish Problem', than to any other single issue. According to George Boyce,

> What made the difference, what transformed the political landscape of Ireland, was the agricultural crisis which began in 1878 and led to the 'Land war' of 1879–1882. But what was equally important was the mood which this crisis engendered among important sections of the Irish tenant farming class – the most numerous, significant and (after 1849) homogeneous part of the population of Ireland.

All that was needed, added Boyce, was 'leadership, propaganda and organisation on a nationwide scale'. The agricultural depression produced all of these and led to the formation of the Land League, and when forged in an alliance with the Home Rule Party the result was the creation of 'a mass movement'.[59] Tenant insecurity, therefore, and the campaign to secure tenants' rights, land tenure and control, and land management, lay at the root of the campaign, and it worked not only to unite rural Ireland, but also to consolidate Irish opinion across industrial Britain, and throughout the Irish diaspora. Indeed, a letter published in the *Glasgow Herald*, in February 1882, expresses clearly this notion:

> There can be little doubt that the Irishmen of Glasgow are today more united and more at one upon the political question concerning Ireland, than they have been for some years past. This happy state of matters is in no doubt due in large measure to the beneficial influence of the Land league ...

'And why should this be a bad thing?' continued the correspondent. 'Surely it was the "duty" of every Irishman to oppose by every means in his power those coercive Liberals'.[60]

The Land League activities in both Ireland and Scotland were thus helping to forge solidarity among the Irish community, and the campaign for Irish Home Rule simply consolidated this movement.[61] Like the *Daily Record and Mail*'s reporting of Zionism 'spreading throughout the Jewish World', so too did the politics of Irish nationalism, and, like Zionism, it too 'became a force to be reckoned with'. It is clear, however, that while Zionism was viewed as a positive political movement with some legitimacy, in Scotland Irish nationalism was never quite held in the same regard. Indeed, many resented the fact that the Irish population 'contrived to make the issue of Irish Home rule a factor in Scottish politics'.[62]

It is well documented that at this time the Jewish community in Glasgow, although considerably smaller than the Catholic Irish community, had, in Mr Michael Simons – elected in October 1883 – the first Jewish councillor on Glasgow Municipal Council.[63] Yet there was no Catholic councillor for Glasgow at this time. This fact had prompted many historians of the Irish to ask the obvious question 'why?' According to letters published in the *Glasgow Observer* (the main Catholic newspaper in Scotland), shortly after its launch in 1885, there were clearly a good many Catholics elected to local councils across Scotland and in areas around Glasgow. For example, there was a councillor in Pollockshaws, two in Maryhill, three in Coatbridge and others in Stirling, Maxwelltown and Dumfries local councils. Indeed, the correspondents noted a longer pedigree, pointing out that there had been a councillor elected in Airdrie, the late Mr J. McAuley, 18 years before in 1867, and another, Robert Carnan (who was also a Baillie) elected at Maxwelltown, in 1865 – perhaps the first Catholic to be elected to a local authority in Scotland. Aberdeen too had had a Catholic councillor, and Dumfries had several Catholic councillors over the years. But Glasgow had none at that juncture.[64]

Indeed, in congratulating the three Catholic councillors elected to Coatbridge Council in 1885, an editorial in the *Glasgow Observer* bemoaned the fact that the same effort had clearly not been made in the west of Scotland: Catholics there seemed more caught up in Parliamentary elections:

> The successful score [that] has just been made is certainly a gratifying one, and leaves room for hope that if so much can be done at Coatbridge, the Irish population throughout the whole of Scotland have much room for hope that, even after a general election, their energies can be usefully employed in asserting their rightful claims to a part in their municipal control of the country.[65]

Irish nationalism and Zionism may have bound together the wider communities of Irish and Jews around the world, but unlike the Irish the Jews of Glasgow did not ignore local political matters. The above editorial perhaps offers some insight into why the Irish of Glasgow were less likely to get involved in local politics, preferring instead to focus on Irish and nationalist issues at the time of general elections. It was 1896 when the first Irish Catholic councillor was finally elected to Glasgow Council and he represented the Independent Labour Party.[66]

Irish and Jewish Relations

The relationship between the Catholic and Jewish religions has not always been one based on mutual respect and toleration. This was clearly articulated in an article published on the death of Cardinal Manning in the 15 January 1892 edition of *Jewish Chronicle*, where it was reported: 'How great is the change in the order of things when it becomes the Jewish community to offer a tribute of affectionate gratitude to a Cardinal Priest of the Roman Catholic Church'. The readership was reminded that he was prominent in the agitations of January and February 1882 on behalf of the persecuted Jews in Russia. He was the first to the fore then and when there was a 'recrudescence' of the Russian Oppression during 1890, 'no one was more eager than Cardinal Manning to manifest indignation to the persecutors, and sympathy with the persecuted'. The report concluded: 'His sympathies were never bounded. They were in the highest sense Catholic'.[67]

Much had patently changed in the relationship between these two great religions and that same sense of toleration and peaceful co-existence was clearly evident at Glasgow. Much of this was due to the actions and attitude of Archbishop Eyre. In a similar fashion to Cardinal Manning, he was first to the fore in the early 1880s, when the initial terrible reports of 'Russian Outrages against the Jews' started to appear in the Glasgow press: indeed, in terms of the breadth and detail of the reports on the 'outrages' only the *Jewish Chronicle*, or perhaps *The Times*, could surpass the *Glasgow Herald* in reporting these events.

The week before the report of Cardinal Manning's death, in January 1892, the *Jewish Chronicle* – in its 'News from the Provinces' section – reported that there had been placed before the Lord Provost of Glasgow a petition to organise a public meeting to raise funds for the 'amelioration of the conditions of the victims of Russian persecutions, and that a committee had been formed to make the necessary arrangements'.[68] Sandwiched between the now regular and greatly detailed eight-page supplement 'A Special Report: Darkest Russia', it was reported that the meeting would be convened by the Lord Provost and was to be held at the Merchant's Hall on 20 January. There, the following motion was moved by Mr J.G.A. Baird MP: 'That this meeting of the citizens of Glasgow express its profound commiserations for those Russian Jews, whose bitter and continued privations and sufferings are the result of their expulsions from their native land'. The motion was seconded by Dr Donald Macleod, who added: 'that on the platform every creed was represented. They were moving together on the broad ground of humanity to do what was right … for the sake of every suffering and starving brother and sister who had been driven out of that great Empire'. Archbishop Eyre, rose to support the resolution, adding: 'That he hoped that good would come out of the present evil, and that the Jews who were forced to leave Russia might be enabled by contributions sent to them to leave under favourable conditions'. The resolution was unanimously carried and all monies raised were sent to the Russo-Jewish Committee which administered the London Mansion House Fund of 1892.[69]

What we were seeing at this time was in every sense a re-run of what had occurred over a decade before at the time of the 1880 pogroms, and it is at this time that we can also build up some picture of a growing relationship with the Glasgow Christian community and the Glasgow Jews. It is also clear that in the extensive and wide-ranging reports printed in the *Glasgow Herald* at this time, the Jewish problem in Russia had the full attention of this leader of the Glasgow press. And the paper did not pull its punches when making judgements on the actions of the Russian authorities when they attempted to distance themselves from what was occurring in Russia at that time.

The Glasgow press did not report with so much detail in the early 1890s what was happening in eastern Europe: by this time they seemed more concerned with accusation of 'sweating' by Jewish employers in Glasgow's southside. However, one letter written to the *Glasgow Herald* suggested that a benevolent public would not be deterred by such a narrow view, especially when set against the 'hideous persecution of the Jews'. In the same edition an anonymous commentator called for 'common sense' on this issue and stressed that what was needed was a common cause for 'true martyrs, sacrificing home comfort and country for complete beggary'. These Russian Jews 'compared favourably with any creed or nationality in sobriety, morality and frugality, honesty and fair dealings'. 'Yes! There were wealthy Jews, and he did not deny them their success, but for every one wealthy Jew', he noted, 'there were thousands struggling for a living in the city of Glasgow'. The letter was lengthy, written in a very erudite and lucid manner, and simply requested that in the current situation 'the citizens of Glasgow maintained their humanity'.[70] There is little evidence to prove it, but this letter may well have been penned by Archbishop Eyre – a point that will be returned too below.

By January 1893 the paper was reporting on the work of the Jewish Relief Fund and the meeting being held at the Merchant Hall concerning the persecution of the Russian Jews, followed by another large meeting in April to takes matters further. There was a full and detailed account of this meeting and the resolution moved by Dr Donald Macleod. In his statement he outlined the extent of the persecution of the Jews all over Europe and other locations, not discounting the history of persecution nearer home in Ireland, and before that England. 'Scotland', he suggested, 'had no such memory to burden them about dealing with Russia (cries of "hear, hear"). Scotland was the only country in the World in which there has never been a persecution of the Jews (Applause)', and therefore they had perfect freedom to rise up and protest against the way the Jews were treated in Russia. Archbishop Eyre was also in attendance and spoke in favour of the motion, adding that the Jews in Russia were honest citizens, and they were proving likewise in Scotland.[71] Within a few days, noted the *Jewish Chronicle*, nearly £2,000 was raised.[72]

The *Jewish Chronicle* made regular reports on Glasgow at these times of distress and in every occasion the Archbishop was present. At one meeting, in 1892, he was noted as saying 'that the Jews might never wish again to return to their native Russia, but would gradually rise themselves in scale ... for which they were so well capacitated by their talents and by their moral conduct'.[73] Archbishop Eyre, just before his death in 1902, was again campaigning to raise funds for the Russian Jews, and before that he was involved in helping to raise funds to build the new Jewish synagogue in the Gorbals. In June 1900, a very successful bazaar was held, and this was 'liberally supported' by fellow citizens of other denominations, among others 'Archbishop Eyre, the Head of the Roman Catholic community in the West of Scotland'. He had made his donation by letter, and expressed that it gave him great pleasure to contribute to the object of the bazaar. In reply, Mr Pinto, the honorary secretary of the Funding Committee, stated that 'the Jewish community appreciated the Archbishop's handsome donation, not only on account of its intrinsic value, but because of the tolerant and broadminded spirit with which it manifested in the donor'.[74] When the foundation stone was laid the Christian community of Glasgow was represented at the ceremony: the synagogue was consecrated in September 1901.

Conclusion

This essay argues a strong and peaceful relationship between the Catholic Irish and the Jews of the Gorbals, and that this was due in no small part to the influence and good grace of Archbishop Eyre. A letter deposited in the Archdiocese Archive in Glasgow written by Archbishop Erye testifies to this. It is a long letter and sets out why those of the Roman Catholic faith should extend the hand of friendship towards the Jewish community in Glasgow. The letter is not dated, but it was likely the notes for his reply to a presentation that was to be made to him by the Jewish Community in Glasgow, by Baillie Simon, some time before Archbishop Eyre's death in March 1902, of which the following is brief extract:

> Allow me to express my sincerest thanks for the address just presented by the Jewish community of our city ... to know what has caused this compliment to be paid to me by that body has been a puzzle to me. During my career in Glasgow I have come very little into contact with the Jews. True, it is on two occasions I raised my voice in common with other Glasgow citizens, amongst whom I may mention Donald Macleod, against an intolerable cruel oppression and persecution of the Jews in Russia. What I said on those occasions may not have had much weight with the Russian Government, but it served to show our fellow citizens our sympathy with the Jews of Russia.[75]

The letter then went on to express that his actions were in accordance with the history and traditions of the Catholic Church. This is certainly a position that not all in the Jewish community would perhaps recognise, but in the Glasgow context, and given that the Archbishop was writing in response to the Jewish community's presentation to him, his words in every sense embodied how he acted in his life. Moreover, certain phrases appear to link him with the anonymous letter referred to previously, when he wrote, 'We may add the same about our own locality. The Jewish body is numerous, is prosperous, and is law-abiding', and concluded,

> on the 17th of this month it was stated in Court, by one of our Magistrates, Baillie Browan, that in his experience in the Police Courts that he had once a Jew before him charged with committing an offence. And in the name of Baillie Simons we all require a man, who is a worthy

representative of the Jewish body, a most useful member of the Corporation, a very successful and upright Glasgow merchant, and a citizen whom we all love and of whom were are all proud.

This response reveals a great deal of mutual respect and admiration. It seems clear that Archbishop Eyre was promoting a common cause with the Jewish community. Perhaps the reason this research could not find any Catholic intolerance of Jews in Glasgow was because of Archbishop Eyre's tolerant attitude. It could so easily have been different, not least when we consider the significant persecution of the Jews in Limerick in 1904, sparked by a Roman Catholic priest speaking in a tone unrepresentative of the Catholic community, and in direct opposition to the thoughts expressed by Cardinal Manning and Archbishop Eyre. Given the considerable concentration of Jews in the Gorbals it is not difficult to imagine serious social conflict taking place had the agitations encouraged in Limerick been replicated.[76]

Indeed, the good work was maintained by Archbishop Eyre's successor, Archbishop McIntosh, seen in his response to the 'Blood Libel Russian Case' protest meeting in Glasgow, in October 1913. It was noted among other things that Glasgow was the first city in Britain to appoint a Jewish Magistrate, and this was followed by a motion moved by Archbishop McIntosh 'against the foul accusations of the Russians'. And it was Jesuit priest, the Rev. Father Hanson, who seconded the motion, stating: 'He was [here] … purely out of an honest desire towards the Jewish race. Being not only a Catholic but a Jesuit he could sympathise with the Jews who as a race had suffered under foul lies' (perhaps the view expressed here was a veiled reference to Scottish intolerance of Catholicism and the Irish people in Scotland). It was noted that the audience was mainly Jewish, but that 'all shades of political opinion' were present, both Catholic and Protestant. But clearly, given that members of the Catholic community both moved and seconded the motion, this serves to demonstrate once again the degree of religious tolerance evident between Jew and gentile in Glasgow.[77]

As for the Gorbals, it remained the main focus of Jewish life in Glasgow, at least until the second half of the nineteenth century. According to Tom Devine, the Jews of the Gorbals were climbing the social ladder by the interwar years, and while they did face prejudice 'they did not experience the same type of systematic discrimination that was the lot of many Scots of Irish Catholic descent'. Indeed, by the interwar period 'some of the best known businesses in Glasgow were Jewish owned'.[78] At the same time, from the 1930s onward, 'Yiddish began to die out as the mother tongue', and is perhaps best illustrated by the fact the Gorbals Yiddish theatre – which had flourished there for decades – closed its doors in the 1930s. Clearly, while the speaking of Yiddish may have declined in use, as Vassilikou shows, the experience of living and working in the Gorbals ultimately favoured Jewish upward social mobility. The process of embourgeoisment was beginning to take place by the interwar years and within another generation the Gorbals Jews would be a memory. But as this process was taking place the Catholic community – seen first and foremost as Irish Catholic in composition – were experiencing a fresh attack from the Protestant community in Scotland. The Jewish community was not perceived as a threat to Protestant Scotland, but the Catholic community was, and even in the 1930s the General Assembly of the Church of Scotland recommended the repatriation of Irish Catholics, because they were 'a completely separate race of alien origins'.[79] Indeed, according to Patrick Reilly, 'the government pondered long and hard before rejecting pleas to stop Irish Catholic immigration and to deport as many of the interlopers as possible' during the early 1930s. Given this ideological climate is it any wonder, he argued, 'that the interwar years were marred by serious sectarian conflict'.[80]

In 1989, the *Observer* newspaper – echoing the words spoken by Dr Donald MacLeod almost 100 years before – claimed that Scotland was the only country in Europe 'that had in recent, or past times, not shed Jewish blood or persecuted the Jews'. It is indeed ironic that this report appeared in the decade that witnessed the first real and tangible diminution of anti-Catholicism in Scotland.[81] Two generations after Scotland's Jews began climbing the 'social ladder' Scotland's Catholic population – many of whom were of Irish descent – was finally experiencing a similar and widespread social mobility. As Vassilikou's model predicted, those descendents of the Irish Catholics in Scotland had ensured 'their group survival', and their experience of life in Scotland did – eventually – 'favour their upward social mobility'. But it was some time coming.

NOTES

1. T.M. Devine, *The Scottish Nation 1700 to 2000* (London: Penguin, 1999), pp.518.
2. Ibid.
3. W. Kenefick, *Rebellious and Contrary: The Glasgow Dockers, 1853 to 1932*, Scottish Historical Review Monograph, No.10 (East Linton: Tuckwell Press, 2000), pp.112–18.
4. Henry Maitles, 'Attitudes to Jewish Immigration in the West of Scotland to 1905', *Scottish Economic and Social History* 15 (1995), pp.47, 49.
5. W. Kenefick, 'The Scottish Trade Union Movement c.1850 to 1914', *History Teaching Review* II (1997), pp.18–25.
6. Maria Vassilikou, 'Greeks and Jews in Salonika and Odessa: Inter-ethnic Relations in Cosmopolitan Port Cities', in David Ceserani (ed.), *Port Jews: Jewish Communities in Cosmopolitan Maritime Trading Centres, 1550–1950* (London and Portland, OR: Frank Cass, 2002), p.156.

7. G. Gordon, 'The City of Glasgow', in J. Butt and G. Gordon (eds.), *Strathclyde: Changing Horizons* (Edinburgh: Scottish Academic Press, 1985), pp.58–60.
8. Kenefick (see note 3), p.57.
9. Maitles (see note 4), p.48.
10. Devine (see note 1), p.520.
11. Ibid.
12. Maitles (see note 4), p.49.
13. Ibid., pp.50–52.
14. *RC on the Poor Laws*, 1910, *British Parliamentary Papers*, Evidence presented by W.H. Raeburn, Q89.877.
15. Maitles (see note 4), p.48.
16. Murdoch Rodgers, 'The Glasgow Jewry', in Billy Kay (ed.), *The Complete Odyssey: Voices from Scotland's Recent Past* (Edinburgh: Polygon, 1996), p.227.
17. Devine (see note 1), p.518.
18. Rosa M Sacharin, 'The Gertrude Jacobson Orphanage: Care of Orphaned Children', *Scottish Jewish Archive Newsletter* 14.1 (Spring 2002), p.5.
19. Harry McShane and J. Smith, *Harry McShane: No Mean Fighter* (Edinburgh: Pluto, 1978), p.11; see also Billy Kay, 'From the Gorbals to Gweedore', in Kay (see note 16), p.6.
20. Kenefick (see note 3), see ch.5, pp.109–25; see also McShane and Smith (note 19); and Kay (see note 16).
21. Maitles (see note 4), p.45.
22. A. Levy, *The Origins of Scottish Jewry* (Glasgow: Jewish Historical Society of England, 1958), p.13.
23. Ibid., p.23.
24. *Jewish Chronicle*, 9 March 1883.
25. Kenneth Collins, *Glasgow Jewry: A Guide to the History and Community of the Jews in Glasgow* (Glasgow: Scottish Jewish Archives, 1992). Based on the two different figures presented in Collins's findings the percentage at the lower level of 758 would have been just under 38 per cent, and at the higher level of 935 the Gorbals Jews would have accounted for 46.7 per cent, just under half of the Glasgow Jewish population.
26. Levy (see note 22), p.22.
27. Maitles (see note 4), p.48; see also C. Hutt and H. Kaplan, *A Scottish Shtetl: Jewish Life in the Gorbals, 1880–1974* (Glasgow: Gorbals Fair Society, 1984); this is corroborated by Ben Barber, *Integration of Jewish Immigrants in Glasgow 1880–1939* (unpublished Ph.D. thesis, University of Glasgow, 1992).
28. Murdoch Rodgers, 'The Glasgow Jewry', in Kay (see note 16), p.227.
29. *Jewish Chronicle*, 4 September 1903, contained in a letter sent by 'Glaswegian'.
30. Callum Brown, *The People and the Pews: Religion and Society in Scotland since 1780*, Studies in Scottish Economic and Social History, No.3 (Dundee: Scottish Economic and Social History Society, 1993), p.25. When Brown made this statement in 1993, he also stressed then that 'Research [was] only in its early stages on the Jewish experience in Scotland'. Perhaps more telling was the remark that this research tended to 'concentrate on ecclesiastical and biographical approaches' indicative of the work of Kenneth Collins.
31. Collins (see note 25), p.7.
32. *Jewish Chronicle*, 9 November 1883.
33. Maitles (see note 4), p.47.
34. *Jewish Chronicle*, 23 September, 1902, 13 February 1903, and 10 November 1905.
35. Collins (see note 25), p.7.
36. Kenneth Collins, *Second City Jewry: The Jews of Glasgow in the Age of Expansion 1790 to 1919* (Glasgow: Scottish Jewish Archive, 1990), p.53.
37. *Jewish Chronicle*, 2 January 1903.
38. Collins (see note 36), p.101.
39. Ibid., pp.83–4.

40. Ibid., p.103.
41. Ralph Glasser, *Growing up in the Gorbals; Gorbals boy at Oxford; Gorbals voices, Siren Songs*, 'Omnibus edition' (London: Lomand Books, 1999), p.22.
42. See Braber (note 27); and Henry Maitles, *Anti-Semitism and Responses to it in the West of Scotland 1880–1939* (unpublished, M.Phil. thesis, University of Strathclyde, 1990).
43. .Braber (see note 27), Introduction.
44. Kenefick (see note 3), pp.116–18.
45. The Jewish Correspondent for the *Daily Record and Mail*, 1 February 2002.
46. *Jewish Chronicle*, 17 July 1903.
47. *Jewish Chronicle*, 1 July 1904
48. Quoted by Maitles (see note 42), p.55.
49. Ibid., p.56.
50. Ibid., p.61.
51. Ibid., p.58.
52. Devine (see note 1), p.487.
53. W. Kenefick, 'Irish Dockers and Trade Unionism on Clydeside', *Irish Studies Review* 19 (Summer 1997), p.23.
54. See Kenefick (note 3), pp.115–16.
55. Michael Lynch, *The Oxford Companion to Scottish History* (Oxford: Oxford University Press, 2001), see section under 'Irish Home Rule', pp.345–6.
56. Devine (see note 1), pp.301, 304.
57. Philip Bull, *Land, Politics and Nationalism: A Study of the Irish Land Question* (Dublin: Gill and Macmillan, 1996), p.7.
58. Various letters in the *Glasgow Herald* over the early months of 1882 testify to the fact that Irishmen were being 'boycotted' by some Glasgow employers. How extensive this practise was is unclear, but it was a response to event taking place in Ireland and the 'boycotts' imposed by Irish tenant farmers against the landlords.
59. D. George Boyce, *Nineteenth-Century Ireland: The Search for Stability* (Dublin: Gill and Macmillan, 1990), p.163.
60. *Glasgow Herald*, 21 February 1882.
61. Michael J. Winstanley, *Ireland and the Land Question 1800–1922*, Lancaster Pamphlets (London and New York: Methuen, 1984), p.29. In October 1882 the Land League was superseded with the Irish National League, and with this and the relative peace that was apparent over the autumn months, the Land War had effectively come to an end.
62. Lynch (see note 55), p 345.
63. *Jewish Chronicle*, 9 November 1883.
64. *Glasgow Observer*, 17 October 1885, letters page.
65. *Glasgow Observer*, 7 November 1885.
66. J.J. Smyth, *Labour in Glasgow 1896–1936: Socialism, Suffrage, Sectarianism*, Scottish Historical Review Monograph No.11 (East Linton: Tuckwell Press, 2000), pp.136–9.
67. *Jewish Chronicle*, 15 January 1892.
68. *Jewish Chronicle*, 8 January 1892.
69. *Jewish Chronicle*, 29 January 1892.
70. *Glasgow Herald*, 9 January 1892.
71. *Glasgow Herald*, 23 April 1892, front page.
72. *Jewish Chronicle*, 28 April 1893.
73. *Jewish Chronicle*, 29 January 1892.
74. *Jewish Chronicle*, 1 June 1900.
75. Handwritten later in response by Archbishop Eyre to the Glasgow Jewish Community's 'Vote of Thanks', Glasgow Archdiocese Archive, IP-E30/19/1 (c.1900 – the time of the 'Bazaar' to raise funds for the Portland Street Synagogue).
76. Dermot Keogh, *Jews in Twentieth-Century Ireland* (Cork: Cork University Press, 1998), see ch.2, 'The Limerick Pogroms 1904'.

77. *Glasgow Herald*, 28 October 1913.
78. Devine (see note 1), pp.521–2.
79. Kenefick (see note 53), p.24.
80. Patrick Reilly, 'Kicking with the Left Foot: Being Catholic in Scotland', in T.M. Devine (ed.), *Scotland's Shame? Bigotry and Sectarianism in Modern Scotland* (Edinburgh and London: Mainstream, 2000), p.32.
81. Devine, 'Then and Now: Catholics in Scottish Society, 1950–2000', in Devine (see note 80), pp.261–3.

Testing Cosmopolitan Tolerance: Port Jews in Cape Town during the Late Victorian and Edwardian Years

MILTON SHAIN, RICHARD MENDELSOHN and VIVIAN BICKFORD-SMITH

Cape Town in the late Victorian and Edwardian periods provides an interesting non-European location for testing the wider applicability of the Sorkin-Dubin 'port Jew' model, including the notion that port cities provide a peculiarly tolerant and welcoming environment, rooted in mercantile imperatives and cosmopolitanism.[1] The model patently has valency in the early modern European setting, in a world where communications were restricted, economies relatively undeveloped and political authority often localised, and where Jews could readily be identified as valuable additions to economy and society and enticed with special privileges. However, when one moves beyond this particular spatial and temporal setting, the notion of the 'port Jew' becomes more problematic, notwithstanding the attempts made by historians to identify 'port Jews' in later periods. Cape Town is especially problematic: at the very time that numerous European ports, including ironically Amsterdam, welcomed Jewish enterprise and industry, the Dutch rulers of the Cape prohibited Jewish (and Catholic) settlement. Thus, even if ports generate a tradition of tolerance and cosmopolitanism, this would not apply to Cape Town.

Jews were relatively late arrivals in colonial Cape Town: the Dutch East India Company which established the original settlement in 1652 as a refreshment station to supply its fleets sailing to the Indies, excluded non-Protestants from its employ and from residence in its colonial possessions. The sprinkling of Jews who appear in the records of the Cape settlement were either converts to Christianity or passed as such. The prohibition was ultimately lifted during the short-lived Batavian period of rule at the Cape between 1803 and 1806. This liberalisation, informed by the principles of the French Revolution, was confirmed with the transfer of authority to the British in 1806. However, only a handful of Anglo-German Jews took advantage of this new opening, and it was only in 1841 that the Cape Town Hebrew

Congregation was founded by 17 men who attended a meeting and religious service on the eve of the Day of Atonement.[2]

Seven years after the congregation's formation, its moving spirit, Benjamin Norden, a local merchant, welcomed – specifically on behalf of the Jewish community – the triumphant Cape governor, Sir Harry Smith, on his return from a battle in the interior. The exchange of pleasantries on that occasion reflected both the Jewish community's good standing and the tolerant and liberal ethos of mid-Victorian Cape society. All religious denominations, noted the governor, were 'equally valid' and Jewish interests were 'as blended with the people at large, for whether a man is a Jew or a Christian, he is equally protected by the law, and I believe equally acceptable in the eyes of God'. Smith's sentiments succinctly reflect classical nineteenth-century British liberalism, rooted as it was in respect and admiration for the Judeo-Christian tradition.[3]

In all likelihood the Jews of Cape Town were generally perceived in much the same way as were their co-religionists in mid-Victorian England. While that image included some negatively charged dimensions, it was on the whole benign. Certainly the 170 Jews in 1855 thrived in a society that separated church and state. An act of 1860 empowering the government to appoint Jews as marriage officers and another act eight years later proscribing any differentiation or penalties on account of religious belief were further indications of tolerance and goodwill.[4]

It needs to be emphasised that this tolerance was not strictly a local phenomenon but rather part of a much broader imperial ethos informed by an assimilationist ideal, albeit one permeated by notions of racial paternalism. Cape Town's status as a colonial port city was at best marginal to its tolerance of cultural and religious difference, in particular its acceptance of Jews. More significant in this regard was its character as an outpost of liberal empire. Similarly, its markedly changed character later in the century was a product of broader forces originating beyond the littoral.

In all probability this mid-Victorian tolerance helped to inspire the enduring myth, only recently challenged, of 'Cape Liberalism', one element of which was the notion that Cape Town was a tolerant and cosmopolitan port city which possessed a 'special tradition of multi-racialism' and where 'fraternization between racial groups ... remained relatively free and unimpaired by laws or even strong and consistent patterns of customary exclusion until well into the twentieth century'.[5] The harsh reality is that 'liberal' Cape Town could not withstand broader shifts in the late nineteenth-century cultural climate. As the decades passed, the assimilationist discourse of the mid-century gave way to a segregationist discourse which contributed to a sharpening of racial and ethnic differences in the city. The frontier wars in the eastern Cape, the mineral revolution associated with the discovery of diamonds and gold in the interior and its attendant insatiable demand for cheap labour, not to mention the legacy of slavery and of the hierarchical social structure inherited from the Dutch period, all impacted on the local *Weltanschauung*.[6]

Critical to this development, and therefore to undermining Cape Town's liberal exceptionalism, was the fact that the British granted Responsible Government to the Cape in 1872. This effectively handed control of the Cape to its white inhabitants. Despite a non-racial franchise, most blacks were too poor to vote. Responsible Government brought the beginnings of party political organisation along the interconnected lines of ethnicity and economic interests at both central and local government levels, in particular between English and Dutch/Afrikaans-speaking members of the Cape's white elite. Taking place against the backdrop of British imperial expansion, there developed an increasingly assertive and racist settler Englishness which informed perceptions both of 'non-whites' and of the Jew. This racism drew on the pseudo-scientific ideas increasingly popular in Britain about racial hierarchy, specifically social Darwinism, phrenology and eugenics. Predictably, Anglo-Saxons were assigned top position in this hierarchy. Segregation – or social separation – became a dominant ideology, and in keeping with this ideology the amount of white/black segregation increased considerably. The latter included the residential segregation of Africans, as well as the segregation of whites from blacks in hospitals, schools, gaols, many places of entertainment, some beaches, several trade unions and most sports.[7]

At the very time that racial attitudes were hardening, Cape Town saw the influx of a sizable number of East European (mainly Lithuanian) Jews fleeing the oppression and poverty of the Pale of Settlement and attracted by the economic opportunities created by South Africa's mineral revolution. Over 10,000 Jews settled in Cape Town and its environs between 1891 and 1904, radically transforming the character of the Jewish community, hitherto largely acculturated and bourgeois.[8] In this racially conscious atmosphere the impecunious newcomers from eastern Europe were increasingly defined in racial terms and rapidly became the targets for abuse and scurrilous stereotyping.

From the early 1890s voices were repeatedly raised against the influx of the conspicuous, strange and heavily accented East European newcomer. The dirty proletariat from the Polish Russian borders were warned to 'avoid our land' by a local German-language newspaper, the *Züd Afrikanische Zeitung*. In 1893, J.T. Molteno successfully moved a resolution in the Cape Parliament that government attention be directed to the increased and increasing immigration of Russians, Poles and Asians, with a view to devising a scheme to check such undesirable immigration.[9] *The Owl*, a Cape Town weekly, focused on the new arrivals as a symbol of urban evil and decay. Its readers were provided with vicious satire and ugly caricatures of semitic financiers controlling South African society. While these ideas were more obviously related to the alleged preponderance of Jews among the Randlords, the mining magnates of the Witwatersrand goldfields a thousand miles from Cape Town, the negative stains also brushed the local variety of Jew. Typical of the denigrating journalese was the following diatribe on the scene at the Parade, Cape Town's principal outdoor marketplace:

> Saturday by Saturday the 'Grand' – Heaven save the word – Parade gets worse. The rotten trash that is put upon the sales there would be a disgrace to Petticoat Lane. Not only this, but the trade is now largely carried out by Polish Jews, who import – no doubt from other Polish Jews in London – the commonest off-scourings of Houndsditch goods. Then these greasy frowzy gentry stand around and sum up things until whoever purchases is sure to be heartlessly swindled ...
>
> The fact is Cape Town at the present time is full of those Polish Jew hawkers, who live in dirtier style than Kafirs [sic], and existing on about half a crown a week each, rob the tradesman of his due. They don't pay rent, rates or taxes, yet they are allowed to sell goods just the same as if they kept a store. Respectable Europeans should order these people from their doors. That is the only way to put them down. Let these people do manual work.[10]

Evidently the East European Jewish presence could not be ignored, especially since the arrival of these hapless victims of Tsarist oppression and discrimination coincided with an increasing concern with public health as manifested in the Cape Colony's Public Health Amendment Act no.23 of 1897.[11] Dr H. Claude Wright, the district surgeon of the suburb of Wynberg, was particularly condemnatory of appalling living conditions in his Public Health and Sanitation Report for 1897. Writing about 'the large influx of Russian and other Jews, who overcrowd and cohabit promiscuously', he noted that 'amongst them filth and vermin abound, and they have great objection to ventilation, the crevices all being wedged up with rags in many of their rooms. Some of these people are *worse than the natives* in these matters' (emphasis added).[12]

These comments need to be seen in the context of new bourgeois obsessions with sanitation and health. 'Sanitation', a major recent history of Cape Town notes, 'was the hallmark of imperial civilization, a gospel carried to the colonies by British middle class immigrants'.[13] Such immigrants increased significantly in number from the 1870s and led strident campaigns for urban reform in Cape Town. English ethnic mobilisation was a critical part of these campaigns. It was promoted by recently established local journals like the *Cape Times* and *Lantern*. Such ethnic mobilisation grew by distinguishing

Englishness from the 'otherness' it perceived in the rest of Cape Town's population – whether Jews, Afrikaners, Coloureds, Africans or Asians – who were duly blamed for most of the city's problems during this period of rapid urbanisation.[14]

By virtue of their substantial numbers and their foreign manners and appearance, the East European newcomers were conspicuously and unmistakably alien. That alienness was reinforced by religious 'deviance' as the Anglican Dean of Cape Town, the Very Reverend William Barnet-Clarke, reminded his flock on Good Friday of 1899. Jews, he warned, were gathered in their synagogues at Passover to curse and anathematise the Gentiles. The Jews, he said,

> were reviling us and praying against us, for they could not countervail the truth that their forefathers crucified Christ on that day. Much as they might admire them as fellow citizens and public spirited men, they could not forget that. It was Caiaphas and his false friends who accepted bribes and bribed as at election time earning their money by the Jewish system of 'shent per shent'.[15]

Here was theology blended with crass prejudice. Consequently the *Cape Times* berated the Dean for speaking 'however unintentionally in the very accents of Judenhetze that disgraces the Continent of Europe, and the anti-Dreyfus fury that degrades France'. It was ridiculous, it said, to 'throw up' the crucifixion at the modern Jew, 'the cultivated ones at any rate', who 'far from reviling profess a high respect for the ethical teachings of Jesus'.[16] Clearly theologically based ideas were not without influence in turn-of-the century Cape Town. They certainly hardened existing divisions between Jew and gentile and consolidated the outsider status of the Jew. By and large, however, Jews in late nineteenth-century Cape Town were characterised in essentially secular terms.

Yet another factor influencing the position and status of Jews in Cape Town, and once again unrelated to Cape Town's character as a port city, was the Anglo-Boer War which began in 1899. Anti-Jewish prejudice was exacerbated during the war, following a large influx of Jewish refugees from the interior. Within months of the outbreak of hostilities, the city's Jewish population swelled from five or six thousand to ten thousand. The newcomers, many of them impecunious, aroused concern and even resentment, and the British High Commissioner, Alfred Milner, was quick to inform the secretary of state, Joseph Chamberlain, of the situation. 'Many of the refugees', he reported,

> are not only penniless, but belong to a very undesirable class. They include the loafers and hangers on of society, and those who made a precarious living by mean and in some cases illegal trades – such as

buying of stolen goods and the sale of liquor to natives. A great number
of then are the low class of Jews known as Peruvians.[17]

Significantly, the term 'Peruvian' had originated on the Witwatersrand,
demonstrating again the easy transmission of ideas between the port and the
hinterland.[18]

Milner's wife, then Lady Cecil, was similarly unimpressed with the quality
of the refugees. The worst of these, she recalled,

> were the Jews who had come to South Africa from the ghettos of
> Eastern Europe (they were known as Peruvians), and had taken British
> nationality and proposed to live on this and on their wits. They remained
> a heavy burden for as long as the war lasted, a curious people, in rags,
> with their belongings in untidy bundles and yet it was often found that
> they were quite well off, and the possessors of valuables.

As the historian Elizabeth Van Heyningen points out, Lady Cecil's remarks
contained 'all the blend of dislike, resentment, prejudice, and ignorance which
the Jewish refugees generally aroused'.[19]

Van Heyningen might have added 'untruths', for despite selfless
benevolence from Jewish individuals and institutions, the refugees remained
conspicuously poverty stricken. Their arrival furthermore aggravated an
already serious housing shortage and, in a city acutely sensitive to the dangers
of overcrowding and poor sanitation, these newcomers posed a potential
health hazard. Indeed, the appalling living and health standards of the Jews
once again featured in the Public Health Report for 1901 of Wynberg's district
surgeon, Dr H. Claude Wright: 'Their houses are filthy in the extreme' and the
children of '80 per cent of that persuasion bathed once a month', he noted.
Wright recommended a 'very rigid supervision' over their health standards
when dealing with the dairy products they vended. One year later his medical
report reiterated the same concerns:

> Dwellings of the Jewish community are much overcrowded and ill-
> ventilated. These people herd together and overcrowd to an alarming
> extent. They are exceedingly afraid of fresh air and ventilation, and close
> every aperture in their rooms, notably when they have any illness. Their
> mode of living is objectionable and dirty in the extreme. They seldom or
> ever bath and their bodies are covered with vermin. They therefore
> remain a sickly crowd, entirely oblivious to decency and sanitation. Many
> of their habitations are unfit to be used as such, and as they are large
> vendors of food, some serious notice should be taken of their mode of
> life and preparation and storage of articles of food. Some time ago I
> came across a manufacturer of caseim or cream cheese at a Jewish
> vendors place. It would baffle description to depict the filth of that place

in which the trade was carried on. I cannot too strongly denounce the state of affairs, and express my emphatic opinion that strict supervision should be given this very undesirable class, look at him from any point of political or sanitary economy you like.[20]

Dr Wright's revulsion was widely shared. A medical expert, Professor W.J. Simpson, went so far as to identify Jewish living conditions as a contributory factor to a major plague epidemic in 1901. Nevertheless, despite these suspicions, Jews did not receive differential treatment during the plague. That they did not can be attributed to respect for the Jewish establishment and to the fact that, as whites, it was felt that East European Jews could be regenerated. There was certainly no consensus that they were beyond improvement; the problem was essentially one of time. Significantly this was not the case for Indians – a primary focus of anti-alien activity and action.[21]

Besides associating Jews with unsanitary living conditions, caricatures linked the Jews to a range of Cape Town's social evils. *The Owl* was particularly malicious, its journalistic invective comparing strikingly with the anti-Jewish journalism in Europe at this time. Especially crude in his depictions of the Jew was *The Owl*'s German-born cartoonist, Heinrich Egersdörfer. 'The Evil of the Hour' and 'Curses of Cape Town' were just two of his many cartoons which reflected his violently anti-Jewish sentiments. But *The Owl* was not alone in its coarse stereotyping. Another periodical, the *Telephone*, claimed that the Jew was prepared to 'do his own brudder'.[22] Even a respectable daily such as the *Cape Times* had few qualms about vulgar stereotyping as evident in the following outburst against Yiddish-speaking fish merchants in the seaside suburb of Kalk Bay:

> A disreputable-looking coterie of the parasites of the social fabric, standing a little apart, conversing in a gibberish of mid-Europe, bare-legged, frowzy-headed, shifty eyed, and nervously sharp, ready to pounce upon the rough handed sons of the seas as they come to land ... The keen-witted specimen of the lower species of the immigrant Hebrew race in unvarnished guise and unreserved demeanour ... Rapacious foreign Hebrew who never risks his own life or safety ... indignantly asks in pig-English 'Call that a fish? Vy, I will haf to give it away.' ... The Peruvian soon pockets his profit, and so he prospers from day to day.[23]

Hostility toward the Peruvian Jew had obviously been exacerbated by the arrival of so many East European refugees during the war. 'A most undesirable crowd', was the way P. Ashendon, the city's engineer in charge of relief, described them. In his view they were appalling labourers, filthy and with a negative attitude toward physical work. One of Ashendon's overseers considered them 'more like wild beasts in a tent than human beings'. These people, concluded the engineer, 'are legitimately the pariahs of society and should be right under police protection, not the public works'.[24]

It was these sorts of sentiments that underpinned the attempt to curtail the influx of East European Jews through the Cape Immigration Restriction Act of 1902. Although primarily aimed at Indians, its language clause – which determined that anyone unable to sign his name in European characters fell within the description of 'prohibited immigrant' – was consciously designed to deal with the 'Peruvian' newcomers. Substantial pressure from the Jewish establishment in Cape Town and Britain, and the shipping companies that stood to lose financially from the loss of East European migrants, led to Yiddish being accepted as a European language for the purposes of the Act. But the anti-alien agitation continued unabated against a backdrop of rising unemployment and economic recession. 'The lowest class of Russian, Polish and German Jews, filthy and evil-smelling, pass in succession through the Dock gates', wrote H.S. Smith to the *Cape Times* in February 1904.[25]

The continuing influx of these newcomers also worried the colonial authorities, as evident in the *Report on the Working of the Immigration Act 1902*, compiled by Dr A.J. Gregory, the Medical Officer of Health for the Cape Colony, in whose hands the general administration of the Act had been placed. '[I]ll-provided, indifferently educated, unable to speak or understand any language but Yiddish, of inferior physique, often dirty in their habits, persons and clothing and most unreliable in their statements', was the way Gregory described the newcomers. 'That a limited number of such immigrants may be of advantage to the Colony is possible, but it would seem that the number actually being admitted constitutes a surfeit in a country, in which the spirit of speculation is already out of proportion to the capacity for production'. The Report went on to comment on the bogus contracts and evasive techniques of the aliens. It concluded that if Yiddish were not classed as a European language in the administration of the Act, the worst and least desirable immigrants would be excluded.[26] *The Owl* was even more direct. Anyone, it commented, working in the vicinity of the docks would realise the undesirability of the aliens. 'They are mainly composed of the exiles from Russia, Poland and Germany, the Semitic scum of these countries'.[27]

Hardening of attitudes towards the East European Jews mirrored the hardening of attitudes towards all non-Anglo-Saxon 'others'. Afrikaners, Coloureds, Africans or Asians were also blamed for crime, dirt and disease in the city. Thus Coloureds, for example, were abused as 'this hopelessly filthy and pestilent hydra' and 'a nightmare and an incubus on the community'.[28] Journalists and correspondents to the press concluded that the deserving white poor had to be rescued from a racially degenerate black residuum. In short, segregation and exclusion were a crucial part of the means by which the city's self-assertively English dominant class maintained social order in a city undergoing rapid economic and demographic growth and change.

Yet, despite the burgeoning prejudice against both East European Jews and 'non-whites', Jews never suffered the fate of the latter; attempts to define them as other than white failed and Jews escaped relegation into the 'lower' category. A powerful strain of philo-semitism, which ran concurrently with the anti-Jewish sentiments, played a crucial part here, as did the well-entrenched position of the acculturated Jewish middle-class establishment. Such philo-semitic sentiments were best exemplified in the words of Olive Schreiner, the famed author and social activist, on the occasion of a protest in 1906 denouncing the outrages against Jews in Russia:

> Therefore I say that I would welcome the exiled Russian Jew to South Africa not merely with pity, but with a feeling of pride ... The study of the history of Europe during the past centuries teaches us one uniform lesson, that the nations which have received and in any way dealt fairly and mercifully with the Jew have prospered, and that the nations that have tortured and oppressed him have written out their own curse.[29]

Those like Schreiner welcoming the Jewish presence in South Africa could well turn to Cape Town's middle-class Jewish elite, comfortably ensconced within the dominant white mercantile ethos, as reinforcing their philo-semitic arguments. Although the impecunious hawker, itinerant pedlar or toiling tailor comprised a significant and visible segment of the Jewish population, a very opulent and substantial Jewish elite enjoyed the benefits of Cape colonial society and contributed to its material prosperity. Indeed just prior to the rapid influx of East European Jews to South Africa in the late nineteenth century, a correspondent to the *London Jewish Chronicle* noted:

> There are three sections – so to speak – amongst us, the highest are the big shopkeepers, the second are the small shopkeepers, and the lowest – well we have no lowest. The conditions of life are eminently comfortable, and existence is not a very difficult problem with the majority.[30]

The fulcrum of Cape Town's Jewish elite was the Cape Town Hebrew Congregation with its synagogue in the public Gardens in the centre of Cape Town. Led by the urbane and Cambridge-educated Rev. Alfred Philipp Bender, the synagogue's members radiated bourgeois respectability and civility. At the time of Bender's appointment in 1895 the congregation was comprised mostly of English and German Jews who had arrived in the 1870s. A few members were of East European origin, but they had on the whole been successful in Cape Town mercantile circles. Although maintaining their foreign accents, they had usually learnt English during a sojourn in England before departing to

South Africa. These East European members of the Cape Town Hebrew Congregation saw English society as their reference model and soon shared a colonial lifestyle with their English co-religionists in the salubrious suburbs of Tamboerskloof, Gardens and Oranjezicht in the 'bowl' of Table Mountain. These middle class Jews formed, as the authors of *Cape Town: The Making of a City* put it, 'an integral part of the local elite of Cape Town', contributing substantially to the economy.[31] They fitted in comfortably with the bourgeois Victorian values of thrift, enterprise and sobriety, and enjoyed, in true Victorian and Edwardian fashion, ongoing public respect as 'cultivated' Jews. Tellingly, the city elected a highly respected Jew, Hyman Liberman, as mayor from 1904 to 1907.

Despite their acceptance into the general society the Jewish establishment of Cape Town was not indifferent to the levels of prejudice experienced by their less-acculturated co-religionists. Young individuals such as Morris Alexander, a Cambridge-educated lawyer and future son-in-law of the famed Jewish scholar Solomon Schechter, and Lionel Goldsmid, the English-born editor of the *South African Jewish Chronicle*, founded in Cape Town in 1902, were not confident of unbounded British goodwill and fair play. For them anti-semitism was an abiding concern. They were fully aware of the ugly anti-semitic currents running throughout the country in the wake of the Anglo-Boer War, particularly the insidious image of the Jew as a cosmopolitan financier. Clearly built on the alleged machinations of the Randlords on the Witwatersrand, this idea had taken root against the backdrop of the war and of the post-war agitation for cheap Chinese labour to work the mines. Cape Town was of course far from the centre of such activities, but the character of the Randlord was instantly recognisable, as evidenced in the birth of the cartoon character, the quintessential Jewish *parvenu*, Hoggenheimer.

Although the Cape Town cartoonist, D.C. Boonzaier, was responsible for the representation, Hoggenheimer was not his creation. This distinction belongs to the English playwright Owen Hall, who created the avuncular millionaire Max Hoggenheimer in his West End musical comedy *The Girl from Kays*. This story of an alluring show dancer who enthralled a South African millionaire opened at London's Apollo Theatre in 1902, playing for 432 performances before being brought to South Africa by the London Gaiety Club under the auspices of Messrs Wheeler and Edwardes. The loud-mouthed Hoggenheimer became an instant favourite with South African theatregoers. By all accounts the English comedian W.W. Walton delighted audiences with his portrayal of the wealthy Jewish financier of Park Lane. It was ten days after *The Girl from Kays* opened at the Good Hope theatre in Cape Town that Boonzaier published his first Hoggenheimer cartoon, acknowledging Owen Hall's creation by appending the caption 'with apologies to "The Girl from Kay's"'. Thereafter Hoggenheimer became a regular feature in a Cape Town daily, the *South African News*.

Hoggenheimer manifestly struck a responsive chord in the popular consciousness. Only in this way can the delight expressed by audiences at Walton's portrayal of the Park Lane millionaire and the enduring popularity of Boonzaier's Hoggenheimer cartoons be explained. The ostensible power of the Randlords, the imperialist nature of the Anglo-Boer conflict, the infiltration of pro-Boer ideology from Britain's radical left, which associated the Anglo-Boer War with Jewish financiers, and the controversial issue of Chinese labour ensured Hoggenheimer's transition from stage character to popular culture. It is no wonder that within two years he became, in the words of one-time Cape Colony Prime Minister J.X. Merriman, 'a classic character'.[32]

Crucially, the anti-Jewish stereotype that evolved in Cape Town was not constructed within the ambit of the city alone. Besides the impact of a new segregationist discourse and its attendant racist paradigm (which coincided with the influx of large numbers of East European Jews), the Jewish presence in other parts of the country critically informed the Cape Town image. This is well illustrated in a letter to the Cape Town weekly, *The Owl*, from 'Rondebosch Britisher'. Having visited Johannesburg, the writer, a resident of Rondebosch, a middle-class Cape Town suburb, was struck 'with considerable force at the presence of representatives of the chosen people'. 'Jewburg', he maintained, was certainly an appropriate appellation for the city. The Jews had after all 'spread in all directions, they permeate every phase of life; they are ubiquitous'. Their 'connections', he maintained, 'extend to the remotest point of the country', and their influence was felt 'everywhere'.[33]

Demonstrably, distinguishing between what is indigenous to Cape Town and what is imposed on it from without, is fraught with difficulty: the 'port' as a distinctive shaper of cultural patterns and social types becomes difficult to sustain. Cape Town's cultural ethos in the late Victorian and Edwardian period cannot easily, if at all, be separated from developments well beyond its immediate locale. Modernity, it would seem, erodes the social space within which Sorkin and Dubin's port Jew thrives; that was unique to the self-contained port city of the early modern period. The close integration of modern port cities with society at large, including their hinterlands, precludes this.

NOTES

1. See David Cesarani (ed.), *Port Jews: Jewish Communities in Cosmopolitan Maritime Trading Centres, 1550-1950* (London: Frank Cass, 2002).
2. Louis Herrman, *The Cape Town Hebrew Congregation 1841-1941: A Centenary History* (Cape Town: n.p., n.d.).
3. Milton Shain, *The Roots of Antisemitism in South Africa* (Charlottesville, VA: University Press of Virginia, 1994), p.10.
4. Ibid., p.11.
5. George M. Fredrickson, *White Supremacy* (New York: Oxford University Press, 1981), p.258.

6. See Hermann Giliomee, *The Afrikaners: Biography of a People* (Cape Town: Tafelberg, 2003).
7. Vivian Bickford-Smith, *Ethnic Pride and Racial Prejudice in Victorian Cape Town* (Cambridge: Cambridge University Press, 1995), pp.149–50. A telling example of these changes is the growth of segregation in cricket. There were mixed race cricket matches in Cape Town from at least the 1850s to the early 1890s. But in 1894 a Coloured bowler who had been picked to play for South Africa was removed from the team, and three years later a whites-only cricket league was established in Cape Town. The *Cape Times*, 13 November 1897, commented that though Coloureds were political equals of whites, 'socially [they were] not so ... both colours should ... pursue a policy of mutual exclusion'.
8. The total population of Cape Town in 1904 was close to 200,000. See Nigel Worden, Elizabeth van Heyningen and Vivian Bickford-Smith, *Cape Town: The Making of a City* (Cape Town: David Philip, 1998), pp.212–13.
9. Milton Shain, *Jewry and Cape Society: The Origins and Activities of the Jewish Board of Deputies for the Cape Colony* (Cape Town: Historical Publication Society, 1983), p.7.
10. *The Owl*, 23 January 1897.
11. Elizabeth van Heyningen, *Public Health and Society in Cape Town 1880–1910* (unpublished Ph.D. dissertation, University of Cape Town, 1989), p.251.
12. G42-1897 Cape of Good Hope, Reports of District Surgeons upon Public Health and Sanitation, *Annexures to the Votes and Proceedings of the House of Assembly*.
13. Worden *et al.* (see note 8), p.211.
14. Bickford-Smith (see note 7), pp.39–66.
15. *Cape Times*, 1 April 1899.
16. *Cape Times*, 3 April 1899.
17. Cited in Diana Cammack, 'The Politics of Discontent: The Grievances of the Uitlander Refugees, 1899–1902', *Journal of Southern African Studies* 8 (1982), p.248.
18. The term Peruvian is probably an acronym for Polish and Russian Union – a Jewish club established in the diamond-mining city of Kimberley in the early days. It has also been suggested that the term refers to those immigrants who had sojourned in Argentina under Baron de Hirsch's settlement scheme before coming to South Africa. If that is the origin of the term, the lack of a geographical distinction between Argentina and Peru needs to be explained. It is interesting to note, however, that in a short story in *The Owl*, 8 February 1901, by J.E. Corbett, the author refers to the English Jews struggling to compete against 'Hebrews from Peru and Argentina'. Similarly the *Johannesburg Times*, 1 April 1896, description of the Peruvian mentions the 'generosity of Baron Hirsch'. Another theory is that the term is derived from 'Peruvia', a mistaken reference to the ancient Latin term for Poland.
19. Elizabeth van Heyningen, 'Refugees and Relief in Cape Town', in Christopher Saunders and Howard Phillips (eds.), *Studies in the History of Cape Town*, vol.3 (Cape Town: Department of History, University of Cape Town in association with the Centre for African Studies, University of Cape Town, 1980), p.81.
20. G66-1903 Cape of Good Hope, Report on Public Health for the Year 1902, *Annexures to the Votes and Proceedings of the House of Assembly*.
21. See Shain (note 3), pp.45–6.
22. *Telephone*, 13 January 1900.
23. *Cape Times*, 20 March 1902.
24. Van Heyningen (see note 19), p.92.
25. *Cape Times*, 5 February 1904.
26. G63-04 *Report on the Working of the Immigration Act 1902*.
27. *The Owl*, 8 April 1904.
28. *Cape Times*, 9 August 1888.
29. *South African Jewish Chronicle*, 20 July 1906.
30. *London Jewish Chronicle*, 3 July 1891.
31. Worden *et al.* (see note 8), p.189.
32. Shain (see note 3), p.62.
33. *The Owl*, 27 November 1903

From Atlantic Hotel to Atlantic Park: Anglo-America, Port Jews and the Invisible Transmigrant

TONY KUSHNER

This essay comes out of the international conference on 'Port Jews' organised jointly by the Universities of Cape Town and Southampton. It is thus appropriate, given the subject matter and the locations of this academic partnership, to start with the arrival of the transport SS *Cheshire* in Southampton from the Cape during the Boer War. Of the 500 on board, some 350 were Jews. Most of these Jews, of recent Lithuanian origin (the so-called Peruvians), had left the Transvaal during the conflict for the coastal towns and, unwanted, had been persuaded by the British authorities to return 'home'. Their stay in Southampton, in the first days of February 1900, was incredibly brief: moored overnight a few miles from the port they were provided with light refreshments in the morning and then immediately whisked off via train to London.[1] From there, some were allowed to stay by the Jewish authorities but others were dispatched to a range of English ports where they continued their journeys.[2] Where they went on to is not known – some probably returned to Lithuania – but it is clear that they were only allowed on the transport ship on condition that they had the means to continue their journeys beyond Britain.[3]

It was the particular moment and especially the xenophobia and nationalism associated with the South African war that led to the case of the SS *Cheshire* developing into one of local, national and international concern.[4] Through the efforts of the *Daily Mail*, the largest circulation newspaper in Britain, it provided the opportunity to articulate a vicious populist anti-alienism that was also blatantly anti-semitic. The *Daily Mail* accused what it portrayed as the unmanly and selfish Jews on board of fraudulently claiming the status of poverty stricken refugees. These undesirables were then contrasted to the worthy Englishmen on the SS *Cheshire* 'who stood by each other in a proud, shame-faced sort of way'. The Englishmen, argued the *Daily Mail*, had left South Africa through no fault of their own, implying that the unsavoury Jews had somehow deserved their fate.[5]

The local solution envisaged with the imminent arrival of the SS *Cheshire*, as the rabbi at Southampton put it, was to 'get the refugees of our faith off as expediciously as possible'.[6] Through the cooperation of the Southampton authorities, this was achieved most smoothly and only the intervention of the *Daily Mail* stopped the dispersal of the refugees passing into total historical obscurity. Its notoriety was brief, however, and after the flurry of excitement the story passed into historical amnesia for close to a century.

I came across this particular voyage of the SS *Cheshire* in the late 1990s whilst researching a much larger project connecting the global, national and local dimensions of refugee movements during the twentieth century. Not surprisingly, given the controversy stirred by the *Daily Mail*, those in the Southampton Hebrew Congregation were concerned about the SS *Cheshire*, and its implications for the Jews of the town. The international diplomacy surrounding the ship, as well as the more mundane practical local issues, featured prominently in the minute books for the first months of 1900.[7] Subsequently, and rather remarkably for a piece of local history, it has been taken up in a national advertising campaign by pro-refugee campaigners in Britain as well as in books and newspaper articles on the nature of anti-asylum seeker prejudice in contemporary Europe.[8]

The story has recently been used to turn the anti-alienism of the *Daily Mail* against itself and to show how almost all refugee groups, even when later regarded as genuine and deserving, have been represented by antipathetical contemporaries as bogus.[9] Yet what has been lost in this instrumentalising of history is a wider sense of the story's significance in highlighting some of the most important features of the modern Jewish experience – that of transmigrancy and the fluidity of Jewish population movements. It is not surprising, given the powerful negative image of the 'wandering Jew', that Jewish historians and others have often emphasised the rootedness of local and national Jewish communities, especially in the West, revealing a sense of belonging, contribution and loyalty. If, in contrast, Zionist historiography has provided a critique of this approach, it has also shared the idea of a stable homeland as the end point or beginning of history.[10]

The concept of the port Jew, whether defined narrowly in chronological and geographical terms, as argued by David Sorkin,[11] or more broadly by Lois Dubin,[12] shows the impossibility of constraining Jewish history into a purely local context – however crucial it is in shaping each community and its particular dynamics. But the international flow of ideas, practices, people and trade make it totally misleading to study any port Jew community, and, to a lesser extent, any Jewish community, in isolation. What has been lacking in existing Jewish historiography is an acknowledgment of the full fluidity of the modern experience, of flows not just from east to west, or *galut* to 'homeland', but also such movements in reverse as well as across such lines of communication and travel. To take the case of British Jewry, the focus of this essay, in the period between the 1870s and 1914, the age of mass migration, some half a million Jews spent at least two years in the country before moving on.[13] Many hundreds of thousands more, probably millions, passed through and many Jews used the port to return eastwards having briefly lived in the West. Yet attention in the existing literature has focused on the small minority of East European Jews, roughly 150,000, who settled more permanently.[14] 'Great Britain', as a contemporary Jewish activist and pro-alien campaigner, argued, 'owing to its geographical position and plenitude of coast-line, [was] a kind of international Clapham Junction and clearing-house for the reception and distribution of passengers and commodities to and from all parts of the world'.[15]

This chapter has started off with the SS *Cheshire* as a symbol typifying this perpetual but far from voluntary motion of the Jewish experience. In similar fashion, Paul Gilroy starts off his path-breaking study of the Black Atlantic by arguing for a theory that is 'less intimated by and respectful of the boundaries and integrity of modern nation states than either English or African-American cultural studies have so far been'. Gilroy adds that he

> settled on the image of ships in motion across the spaces between Europe, America, Africa and the Caribbean as a central organising symbol for this enterprise and as his starting point. The image of the ship – a living, micro-cultural, micro-political system in motion – is especially important for historical and theoretical reasons. Ships immediately focus attention on the middle passage, on the various projects for redemptive return, on the circulation of ideas and activists as well as the movement of key cultural and political artefacts.[16]

In the case of Southampton's history, the significance, meaning and symbolism of ships has varied immensely in function as well as time. For its small Jewish community, as well as the town as a whole, either directly or indirectly, the prosperity of its shipping trade was crucial to its overall economic well being. Nevertheless, the growth of its international passenger trade in the second half of the nineteenth century and beyond, whilst crucial to the port, also began to threaten the civic respect that the Jews of Southampton had nurtured, largely successfully, across the nineteenth century.[17]

Considering its size, the civic contribution of Southampton Jewry in the Victorian era was heavily disproportionate. For a community that before the First World War never claimed more than 100 members, or at most one-eighth of one per cent of the local population, it produced as many as three mayors as well as numerous sheriffs, JPs, bailiffs and coroners. Indeed, Abraham Abraham, in 1838, was voted the first Jewish councillor in Britain. He risked prosecution by refusing to take a Christian oath, if, as the mayor put it, 'anyone had the bad taste to do so'.[18] The positive example of Abraham was used by contemporaries such as David Salomons, the principal campaigner in the gradualist campaign for Jewish emancipation in Britain.[19] It was also championed within 'liberal' Southampton to show the town's 'attachment to the great principles of civil and religious liberty'.[20] Outside the world of local governance, Abraham's son, aside from being mayor, was deputy chairman of the Pier and Harbour Board, director of the Chamber of Commerce and prominent in school and higher education governance within Southampton.[21]

The historian of Southampton, Temple Patterson, has argued that the city was transformed from the 1830s not so much by the extension of the municipal franchise but by

> a different kind … of people … the emergence of a new and frequently nonconformist type of business man, often not born in the town but coming into it because of the new opportunities it now offered, enterprising, sceptical and impatient of old ways … sometimes self-made and selfish but also sometimes imbued with Christian zeal and humanitarian ideals.[22]

Obviously, in this context Temple Patterson did not have immediately in mind the Jews of Southampton. Nevertheless, if 'Jewish zeal' is replaced for 'Christian', then his model fits neatly those that were prominent in the town's Hebrew Congregation and who also contributed so much to the wider society (even if, ironically, most of the Jewish leading figures that emerged were Conservatives). Indeed, Temple Patterson believed that it was the 'civic prominence and the respect' for Abraham Abraham that prompted the town's support for Jewish emancipation as early as 1841.[23] If further evidence of the full political, economic, cultural and social integration of the Jews of Victorian Southampton was required, it would be provided by the example of Michael Emanuel, mayor of the town in 1895. He made his Jewishness a major feature of his period of office, organising a special service given by the Chief Rabbi to which all the town's civic leaders and dignitaries were invited.[24] Emanuel also made no pretence of his occupation – aside from being a silversmith he was also a leading pawnbroker, quipping when he was accepted as a mason – he was Master of the Lodge of Peace and Harmony – that the members would have to start getting used to calling him 'brother' as well as 'uncle'.[25] More generally, the place of prominent Jews in local freemasonry, a critical meeting place between business and civic government, revealed their integration within the power structures of Southampton.

Here, on the surface, is a story of a port Jew community that developed and benefited greatly from the opening up of a town from an Anglican oligarchy of gentlemen, older-style merchants and retired officers in the eighteenth and early nineteenth centuries into a flourishing modern, diverse, international port.[26] It is thus possible to produce a Whiggish narrative with the emphasis placed on increasing tolerance and inclusivity, which, in turn, enabled religious nonconformists, including Jews, to play a leading role in the creation of what was to become one of the most important commercial maritime centres in the western world. But we know from other port Jewish communities that tolerance can run simultaneously alongside intolerance – most blatantly where Jews were more or less integrated into white society in slaveholding societies, as the work of Jonathan Schorsch on Amsterdam and Gemma Romain on Charleston emphasises.[27] In Southampton, throughout the nineteenth century, hostility towards nonconformists and Roman Catholics persisted. Furthermore, whilst the town had flourishing anti-slavery societies, there were also many in Southampton who owned estates in the West Indies.[28] Its civic leaders therefore were wary of taking strong leads on some of the leading moral questions of the day. Indeed, the first Jewish mayor of the town, S.M. Emanuel (father of Michael), caused a national scandal in 1866 by welcoming and feting ex-governor Eyre after his return from the brutal and racist repression of the Jamaican rebellion. It was all very well, Emanuel joked, in proclaiming, as did liberals and radicals in the town, that the black man was 'a man and a brother', 'but would these people have him as a brother-in-law?' Pausing for laughter, he continued by asking 'Would they be willing to have their beautiful and elegant sisters allied to the Negro – debased and despised as he was?'[29]

The importance of Southampton's support of what was Britain's first Jewish councillor and of Jewish emancipation more generally should not be dismissed. Yet the numbers of Jews locally were so low that these were relatively painless gestures to make. Even then, the failure of Abraham Abraham to become mayor, as was expected, in 1842, points to a residual hostility.[30] Moreover, it is clear from the records of the Hebrew Congregation, as well as the public behaviour of the Jewish leaders of the town, that integration and acceptance was conditioned by size and behaviour. That many of its major figures were prominent within the 'inner counsels of the Conservative party' is revealing in itself.[31] Local patriotism was particularly pronounced within the Jewish leadership, hence the remarkable record of civic contribution, including within the Hampshire Regiment and supporting Christian charities. Such local pride was never at the expense of denying Jewishness, but the emphasis was placed on the two going hand in hand in mutual reinforcement. Anti-semitism could be anticipated, and therefore deflected, as with Michael Emanuel's poking fun at himself and his status as a pawnbroker. That such occupational associations were quickly drawn was shown on another occasion when visitors to the town were given a tour of Southampton's Electric Light Works. Fearing damage to their watches through the presence of powerful dynamos, it was decided to deposit them for safekeeping: "'The Chairman of the Watch Committee [i.e. Michael Emanuel] is the proper person to take charge of them", a wag declared'. Emanuel was forced to join in the merriment by giving the men 'tickets' for their goods.[32] Similarly, his father's crude anti-black racism at the time of the Eyre controversy revealed a desperate desire to be part of elite culture at a point when many in Britain perceived the Jews as being racially distinct. S.M. Emanuel's remarks were made at a banquet which he had provided in Eyre's honour. He relished the attendance of aristocrats and churchmen at the banquet, representing 'traditional' England. Amongst those attending were the Earls of Hardwicke, Shrewsbury and Cardigan.[33]

More generally, as part of its general strategy to gain local acceptance, the Southampton Jewish community did its best to dissuade Jews without means from settling in the area. But the growth of transmigrancy, and Southampton's increasing importance in the trade, made this objective increasingly hard to achieve. In 1905 the secretary of the Hebrew Congregation, Nathan Levy, wrote to the *Jewish Chronicle* to revoke a charge that had been made in the *Empire Review* by a leading anti-alienist, C. Kinloch Cooke. Cooke had stated that he remembered

> a batch of Jewish immigrants being sent back from the United States and landing at Southampton. These aliens were taken to the workhouse, as they had no money to support themselves, and neither their co-religionists nor fellow countrymen would come to their aid.[34]

Levy responded that, in fact, the Southampton Hebrew Congregation 'had always made it a special duty to see after poor Jewish emigrants or immigrants'. Levy gave an example of ten poor Russian Jews arriving from America on board the *St Louis*. 'We provided for their immediate needs and on Monday paid their railway fare to their destination'. Significantly, Levy argued that anyone still believing this 'libel on the Jews of Southampton' should seek the truth from the chairman of the Southampton Board of Guardians, the master of the workhouse or the Chief Constable of the town. Jewish transmigrants slipping through the net were, it is clear, in the mind of local government, the responsibility of the local Jewish community. The task of the Jewish community was to send them onwards as humanely but as quickly as possible. As Levy put it: 'We have the greatest difficulty in providing means for these poor men, who are hunted from pillar to post, and who appeal to us so strongly for sympathy and help'.[35]

The scale of transmigrancy was growing enormously in importance in the latter part of the nineteenth century. From the 1890s, transatlantic trade shifted more and more from Liverpool to Southampton, marked by the move in ports by the American Shipping Line in 1893. With its strong continental and South African links, it is not surprising that Southampton was able to take advantage of the huge increase in world passenger movements and begin to take over Liverpool's supremacy.[36] It is through transmigrancy that the other side to the town's ambivalence towards Jewishness increasingly became apparent. Until the 1920s, the town was inadequately prepared to deal with the numbers of transmigrants passing through the port. Nevertheless, in 1893 an attempt was made to confront the scale of transmigrancy through the opening of an Emigrants' Home, soon to become known as Atlantic Hotel. Rather than having steerage transmigrants lingering in the unsatisfactory hostel in Blackwell in the docks of East London, it was agreed that it was essential that they be sent to Southampton direct whilst waiting for their transatlantic passage.[37]

The opening of the Emigrants' Home revealed the various forces calling for such an institution. Aside from the mayor and representatives of the council, there were also representatives from the American Shipping Line, who dominated the proceedings, and the American consul in the town.[38] The records of the American consul before the opening of the hostel make clear that the American authorities had major concerns about the health risks posed to emigrants through the poor conditions and lack of medical inspection at Blackwall.[39] In 1891 the first permanent infrastructure to control alien immigration had been implemented in the United States, increasing inspection, especially the medical examination, of aliens. In 1892 semi-hysteria against emigrants on health grounds developed in Germany and America as a result of the cholera epidemic in Hamburg and the typhus epidemic in New York, both of which were blamed on Russian Jews. Although in the United States a more powerful immigration bill failed in 1893, a Quarantine Act was enforced in that year.[40] The opening of Atlantic Hotel, on one level an obvious answer to a local need, was, on another, a part of an international concern and moral panic about the fitness of emigrants and transmigrants in which the American authorities played a leading part.

The American involvement in creating Atlantic Hotel should not disguise the local and national initiatives in the growing medical inspection of aliens during the 1890s. Indeed, in 1892 the Southampton Port Authority employed the town's medical officer to write a detailed report on the precautions needed to avoid the importation of cholera. One particular fear was that those rejected at New York 'might be transhipped back to Europe and prove a source of danger to ourselves'. At its own expense, the municipal government hired a floating port sanatorium. Any passengers examined on board suspected of carrying infectious diseases were quarantined on it.[41] It was clear that such action was not simply to protect the local population. At the annual meeting of the Association of Port Sanitary Authorities held in Southampton in 1902, Alderman Walton, who was hosting the event, emphasised the 'vast responsibility [that] rested upon the ports of this country not only to keep a clean bill of health for themselves, but also the whole country of which they were the front doors'.[42]

Aside from local initiatives, central government, well before the implementation of formal alien restriction through the 1905 Aliens Act, had implemented a system of medical inspection. It was limited to those travelling steerage – an indication of the class as well as racial prejudices behind such measures. Colonel Swalm, the American Consul in Southampton, described as a 'virile Anglo-Saxon', had, as one contemporary put it, 'decidedly strong views on the "Alien"', having 'no use for the pauper immigrant'. In several detailed reports to the Assistant Secretary of State, Swalm described the medical inspection procedures at Southampton, the thoroughness of which he totally approved. Each emigrant was doubly examined, by a ship's surgeon and then by a surgeon representing the Board of Trade. With the one exception of trachoma, the virulence of which he linked to Russian Jews from the East End of London, Swalm felt that 'all is being done that rational sanitary care and science can suggest'.[43]

Swalm could only witness the medical inspections in the port. Outside it, however, the American authorities – the shipping companies alongside the consul – continued to monitor closely and examine the transmigrants housed in Southampton hostels where they had assumed control as well as those in American-owned vessels in which the consul provided its own surgeon.[44] The 1905 Aliens Act formalised much of the medical inspection, although it changed little of what was already taking place in Southampton – one of the designated immigration ports. Whilst the restriction of pauper aliens was controversial, few disputed the need either before or after the act to keep out those deemed to physically or mentally diseased.[45] Meanwhile, the number of aliens passing through Southampton increased rapidly. In 1907 those from the continent alone totalled some 36,435.[46] It is significant, however, that the racialised discourse of Colonel Swalm, especially his fears about the health of Russians of 'the Jewish type' was not fully shared within the world of port health inspection. Indeed, it has been suggested that generally 'Medical Officers of Health [were] favourably disposed towards Jewish immigrants'.[47] On a very practical level, it was not aliens but British sailors and returning soldiers who posed the most pressing problems for Southampton's health authorities.[48] Even so, the medical inspection of aliens had now been formally instituted. Although the initial impact was relatively minor, a precedent had been set and a link had been made between aliens, infectious diseases, inspection and immigration control procedures.

The 1905 Aliens Act did not apply to transmigrants and was limited to those travelling steerage. In contrast, the 1919 Aliens Restriction Act and the subsequent aliens orders imposed almost total control with even greater emphasis on medical inspection. Nine pages of detailed instructions were provided for the medical inspectors in the ports, including, for the first time, clear responsibilities with regards to transmigrants. The shipping companies were now liable for any expenses incurred in keeping and returning transmigrants who were medically rejected.[49] The shipping companies, hoping for a return to the lucrative pre-war trade in international passenger movement, inadvertently found themselves victims of worldwide alien restrictionism, especially that implemented in the US through the 1921 and 1924 Quota Laws.[50] The net result, locally, was the creation of a huge transmigrant camp, Atlantic Park, a 30-acre site four miles outside Southampton and the site of a former United States naval airbase during the First World War.[51] It was intended not only as a money-making enterprise where the aliens could wait for their ships but also as a place of detailed medical inspection by the British and American authorities. Indeed, the government became worried about disease spreading through the 'use of undesirable and insanitary lodging houses and so-called hostels' housing the increasing number of stranded transmigrants which they thought would lead to another epidemic.[52] Hostels such as Atlantic Hotel were no longer enough to deal with the racial hygiene problem posed by the alien presence. The medical function of Atlantic Park came very much to the fore, employing bathing, de-lousing and detailed medical examinations. As the American consul, John Savage, put it in a detailed report (in which, significantly, the section on quarantine came first): on arrival each emigrant would be 'registered, cleansed and their baggage disinfected ... irrespective'.[53] Its commercial aims, however, were lost as the shipping companies found themselves responsible for a group of over 1,000 Ukrainians, mainly Jews but also some Menonites, who had been turned back from Ellis Island, caught in the new American racist immigration quotas of 1921 and 1924. Official British racial discourse by this time had caught up with that in parts of the continent and the US – these stranded Jews, in the words of Home Secretary Joynson-Hicks, were the 'class of people ... we do not want, and America does not want them either'.[54]

John Savage described the medical inspection routine at Atlantic Park:

Each passenger will be provided with a dressing room in which to disrobe, the clothing being immediately removed and placed in a canvas bag and treated in a disinfector while the emigrant is being bathed ... Numerous shower baths and a few bath tubs for special cases are provided, and after the bath has been taken the emigrant is then examined by the resident surgeon or one of his assistants to ascertain if the passenger is free of nits and lice. If found clean they will then be allowed to proceed to a second dressing room where the clothing which has been disinfected will be returned. In this section there is also a

special room for the treatment of hair. If passengers are not found clean
in every respect they will be detained in the quarantine section and the
operation repeated as often as is found necessary.[55]

Not surprisingly, the few fragmentary autobiographical accounts of Atlantic
Park that have come to light have emphasised the impact of the medical
inspections, especially the naked bathing examinations. Often so great was the
traumatic memory that it was passed on to later generations. Cyril Orolowitz's
mother, Liza Shleimowitz, then a 13-year-old orphan with her four sisters and
young brother, having escaped civil war and pogroms in the Ukraine, was
'interned' at the camp. Cyril recalls his mother relating the misery caused by
having her hair shaved and being sprayed with disinfecting water: the 'four
sisters form[ed] a circle to protect their baby brother, Izzy, while they were
being hosed down'. The children were to spend several years in the camp.[56]
Similarly, Jacob Klassen, a Menonite, left Russia in 1926 and had an extended
and unintended stay in Atlantic Park. His memoirs, from the point of
departure from Russia, are dominated by medical inspection. At Riga he
remembered the 'laundry, bathing, combing, disinfecting and most important,
the eye examinations'. Arriving at the 'famous Atlantic Park', 'another
examination was requested, [h]opefully the last'. It proved to be anything but
– concern about possible trachoma, periods of quarantine, hospitalisation and
endless re-examinations extended Klassen and his family's stay at Atlantic Park,
leading to massive disorientation. Eventually Jacob had to leave for Canada
without his wife and youngest child.[57]

Experiences of people such as Liza Shleimowitz and Jacob Klassen have
not got the attention they merit in studies of migration – it is significant that,
to a long-suffering transmigrant like Jacob Klassen, Atlantic Park was 'famous',
but that it has subsequently been subject to historical and popular amnesia.
Studies of emigration have often been limited to official responses or crude
statistics and, as a result, the humanity of those in transit has been sidelined or
ignored. Historians and others would do well to recall the words of Mary
Antin, who suffered the distress of medical inspections en route from Polotzk
to Boston: 'The plight of the bewildered emigrant on the way to foreign parts
is always pitiful enough, but for us who came from plague-ridden Russia the
terrors of the way were doubled'.[58] Never properly explained and crudely
executed, medical examinations and procedures were particularly frightening
to the already dislocated transmigrants.

Before 1914, the medical inspection of aliens in Southampton was done on
board outside the port outside the public gaze, as were those on the sanitation
ship. After the war, Atlantic Park was similarly a cut-off world. For the most
part, the settled Jewish community of Southampton were thus in separate
spatial worlds to the Jewish transmigrants who hugely outnumbered them.[59] In

terms of place identity, the organised community behaved, with good reason, as if its acceptance was dependent on keeping the required distance from the floating Jews who were largely out of sight. For a small community they did their best to ensure that on a temporary basis the transmigrants' immediate needs were met, but on condition that they did not settle permanently.

The port Jews of Southampton thus in many ways presented a true of image of the town to itself. The settled community did much to make it the globally important port it had become by the early twentieth century. The transmigrants, whilst largely invisible, typified a city that, as a contemporary stated, 'in comparison with its size has a very large floating population' and to which Southampton stood ambiguously.[60] On the one hand, it brought the expense of medical inspection and the fear of infection. On the other, it helped the prosperity of the town as a whole. Rather than the dichotomy of the slave-owning communities, with its tolerance of one minority and stigmatisation of another (the town was split down the middle over slavery and the treatment of ex-slaves), Southampton had a fundamental ambiguity to its Jewish minority. There was praise, but perhaps only conditional acceptance, of the settled Jews and fear of the transmigrants alongside recognition of the money they brought in.

The medical historian Paul Weindling, referring to de-lousing in the mid-twentieth century, writes that it has

> a prehistory in the more generalised medical screening of transmigrants from the East, as they made their way via such ports as Bremen and Hamburg, Antwerp and Liverpool to Ellis Island: here we find a sequence of routines imposed under different state regulatory systems on suspect ethnic carriers of 'Asiatic' epidemics like cholera, trachoma and typhus.[61]

His list of ports is selective but could have easily included Southampton, as we have seen. Antony Sher's remarkable novel *Middlepost* (1988) not only provides an evocation of Jewish emigration to South Africa from eastern Europe but also acts as a metaphor for the country as a whole. His character 'Smous' enters Cape Town and waits to see whether he will receive the stripping, showering and medical inspection he received at Libau or the sulky help he had received from the 'overworked Jewish Immigration people' at Southampton 'who had arranged ... transportation to the hostel'.[62] We need to add to the imaginative work of Sher and the detailed research of Weindling the knowledge that ports such as Southampton in Britain were part of a racial hygiene process that had, by the 1920s, through its local and national contributions, become truly internationalised and cross-pollinating. Hamburg, Bremen, Libau, Antwerp, New York but also Southampton were thus at the forefront of the inspection of alien Jews which moved from tentative steps to extreme and harrowing medical intervention and to the misery of increasing numbers of stateless people. The worldwide port medical inspection of transmigrants thus needs to be added to the overall story of port Jews – indeed, in many respects it provided a perverse mirror image of the port Jew: a mutually reinforcing global network of modernised expertise to stop the free flow of people. In the case of Southampton, whether in the form of its tiny but dynamic community, or in the sizeable but invisible transmigrant population and the medical response to it, the Jews were the essence of the port.

To bring this overview to a close: Ruth Ellen Gruber has recently described post-war Europe as representing a remembered presence of Jews and Jewish space through museums, restoration of buildings and quarters and exhibitions but with an actual absence of Jews.[63] In contrast, our case study had real Jews, permanent and transitory, whose impact on the town was profound, in spite of their lack of visible presence at the time and amnesia towards their existence subsequently. Their experience, positive and negative, has to be added to those coming under the umbrella of the port Jew. The port of Southampton, therefore, in a very different way to that outlined by Gruber, was also 'virtually Jewish'.

NOTES

1. The details of the episode are covered in the *Jewish Chronicle*, 9 February 1900, and *Southampton Times*, 3 February 1900. For an overview, see Tony Kushner and Katharine Knox, *Refugees in an Age of Genocide: Global, National and Local Perspectives during the Twentieth Century* (London: Frank Cass, 1999), pp.22–6.
2. Information about the fate of the refugees beyond Southampton provided by Aubrey Newman at the conference based on material in the Jews Temporary Shelter archive which is not fully accessible to scholars.
3. *The Times*, 22 January 1900, and correspondence between Mr Soulsby of the Transvaal Refugees Fund to Mr Stephany of the Jewish Board of Guardians, 15 February 1900, in Jewish Board of Guardians archive, MS 173/1/11/2, University of Southampton archive (SUA).
4. See Milton Shain, *The Roots of Antisemitism in South Africa* (Charlottesville, VA: University Press of Virginia, 1994), chs.2 and 3.
5. 'So-Called Refugees', *Daily Mail*, 3 February 1900.
6. Rabbi Holdensky to Stephany, 29 January 1900, in MS 173/1/11/2, SUA.
7. Minute books of the Southampton Hebrew Congregation, January–February 1900, in the archive of the Hebrew Congregation.
8. For example, it was used by the Refugee Council in adverts connecting the hostility of the *Daily Mail* across the twentieth century and featured prominently in Jeremy Harding, *The Uninvited: Refugees at the Rich Man's Gate* (London: Prospect Books, 2000), pp.48–9.
9. This theme is explored further in Tony Kushner, 'Meaning Nothing But Good: Ethics, History and Asylum-Seeker Phobia in Britain', *Patterns of Prejudice* 37.3 (2003), 257–76.
10. For succinct overviews, see David Myers and David Ruderman (eds.), *The Jewish Past Revisited: Reflections on Modern Jewish Historians* (New Haven, CT: Yale University Press, 1998).
11. David Sorkin, 'The Port Jew: Notes Towards a Social Type', *Journal of Jewish Studies* 50.1 (1999), 87–97; and idem, 'Port Jews and the Three Regions of Emancipation', in David Cesarani (ed.), *Port Jews: Jewish Communities in Cosmopolitan Trading Centres, 1550–1950* (London: Frank Cass, 2002), pp.31–46.
12. Lois Dubin, *The Port Jews of Habsburg Trieste* (Stanford, CA: Stanford University Press, 1999); and

idem, 'Researching Port Jews and Port Jewries: Trieste and Beyond', in Cesarani (see note 11), pp.47–58.

13. Lloyd Gartner, 'Notes on the Statistics of Jewish Immigration to England, 1870–1914', *Jewish Social Studies* 22.2 (1960), 97–102; Jonathan Sarna, 'The Myth of No Return: Jewish Return Migration to Eastern Europe, 1881–1914', *American Jewish History* 71 (1981), 256–68; and S.A. Hochberg, 'The Repatriation of Eastern European Jews from Great Britain: 1881–1914', *Jewish Social Studies* 50.1–2 (1988–92), 49–62.

14. The best account remains Lloyd Gartner, *The Jewish Immigrant in England: 1870–1914*, 3rd edn. (London: Vallentine Mitchell, 2001). For recent syntheses of British Jewish history, see Todd Endelman, *The Jews of Britain, 1656 to 2000* (Berkeley, CA: University of California Press, 2002); William Rubinstein, *A History of the Jews in the English-Speaking World: Great Britain* (London: Macmillan, 1996); Geoffrey Alderman, *Modern British Jewry*, 2nd edn. (Oxford: Clarendon Press, 1998).

15. M.J. Landa, *The Alien Problem and Its Remedy* (London: P.S. King, 1911), pp.54–5.

16. Paul Gilroy, *The Black Atlantic: Modernity and Double Consciousness* (London: Verso, 1993), p.4.

17. Southampton has not been well-served by historians, but see the three volume history by A. Temple Patterson, *A History of Southampton 1700–1914*, 3 vols. (Southampton: University of Southampton Press, 1966–75); and, of particular relevance here, Bernard Knowles, *Southampton: The English Gateway* (London: Hutchinson, 1951).

18. See the Council minutes reproduced in A. Temple Patterson (ed.), *A Selection from the Southampton Corporation Journals, 1815–35 and Borough Council Minutes, 1835–47* (Southampton: University of Southampton Press, 1965), pp.94, 105; idem (see note 17), vol.2, *The Beginnings of Modern Southampton 1836–1867* (1971), p.41 n.1.

19. M.C.N. Salbstein, *The Emancipation of the Jews in Britain: The Question of the Admission of the Jews to Parliament, 1828–1860* (London: Associated University Presses, 1982), p.131. Salomons also referred to Jewish councillors in Birmingham (1839) and Portsmouth (1841).

20. Editorial, 'The Shrievalty', *Southampton Times*, 12 November 1864.

21. Details from Sidney Weintraub, 'History of the Southampton Hebrew Congregation', Southampton Hebrew Congregation archives.

22. Temple Patterson (see note 17), vol.2, p.1.

23. Temple Patterson, *A Selection from the Southampton Corporation Journals* (see note 18), p.107.

24. See the obituaries in *Jewish Chronicle*, 10 February 1911, and *Southampton Times*, 4 February 1911.

25. *Southampton Times*, 11 February 1911.

26. As outlined in the title of Temple Patterson (see note 17), vol.1, *An Oligarchy in Decline 1700–1835* (1966).

27. Jonathan Schorsch, 'Portmanteau Jews: Sephardim and Race in the Early Modern Atlantic World', in Cesarani (see note 11), pp.59–74; Gemma Romain's contribution to this volume, 'Ethnicity, Identity and "Race": The Port Jews of Nineteenth Century Charleston', pp.123–40.

28. On slavery and anti-slavery in the town, see J.R. Oldfield, 'Southampton and Anti-Slavery, 1823–1870', *Southern History* 9 (1987), 90–102; and Temple Patterson (see note 17), vol.1, pp.85, 149–51, 172; for Catholics and nonconformists and reactions to them, see ibid., vol.2, pp.70–71, 76–7.

29. *Southampton Times*, 25 August 1866. See also his obituary in *Southampton Times*, 16 June 1894, which refers to the 'stir' caused by Emanuel's feting of Eyre. For a superb overview of the local politics at the time, and the importance of 'race' within it, see Gwen Oliver, *Southampton and the Governor Eyre Controversy* (unpublished dissertation, Department of History, University of Southampton, 2000).

30. Abraham was also linked to a political bribery scandal in which his Jewishness became an issue. See Temple Patterson (note 17), vol.2, pp.41–5.

31. *Jewish Chronicle*, 15 June 1894 and 10 February 1911.

32. *Southampton Times*, 11 February 1911.

33. See the essays in Todd Endelman and Tony Kushner (eds.), *Disraeli's Jewishness* (London: Vallentine Mitchell, 2002), on the contemporary racialisation of the Jew; *Southampton Times*, 25 August 1866.

34. Kinloch Cooke, in *Empire Record*, quoted in 'Labour and the Aliens Bill', *Jewish Chronicle*, 6 January 1905.

35. *Jewish Chronicle*, 13 January 1905.

36. Temple Patterson (see note 17), vol.3, *Setbacks and Recoveries 1868–1914* (1975), esp. ch.9.

37. *Southampton Times*, 11 November 1893.
38. Ibid.
39. United States Diplomatic Records: Despatches from the US Consul in Southampton 1790–196 (T239), vol.8, minutes and correspondence, March–April 1893.
40. John Higham, *Strangers in the Land: Patterns of American Nativism 1860–1925* (New York: Atheneum, 1978), pp.99–100; Howard Markel, *Quarantine! East European Jewish Immigrants and the City Epidemics of 1892* (Baltimore, MD: Johns Hopkins University Press, 1997); Richard Evans, *Death in Hamburg: Society and Politics in the Cholera Years, 1830–1910* (Oxford: Clarendon Press, 1987), ch.4.
41. A. Wellesley Harris, 'A Detailed Report on the Precautions Adopted by the Southampton Port Sanitary Authority Against the Importation of Cholera' (1892), in Southampton Record Office (SRO), SC/H/1/16.
42. Minutes of the Association of Port Sanitary Authorities, 19 August 1902, SRO SC/H/24/9/1.
43. See the *Annual Reports of the Port of Southampton* from 1893–1905; and United States Diplomatic Records, Despatches from US Consuls in Southampton 1790–1906, reports from Albert Swalm, 9 August 1904 and 27 November 1905; and the description of Swalm in *The Syren and Shipping*, 15 March 1905. On the concern about trachoma in America, see Howard Markel, '"The Eyes Have It": Trachoma, the Perception of Disease, the United States Public Health Service, and the American Jewish Immigration Experience, 1897–1924', *Bulletin of the History of Medicine* 74 (2000), 525–60.
44. Swalm report, 8 December 1905, US Consul Records.
45. *Aliens Act, 1905* (11 August 1905, 5 EDW.7). More generally, see Bernard Gainer, *The Alien Invasion: The Origins of the Aliens Act of 1905* (London: Heinemann, 1972); and Bernard Harris, 'Anti-Alienism, Health and Social Reform in Late Victorian and Edwardian Britain', *Patterns of Prejudice* 31.4 (1997), 3–34.
46. *Annual Report on the Port of Southampton for the Year 1907*, SRO SC/H/1/16.
47. Bernard Harris, 'Pro-alienism, Anti-alienism and the Medical Profession in Late-Victorian and Edwardian Britain', in Waltraud Ernst and Bernard Harris (eds.), *Race, Science and Medicine, 1700–1960* (London: Routledge, 1999), p.209. For a local study, see Kenneth Collins, *Be Well! Jewish Immigrant Health and Welfare in Glasgow, 1860–1914* (East Linton: Tuckwell Press, 2001), chs.4 and 5.
48. See the annual reports for the 1890s and 1900s.
49. 'The Aliens Order, 1920, Instructions to Medical Inspectors', SRO SC/H 24/9.
50. Higham (see note 40), ch.11.
51. For its full history, see Kushner and Knox (note 1), ch.3.
52. Jews' Temporary Shelter, *Thirty-Third Report for the Year Ending October 31st, 1922* (London: Chas. Knight and Co., 1923), p.8.
53. Report of John M. Savage, 27 January 1922, Department of State, National Archives, Washington, DC (NA), 841.56/15.
54. Joynson-Hicks, *Hansard* (HC) vol.180, cols.313–14 (11 February 1925).
55. Savage report, 27 January 1922 (see note 53).
56. Cyril Orolowitz, interview with the author, Southampton, 1 June 1994.
57. Jacob Klassen, 'A Historical Autobiographical Sketch', translated by his great granddaughter, Barbara Bradshaw, in the possession of the author.
58. Mary Antin, *The Promised Land* (Princeton, NJ: Princeton University Press, 1969 [1912]), pp.174–5.
59. The transmigrants hardly feature in the minutes of the congregation but there is a 'collective memory' of the help given with regards to weddings and festivals.
60. Annual Report for the Port of Southampton, 1910, SRO SC/HI/32a.
61. Paul Weindling, 'A Virulent Strain: German Bacteriology as Scientific Racism, 1890–1920', in Ernst and Harris (see note 47), p.221.
62. Antony Sher, *Middlepost* (London: Chatto and Windus, 1989), p.21. Sher's origins were similar to that of the principle character. See his autobiography, *Beside Myself* (London: Arrow Books, 2001). A powerful testimony of a Lithuanian-Jewish immigrant who contracted trachoma in the port of Libau and had to spend six months in a hostel recovering, before being detained for the same reason in London, is provided in Bernard Sachs, *Mist of Memory* (London: Vallentine Mitchell, 1973), pp.46–9.
63. Ruth Ellen Gruber, *Virtually Jewish: Reinventing Jewish Culture in Europe* (Berkeley, CA: University of California Press, 2002).

An Island of Humanity in a Sea of Barbarism? Hamburg Jewry during the Nazi Period, 1933–45

RAINER LIEDTKE

In late August 2002, Ronald Barnabas Schill, Senator for the Interior and Second Mayor of the City and State of Hamburg, spoke in the German Parliament as a representative of that state. The occasion was a debate on how to finance aid for the victims of the devastating flooding of the River Elbe in East Germany the previous summer. Schill, a judge by trade who had founded a party on a law-and-order ticket only a year earlier, had been tremendously successful in the Hamburg state elections and was now forming a coalition with the Conservatives to rule Hamburg. He used his time mainly to deride the politics of the Social Democratic/Green government and argued time and again that since the 1970s too much money has been spent in Germany for supporting foreign refugees, for giving aid to developing countries and for making the lives of imprisoned criminals comfortable, so that nothing was left in such a time of crisis for compensating hard-working German citizens hit by the flood.

The speech was repeatedly interrupted not only by members of the government parties who heavily criticised Schill's tirades, but also by members of the Christian Democratic opposition who voiced approval for some of his arguments. Schill's presentation ended in controversy when he refused to leave the lectern after the president of the parliament told him his time was up and his microphone was switched off.[1]

Obviously, this minor scandal is merely a footnote in Germany's political history in as much as Schill and his already disintegrating party, as most observers expect, are merely a passing phenomenon in the history of Hamburg's city government. However, in the further reactions to this speech we can find a significant reflex that is all-pervasive in Hamburg's historical tradition. Ole von Beust, the conservative head of Hamburg's government, whose Christian Democrats are the senior partner to Schill in the coalition to which the Liberal Democrats also belong, found himself compelled to criticise the ranting of his associate. He had to tread cautiously though, because his government depended upon Schill's continuing support.

Most interestingly, von Beust employed historical rhetoric to rebuke Schill. He said that one only needs to look at the preamble of the coalition contract of 2001 which states that 'Hanseatic virtues like cosmopolitanism and tolerance are indispensable values. They forbid any discrimination of minorities'. This is one of the first sentences in the coalition contract of 2001, drafted by a conservative law-and-order government in order to pacify its critics.² But in Hamburg this line of argument has a longer-standing history.

As the Second World War came to a close, Hamburg tried to come to terms with its immediate past. Rudolf Petersen, a merchant and the mayor installed by the occupation authority, addressed a memorandum to the British in the summer of 1945 in which he postulated that in comparison to the Reich in general, National Socialism had gained comparatively little ground in Hamburg over the previous 12 years. To Petersen it was a plain fact that Hamburg was not affected in the same way as almost all parts of Germany by the 'crimes and immoderateness' of National Socialism. The most important proof for this was that Karl Kaufmann, as *Gauleiter* and *Reichsstatthalter*, the top-ranking Nazi, had surrendered the city to advancing British troops without further resistance five days before Germany as a whole capitulated to the Allies. He had done so against the explicit orders of Hitler. Thereafter the city upheld the notion that it was a kind of enclave that had to the best of its abilities resisted the worst excesses of National Socialism due to the virtues of Hanseatic liberalism.

Hamburg thus claimed to be a 'good port city', to which some of the central hypotheses of this volume apply. As a port city, it supposedly created an open and tolerant environment, since it depends on the free exchange of goods and people. In this liberal milieu, one should assume, minorities of whatever kind were also more respected than in a location that does not have that kind of exchange with the outside world. So, what better way is there to test this notion than to look at the fate of Hamburg Jewry between 1933 and 1945, in its period of extreme crisis?

Let us first look very briefly at some key figures and events, as they relate to Jews, between the coming to power of the Nazis and the liberation of the city by the British. Hitler became Germany's chancellor on 30 January 1933 and his party, the NSDAP, won the general election of March of that year. Hamburg's city government, the Senate, newly constituted itself on 8 March 1933 and now included a weighty contingent of the Nazi Party.

In early 1933 about 20,000 Jews resided in Hamburg, approximately one per cent of the overall population of Germany's second biggest city. Their persecution began almost immediately, and the first anti-Jewish measures were aimed at isolating and ostracising the minority. They commenced with a boycott of Jewish shops, organised by the party's *Schutzstaffel*, the SA, on 1 April 1933, which was as successful or, in small parts, unsuccessful in

Hamburg as it was anywhere else in Germany. Persecution accelerated with the passing of a law, a few days later, which effectively removed Jewish civil servants from their offices. Associations of all sorts imitated this and incorporated so-called 'Aryan paragraphs' into their statutes which allowed them to exclude Jews. As a consequence many Jews were deprived of their livelihoods and social contacts. Quickly, an undefined but clearly visible Jewish ghetto developed, which did not look different in Hamburg than elsewhere in Germany.

The Nuremberg Laws of summer 1935 relegated Jews to second-class citizens by excluding them from Reich citizenship and prohibiting them from marrying or having sexual relations with persons of 'German or related blood'. Supplementary ordinances disenfranchised Jews and deprived them of most political rights. After a period of comparative calm, largely due to the need to present a peaceful and tolerant Germany in connection with the Summer Olympics in Berlin in 1936, persecution accelerated again and culminated in the pogrom night of 9 November 1938, during which Jewish property was systematically destroyed all over Germany and many Jews were arrested, mistreated and sometimes killed in concentration camps and prisons.

Many Hamburg Jews reacted to all this with their feet and between 1933 and summer 1941, when immigration was forbidden, some 9,000 to 10,000 of them had left the city through legal channels. What followed for the remnant was deportation and mass murder. The first transport of Hamburg Jews to the ghettos and extermination camps of the East took place in October 1941 and by the end of 1942 only 1,805 Hamburg Jews, most of them 'protected' by a marriage with a non-Jewish partner, remained in the city. Some of those were deported later on but exact figures are hard to come by. After the war fewer than 1,300 Jews resided in the city, some who had lived through the war underground, others survivors of the camps or displaced persons. Many did not stay and in the early 1990s the community had not grown any larger. Only then was it augmented significantly by the arrival of Jews from the disintegrating Soviet Empire.[3]

Although the above figures are specific to Hamburg, the events and the development of persecution were not particularly different in the Reich as a whole. So what are the specificities of Hamburg when it comes to Jews? What is the basis for the notion that the city was an island of liberalism in a sea of monstrous crimes? It has to be borne in mind that there was significant room for variety in anti-Jewish politics under the Nazis. Individual initiative or inactivity could make quite a bit of difference in a regime that was based on conflicting competencies between all sorts of decision-making levels. Let us therefore look at some details.

The first issue that deserves closer consideration is how Hamburg Jewry experienced *Kristallnacht*, the pogrom night of 9 November 1938, during which

Jewish businesses, public buildings and private homes were systematically looted and destroyed all over Germany and during which a large number of Jewish individuals was arrested and taken into so-called protective custody (*Schutzhaft*). Were the events in Hamburg any different from what happened in other German cities? Laurence Milner Robinson, the British Consul General in Hamburg at the time, certainly thought so. In a report to London, he argued that the Berlin government had its doubts that anti-Jewish measures in Hamburg would be carried out with the necessary brutality and therefore had ordered SS men from other locations to be present in Hamburg on the day.[4] This argument, which *Gauleiter* Kaufmann had also used in his self-defence during the Nuremberg trials, has been exposed as myth in a finely researched article written by an archivist of the Hamburg State Archive.[5] If some Nazi personnel from outside the city were participating in the pogrom, then this was due to the fact that, owing to an inefficient communication system, not enough Hamburg Nazis could be mobilised quickly enough to stage the 'spontaneous action of the common people' against the Jews. But in pre-war times, it seemed advisable to downplay the violent potential of a city whose economic fortunes were still largely based on trade with foreign partners. It is likely that Milner Robinson had been used deliberately by his regime contacts to spread the rumour about outside intervention.

The pogrom was carried out as ruthlessly in Hamburg as elsewhere. While only one synagogue and one Jewish funeral hall were burned down, a large number of Jewish-owned shops in the central business district were attacked and, more importantly, a very sizeable number of Jews were arrested and brought to the Fuhlsbüttel prison, at that time run by the Gestapo. The Hamburg secret police was hunting for Jews for one week after the pogrom night. The exact number of arrested Jews is hard to establish, but was most likely between 600 and 1,200, many of whom disappeared for good or were severely mistreated before their release. During the pogrom itself the local Nazi administration did not, as it claimed after the regime had collapsed, protect Jewish individuals or property against atrocities. Rather it confined itself to securing the property of non-Jews located adjacent to Jewish shops or public buildings.[6]

The second topic that deserves closer consideration is how Hamburg applied the so-called 'law for the Protection of German blood and German honour', passed as part of the Nuremberg Laws in 1935, which prohibited marriages and any sexual relations between Jews and German citizens carrying 'German blood' (that is, everybody else). It also forbade Jews from employing non-Jewish female servants under the age of 45.

Offenders were charged with having committed *Rassenschande*, or disgracing the race. However, a law on paper is somewhat different from how courts and public prosecutors handle it in practice. In particular, with such a law there is plenty of room for interpretation. A highly interesting study carried out in the early 1960s by Hans Robinsohn, a non-Jewish Hamburg merchant and Liberal politician who was active in the resistance against the Nazi regime, investigates how forbidden sexual contacts between Jews and non-Jews were treated by the Hamburg jurisdiction. Interestingly, the study found a publisher only in 1977.[7]

Between 1936 and 1943, investigations of 1,150 individuals suspected of perpetrating *Rassenschande* were carried out. A total of 429 of these were brought to trial, all of whom were convicted. Of these 270 were Jews, the rest their non-Jewish partners. That would not be particularly remarkable, since such prosecutions and convictions existed everywhere in Germany. However, if one compares Hamburg to two other big cities, Frankfurt and Cologne, as Robinsohn has done, it becomes apparent that the prosecution was much stricter in the Hanseatic city than elsewhere. Frankfurt, at the time of the sample, had less than a third of Hamburg's population and an even slightly larger number of Jews. Nevertheless, only 92 people altogether, that is slightly more than a fifth of the Hamburg figure, were convicted of crimes labelled *Rassenschande*. The ratio is similar for Cologne, which was and still is bigger than Frankfurt but also had fewer Jewish citizens. Only 62 people (Jews and non-Jews) received a sentence in that city.

One cannot assume that the sexual habits of Jewish men in Hamburg differed significantly from the habits of those living in the other two cities and neither was their intention to break the law five times bigger than that of their co-religionists in Frankfurt and Cologne. The only explanation for the huge difference is that prosecution and court practice in Hamburg were much stricter than elsewhere.

Hamburg's legal authorities treated *Rassenschande* cases differently from others. It not only prosecuted them more zealously, but also usually handed down the most severe sentences possible. Moreover, while the law did not distinguish between Jewish and non-Jewish 'perpetrators' of that 'crime', Hamburg courts punished the Jewish partner much harsher than the non-Jewish one. Thus, Hamburg prosecutors and judges used the 'protection of German blood and honour' primarily as a political tool to isolate Jews and to rid society of them. That was obviously what the law had intended, but the Nazi obsession with legality in dealing with self-defined enemies, at least until the Second World War, did not force the courts to act in that way. They did it voluntarily.

The courts in Hamburg that were concerned with *Rassenschande* offences did not consist of overt Nazis, at least no more than average. The jurists were not handpicked to serve in this area because they qualified based on their anti-semitic attitudes. Like the jurisdiction generally, they were in their backgrounds representative of Hamburg's elite. Traditionally, the law profession was closely intertwined with the city's commercial bourgeoisie, not only through family ties but also because for centuries Hamburg's constitution prescribed that an equilibrium be maintained in the city government between lawyers and merchants.

This educated and propertied middle class, most of whom had little or no contact with the Nazi Party before 1933, had internalised the racial ideology of National Socialism sufficiently to believe that non-Jewish Germans must be protected from mixing with Jewish ones. A further indication of how ardently most members of the law profession supported the regime is the persecution of Jewish lawyers in Hamburg. Not only were they ostracised from their trade as soon as the Nazis had come to power, they were also especially harshly prosecuted through the Hamburg courts, if there was any basis, constructed or not, for doing so. Those Jewish lawyers who had defended Social Democratic organisations or individuals in trials against Nazis during the final years of the Weimar Republic were particularly sought after.[8]

Like the courts the administration of Hamburg hurried ahead when it came to preventing *Rassenschande*. The case study of a Jewish/non-Jewish couple with two children, meticulously researched and documented during the 1990s by a surviving daughter, showed that this couple was denied permission to marry in Hamburg one month before the relevant law prohibiting this act came into effect in 1935. In this case, the male partner was not Jewish and, since he stood by his wife and children, was incarcerated and later pressed into military service in a kind of parole battalion, where he was killed in action. The fact that the man kept coming back to his family after he was released from prison was even reported in the local press as a particularly severe case of *Rassenschande*. The Jewish woman was killed in a concentration camp.[9]

The final topic to be addressed here in assessing anti-Jewish measures is the forcible sale or expropriation of Jewish businesses and assets, the so-called Aryanisation process. Especially here, local initiatives determined the speed and efficiency with which Jews were stripped of their property. This was particularly relevant when it came to determining what assets a Jew who was willing to emigrate could take with him and thus had an important influence on many decisions to leave or to stay put.

At first glance, there seems to be room here for the argument that the situation of the Jews in Hamburg in the first three to four years of Nazism was not as bad as in many other places in Germany. Admittedly, from the moment the Nazis came to power, non-Jewish competitors at all levels of the economy attempted to oust Jews from their businesses and, if possible, acquire their assets cheaply.[10] However, the city government, in stark contrast to the pattern described in connection with the *Rassenschande* trials, did not support a systematic campaign against Jewish businesses. On the contrary, a number of historical studies point out that in Hamburg, unlike most other places, Jews also participated in the economic upturn during the pre-war years and companies owned by Jews even increased their profits.

This fact was central to the notion that Hamburg was less receptive to National Socialist ideas than most other places in Germany. Is there perhaps a kernel of truth in it? It does not look like it. Especially if one takes into consideration the specific structure of the Hamburg economy in the 1930s and Nazi economic policy on the whole, there is a fairly rational explanation for the initial hesitation in making life difficult for Jewish businessmen.

The politics of rearmament and autarchy in particular favoured industry and farming, not commerce and trade and particularly not export trade, on which Hamburg largely depended. Therefore, Hamburg recovered only very slowly from the slump of the early 1930s and suffered from especially high unemployment. About 1,500 businesses in the city were owned by Jews, and any aggressive measures against them unquestionably would have exacerbated the economic crisis considerably and would have provoked adverse reactions among the general public. Furthermore, the economic elite of the city, which was practically synonymous with the political leadership, generally resented any form of state intervention (meaning the central state!) into their business affairs. Measures against Jewish businesses were therefore viewed as a potential threat to one's own position, since they could set a paradigm. Needless to say, these considerations did not translate into solidarity with or support for beleaguered Jewish businessmen.

But this period of comparative calm was short-lived. In 1937 a special economic advisory office, manned by ideologically uncompromising younger Nazis, was opened in Hamburg with the express purpose of accelerating the sale of Jewish businesses. The local authorities gave free rein to the activities of this office, because it was hoped that the central state would also focus its economic activities largely on this and not on other issues that concerned Hamburg's economic well being. The economic climate in the Hanseatic city had also changed. Unemployment was declining, the city was finally participating in the economic boom preceding the war and the National Socialist regime had demonstrated, not least through its foreign policy, that it could be successful and was there to stay for some time to come. It no longer seemed necessary to protect Jewish businesses in the interest of overall economic stability and it seemed highly unwise to counteract the measures of winners. As everywhere else in Germany, the Pogroms of 9 November 1938 hastened the forcible takeover of Jewish businesses and assets by non-Jews, not least because many Jewish businessmen had been incarcerated and their companies had fallen into the hands of trustees who sold everything without the owner's consent.[11]

A small detail may illustrate further that Hamburg was also in the earlier 1930s not exactly favourably predisposed towards Jewish business interests.

From early 1933 onwards, a number of non-Jewish Hamburg businessmen continuously protested that Jewish companies were still allowed to supply goods to the general public welfare offices (prostheses, glasses, medical supplies and so on). The German government decreed in 1933 that local welfare offices should not exclude Jewish suppliers and that recipients of welfare had the right to buy their aids wherever they chose. The welfare department of Hamburg's government paid no attention to this order and successfully circumvented it through a number of executive orders and administrative tricks. All to serve the business interests of non-Jewish competitors. When the government of the Reich finally changed the practice and decreed that Jewish companies should not at all be allowed to work in or for public services, there was practically no further need to change anything at the local Hamburg level.[12]

While Hamburg was not particularly vicious in expropriating Jewish assets, at least not in comparison with other cities such as Munich, it cannot at all be argued that it was in any way more lenient. That did not prevent Mayor Petersen from claiming after the war that Hamburg always made an effort to enact anti-Jewish laws passed for the Reich as a whole more hesitatingly and in a more considerate fashion. Frank Bajohr, who has carefully researched 'Aryanisation' in Hamburg, has come to the conclusion that anti-Jewish laws and measures called for by the central government were swiftly and ruthlessly enacted in Hamburg and that the city can by no means claim to have been an 'island of humanity in a sea of anti-semitic barbarism'.[13]

The port city of Hamburg, when put to the test, did not treat its Jewish minority in its time of extreme crisis any better than elsewhere. On the contrary, there were areas where the prosecution of Jews was worse in Hamburg than in other German cities or regions. And that might have to do precisely with the fact that Hamburg was a port city that for centuries had been run by a close knit group of 'grand families'. These were active in trade and commerce and also dominated the law profession, the two cornerstones of Hamburg's existence. Outsiders of any kind were only very reluctantly admitted into this circle and the Nazi period provided an opportunity, in a sense, to purify the elite of the city again and rid it of 'foreign' elements.

An enquiry into the economic policy of Hamburg in the 1930s and 1940s concludes that soon after the Nazi Regime took root, a barely hidden racial anti-semitism emerged in Hamburg's economic elite, which, combined with an opportunity for material gain, provided the basis for a parallel, mafia-like structure of business and administration that exploited Jewish citizens to the maximum. This system allowed non-Jewish business leaders to interact closely with the regime for the purpose of protecting German interests, without being accused of being greedy capitalists, that other enemy of the people sketched out in Nazi ideology.[14]

As I pointed out in my contribution to the previous volume on the history of Jews in port cities, where I looked at Hamburg Jewish history before the Nazi period, Hamburg was in no sense a tolerant environment.[15] Its tolerance was based on economic utility but very little else. When Jews appeared not to be needed any more to further the economic progress of the city or, worse, when it became apparent that there were 'legal' ways of expropriating them, this kind of toleration evaporated very quickly.

Finally, a personal note. While the myth that Hamburg was less receptive to National Socialism than other places in Germany has been exposed by academic research in the 1980s and 1990s and no respectable scholar sustains it today, this cannot be said about the popular mind. When I started researching Hamburg Jewish history in the early 1990s, I was confronted by statements that the Nazi period was not quite as bad for the Jews there than elsewhere, made by people who were themselves genuinely interested in Jewish history and sympathetic to the plight of the Jews. It seems, therefore, that the 'port city' bonus is still working for Hamburg.

NOTES

1. The entire speech can be found at: http://www.contra-schill.de/hamburg/rede.html.
2. In the original: 'hanseatische Tugenden wie Weltoffenheit und Toleranz [sind] unverzichtbare Werte gerade unserer Stadt ... [und] verbieten jegliche Diskriminierung von Minderheiten'. The coalition contract can be found at: www.cduhamburg.de/content/regierung/koalitionsvertrag.pdf.
3. Ina S. Lorenz, 'Die jüdische Gemeinde Hamburg 1860–1943: Kaiserreich–Weimarer Republik–NS-Staat', in Arno Herzig (ed.), *Die Juden in Hamburg 1590 bis 1990* (Hamburg: Dölling und Galitz, 1991), pp.92–9.
4. Anthony Read and David Fisher, *Kristallnacht* (New York: Random House, 1989), p.81.
5. Jürgen Sielemann, 'Fragen und Antworten zur "Reichskristallnacht" in Hamburg', in Hans Wilhelm Eckardt and Klaus Richter (eds.), *Bewahren und Berichten: Festschrift für Hans-Dieter Loose*, Zeitschrift des Vereins für Hamburgische Geschichte 83.1 (Hamburg: Verein für Hamburgische Geschichte, 1997), pp.473–501. Kaufmann's supposed 'aversion' to violence against Jewish citizens of Hamburg has also been stated by otherwise serious historians, such as Robert Gellately, who in his *The Gestapo and German Society: Enforcing Racial Policy, 1933–1945* (Oxford: Clarendon Press, 1990), p.121, has argued that the Hamburg *Gauleiter* was not keen on starting a pogrom and that therefore the action in the Hanseatic city had been milder than elsewhere. In this assertion Gellately relies partially on Kaufmann's own testimony.
6. Sielemann (see note 5), passim.
7. Hans Robinsohn, *Justiz als politische Verfolgung: Die Rechtsprechung in 'Rassenschandefällen' beim Landgericht Hamburg, 1936–1943* (Stuttgart: Deutsche Verlags-Anstalt, 1977).
8. Wilfried Weinke, 'Die Verfolgung jüdischer Rechtsanwälte Hamburgs am Beispiel von Dr. Max Eichholz und Herbert Michaelis', in Angelika Ebbinghaus and Karsten Linne (eds.), *Kein abgeschlossenes Kapitel: Hamburg im 'Dritten Reich'* (Hamburg: Europäische Verlags-Anstalt, 1997), pp.248–65.
9. Irene Eckler, *Die Vormundschaftsakte 1935–1958: Verfolgung einer Familie wegen 'Rassenschande': Dokumente und Berichte aus Hamburg* (Schwetzingen: Horneburg, 1996), pp.13, 29–31.
10. A particularly telling example is that the Hamburg chapter of the *Ring Deutscher Makler*, the umbrella organisation of German real estate agents, expelled its Jewish members in 1933 against the explicit orders not only of the central directorship of the organisation but also of the Ministry of the Interior, run by National Socialists from the time Hitler had become chancellor.

See Frank Bajohr, *Arisierung in Hamburg: Die Verdrängung jüdischer Unternehmer, 1933–1945* (Hamburg: Christians, 1997), p.34.

11. Ibid., passim.
12. Uwe Lohalm, 'Hamburgs öffentliche Fürsorge und die Juden 1933 bis 1939', in Herzig (see note 3), pp.499–514.
13. Bajohr (see note 10), pp.121–2.
14. Karl Heinz Roth, 'Ökonomie und politische Macht: Die "Firma Hamburg" 1930–1945', Ebbinghaus and Linne (see note 8), pp.15–176 (at 57).
15. Rainer Liedtke, 'Germany's Door to the World: A Haven for the Jews? Hamburg 1590–1933', in David Cesarani (ed.), *Port Jews: Jewish Communities in Cosmopolitan Maritime Trading Centres, 1550–1950*, 2nd edn. (London: Frank Cass, 2002), p.75–86.

Singapore, Manila and Harbin as Reference Points for Asian 'Port Jewish' Identity

JONATHAN GOLDSTEIN

The Jews of East and Southeast Asia resemble their European counterparts in one fundamental respect: both continents contain multitudes of geographically, linguistically, ethnically and theologically diverse Jewish diasporas. In an attempt to generalise about the history of sixteenth- to twentieth-century Sephardi and Italian Jews living in Mediterranean, Atlantic and West Indian seaports, historian David Sorkin advanced the concept of 'port Jews.' Some of Sorkin's criteria may apply to East and Southeast Asian Jewish communities. What are these distinguishing traits and to what extent do they appear in Singapore, Manila and Harbin – three geographically, linguistically, ethnically and theologically distinct reference points for Asian Jewish identity?

First, Sorkin cites the good fortune of Jewish merchants to be situated in societies that valued international trade. He then emphasises the specialised skills that Jews could contribute to those communities. He writes that:

> in an age without a developed banking system, these [Jewish] merchants had the great advantage of being able do business with, and draw bills of exchange on, relatives, friends, or business associates whom they could trust.[2]

Jewish merchants were thereby able to create distinct patterns of migration and commerce which linked old Mediterranean routes with the Atlantic economy.

Second, Sorkin stresses the valuation of commerce. He argues that it was the commercial utility of Jews to host societies which valued international trade that assured Jews a relatively long 'admission to, or continuing residence in, a polity'.[3]

Third, the Jews' commercial utility also gained them forms of social acceptance and legal status beyond mere residential privilege. (Examples of this phenomenon would include the acceptance of Jews in chambers of commerce, the Masonic order, and honorary and appointed offices of municipal government.) Their enhanced social status along with gradual increases in legal privilege enabled Jews to move toward full emancipation.

Fourth, Sorkin notes significant intellectual ferment in these nurturing political and economic environments. He refers to specific kinds of intellectual development as 're-education' and '*haskalah avant la lettre*'. For some Jews 're-education' meant an intensification of Rabbinic Judaism. 'New Christians', or Jews who had converted to Christianity as a self-defence mechanism during the reign of the Inquisition and who were derided as *marranos* (pigs) by their Christian adversaries, were able to reconvert to Judaism. Others who had remained Jews all along had the opportunity to deepen their commitment to faith and practice in the relatively unrestricted environment of port cities. Most significantly, *haskalah avant la lettre* meant that some Jews, without any formal exposure to Enlightenment tracts by Voltaire, Locke or Moses Mendelsohn, were nevertheless able to access and imbibe aspects of a broad secular culture. Simultaneously they retained and expanded upon Judaic beliefs. Sorkin cites the example of the Etz Haim Yeshiva of Amsterdam, which

> integrated secular subjects such as vernacular language, arithmetic and geography into a curriculum of Jewish subjects that included the independent study of the Bible and Hebrew language alongside study of the Talmud.[4]

Fifth, Sorkin broadly defines 'Jewish identity' as it existed in port cities. He stresses that some Jews who were 'lax if not altogether neglectful in observance ... remained identifiable Jews through their loyalty to the community'. They expressed 'non-religious' forms of solidarity with the community, particularly philanthropy and political intercession. He offers the example of a Portuguese Jew who 'did not keep the dietary laws, selectively observed the holidays, and in general questioned the authority of the Oral Law. Nevertheless he [was] always ready to contribute funds ... to both secular and religious education ... and to intercede with the authorities'. Sorkin describes 'wealthy Sephardi merchants [in London] who lived like Christian gentlemen ... at a distance from the synagogue'. They nevertheless continued 'to support the community with their wealth and influence'.[5]

The philanthropic behaviour and communal advocacy which Sorkin saw in the fifteenth to mid-nineteenth centuries had their counterparts in institutions not mentioned by Sorkin, in late nineteenth- and early twentieth-century Jewish communities in Europe, the Americas, the Levant, South Africa and East and Southeast Asia. These latter-day forms of philanthropy and activism, like the institutional behaviour which Sorkin does describe, were rooted in a synagogue-based religion. They included the establishment and/or endowment of Jewish communal social service agencies, especially those servicing immigrants; settlement houses, soup kitchens and shelters for the infirm, aged, homeless and orphaned; youth, sport, fraternal, political and

Zionist organisations; and quasi-secular as well as religious schools, libraries and publishing enterprises.

In an attempt to assess the extent to which 'port Jewish' criteria may apply in East and Southeast Asia, we will first examine Singapore, then Manila and finally Harbin.

Singapore Baghdadis' Communal Origins and Commercial Activity

Beginning in the late eighteenth century, Baghdadi Jewish merchants began moving eastward to Bombay, where they took advantage of favourable economic conditions created by the British colonial presence. The pioneer Baghdadi immigrant to India was Suleiman Ibn Yakub, who was active in the Bombay opium export trade between 1795 and 1833. He and other Baghdadi Jews duplicated the economic strategies of contemporaneous Parsee merchants as well as those of Boston, New York and Philadelphia entrepreneurs who had been trading in the Far East since 1784. All these traders shrewdly reinvested their opium profits in the import and export of other commodities, in real estate development and in early forms of manufacturing, especially textiles.[6] In the case of the Baghdadi Jews, this strategy was perfected by David Sassoon (1772–1864), who fled persecution in Iraq and arrived penniless in Bombay in 1833. Within a generation, Sassoon and his sons had built their own docks in Bombay harbour and were known as the 'Rothschilds of the Orient'. Sassoon's sons extended their empire eastward to Calcutta.[7]

By the mid-nineteenth century Baghdadi Jewish merchants reached Singapore. The Jewish community in this British colonial island/seaport/city had all the legal and commercial characteristics of 'port Jewry'. Jews enjoyed residential permission, civic inclusion and full commercial privilege in Singapore from their moment of arrival. Because they spoke Arabic (and readily learned English but not Chinese) they tended to trade with other Baghdadi Jewish as well as Arab traders, particularly those from Hadramaut who had settled in India, Penang, Sumatra and Borneo. In Singapore, as in Bombay, Baghdadi Jews engaged in the opium trade. They re-exported the drug further east to Canton, Macao, Hong Kong and Shanghai. In 1858, when Yaakov Saphir visited Singapore on a fundraising mission for Jewish institutions in the Land of Israel, he wrote that for 20 Jewish families, 'their means of livelihood was mainly the legalised opium trade that flourished between India and China and their generosity depended on the swings of the trade, for it was like putting money on the horns of a bull'.[8] Because of fluctuations in the opium trade, Singapore Jewish merchants, like other opium merchants, began to invest their profits in more stable commodities. Ultimately they purchased real estate. By 1907, Baghdadi trader and stockbroker Nissim

Adis had built Singapore's Grand Hotel de l'Europe. Somerset Maugham is reputed to have said, 'You may stay at the Raffles, but dine at the Grand'. For his private residence Adis built 'Mount Sophia', described as 'one of the finest mansions east of Suez'.[9] In 1926 a Jewish merchant visiting from Shanghai marvelled that

> Singapore is an ideal place for trade, the country being peaceful and free from unrest and turmoil, to which China is afflicted. The ups and downs to which merchants are subjected [in China] are totally unknown in Singapore, which is under the benign rule of Great Britain.[10]

Menasseh Meyer was Singapore's supreme Jewish entrepreneur and, by one account, 'the community's revered benefactor'.[11] He was born in Baghdad in 1846, raised in Calcutta, and arrived in Singapore in 1873 to join his uncle's opium trading business, the largest in the port. He expanded the firm's real estate holdings to include the Adelphi and Sea View hotels. By 1900 he owned about three-quarters of the island. One contemporary described Meyer as 'the richest Jew in the Far East', exceeding even the Sassoons.[12] Another source asserts that Meyer 'eventually owned more real estate in Singapore than any other person'.[13] Meyer was knighted by Edward VII in 1906 and, by all accounts, dominated and shaped the identity of the Jewish community for 60 years.[14]

Singapore Baghdadis' Intensification of Belief and Quasi-Secular Jewish Identity

The institutional and ideological evolution of Singapore's Baghdadi Jews exemplified, with the exception of re-conversion, the criteria for port Jewry. In the nurturing political and economic environment of Singapore, Judaic belief intensified and simultaneously Jews participated in secular culture, philanthropy and communal activism. Singapore historian Charles Buckley notes that, as early as the mid-nineteenth century, the pioneering Jewish merchant Abraham Solomon, while having much to do with the synagogue, educated his children 'in an English school here, an advantage Baghdad did not offer'.[15] This custom was followed by many anglophile Baghdadis, including Sir Menasseh Meyer, who sent his children to English schools and simultaneously oversaw the building of the monumental Magen Aboth synagogue and its religious school (*Talmud Torah*). In 1905, after a disagreement over who should run Magen Aboth, he built a second palatial synagogue, Chesed El, adjacent to his home.[16]

Sir Menasseh is distinct from his Baghdadi predecessors in his adoption and active promotion of what a visiting rabbi later characterised as 'a positive interest' in the building up of Palestine.[17] Sir Menasseh's enthusiasm for Jewish institutions in Palestine should not be conflated with the roughly contemporaneous development of European Zionism. In an important article in *Commentary* in 1963, historian Hugh Trevor-Roper demonstrated that European Zionism was very much a product of the Enlightenment in Europe.[18] Meyer, on the other hand, was influenced by the pre-Herzlian religious Zionism of Rabbi Hakham Joseph Hayyim of Baghdad, who officiated there from 1859 to 1909 and inspired in many Jews of Iraqi origin a great longing for visiting and dwelling in the Holy Land.[19] Meyer took his family on a visit to Jerusalem in order 'to inculcate in them a love for Israel'.[20] In Palestine he maintained a house for Talmudic study (*Beth Ha-midrash*) as well as a small synagogue for Baghdadi Jews. Like other Baghdadis, Meyer subsequently affiliated with Herzl's World Zionist Organisation. By 1921 he contributed £3,000 to World Zionist Organisation activities, the largest individual gift Anglo-Jewish emissary Israel Cohen received on his Asia-Pacific fundraising tour of that year. In the following year Meyer became the founding president of Singapore's Zionist Society, a branch of the worldwide organisation. His home then became, according to one contemporary, a 'beehive' of Zionist activity.[21] In 1922, when Albert Einstein passed through Singapore on a fundraising mission for the Hebrew University of Jerusalem, Meyer hosted a reception for 200 people which resulted in £10,000 worth of pledges for the school.[22]

During Sir Menasseh's later years his daughter Mozelle Nissim further broadened the scope of his Zionist activity and philanthropy. In 1929 she committed £3,000 for the construction of a school at Kfar Vitkin, then the northernmost Jewish settlement in Palestine. South Asian Zionist emissary A. Goldstein (no relation to the author) wrote to the Zionist Executive that Mrs Nissim 'is really one of the best women our movement should be proud to have'.[23]

After Sir Menasseh's death in 1930, the Zionism which he had promoted among Singapore Baghdadis continued to thrive. On 1 October 1936, in what may be perhaps the fullest expression of the local spirit of this movement, Montague Ezekiel and his two brothers wrote to the Jewish Agency for Palestine:

> We [the Singapore Zionists] have done much for Zionism here and our efforts were praised by *Israel's Messenger* and the *Jewish Tribune* [arguably the pre-eminent English-language Jewish newspapers in the Far East, Shanghai and Bombay respectively]. We are not the type of Jews to be intimidated by riots and Arab violence. Our reply to anti-Zionism is 'more and more Zionism' and to anti-Semitism 'more and more Judaism'. We are ready to work on the soil of Eretz Israel right now. If [Palestine immigration] certificates are sent [the Baghdadi] community

will be overjoyed and Singapore will be in the future another Zionist fortress.[24]

In early 1941 Singaporean Flora Shooker, in the tradition of her Baghdadi predecessors, established an educational trust for use in Palestine, Baghdad and Singapore.[25] Although Singapore was overrun by the Japanese shortly thereafter and most of its Jews incarcerated, after the Second World War the Baghdadi community and its Zionist movement rebounded. In 1955 one member of the community, David Saul Marshall (1908–95), was elected Singapore's first Chief Minister. In that capacity he gave Singapore its first measure of internal self-government and set the colony on its path to complete independence, which was achieved shortly after Marshall left office.[26]

Jews in independent as well as in colonial Singapore enjoyed full equality. Judaism became one of the multi-ethnic nation's eight officially recognised religions. In 1977 the magazine *Israel Report* expressed what it saw as the commercial rationale behind this equality, an argument similar to Sorkin's assertion about the economic utility of Jews in port cities:

> Lee Kuan Yew's regime, which makes a point of displaying openness both internally and externally, is considerably interested in having Jews live in Singapore. For this country, which is a crossroads and commercial centre, there is a clear advantage in the existence of a synagogue alongside temples, mosques, and churches.[27]

Prime Minister Lee and other leaders of independent Singapore came to realise that there was much to be learned from the newly independent Jewish state. In 1956, in one of the earliest expressions of that awareness, Frances Thomas, the Minister for Communications and Works, argued that Singapore, 'now on the threshold of independence, could learn a lot from the spirit which has turned the small State of Israel from a desert into a garden'.[28] Singaporean Zionists laboured diligently to solidify two-way ties. In 1946 a Singapore branch of the Labour Zionist youth group Habonim was established, followed several years later by a local affiliate of the Women's International Zionist Organisation (WIZO).[29] A 1953 visit by *Jerusalem Post* founding editor Gershon Agron resulted in contributions of US$6,740 to the United Israel Appeal and a simultaneous communal commitment to assist Singaporeans wishing to emigrate to Israel. An internal community assessment of the results of Agron's visit includes the comment:

> During Mr. Agron's visit, steps were taken to assist the immigration to Israel of five young Jewish girls and a woman of sixty years. They travelled to Bombay with funds provided by various donors, whose generosity deserve our appreciation. This should be an encouragement both to our youth, who really feel they could do better in Israel, as well

as to our donors, who will have the satisfaction of knowing that the money was well spent.[30]

In 1956 the *Singapore Standard* reported that an '"Israel Today" photographic exhibit is the biggest postwar public event organised by the Colony's 900-strong Jewish community'.[31] In that same year outgoing Israeli Foreign Minister and former Prime Minister Moshe Sharett remarked after a visit to Singapore that 'the gathered people's thirst to listen and understand is endless'.[32] A March 1962 visit and lecture by Keren Hayesod Director Shlomo Temkin netted contributions of US$2,443 to assist new immigrants in Israel. This visit was followed by a series of trade and technical aid agreements between Singapore and Israel and ongoing visits by ministers, public figures and senior officials. In 1969 this process culminated in the establishment of full diplomatic relations between an independent Singapore and the Jewish state.[33]

The strengthening of Baghdadi Jewish life in Singapore and of ties between Singapore and Israel occurred simultaneously with the almost complete disintegration of Jewish communal life in Iraq. While Jews had experienced periods of both toleration and persecution under the Ottoman Sultanate as well as in independent Iraq, until 1948 the community as a whole had no realistic alternatives other than trying to cope with mercurial rulers. After the creation of an independent Jewish state in 1948 there was a concrete alternative. In 1949–50 over 150,000 Iraqi Jews evacuated en masse to Israel. Because of many Iraqis' high educational level and prominence in business, law and government, they, unlike other Oriental Jewish immigrants, integrated relatively smoothly into the then-overwhelmingly Ashkenazi power structure of the Jewish state. Their success stories ranged from that of Shlomo Hillel, Israel's first minister of police, to a number of Chief Rabbis, to writers Shimon Ballas and Sami Michael, academics Sasson Somekh (who completed high school in Baghdad) and Sammy Smooha, parliamentarian Mordechai Ben Porat, Defence Minister and Labour Party Chief Benjamin Ben Eliezer, Army Chief of Staff Moshe Levy, and Ambassador Zvi Gabbay, in 2003 the Deputy Director General of Israel's Foreign Ministry, with jurisdiction for all of East, South and Southeast Asia.

At precisely the time when many Iraqi Jews were integrating into Israeli society, an ethnically diverse Jewish community was forming in Singapore. Traditional Baghdadi communal institutions were also being preserved. Two other Jewish populations grew up alongside the Baghdadis. Starting in 1965, when Israeli experts began to train Singapore's new armed forces, Israeli diplomats, consultants and business people arrived on temporary assignments. There was an additional influx of non-Israeli, overwhelmingly Ashkenazi diplomats, professionals, business people, students and other temporary residents. This group has initiated informal gatherings on Reform Jewish lines and imports a rabbi to conduct High Holiday services at a hotel.

The core of Jewish residents of Singapore with Singaporean citizenship remains overwhelmingly Baghdadi. Indeed if one wishes to see a functioning Baghdadi Jewish community in 2003, one only needs to visit Singapore. The community consists of about 180 people. An American academic who attended a Sabbath service in one of the Baghdadi synagogues in Singapore in 2000 observed both the recent diversity and traditional characteristics of the community. She wrote:

> On the right side sit the old-timers, the men of Baghdadi origin who lived through the Japanese occupation. On the left side sit the wealthier members of the community and the younger generation of Jews and expatriate Israelis, some of whom have become important, active members of the community ... When Frank Benjamin, President of the Jewish Welfare Board, stepped down from participating in the Torah service, he walked the room and wishes *Shabbat shalom* [Sabbath peace] to all. The gesture is heartfelt and inclusive, consistent with his determination to bring all Jews living in Singapore together ... Frank Benjamin and others are determined to keep their [community] vibrant and alive without sacrificing the basic orthodox traditions that inspired Singapore's first Baghdadi Jews over 160 years ago.[34]

Apart from the fact that there is no evidence of 'new Christians' reconverting in Singapore, the Baghdadi community of Singapore exemplifies all port Jewish characteristics. Singapore represents Jewish communal longevity and vitality in what was, in the 1970s, the largest seaport in the world. Two other cases – Manila and Harbin – represent somewhat different reference points for Asian Jewish identity.

Manila Jews' Communal Origins and Commercial Activity

The 'new Christian' brothers Jorge and Domingo Rodriguez are the first Jews who are recorded to have arrived in the Spanish Philippines. They reached Manila in the 1590s. By 1593 both were tried and convicted at an *auto-da-fe* in Mexico City because the Inquisition did not have an independent tribunal in the Philippines. The Inquisition imprisoned the Rodriguez brothers and subsequently tried and convicted at least eight other 'new Christians' from the Philippines.[35]

A second group of Jews arrived in the Philippines in the late 1800s. After the Franco-Prussian War of 1870 two Levy brothers fled Alsace with a stash of diamonds. They first established a jewellery store and then a general merchandising business, Estrella del Norte, which exists in Manila today.

Their enterprise branched out from the importation of gems to pharmaceuticals and automobiles. By 1898, when the United States took over the Philippines from Spain, the Levys had been joined by Turkish, Syrian and Egyptian Jews, creating a multi-ethnic community of approximately 50 individuals.[36]

Unlike Singapore, where there is no record of the existence of any 'new Christians', we know that a 'new Christian' community existed in Manila. Before 1898 they simply may have been too intimidated to reconvert, precisely the result which the Inquisition intended. Nevertheless, once the Spanish departed in 1898, there is no record of any Filipino 'new Christian' reconverting to Judaism, as Sorkin and others observed in a Mediterranean-Atlantic context. But Manila Jewry grew by other means. By 1918, 20 years after the American takeover, Manila Jewry consisted of about 150 people. These new immigrants, according to historian Annette Eberly, considered Manila 'a second frontier ... a place for the young and ambitious to flee to. It was especially attractive to those who chafed at limitations on social and economic mobility in their native lands'.[37] The newcomers were mainly American servicemen discharged in Manila after the Spanish-American and First World Wars plus Russian Jews fleeing the Bolshevik Revolution of 1917. These arrivals, like their Singapore brethren, engaged in import and export trade and in portside real estate development. But they did not interact with a cohesive international Jewish merchant diaspora. In this respect Manila Jews differ from Sorkin's European and Mediterranean Jews, whose commerce was overwhelmingly characterised by ethnic networking.

Jewish Institutional Development in Manila

By 1920 Manila Jewry included the founder of the Makati Stock Exchange, the conductor of the Manila Symphony Orchestra, physicians and architects.[38] Apart from these purely secular achievements, 22 years after the commencement of the American occupation there had been almost no Jewish institutional development. Spanish repression may explain this phenomenon before 1898. It does not account for the absence of institutional development under the Americans. In 1920 the aforementioned Zionist fundraiser Israel Cohen, who was greatly impressed by the institutional and intellectual development of Singapore Jewry, visited Manila. He lamented that although

> there were several hundred Jews, they had not formed a synagogue ...
> Only those who still had a flickering of Jewish consciousness met
> together on the two most solemn days of the Jewish calendar ... after
> which they hibernated for another twelve months.

Despite the fact that

> they were there twenty years, there was no Jewish organization or
> institution of any kind. If a Jew wished to get married, he took a day trip
> to Hong Kong. I left wondering whether all the fortunes of the rich Jews
> of Manila are worth the soul of one poor Jew of Zamboanga [a Syrian Jew
> he had met on one of the outer Philippine islands, who told Cohen 'we feel
> here in Galuth ... soon we hope to get back to the land of Israel'].[39]

A wealthy Ashkenazi benefactor finally built a synagogue in Manila in 1924.
Full-time clergy rarely serviced it. The community imported rabbis and cantors
from Shanghai and elsewhere for short stints. At one point an itinerant rabbi
commuted between the Philippines, Thailand and Vietnam.[40] In 1930 an
American journalist reported that the 80 Jewish families and 50 single Jews in
the Philippines

> are all well established yet indifferent to their Judaism. They have no
> interest in a Jewish community. There is a handsome synagogue, but it is
> used only on [the Jewish high holidays of] Rosh Hashonah and Yom
> Kippur. There was a religious school, but it was closed on account of the
> scarcity of teachers. Thus, most of the children receive absolutely no
> Jewish education and the religious indifference of their parents plus the
> lack of knowledge of Jewish affairs of the children counts these families
> as a total loss to Judaism.[41]

Manila's Jews clearly experienced precious little of the type of intensified
Rabbinic Judaism as occurred in Singapore. While some Manila Jews faded
completely into the seductive woodwork of what historian Eberly calls 'the
good life out there', there is evidence that others assumed secular aspects of
Jewish identity, the fifth criterion for port Jewish life.[42] The fullest expression
of this identity was the significant aid which Philippine Jews gave first to
refugees from Hitler and thereafter to Zionism. For many Philippine Jews
these two forms of philanthropy were inseparable.

Philippine Jews' Assistance to Holocaust Refugees

The rise of Hitler mobilised some of Manila's most secularised Jews into
communal service. The niece of the founder of the infrequently-used Manila
synagogue observed that 'we only became Jewish conscious in a deep way
when the terrible threat came out of Europe and suddenly there were Jews in
desperate need of help'.[43]

Although the Philippines became an American territorial possession in
1898, by the mid-1930s, as a self-governing commonwealth, it came to control
its own immigration policies. Thus it was largely exempt from the severe

immigration restrictions imposed by the United States Congress in 1924. A 'Jewish Refugee Committee' of Manila, organised in 1937, sought to take maximum advantage of this loophole in American immigration law in an effort to assist Jews fleeing Hitler. Jack Rosenthal, an American-Jewish friend of Philippine President Manuel A. Quezon, was able to interest the islands' chief executive in the plight of European Jewry. More particularly, Rosenthal and ultimately Quezon took note of the skills that many Jewish immigrants could bring to the underdeveloped Philippine islands. On 15 February 1939, President Quezon sent a message to the Philippine congress, which technically oversaw immigration matters, urging the admission of 10,000 German-Jewish professionals plus a Philippine $300 million subsidy to assist them in settling Mindanao island.[44] While this grandiose scheme never materialised, Rosenthal was able to persuade Quezon independently to authorise the admission of perhaps as many as 1,000 Nazi-persecuted Jews. Even these admissions were problematical as the Philippines had no independent consular service and relied on United States diplomatic personnel for the worldwide implementation of its immigration policy. In the blunt words of the son of Manila Jewish community president Morton Netzorg, 'wherever the American consular staff was friendly to the Jewish people Jews got out, and where they shrugged their shoulders Jews did not get out'.[45]

By a variety of means about 1,000 Jewish refugees reached Manila before the December 1941 Japanese attack and subsequent occupation of the entire archipelago. Most arrived penniless and on two-year temporary visas. The refugee population included a full-time rabbi and his wife who served the Manila community until moving abroad in 1949. The American Jewish Joint Distribution Committee aided these refugees until the Japanese attack. Some aid before that date and all assistance for the duration of the war came from the Manila Jewish community itself. Of particular help were those community members who held Iraqi, Filipino and – ironically – German passports and who thereby escaped Japanese internment.[46] Morton Netzorg's son recalled that although 'the Jewish community was very small [it] practiced tithing to help the refugees. Five hundred were brought over in a three year period'.[47] This effort becomes all the more impressive when one considers that after 7 December 1941 the Philippines were a combat zone and the community itself was under bombardment. This was especially heavy during the Battle of Manila in 1945, when 79 individuals, or approximately 10 per cent of the Jewish community, became wartime casualties, a rate similar to that experienced by Manila's overall population.[48]

Despite these hardships the Jewish Community of Manila spared perhaps as many as 1,000 Jews from almost certain obliteration at the hands of the Nazis. One of the Austrian-Jewish survivors asserts that you could never find as generous and solid a group of people [as the Philippine Jewish community] anywhere else in the world. They gave – and give – unstintingly in times of crisis. They have never neglected the needs of the destitute and the sick. Even before the Japanese came the community set up a special home for the Jewish indigent in Marakina. It was kept up for years long after the war was over.[49]

The Philippine-Jewish Community's Embrace of Zionism and Assistance to the State of Israel

When the aforementioned Zionist fundraiser Israel Cohen visited Manila in 1920 he was greatly disappointed at the lack of support from the its Jewish community, lamenting that 'I spoke to quite a number of Jews, but they simply would not hear of it, and not a single god damn cent did I get'.[50] Within 25 years many members of the community had made a complete turnaround on the issue of Zionism. In their minds the embrace of Zionism was a natural outgrowth of their own wartime losses at the hands of Hitler's allies plus their significant and simultaneous sacrifices to assist European refugees. In 1947 members of the community who were close to post-war Philippine President Manuel A. Roxas were instrumental, along with key advisors to US President Harry Truman, in convincing the Philippine delegation to the United Nations to vote in favour of the partition of Palestine and the establishment of a Jewish state. The Philippines thus became the only Asian nation to vote for Israeli independence. It was also among the first to establish diplomatic relations with Israel.[51]

As was the case in independent Singapore, the local Jewish community cultivated Philippine–Israel relations. In 1951 the Philippines signed an aviation agreement with Israel. In that same year, retired Israeli Defence Forces Lt. Col. Shaul Ramati paid a fundraising visit. As a result of that campaign, Israeli Consul Ernest E. Simke was able to write to the Central Zionist Executive that 'the appeal yielded approximately P$60,000. It was the highest collection ever made in the Philippines'.[52] In 1956 Simke wrote that 'although the community is small, there is a strong Zionist sympathy'.[53] In that same year the Philippines welcomed Moshe Sharett, Israel's outgoing foreign minister and former prime minister, on a semi-official visit.[54]

Emigration from the Philippines to Israel and elsewhere shrunk the Manila community from an immediate post-war peak of perhaps 2,500, to 1,000 in 1946, 400 in 1949, 250 in 1968, and to approximately 80 families in 1987.[55] Some families, such as the Simkes, took out Filipino citizenship and chose to remain. The community remains a mix of ethnically Filipino spouses and/or converts, Ashkenazim, Sephardim, Oriental Jews, Americans, Israelis and others. Its history validates the fifth port Jewish characteristic of secularised Jewish identity. Manila never had been a *yiddishe gemeinde*, or Jewish community, in the classic European or even Baghdadi sense. Although small in numbers and weak in formal aspects of religiosity, the Jewish community in the fourth largest seaport in Southeast Asia remains secular, Jewish, Filipino and overwhelmingly Zionistic.

Harbin Jews: Inlanders with Seaport Characteristics

While Singapore, perhaps better than any other Far Eastern Jewish community, exemplified and exemplifies virtually all port Jewish characteristics, and Manila moderately so, one final example is counterfactual. The experiences of Jews in the Chinese city of Harbin, 1,500 miles inland, also reflect all port Jewish characteristics except re-conversion. Harbin was a railroad hub, constructed in 1898 in China's most northeasterly province of Manchuria. Tsarist Russia leased the land from Imperial China. Here Jews enjoyed residential permission plus an array of other economic and political rights under laws far more favourable than in Tsarist Russia itself. These fundamental rights remained when the railroad zone passed through various ownerships, including the Soviet Union's sale of the zone to Japan in 1936. The peculiar legal status of China's railway zone was not unlike that of the United States' Panama Canal Zone, established just three years after the Russians got their leasehold in Harbin.[56]

After 1898, in Harbin and other trackside settlements, Russian Jews developed a Sephardi-, Italian-Jewish-, or Singapore-Baghdadi-like trading infrastructure. They exchanged goods and services with their kinsman in European Russia, China, Japan, Korea and America as well as with ethnic Russians, Chinese, Japanese, Koreans and native Siberian peoples. Under these nurturing political and economic conditions, the Russian Jews of Harbin developed a particular kind of intellectual profile. Many *Harbinetsi* were already well-educated people, trained in the West and conversant in Enlightenment ideas before every migrating to China. Prime exemplars were Harbin Jewish hospital director Avraham Yosifovitch Kaufmann (1885–1971) and his first wife, both of whom, although Russian, had matriculated in medicine in Switzerland. Other Jewish émigrés to Harbin had the good fortune of being among the microscopic number of Russian Jews accepted into the universities, academies and training schools of Tsarist Russia. Still others acquired a western education in Harbin itself, both in technical colleges and in western-style high schools, notably the German-run Hindenburg *schule*.

Because of Harbin's peculiar legal and diplomatic status, these émigrés enjoyed an intellectual environment much freer than that in European Russia itself, both Tsarist and communist. While countless Russian intellectuals ranging from Lenin to Chaim Weizmann fled to freedom in the West, other Russians with an entrepreneurial instinct simultaneously fled east. Thus in Harbin a distinct form of Jewish intellectuality thrived. It was outwardly different from the earlier intellectual development in Mediterranean and Atlantic seaports, or among Singapore Jews with Oriental roots and distinct forms of pre-Herzlian Zionism. A publishing industry brought forth both the Hebrew- and Russian-language tracts of Harbin's long-serving Rabbi Aharon Moshe Kisilev (1866–1949), who had embraced the pre-Herzlian religious Zionism of Rabbi Shmuel Mohilever while a student at the Volozhin Yeshiva. Kisilev's fellow students at Volozhin included future Hebrew national poet Hayyim Nachman Bialik and future Ashkenazi Chief Rabbi of Palestine Avraham Yitzhak Kook. It was under Kisilev's influence, from 1913 to 1949, that the Harbin Jews became overwhelmingly Zionistic. The left-leaning Yiddish-language newspaper *Der Vayter Mizrekh* (The Far East) competed with the Russian-language Zionist publications *Evreiskaia Zhizn'* (Jewish Life) and *Gadegel* (Cyrillic rendition of the Hebrew word for 'the [Zionist] flag'). Lazer Epstein's anti-Zionist Jewish Workers' Bund contested Avraham Kaufman's Herzlian Zionism as well as the ultra-religious non-Zionist Agudat Israel. Harbin was the East Asian point of entry for Vladimir Zev Jabotinsky's Zionist Revisionist movement, which counted among its adherents future Israeli parliamentarian Yaakov Lieberman and Motti Olmert, father of one-time Jerusalem Mayor Ehud Olmert. Even Harbin's two major Jewish sports organisations reflected the intellectual diversity of the community: Maccabi for the General Zionists and Brit Trumpeldor (Betar) for the Revisionists. These two groups would cooperate at times of natural disaster, such as floods on the Sungari River. They also buried their ideological differences and united to combat the virulent anti-semitism of some of Harbin's White Russian organisations, which also thrived in this relatively unrestricted political environment.[57]

Perhaps the fullest description of Harbin's vibrancy appears in Israel Cohen's account of 1920. He visited the community on a fundraising mission. He was impressed by Harbin's 'vigorous Jewish consciousness' which

> manifested itself in a struggle of parties, in which the Right, Centre, Left, and Extreme Left were always engaged. There were ceaseless public discussions, especially on Saturday night, between the rival adherents of Zionism pure and simple, Zionism without Orthodoxy, Orthodoxy without Zionism, Zionism with Socialism, Socialism without Zionism, Hebraism in Manchuria, and Yiddishism in Palestine … I soon realized that there were … hundreds of Jews in Harbin who were eager to go to Palestine … There was therefore no need for me to gain converts: my task was confined to spreading information and obtaining donations from a relatively small group.[58]

Cohen's observations about Harbin's intellectual vitality suggest broadening the argument that the special conditions of seaports helped Jews win political privileges and fostered intellectual development. Although Harbin was not a seaport, it was a trading and distribution centre and an entrepôt where long-distance merchants made their headquarters and to and from which goods were shipped. The same dynamics which influenced seaports and produced intellectual vitality there also influenced Harbin. At least two other hypotheses, over and beyond the port Jews theory, may help to explain Jewish development in Harbin. All across Siberia, one of the world's vastest wildernesses which ultimately straddled three independent countries, Jews served as commercial middlemen. They literally arrived on the first trains into the region and set up shop alongside the tracks, as they did simultaneously in the American West. Perhaps it was the dynamics and opportunities of a frontier environment, as suggested by historian Frederick Jackson Turner and amended by George Mosse with specific reference to Jews, that gave Jews the wherewithal to evolve economically, politically and ideologically.[59] A second hypothesis derives from sociology. Many Siberian whistlestops and jerkwaters, including Harbin, ultimately turn into substantial metropolises where Jews retained commercial prominence. Perhaps it was the dynamics of an urban environment *maritime or inland*, as postulated by sociologist Robert E. Park, which accounts for Jewish economic, political and ideological evolution in East and Southeast Asia.[60] On the basis of a comparison of Singapore, Manila and Harbin, it is clear that additional research is needed to validate the important suggestions about 'port Jewry' advanced by Professor David Sorkin.

NOTES

The author wishes to thank the University of West Georgia's College of Arts and Sciences for providing the released time which made the writing of this essay possible, at the University of Cape Town, at Oxford, UK's Centre for Hebrew and Jewish Studies, and at Jerusalem's Central Zionist Archives. I am also most grateful to West Georgia's Learning Resources Committee for funding this research and to West Georgia's Dean Donald R. Wagner and the Oxford Centre's David Patterson for repeated and invaluable encouragement. The following librarians assisted in ferreting out the arcane materials necessary for this study: Myron House of West Georgia's Ingram Library; Raymond Lum of the Harvard-Yenching Institute Library; and the entire staffs of the University of Southampton Hartley Library and of the Central Zionist Archives. Joan Bieder of the University of California, Jacques M. Downs of the University of New England, William Gervase Clarence Smith of the University of London's School of Oriental and African Studies, Lois C. Dubin of Smith College, Teddy Kaufman of Tel Aviv's *Igud Yotsei Sin* (Association of Former Jewish Residents of China), and Jean Marshall of Singapore made numerous helpful suggestions in the writing of this text. Final responsibility is, of course, the author's alone.

1. David Sorkin, 'The Port Jew: Notes Toward a Social Type', *Journal of Jewish Studies* 50.1 (Spring 1999), 87–97. Among the works Sorkin drew on were Lois C. Dubin, *The Port Jews of Habsburg Trieste: Absolutist Politics and Enlightenment Culture* (Stanford, CA: Stanford University Press, 1999). Dubin has subsequently offered port Jewish characteristics of her own, which differ from those of Sorkin, '"Wings on their feet ... and wings on their head": Reflections on the Study of Port Jews', in this volume, pp.14-30 (paper presented at the conference on 'Port Jews and Jewish Communities in Cosmopolitan Maritime Trading Centres', University of Cape Town, 6 January 2003). Since Dubin's criteria have not yet appeared in final published form as of this writing, I refer only to Sorkin's five published characteristics. Arabic-speaking Jews from Baghdad, who have also been referred to as Levantine Jews, should not, strictly speaking, be classified as 'Sephardim', Jews of Iberian origin

who retained Medieval Spanish or Portuguese as their mother tongue in varied places of exile. Nor should those Italian or Greek Jews whose forebears never lived in Iberia.

2.   Sorkin (see note 1), pp.89–90. The Sephardi and Italian-Jewish international trade infrastructure was similar to that which bound early American merchants from a particular city with each other and with their overseas financiers and agents. Economic historian Thomas C. Cochran observed that 'in spite of intercolonial trade in some items, each major [early American] port was a separate business community remote from its neighbors. The personal ties that bound the business world together were more often between American merchants and the houses of Liverpool or London than between men on this side of the Atlantic. Businessmen of Charleston were more at home in London than in Boston'. Thomas C. Cochran, *Basic History of American Business* (Princeton, NJ: Van Nostrand, 1968), p.28. On Philadelphia Quakers as a case in point, see Richard Waln, Jr., *Walnford Mill Accounts, 1772* (manuscript copies in the Historical Society of Pennsylvania, Philadelphia); [Stephen Winslow], *Biographies of Successful Philadelphia Merchants* (Philadelphia: James K. Simon, 1864), pp.129–32; and Jonathan Goldstein, *Philadelphia and the China Trade, 1682–1846 Commercial, Cultural, and Attitudinal Effects* (University Park and London: Penn State University Press, 1978), pp.11–12 and passim. A second case in point of networking in colonial and early national American trade are the Huguenots. In nineteenth-century East, Southeast and South Asia, the major ethnic networkers in maritime trade apart from Baghdadi Jews were the Parsees, Armenians and various communities of Chinese. See Assiya Siddiqi, 'The Business World of Jamsetjee Jejeebhoy', *Indian Economic and Social History Review* 19.3–4 (1982), 301–24.

3.   Sorkin (see note 1), p.90.

4.   Ibid., p.94. 'Enlightened' Jewish nationalists in the Far East included Anglophile Baghdadi Jews like Shanghai's Nissim Elias Benjamin Ezra (1883–1936), who edited and published the Zionist monthly *Israel's Messenger* from 1904 to 1936, and Harbin General Zionist leader and hospital director Dr Avraham Iosifovitch Kaufmann (1885–1971). Ezra, significantly, is representative of a generation which came after that of Sir Menasseh Meyer, which was influenced by traditional Baghdadi, pre-Herzlian 'love of Zion'. The ideologies of Ezra, Kaufman and their comrades and followers closely resembled those of eighteenth-to-twentieth-century American, Irish, Italian and Scottish nationalists who took Enlightened world views but simultaneously and proudly affirmed their national identities. On Zionism and other nineteenth-century nationalisms as expressions of European Enlightenment thinking, see Hugh Trevor-Roper, 'Jewish and Other Nationalisms', *Commentary* 35 (January 1963), 19–20. He writes that Zionist leaders were 'Europeans of the Enlightenment [who] were not content with distant memories or merely religious traditions. If they revived the Hebrew language it was not merely to study the Scriptures or the Law. If they remembered their history it was not merely their ancient, sacred history. It was a Jew of the Emancipation, Heinrich Graetz, who wrote the first continuous history of the Jewish nation, carrying it through the destruction of the Second Temple, over the intervening centuries, to his own time. It was a Jew of the Emancipation, Moses Hess, who first urged escape from Europe to Jerusalem, and he urged it explicitly as a nationalist, secular movement, in imitation of the nationalist, secular Italian Risorgimento. If Zionism was the age-old hankering of Jews for the Holy Land, it was that hankering secularized: a return to Israel without waiting for the Messiah, or led by a secular Messiah – one, moreover, who was half-assimilated into Europe ... If [Zionism's] faithful masses came out of the Russian Pale, [their movement] was headed by half-assimilated men whom strict Jews might regard as little better than Gentiles and whose life was led in the Western Cosmopolitan cities of Paris and Vienna'. On the connection between European Enlightenment thought and American, Irish and Scottish nationalism, see David Dickson, 'Paine in Ireland', and John Burns, 'Scottish Radicalism and the United Irishmen', both in David Dickson, Daire Keogh and Kevin Whelan (eds.), *The United Irishmen: Republicanism, Radicalism, and Rebellion* (Dublin: Lilliput Press, 1993), pp.134–50 and 151–66 respectively. Historian Eric Foner notes that, in spite of all his propagandising for an Enlightened internationalism, Tom Paine both 'called himself a "citizen of the world"' and 'was an early advocate of a strong central government for America'. Eric Foner, *Tom Paine and Revolutionary America* (London: Oxford University Press, 1976), p.xix. On the 'new Christians', see Yehuda Bauer, *A History of the Holocaust* (New York: Franklin Watts, 2001), p.32.

5.   Sorkin (see note 1), pp.95–6.

6.   Goldstein (see note 2); Siddiqi (see note 2).

7.   Primary sources on Far Eastern Baghdadi Jews include manuscript materials and printed, often

mimeographed, reports in two repositories: the records of the British Commonwealth Jewish communities in the Hartley Library of the University of Southampton, UK (hereafter HL); and Jerusalem's Central Zionist Archives (hereinafter CZA). Other sources include Israel Cohen, *A Jewish Pilgrimage* (London: Vallentine Mitchell, 1956), pp.194–6; Ezekiel Musleah, *On the Banks of the Ganga* (North Quincy, MA: Christopher, 1975), passim; Joan Roland, 'Baghdadi Jews in India and China in the Nineteenth Century: A Comparison of Economic Roles'; Chiara Betta, 'Silas Aaron Hardoon and Cross-Cultural Adaptation in Shanghai'; and Maruyama Naoki, 'The Shanghai Zionist Association and the International Politics of East Asia Until 1936', all three in Jonathan Goldstein, *The Jews of China*, vol.I (Armonk, NY and London: M.E. Sharpe, 1999), pp.141–56, 216–29 and 251–66 respectively; Cecil Roth, *The Sassoon Dynasty* (London: Robert Hale, 1941); Maisie J. Meyer, *The Sephardi Jewish Community of Shanghai 1845–1939 and the Question of Identity* (Ph.D. dissertation, London School of Economics, University of London, 1994); and Joan Roland, *Jews in British India: Identity in a Colonial Era* (Columbia, SC: University of South Carolina Press, 1993).

8. Saphir, quoted in Eze Nathan, *History of Jews in Singapore* (Singapore: HERBILU, 1986), p.3. In 1883 the Singapore merchant W.G. Gulland asserted that 'the opium trade ... is wholly in the hands of Jews and Armenians ... and forms an important part of the Native trade of this city, as of almost all other eastern settlements'. LEGCO 1883 Straits Settlements, *Straits Settlements Legislative Council Proceedings* (Singapore: Government Printing Office, 1883), p.8. Twentieth-century Singapore community historian Nathan described the opium trade of Singapore Jews as 'a legitimate short cut to wealth'. Nathan, *History of Jews in Singapore*, pp.8–9. Additional sources on the early history of Singapore Jewry include censuses reproduced in ibid., passim; Jacob Tomlin, *Missionary Journals* (London: James Nisbet, 1844), p.23; 'The Jews of Bagdad [sic]', J[ohn] T[urnbull] Thomson, *Some Glimpses of Life in the Far East* (London: Richardson, 1864), ch.43, pp.242–49; Charles Buckley, *Anecdotal History of Old Time Singapore*, vol.1 (Singapore: Fraser and Neave, 1902), p.311; Israel Cohen, *Journal of a Jewish Traveller* (London: John Lane, 1925), pp.198–208; Ida Cowen, *Jews in Remote Corners of the World* (Englewood Cliffs, NJ: Prentice-Hall, 1971), pp.141–7; Moshe Yegar, 'Le-Toldot Ha-Kehillah Ha-Yehudit Be-Singapoor' (Hebrew: On the History of the Jewish Community in Singapore) *Gesher* 1.78 (1974), 50–65; and Lionel Simmonds, 'An Asian Odyssey', *Jewish Chronicle Magazine* (London), November 1983, pp.16–17. Some Singapore Jews of Baghdadi origin did face a certain amount of social/employment discrimination in the colonial period as they were categorised not as 'Jews' but as Asians.

9. Phyllis Funke, 'Singapore'. *Hadassah Magazine* 76.3 (November 1987), pp.22–23; Tudor Parfitt, *The Thirteenth Gate: Travels Among the Lost Tribes of Israel* (London: Weidenfeld and Nicolson, 1987), p.72.

10. 'The Jews of Singapore: Special Interview with John Solomon', *Israel's Messenger* (Shanghai), 2 April 1926, p.21.

11. Simmonds (see note 8), p.16.

12. Cohen (see note 8), p.199; Cohen (see note 7), p.208; Funke (see note 9), p.22; Parfitt (see note 9), p.72.

13. Joan Bieder, 'Jewish Identity in Singapore: Cohesion, Dispersion, Survival', unpublished paper (2002), p.11.

14. Simmonds (see note 8), p.16; Warren Freedman, 'The Jews of South-East Asia', *Jewish Post*, 20 September 1979, p.74; Bieder (see note 13), pp.11–18. While the great majority of the permanently-resident Singapore Jews have always been Baghdadi, there have been significant figures with other origins, such as long-resident Romanian diamond merchants and some businessmen and medical doctors who escaped from Europe before the Holocaust and for whom members of the community sought work and residential permits. Jean Marshall, Singapore, email to the author, 31 March 2003.

15. Buckley (see note 8), vol.1, p.311. Buckley adds that Solomon also took 'an enthusiastic interest in the manners, customs, and literature of the East'.

16. When Albert Einstein visited Meyer in 1922, he referred to Meyer as 'Croessus' (the legendary king of Lydia). Einstein viewed Chesed El as 'a magnificent synagogue which was actually built for the purpose of communication between Croessus and Jehovah'. Bieder (see note 13), pp.1–2, 22–3; Parfitt (see note 9), p.72.

17. Louis Rabinovitz, *Far Eastern Mission* (Johannesburg: Eagle Press, 1952), p.158.

18. See note 4.

19. David Sassoon, *History of the Jews in Baghdad* (Letchworth, UK: S.D. Sassoon, 1949), p.217.

20. Cohen (see note 8), p.208; Freedman (see note 14), p.74.
21. Cohen (see note 8), p.208; 'The Jews of Singapore' (see note 10), p.21; Orly Baher, 'The Baghdadi Jewish Community in Shanghai and Singapore', *Points East* (Menlo Park, CA) 17.2 (July 2002), p.15. Apart from the visible activism of the Menasseh Meyers, there were always unaffiliated and apathetic Jews and non-Zionists within the Singapore Jewish community.
22. Joan Bieder and Hanoch Gutfreund, 'Einstein in Singapore: A Genius Abroad', *The Straits Times* (The Sunday Plus Times Section), 2 January 2000, p.20; Bieder (see note 13), pp.1–3, 22–3; Baher (see note 21), p.15.
23. Letters: A. Goldstein, Kandy, Ceylon, to Zionist Executive, Jerusalem, 7 January 1927, KH4 9610; Dr A. Bension, Singapore, to Leo Herrmann, Jerusalem, 9 April 1929, KH4 12347; M. Nissim, Singapore, to Keren Hayesod, Jerusalem, 9 April 1929, KH4 12347; Zvi Herman [sic], Jerusalem, to Mrs. S. Nissim, Singapore, 14 October 1952, KH4 12347, all CZA; Baher (see note 21), p.15.
24. Letter: Montague Ezekiel, Singapore, to Jewish Agency, Jerusalem, 1 October 1936, 56 3797, CZA.
25. Copy of Last Will of Flora Shooker, Singapore, 4 April 1941, KH4 12421, CZA.
26. On Singapore in general during the Japanese occupation, see George M. Kahin, *Governments and Politics of Southeast Asia* (Ithaca, NY and London: Cornell University Press, 1969), pp.288–9. On the fate of Jews in particular, see personal account by Nathan (note 8), p.109; Moshe Yegar, 'A Rapid and Recent Rise and Fall', *Sephardi World* (Jerusalem) no.3 [July–August 1984], p.10; and Beider (see note 13), p.24. A South African rabbi who spoke with Mozelle Nissim after the war recorded that she 'had harrowing tales to tell of her adventures before she reached a haven of refuge in India, as had most of the Singapore Jews who had suffered either in concentration camps in Japan [e.g. David Saul Marshall, a POW in Hokkaido] or under forced labor in Malaya'. Rabinovitz (see note 17), p.158. On Marshall's life and career, see Letters: David Marshall, Singapore, to Charles S. Spencer, London, 6 May 1955; Michael Cohen, Singapore, to Charles Spencer, London, 15 August 1955; 'Bulletin of Jewish Welfare Board, Singapore' (mimeographed), 1962, passim; 'Profile: David Marshall', *Sunday Times* [London], n.d., ca. 1956, all HL; Terrys Glick, 'Jews in Southeast Asia', *Chronicle Review* (December 1970), p.103; Denis D. Gray, 'Conscience of Singapore speaks out fearlessly', *Atlanta Constitution*, 1 May 1994, p.C6; Gray, 'Jewish lawyer is Singapore's crusading conscience', *Jerusalem Post*, 1 May 1994, p.3; Rabinovitz (see note 17), p.157; Cowen (see note 7), pp.146–7; Nathan (see note 8), pp.69, 80–81; and Chan Heng Chee, *A Sensation of Independence: A Political Biography of David Marshall* (Oxford and New York: Oxford University Press, 1984). On Marshall's 1956 intervention with Zhou Enlai which enabled Chinese Jews to immigrate to Israel, see David Marshall, *Letters from Mao's China* (Singapore: Singapore Heritage Society, 1996); and Josef and Lynn Silverstein, 'David Marshall and Jewish Emigration from China', *China Quarterly* 75 (September 1978), pp.647–54.
27. Lee Kuan Yew was the long-term leader of independent Singapore. 'Jews in Singapore', *Israel Report* no.5 (5 March 1977). The significant role Jews have played in Singapore's economic and political development, Singapore's overwhelmingly non-Muslim population, and the commonality of interests between Singapore and Israel in trade, technological and military matters, may explain why Lee Kuan Yew was willing to 'take the heat' from Arab and Muslim states for Singapore's ties with Israel. Israel's President Chaim Herzog wrote that when he paid an official visit to Singapore in 1986, Malaysia, Indonesia and Brunei withdrew their ambassadors from Singapore 'for consultation' for a few days. There were threats in Malaysia 'to cut off Singapore's water supply'. According to Herzog, 'thanks to Israel and its military mission in Singapore, the country was well equipped to defend itself and to deter Malaysia'. Chaim Herzog, *Living History* (London: Phoenix, 1998), p.308.
28. Francis Thomas, quoted in *Singapore Standard*, 20 February 1956.
29. CZA file F49 634/1 contains approximately 100 letters between Fay Grove, chairperson, and other officials of WIZO and Alice Blitz and other Singapore Jewish women, concerning the formation of an active WIZO chapter in Singapore between the years 1956 and 1970; Yegar (see note 26), p.9.
30. 'Report and Accounts of the Jewish Welfare Board [Singapore], January to December 1953', HL. There also was a small return exodus of Singaporean Jews who migrated to Israel. See 'Repatriation of Jews from Israel to Singapore, 1952', and Letter, Consular Section, British Embassy, Tel Aviv, to Consular Department, Foreign Office, 30 September 1952, CO/022/374, The National Archives, Kew, UK.
31. *Singapore Standard*, 20 February 1956.
32. Moshe Sharett, *Mi-shut be-Asyiah: Yoman masa* [Hebrew: From Travelling in Asia: A Travel Diary] (Tel

Aviv: Davar/Am Oved, 1964), p.87.
33. 'Bulletin of Jewish Welfare Board, Singapore, 14 March 1962', mimeographed, File MS 137, A5/95/76, HL; *Encyclopedia Judaica* 14 (Jerusalem: Keter, 1971), pp.1608–10. Singapore Jewry turned out in force at a 1983 Israel Independence Day celebration given by Ambassador Nahum Eshkol at the Hyatt Regency Hotel, where the guests included the Egyptian chargé d'affaires, British diplomats, and leading figures in Singapore's political, commercial and professional life. Simmonds (see note 8), p.16.
34. Bieder (see note 13), pp.46–8.
35. George Kohut, 'Jewish Heretics in the Philippines in the Sixteenth and Seventeenth Century', *Publications of the American Jewish Historical Society* 12 (1904), 149–56; Henry Lea, *The Inquisition in the Spanish Dependencies* (New York: Macmillan, 1908), p.304.
36. Email William Clarence-Smith to Joan Bieder, 4 July 2002, courtesy of Joan Bieder; Lewis E. Gleeck, *History of the Jewish Community of Manila* (n.p., n.d., c.1989), p.34; *Encyclopedia Judaica* 13 (see note 33), pp.395–6.
37. Annette Eberly, 'Manila? Where? Us? The Good Life Out There', *Present Tense* 2.3 (Spring 1975), 162–3.
38. John Griese, *The Jewish Community in Manila* (unpublished M.A. thesis, University of the Philippines, 1954), pp.21–2.
39. Cohen (see note 8), pp.108–114; Cohen (see note 7), p.193. The absence of Jewish institutional development in Manila occurred simultaneously with social, albeit not legalised, anti-semitism. The Manila Polo Club was founded by Philippine Governor General W. Cameron Forbes, according to one contemporary, 'for white men only. It excluded Filipinos and mestizos. It frowned pointedly on Jews'. In Boston, New York, Philadelphia and Atlanta, Jewish exclusion from overwhelmingly Christian clubs and institutions induced the formation of Jewish counterparts. This did not happen in Manila. Florence Horn, *Orphans of the Pacific* (New York: Reynal and Hitchcock, 1941), p.132.
40. Jack Netzorg, *Manila Memories* (Laguna Beach, CA: Pacific Rim Books, n.d., c.1990), pp.29, 66; Cowen (see note 8), pp.129–38; World Jewish Congress, *The Jewish Communities of the World* (New York: World Jewish Congress, 1963), p.49; Gleeck (see note 36), pp.16–17; Griese, (see note 38), pp.21–2.
41. 'Jews in the Philippines Not Religious', *Jewish Advocate* (Boston), 25 March 1930.
42. Eberly (see note 37), p.60.
43. Minna Gaberman, Manila, quoted in Eberly (see note 37), p.60.
44. [Manuel E. Quezon], *Messages of the President*, V, Part One (Manila: Bureau of Printing, 1941), p.427; Griese (see note 35), p.28. According to one contemporary, after Quezon suggested the admission of Jewish refugees, the Philippines' indigenous Chinese minority 'wonder, ironically, at this generous hospitality. For the Jews, like the Chinese, eventually, work their way into trade, no matter how they start their lives in any country'. Horn (see note 39), p.146.
45. Netzorg (see note 40), p.4. In a 1947 speech to the United Nations General Assembly, Philippines Foreign Minister Felix Romulo reminded delegates that 'during the dispersal of the Jews from Hitlerite Germany the Philippines was among the very few countries that opened their doors to Jewish refugees and extended to them a cordial welcome. We gave them a haven in our country, we accepted them among us, and today they live and work with us in complete harmony and understanding'. United Nations, *Official Records of the Second Session of the General Assembly Plenary Meetings: 16 September–29 November 1947* (Lake Success, NY: United Nations, 1947), vol.2, p.1315.
46. On the Philippines in general during the Japanese occupation, see Kahin (note 26), pp.695–7. On the fate of Jews in particular, see S[olomon] S. Seruya, 'The Jews of Manila', *Jerusalem Post*, 11 April 1979, p.8; Freedman (note 14), pp.74–5; Eberly (note 37), pp.62–3; Gleeck (note 36), p.34; and Griese (note 38), pp.31–3.
47. Netzorg (see note 40), p.3.
48. Yegar (see note 26), p.10; and Cowen (see note 8), p.131.
49. Eberly (see note 37), p.61.
50. Cohen (see note 8), p.110. Cohen called his Manila sojourn 'the least lucrative gathering in the whole of my tour'. Cohen (see note 8), p.193.
51. Eberly (see note 37), p.64; *Encyclopedia Judaica* 13 (see note 33), pp.395–6.
52. Letter: Ernest E. Simke, Manila, to Central Zionist Executive, Jerusalem, 28 May 1951, S5/12.170, CZA.

53. Letter: Ernest E. Simke, Manila, to Office of the 24th Zionist Congress, Jerusalem, 20 February 1956, S5/12.165, CZA.

54. *Manila Chronicle*, 29 September 1956; *Manila Times*, 29 September 1956; *Evening News* (Manila), 3 October 1956; Sharett (see note 32).

55. Letter: Dina Thischby, Manila, to Mrs Gordon of WIZO, Jerusalem, 23 November 1958, CZA; Letter: Simke (see note 49); World Jewish Congress (see note 40), pp.48–9; Susan Bures, 'Behind the Headlines', *Jewish Telegraphic Agency Daily News Bulletin*, 12 September 1984, p.4; 'Tiny Jewish Groups', *Forward* (New York), 3 April 1987; *Asia-Pacific Survival Guide* (Melbourne: Asia-Pacific Jewish Association, n.d., c.1988), pp.85–8; Seruya (see note 46), p.8; Griese (see note 38), pp.21–2; *Encyclopedia Judaica* 13 (see note 33), pp.395–6.

56. On the origin and development of the Harbin Jewish community, see Alexander Menquez [pseud.], 'Growing Up Jewish in Manchuria in the 1930s: Personal Vignettes', in Goldstein (see note 7), vol.II, pp.70–84; Mantetsu Chosa Bu [Japanese: South Manchuria Railway Company, Research Department], *Zai-Man Yudaya Jin No Keizai-Teki Kako Oyobi Genzai* [The Economic Past and Present of Jews in Manchuria] (November 1940), Yudaya Mondai Chosa Shiryo Dai 27 Shu [No.27 in the Jewish Problem Investigation Materials Series], marked 'Gokuhi' [Top Secret], pp.20–21, 44–6, cited in Menquez, 'Growing Up Jewish in Manchuria in the 1930s', p.70; Israel Epstein, 'On Being a Jew in China: A Personal Memoir', in Goldstein (see note 7), vol.II, pp.85–97; Yosef Tekoah, 'My Developmental Years in China', in Goldstein (see note 7), vol.II, pp.98–109; Boris Bresler, 'Harbin's Jewish Community, 1898–1958: Politics, Prosperity, and Adversity', in Goldstein (see note 7), vol.I, pp.200–15; Zvia Shickman-Bowman, 'The Construction of the Chinese Eastern Railway and the Origins of the Harbin Jewish Community, 1898–1931', in Goldstein (see note 7), vol.I, pp.187–99; Joshua A. Fogel 'The Japanese and the Jews in Harbin, 1898–1930', in Robert Bickers *et al.*, *New Frontiers: Imperialism's New Communities in East Asia, 1842–1953* (Manchester: Manchester University Press, 2000), pp.88–108; Herman Dicker, *Wanderers and Settlers in the Far East* (New York: Twayne, 1962), passim; Soren Clausen and Stig Thogerson, *The Making of a Chinese City: History and Historiography in Harbin* (Armonk, NY and London: M.E. Sharpe, 1995); David Wolff, *To the Harbin Station* (Stanford, CA: Stanford University Press, 1999); Yaakov Liberman, *My China* (Jerusalem and New York: Geffen, 1997), passim; and Isador A. Magid, '"I Was There": The Viewpoint of an Honorary Israeli Consul in Shanghai, 1949–1951', in Jonathan Goldstein (ed.), *China and Israel, 1948–98: A Fifty Year Retrospective* (Westport, CT and London: Praeger, 1999), pp.41–5.

57. Aharon Moshe Kisilev, *Mishbere Yam: Sheelot U-Teshuvot Be-Arbaah Helke Shulkan Arukh* [Hebrew: The Waves of the Sea: Response on the Four Parts of 'The Set Table'] (Harbin: Defus M. Levitin, 5686 [1925/26]; reprinted Brooklyn, NY: Katz Bookbinding, 1981); Kisilev, *Natsionalizm I Evreistvo: Stat'i, Lektsii, I Doklady* [Russian: Nationalism and the Jews: Articles, Lectures and Reports] (Harbin: Evreiskaia Zhizn', 1941); Kisilev, *Imre Shefer* [Hebrew: 'Good Words' or 'Beautiful Sayings'], a collection of sermons published posthumously in Tel Aviv by Bezalel-Levitsky with a 1951 introductory letter from Israel's Ashkenazi Chief Rabbi Isaac Herzog; *Evreiskaia Zhizn'* [Jewish Life] (Harbin) no.47 (2 November 1938), pp.14–16, 23–5; no.48 (25 November 1938), pp.7–10, 24–5; interview, Jonathan Goldstein with Teddy Kaufman, Tel Aviv, 2 January 2002; Violet Gilboa (comp.), *China and the Jews* (Cambridge, MA: Harvard University Library, 1992), pp.40, 43; Shickman-Bowman (see note 52), p.196; and *Passage Through China: The Jewish Communities of Harbin, Tientsin, and Shanghai* [*Derekh Erets Sin: Ha-Kehillot Ha-Yehudiot Be-Harbin, Tiyeng'tsin Ve-Shanghai*] (Tel Aviv: Nahum Goldman Museum of the Jewish Diaspora, 1986) [exhibition catalogue], pp.vii–xii; Dicker (see note 56) pp.21–60; Liberman (see note 56), passim.

58. Cohen (see note 8), pp.203–4.

59. For insights into Frederick Jackson Turner's frontier thesis from a Jewish perspective, see George L. Mosse, *Confronting History: A Memoir* (Madison, WI: University of Wisconsin Press, 2000), pp.152–63.

60. According to sociologist Robert E. Park, the emancipated Jew's 'pre-eminence as a trader, his keen intellectual interest, his sophistication, his idealism and his lack of historical sense, are the characteristics of a city man, the man who ranges widely ... who, emerging from the ghetto in which he lived ... is seeking to find a place in the freer, more complex and cosmopolitan life of [the] city'. Robert E. Park, 'Human Migration and the Marginal Man', *American Journal of Sociology* 33.6 (May 1928), 892.

Conclusion

GEMMA ROMAIN

Since Lois Dubin and David Sorkin formulated and developed the concept of the port Jew in the late 1990s, research on individual port Jewish communities along with theoretical elucidations of the concept have proliferated and gone from strength to strength. Of course there was a range of exciting and innovative research being carried out on the early modern Sephardi diaspora and its relationship to the port and the littoral prior to and concurrent with Dubin's and Sorkin's work.[1] However, with the recent development of the port Jew concept there now exists a valuable framework with which to study not only the particularities of the Sephardi diaspora, but also to examine other Jewish histories across time and space which may also fit into a broader understanding of the model.

The model conceived by Sorkin was devised in a restricted manner – specifically to apply to the early modern 'merchant Jews of Sephardi or, to a lesser extent, Italian extraction who settled in the port cities of the Mediterranean, the Atlantic seaboard and the New World'.[2] During the first port Jews symposium in 2001, these limitations were challenged and although contributors acknowledged the importance and usefulness of the term as a research tool, they sought to expand it, particularly by incorporating non-elitist, Ashkenazi history, and the modern period within the working definition. Lois Dubin argued 'the multiplication of examples will enrich our understanding of the realities of port Jews; broadening the concept *port Jew* need not dilute or weaken it'.[3] She championed use of the terms port Jewry or port Jewish community to signify difference from the specific 'social type' identified by Sorkin. Although the term has thus been reshaped and redefined, most participants saw this process as a part of the term's evolution rather than a criticism of the foundations of the term. Sorkin does however make a convincing case for keeping the original conception as specific to the early modern Sephardi diaspora.[4]

Various ideas and dilemmas were thus brought to the fore during the Port Jews conference of January 2003. The range of speakers at this gathering exemplified the attractiveness of the term as a means of describing a range of different yet connected Jewish histories. Nick Evans in his discussion on the port Jews of Libau provided an exploration of both Ashkenazi and transmigrancy history – answering Tony Kushner's call for these histories to be included in the 'paradigm' of Port Jewish studies. Indeed, the history of Jews and transmigration is one of the most important aspects of Jewish littoral history in the modern era. In transmigrancy we see Jews being 'shipped' around the globe rather than being merchants, living within the port locale yet being hidden from view, and sometimes excluded from the local port milieu. Kenefick has provided a further exploration of this Ashkenazi port Jewish community in modern migration history, which can fit into the broader framework conceived by Dubin.

Many essays in this collection, particularly those by Cesarani, Kushner, Evans, Shain, Mendelsohn and Beckford-Smith, and Liedtke show the less than tolerant atmosphere towards Jews that arise from the specific port locale. In all of these locations Jews were subjected to immigration restrictions and anti-semitic stereotyping and were represented as carriers of disease and the cause of various societal problems. Tony Kushner's argument that we need to look at the port also as a site of intolerance certainly carries weight, as does Shain's assertion that it was in fact the modernity of the port and its influence from the hinterland that made Sorkin's particular model untenable when used in a modern, non-European context.[5]

The economic activity and profile of the port Jew was also examined at the 2003 conference. For example, Evans asks the question 'can the concept of port Jewry be applied to a port whose Jewish residents were predominantly of working-class or mercantile status?'[6] Both he and Gekas point out that Jews who fit many criteria of the port Jews also happened to be of working-class origins, in the case of Corfu Jews, porters and labourers – essential jobs within the port economy – as well as olive oil merchants.[7]

The subject of Oliel-Grausz's work exemplifies in many ways the 'classic' port Jew of the early modern Sephardi diaspora. Yet she goes on to tease out further Sorkin's description of the cross-cultural trading networks that characterised these Jews. It is these networks that need to be explored in a holistic way, which is difficult to achieve if the focus is solely on Jews in one port location.[8]

The conference also raised lively discussion and debate on the nature and appropriate definitions of the terms *tolerance* and *cosmopolitanism*. Liedtke's essay introduces important questions concerning the assumption that port milieus were always more tolerant places for Jews. In his study of Hamburg during the Nazi era, we can see the port as a place of illiberalism, which is specifically fostered by local conditions of trade and competition within a closely-knit elite of mercantile firms and families.[9] An additional thesis is raised in my own work on the subject of the Jews of Charleston, which shows that port city society can be liberal to one group of people and at the same time be extremely ruthless to another, the enslaved African. It also indicates that port Jews can and have fitted into assumed notions of whiteness and racial difference as well as participating in the day to day life of a slaving society such as Charleston. Cesarani makes a similar observation in his study of Bristol and Liverpool, where Jews faced anti-Jewish discrimination while at the same time benefiting from an economy founded on slavery.[10] The ports of Charleston, Bristol and Liverpool were sites of transportation of enslaved people, as well as the transhipment of goods and produce emanating from the transatlantic slave trade. The modern port was thus a site of ruthless repression, immigration restriction and policing, as well as vibrancy and economic activity. And yet, cosmopolitanism flourished in these same ports. In this context it is important to recognise that cosmopolitanism does not equate to liberalism, and in studying the port city as a site of cosmopolitanism it must be strictly defined, as Sutcliffe has suggested, as 'one that hosts a diversity of cultures and religions, and thrusts these contrasting life worlds into everyday contact with each other'.[11]

Some participants at the conference whose work is multidisciplinary were reminded of similar conversations taking place in other academic fields, which leads onto the question of the usefulness of comparative, interdisciplinary research for Port Jewish studies. Many of the essay in this volume (if not geographically, then on the basis of its theoretical rudiments) could easily fit into what has been termed 'Atlantic Studies' and perhaps more significantly an interrelated discipline, which has come to be known as 'littoral studies'. Linda Rupert's work, along with my own and others, has been greatly influenced by Atlantic Studies and World History.[12] Lois Dubin has not only reformulated the port Jew concept in a wider form, but is also involved in exploring the possible connections with Atlantic Studies. For example, Arthur Kiron, Holly Snyder and Wim Klooster, with Dubin as Chair and Respondent, presented a session entitled 'Port Jews in the Atlantic World' at the 2003 Association for Jewish Studies conference in Boston. As stated by the panel, 'Both the study of "Port Jews" and "Atlantic" history highlight the need to explore the multiple layers of commercial, social, religious, and indeed biological boundary crossings that occurred among diverse groups of people, especially during the 16th–18th centuries, living under the aegis of expansionist European states'.[13]

Similarly, the rationale behind the 2003 *Seascapes, Littoral Cultures and Trans-Oceanic Exchanges* conference organised by the American Historical Association and the Library of Congress, Washington, DC, could in many ways be extended to Port Jewish studies by its aiming 'to go beyond area studies and to cross the usual national, geographical, and cultural boundary lines of scholarship by examining the role of oceans and sea basins as highways of exchanges between world areas as well as social and cultural sites in their own right'.[14] It is important for Port Jewish studies to be integrated within the fabric of this newly emerging school. Similar issues and problems to those discovered in Port Jewish studies have been seen in 'littoral studies'. Kerry Ward's discussion of Cape Town as a cross-oceanic port city echoes Tony Kushner's concern to look at movement rather than just settlement. Ward argues that 'one of the problems with examining port cities or littoral societies is that it downplays the importance of shipping as the process of voyaging rather than in terms of transportation of commodities or people from point-A to point-B', but that with a new type of examination which analyses movement 'the incorporation of processes of the movement of people as settlers, slaves, sojourners, sailors and soldiers, convicts and exiles comes to the fore'.[15]

Ideas of diaspora, transnational connectedness, boundary crossing and diversity are being explored by scholars looking at the black or African diaspora, the Armenian diaspora, the Southeast Asian diaspora and the Irish diaspora, as well as that of the Jewish.[16] Another way in which the term can be taken forward is to engage in current debates over mobility, globalisation and transnationalism, particularly to challenge the assertion that the massive, global circulation of goods, ideas and people is unique to the modern era.[17] There are of course numerous other ways in which the concept could be applied. It will be fascinating to see how the model develops over the coming years and it would be a constructive outcome if more comparative research could be undertaken along the lines called for by Oliel-Grausz. Having done so much to develop the concept and to establish a valuable archive of case studies, rich in empirical data, it is essential for researchers of port Jews and port Jewish communities to interact with other interrelated schools, studies and theories, and attempt to synthesise and contextualise their work with that in other, related fields.

NOTES

1. For example, see Miriam Bodian, *Hebrews of the Portuguese Nation: Conversos and Community in Early Modern Amsterdam* (Bloomington, IN: Indiana University Press, 1997); Frances Malino, *The Sephardic Jews of Bordeaux* (Tuscaloosa, AL: University of Alabama Press, 1978); and Daniel M. Swetschinski, *Reluctant Cosmopolitans: The Portuguese Jews of Seventeenth-Century Amsterdam* (London: Littman Library, 2000).
2. David Sorkin, 'The Port Jew: Notes Towards a Social Type', *Journal of Jewish Studies* 1.1 (Spring, 1999), 87–97 (at 88).
3. Lois Dubin, 'Researching Port Jews and Port Jewries: Trieste and Beyond', in David Cesarani (ed.), *Port Jews: Jewish Communities in Cosmopolitan Maritime Trading Centres, 1550–1950* (London and Portland, OR: Frank Cass, 2002), pp.47–58 (at 56–7).
4. David Sorkin, 'Port Jews and the Three Regions of Emancipation', in ibid., pp.31–46.
5. See also David Cesarani, 'The Forgotten Port Jews of London: Court Jews Who Were Also Port Jews', in ibid., pp.111–24.
6. Nicholas J. Evans, 'The Port Jews of Libau, 1880–1914', in this volume, pp.197–214.
7. See also Maria Vassilikou, 'Greeks and Jews in Salonika and Odessa: Inter-ethnic Relations in Cosmopolitan Port Cities', in Cesarani (note 3), pp.155–72.
8. Evelyne Oliel-Grausz, 'Networks and Communication in the Sephardi Diaspora: An Added Dimension to the Concept of Port Jews and Port Jewries', in this volume, pp.61–76.

9. Rainer Liedtke, 'An Island of Humanity in a Sea of Barbarism? Hamburg Jewry during the Nazi Period, 1933–45' in this volume, pp.261–70.

10. See Gemma Romain, 'Ethnicity, Identity and "Race": The Port Jews of Nineteenth-Century Charleston', and David Cesarani, 'The Jews of Bristol and Liverpool, 1750–1850: Port Jewish Communities in the Shadow of Slavery', in this volume, pp.123–40 and 141–56 respectively.

11. Adam Sutcliffe, 'Identity, Space and Intercultural Contact in the Urban Entrepôt: The Sephardic Bounding of Community in Early Modern Amsterdam and London' in this volume, pp.93–108.

12. Important centres and initiatives looking at Atlantic Studies include the Atlantic History Seminar, established at Harvard University in 1995 by Bernard Bailyn, under the auspices of the Charles Warren Center for Studies in American History and with the support of the Andrew W. Mellon Foundation. For a useful discussion of Atlantic Studies as a discipline, see Bernard Bailyn, 'The Idea of Atlantic History', *Itinerario* 1 (1996); and David Hancock, 'The British Atlantic World: Co-ordination, Complexity, and the Emergence of an Atlantic Market Economy, 1651–1815', *Itinerario* 2 (1999).

13. Association for Jewish Studies, 35th Annual Conference, Conference Proposal Abstracts, http://www.brandeis.edu/ajs/Abstracts2003.html.

14. *Seascapes, Littoral Cultures and Trans-Oceanic Exchanges*, Library of Congress, Washington, DC, 13–15 February 2003, organised by the American Historical Association and the Library of Congress. Within this conference there were presentations on the organisation of oceanic empires, maritime ideologies in the Southeast Asian littoral and their relation to political-economic contexts, concepts and definitions of littoral societies, as well as my own work on the port Jews of Charleston.

15. Kerry Ward, '"Tavern of the Seas"? The Cape of Good Hope as an Oceanic Crossroads during the Seventeenth and Eighteenth Centuries', *The History Cooperative: Conference Proceedings, Seascapes, Littoral Cultures, and Trans-Oceanic Exchanges*, http://www.historycooperative.org/proceedings/seascapes/ (© 2003 American Historical Association; compiled by Debbie Ann Doyle and Brandon Schneider; format by Chris Hale).

16. See Avtar Brah, *Cartographies of Diaspora: Contesting Identities* (London and New York: Routledge, 1996); Phil Cohen, 'Rethinking the Diasporama', *Patterns of Prejudice* 33.1 (1999), 3–22; Robin Cohen, *Global Diasporas: An Introduction* (Seattle, WA: University of Washington Press, 1997); Mary Chamberlain (ed.), *Caribbean Migration: Globalised Identities* (London: Routledge, 1998); Paul Gilroy, *The Black Atlantic: Modernity and Double Consciousness* (London: Verso, 1993); and Caren Kaplan, *Questions of Travel: Postmodern Discourses of Displacement* (Durham, NC and London, Duke University Press, 1996).

17. See the essays in A.G. Hopkins, *Globalization in World History* (London: Pimlico, 2002).

Abstracts

Introduction
DAVID CESARANI

In January 2003 an international conference in Cape Town enlarged on the port Jew concept, explored the value of port Jewry and port Jewish community as an analytical tool, and interrogated the specific ingredients of the port city milieu.

'Wings on their feet ... and wings on their head': Reflections on the Study of Port Jews
LOIS C. DUBIN

This essay surveys previous scholarly work on port Jews and sets forth a range of questions for further investigation. Developing a seventeenth-century image of merchants that represents them by Mercury's winged feet and cap, that is, with 'wings on their feet ... and wings on their head', it stresses the distance, movement, networks and boundary-crossing inherent in commercial exchange. It thereby highlights a relatively neglected aspect in the first studies of port Jews which had focused on their distinctive paths toward settlement and emancipation in early modern Europe. This essay also seeks to distinguish between the respective roles of Neptune and Mercury, that is, the sea and commerce, in the analysis of port Jews. In exploring possible relations between commerce, culture and cosmopolitanism, it emphasises connection, communication and cultural mediation within and among commercial cities and minority communities.

The Port Jews of Livorno and their Global Networks of Trade in the Early Modern Period
FRANCESCA TRIVELLATO

This essay aims to contribute to the ongoing debate about 'port Jews' in two ways. It examines the large and important Sephardic community of Livorno before emancipation, and finds numerous similarities to and important differences from the Sephardic settlements of north-western Europe. It also stresses the significance of the diasporic dimension of Sephardic identity, and establishes the existence of several (sometimes overlapping) networks within the Sephardic diaspora itself. The importance of these transnational, 'ethnic' networks is evident in the marriage strategies of affluent Sephardic families of Livorno, their close ties to the Ottoman Empire and their business relations with non-Jews in long-distance trade.

Port Jews in Copenhagen: The Sephardi Experience and its Influence on the Development of a Modern Jewish Community in Denmark
THORSTEN WAGNER

In spite of the small number of Sephardic immigrants to Denmark, the concept of the Port Jew seems applicable to some degree to the transformation of Jewish life in eighteenth- and nineteenth-century Denmark. Especially in Copenhagen the general appreciation of commerce seems to have contributed significantly to an early rapprochement between Jews and non-Jews, preparing the ground for social inclusion. The port Jewish presence seems to have had a decisive influence in creating a social and legal setting that ended up determining crucial dimensions of the process of Jewish emancipation and integration. The 'Portuguese' community played a crucial role in the formative beginnings of a modern Jewish culture in Denmark as well: Sephardi merchants constituted the core of a counter-elite challenging the rabbinic establishment from the 1780s. This essay argues that Copenhagen is a case in point, both illustrating the usefulness of the port Jew category and at the same time requiring an approach that does not push the dichotomies between court Jews and port Jews too far, but rather focuses on the interplay and simultaneity of these phenomena.

Networks and Communication in the Sephardi Diaspora: An Added Dimension to the Concept of Port Jews and Port Jewries
EVELYNE OLIEL-GRAUSZ

The relevance and utility of the concept of port Jews, from both a historiographical and heuristic point of view, is beyond discussion. However, the Sorkin–Dubin dialogue is missing one dimension, that of the relations between port Jewries, on the multifaceted networks shaping the diasporic space, and ultimately on the issue of communication. Confronting a multiplicity of sources, this essay provides a global sketch of these networks and interactions.

Were Merchants More Tolerant? 'Godless Patrons of the Jews' and the Decline of the Sephardi Community in Late Seventeenth-Century Hamburg
KLAUS WEBER

This essay provides a chronology of the Sephardi merchant community in seventeenth-century Hamburg and describes its decline, caused mainly by anti-Jewish pressure from the guilds and the Lutheran clergy. In particular, it examines the discourse between the Senate and the wealthy maritime traders on one hand, who tried to protect the Portuguese Jews, and the largely hostile guilds and preachers on the other. By contextualising this conflict in light of pastors' and citizens' attitudes towards other minorities such as Calvinists and Roman Catholics, more general conclusions may be drawn, showing that pressure on Jews was only one element from a larger set of intolerant measures exercised in general by the Lutheran community in Hamburg.

Identity, Space and Intercultural Contact in the Urban Entrepôt: The Sephardic Bounding of Community in Early Modern Amsterdam and London
ADAM SUTCLIFFE

The pattern of Sephardic social transformation in Amsterdam and in London during the seventeenth and eighteenth centuries was broadly similar. Both communities faced intense challenges to their integrity in the economically dynamic and culturally cosmopolitan environments of these key trading entrepôts. However, the sheer size of London, and also the intensification of assimilatory pressures in the eighteenth century, led to that city experiencing a more dramatic erosion of Sephardic collective cohesion.

Trading Globally, Speaking Locally: Curaçao's Sephardim in the Making of a Caribbean Creole
LINDA M. RUPERT

During the eighteenth century the Sephardic community of Curaçao, a Dutch Caribbean entrepôt, played a key role in developing Papiamentu, a creole language that was spoken widely across social class, race and ethnicity. Their role in Papiamentu's success indicates that, far from being an isolated, internally focused enclave, Curaçao's port Jews helped to forge a strong inter-ethnic colonial identity in the local society at the same time they were consolidating far-flung regional and global trade networks. Their case raises compelling questions about the wider role of port Jews in creolisation processes throughout the early modern Atlantic world.

Ethnicity, Identity and 'Race': The Port Jews of Nineteenth-Century Charleston
GEMMA ROMAIN

This essay examines the identity of the port Jews of antebellum Charleston and the way in which their ethnicity was formulated. The Jewish community of Charleston has been characterised as the pre-eminent American community of the antebellum period – accepted into the elite of society and equally embracing of white Charlestonian culture. Utilising the concept of the port Jew, formulated by Dubin and Sorkin, I interrogate and discuss the accuracy of this description and also whether the particularities of Charleston's port economy and society were reasons for this seeming cultural accord. I explore the local and transnational identities of the Jews of Charleston and also interrogate Jewish/non-Jewish relations in the city.

The Jews of Bristol and Liverpool, 1750–1850: Port Jewish Communities in the Shadow of Slavery
DAVID CESARANI

In the mid-nineteenth century the Jewish communities of Liverpool and Bristol were amongst the oldest, largest and best developed in England. They attracted Jewish settlers during a period of economic growth that was largely fuelled by the transatlantic slave trade. Yet historians of the Jews in Britain have hardly examined the interconnections between the slave trade and Jewish settlement. While Jews had little direct involvement in the slave trade, they were enmeshed in the local economy that was driven by it. Nevertheless, the fiercely commercial and utilitarian ethos of the slave-trading cities did not result in a favourable attitude to Jewish settlers. Mercantile interests could militate against the Jews, who were perceived as a source of competition. Contrary to the benign model of the port city this essay suggests that some mercantile centres may have been a dead end on the road to modernity while others may have fostered sectarianism.

The 'Jewish Nation' of Livorno: A Port Jewry on the Road to Emancipation
CARLOTTA FERRARA DEGLI UBERTI

The Letters Patent of 1591–93, known as *Livornine*, were aimed in the first place at Jews, and guaranteed, among other privileges, the right to profess their own religion, the possibility to acquire real estate without any limitations, and tax amenities for trading activities connected with the port. The Jewish Nation of Livorno took shape as a substantially independent administrative structure, with full legitimisation and strictly associated with the cosmopolitan environment created by the port. In the course of the nineteenth century the process of legal emancipation caused profound changes in the relationships between the Jewish Nation, the rest of the population and the state institutions.

The Port Jews of Corfu and the 'Blood Libel' of 1891: A Tale of Many Centuries and of One Event
SAKIS GEKAS

The history of the Jews of Corfu has not been a particularly popular object of study and as a result the history of this community remains basically unknown. In an attempt to fill this gap but also engage with the debate on port Jews, this essay explores first the history of Jews during the ages and especially during the period of British rule in Corfu, the commercial centre of the Ionian State. The occupational classification of the Jews who became Greek citizens in 1864 aims at discerning the role of Jews in the port economy. Finally the essay also investigates the events of 1891, when a blood libel resulted in the first persecution of Jews in Greece. Economic factors, which led to the decline of Corfu as a port towards the end of the century, and the emergence of a local anti-semitism and an aggressive nationalism were the basic reasons for the outbreak of anti-semitic violence in 1891, a by and large unknown event of Greek history.

The Port Jews of Libau, 1880–1914
NICHOLAS J. EVANS

The Baltic port of Libau expanded rapidly during the end of the nineteenth century as the harbour, and the transport connections to it, were developed by Imperial Russia. Despite the constant erosion of the rights of the Jews living in this port, the influence the Jewish mercantile classes had in port commerce inflated their status in port life. The role played by the port Jews of this forgotten port city typified the fluidity of Jewish life at the end of the nineteenth century as Jews sought to migrate for religious, economic or political reasons. Such movement enabled the development of important business networks between Russian and North Seas ports. It is the role of port Jews of Libau that this essay discusses.

Jewish and Catholic Irish Relations: The Glasgow Waterfront c.1880–1914
WILLIAM KENEFICK

Jewish immigration into Scotland was never large-scale, but before 1914 perhaps as many as 10,000 Jews had made Scotland their home. They were relatively new rivals, mainly from Russia, who settled largely in the Gorbals area, south of the river Clyde near the bustling inland port of Glasgow. There were also a great many Irish working along the Glasgow waterfront and living 'cheek by jowl' with the Jews in the Gorbals 'Ghetto of commerce'. What type of relationship developed between the Irish and the new Jews? Was it marred by inter-ethnic conflict and communal violence, or do we see the development of a tolerant and pluralistic community? It is the type of community that developed from this intermingling and its relationship with the host society that is examined in this essay.

Testing Cosmopolitan Tolerance: Port Jews in Cape Town during the Late Victorian and Edwardian Years
MILTON SHAIN, RICHARD MENDELSOHN and VIVIAN BICKFORD-SMITH

The essay uses Cape Town in the late Victorian and Edwardian period to test the wider applicability of the Sorkin-Dubin 'port Jew' model, including the notion that port cities provide a peculiarly tolerant and welcoming environment, rooted in mercantile imperatives and cosmopolitanism. It argues that when one moves beyond the early modern European setting, the notion of the 'port Jew' becomes problematic. Modernity, it would seem, erodes the social space within which Sorkin and Dubin's port Jew thrives. The close integration of modern port cities, like Cape Town, with society at large, including their hinterlands, might preclude them from acting as the distinctive shaper of cultural patterns and social types. Demonstrably, distinguishing between what is indigenous to Cape Town and what is imposed on it from without, is fraught with difficulty: the 'port' as a distinctive shaper of cultural patterns and social types becomes difficult to sustain. Cape Town's cultural ethos in the late Victorian and Edwardian period cannot easily, if at all, be separated from developments well beyond its immediate locale. Modernity, it would seem, erodes the social space within which Sorkin and Dubin's Port Jew thrives; that was unique to the self-contained port city of the early modern period. The close integration of modern port cities with society at large, including their hinterlands, precludes this.

From Atlantic Hotel to Atlantic Park: Anglo-America, Port Jews and the Invisible Transmigrant
TONY KUSHNER

This essay argues that the concept of the port Jew needs to include, as an essential element, the centrality of movement. In the latter part of the nineteenth century and first half of the twentieth century, Jewish transmigrancy grew on a massive scale. This aspect of the Jewish experience has not received sufficient attention but its inclusion complicates the understanding of the port Jew in the modern era. The focus is on the British port of Southampton, whose growth into one of the major world maritime centres in the nineteenth century and beyond was partly stimulated by transmigrant trade. The experiences of the settled Jewish community in the town are contrasted to those of the transmigrants and the wider significance of Southampton in world and Jewish history is explored further through the issue of medical inspection of aliens. Ultimately, this essay points to the negative potential of ports in the Jewish experience, one that has to be considered alongside the potential benefits brought through cosmopolitanism.

An Island of Humanity in a Sea of Barbarism? Hamburg Jewry during the Nazi Period, 1933–45
RAINER LIEDTKE

After the Second World War Hamburg has claimed that it has been a kind of enclave that had resisted the worst excesses of National Socialism. It has built up a popular image as a cosmopolitan and tolerant city which has always treated outsiders well. The investigation of anti-Jewish measures during the Nazi period reveals that the minority had been persecuted at least as vigorously as in other German cities, and in some instances more violently. This essay looks in particular at the developments during the November pogrom of 1938, the prosecution of Jews who had committed *Rassenschande* (defiling 'German blood' by having intimate contacts to non-Jews) and the expropriation of Jewish assets. It demonstrates that the elite that had run this port city for centuries used all opportunities to rid the city of 'foreign' elements and competitors. In Hamburg tolerance was based purely on economic utility.

Singapore, Manila and Harbin as Reference Points for Asian 'Port Jewish' Identity
JONATHAN GOLDSTEIN

Historian David Sorkin has argued that, in late nineteenth- and early twentieth-century Atlantic and Mediterranean seaports, conditions of civic inclusion and economic and political equality enabled Jews to prosper, flourish intellectually and move toward full emancipation. Nearly simultaneously approximately 2,000 Jews settled in the British city/colony of Singapore while another 2,000 reached Manila in the American-occupied Philippines. Does the Sorkin thesis apply in an Asian context? In both Asian cities Jews enjoyed rights comparable to those of their Atlantic and Mediterranean seaport brethren and flourished commercially and intellectually. However, almost exactly the same phenomena can be observed in the same-sized Jewish community of Harbin, China, located 1,500 miles inland. Harbin was a major railroad hub, suggesting that the Sorkin thesis might be broadened to include all major trading and distribution centres and entrepôts which had civic inclusion and economic and political equality. His conditions and criteria would not exclusively apply to seaports.

Notes on Contributors

David Cesarani is Research Professor in History at Royal Holloway, University of London. From 2000 to 2004 he presided over the port Jews project as Director of the AHRB Parkes Centre for the Study of Jewish/non-Jewish Relations, Southampton University. His publications include (ed.) *Port Jews: Jewish Communities in Cosmopolitan Maritime Trading Centres, 1650–1950* (2002), and *Eichmann: His Life and Crimes* (2004).

Gemma Romain works at The National Archives, Kew on a Heritage Lottery Fund project, 'Your Caribbean Heritage', cataloguing and researching colonial office correspondence from the British Caribbean. Her postdoctoral fellowship at the AHRB Parkes Centre, University of Southampton, explored diasporic and ethnic identities of Jews in Charleston, South Carolina, and Jamaica. She is the author of *Connecting Histories: A Comparative Exploration of African-Caribbean and Jewish History and Memory in Modern Britain* (2005). She was a researcher and writer for the 'Connections: Hidden British Histories' exhibition exploring Asian, Caribbean and Jewish history in Britain.

Lois C. Dubin is Associate Professor of Religion at Smith, where she teaches courses in Jewish history and thought. She is author of *The Port Jews of Habsburg Trieste: Absolutist Politics and Enlightenment Culture* (1999), and guest editor of a forthcoming issue of *Jewish History* 20 (2006) on Port Jews in the Atlantic World. She also works on civil marriage and divorce in modern Jewish history, and on feminist theology and ritual.

Francesca Trivellato is Assistant Professor of Continental Early Modern European History at Yale University. Her publications on Jewish history include 'Les juifs d'origine portugaise entre Livourne, le Portugal et al Méditerranée (c.1650–1750)', in *La Diaspora des Nouveaux Chrétiens d'origine portugaise* (2004); and with Giovanni Favero, 'Gli abitanti del getto di Venezia in età moderna: dati e ipotesi', *Zakhor: Rivista della storia degli ebrei in Italia*, VII (2004).

Thorsten Wagner is affiliated with the Danish Centre for Holocaust and Genocide Studies, Copenhagen, and the Jewish Museum of Berlin. He is presently completing his dissertation on the emancipation and acculturation of Danish Jewry 1780–1849 in a comparative European perspective. Recent publications include 'Overcoming Prejudice: The Danish Church and the Jews

1918–1945: Stepping into the Breach or Relativizing Antisemitism?' *Kirchliche Zeitgeschichte* 16 (2003); and 'Holocaust i erindring og på museum', in Hans Sode-Madsen (ed.), *I Hitler-Tysklands Skygge: Dramaet om de danske jøder 1933–1945* (2003).

Evelyne Oliel-Grausz teaches in the Faculté de Philosophie et Lettres, Université Libre de Bruxelles.

Klaus Weber's thesis on German merchants in early modern Atlantic trade has recently been published as *Deutsche Kaufleute im Atlantikhandel 1680–1830* (2004). He researched Atlantic commerce and migration at the Centre for the Study of Human Settlement and Historical Change, National University of Ireland, Galway. In cooperation with David Cesarani he is now directing a research project on Jewish and non-Jewish philanthropy in nineteenth- and twentieth-century Europe, at Royal Holloway, University of London, and the Rothschild Archive.

Adam Sutcliffe is Associate Professor of European Jewish History at the University of Illinois at Urbana-Champaign. He is the author of *Judaism and Enlightenment* (2004), and the co-editor with Ross Brann of *Renewing the Past, Reconfiguring Jewish Culture: From Al-Andalus to the Haskalah* (2004). He is currently working on a history of ideals of friendship in the eighteenth century.

Linda M. Rupert is a doctoral candidate in history at Duke University. She has received dissertation research fellowships from the J. William Fulbright Foundation and the Social Science Research Council, and was the 2004 recipient of the Ida B. Wells Award from the Coordinating Council for Women in History. She has written *Roots of our Future: A Commercial History of Curaçao* (1999), and 'Rethinking Curaçao's Commercial History: Black Seafarers and Jewish Merchants', *Lanternu: Journal of the Central Historical Archives of the Netherlands Antilles*, 20 (2001).

Carlotta Ferrara degli Uberti took her degree in History in 2001 at the University of Pisa. She is currently a Ph.D. student at the Scuola Normale Superiore, Pisa, and at the Université de Paris 1 (Panthéon-Sorbonne). She is working on Italian-Jewish periodicals in the context of European Jewry between the 1840s and the First World War, and on the Jewish Community of Livorno in nineteenth-century Italy.

Sakis Gekas is a Teaching Fellow at the Economic History Department, London School of Economics. His research interests include the economic and social history of Mediterranean port cities during the eighteenth and nineteenth centuries. His publications include 'The Merchants of the Ionian Islands between East and West: Forming Local and International networks', in M.S. Beerbuhl and J. Vogele (eds.), *Spinning the Commercial Web: International Trade, Merchants and Commercial Cities, c.1640–1939* (2004).

Nicholas J. Evans is a Research Fellow at the AHRB Centre for Irish and Scottish Studies at the University of Aberdeen. His Ph.D. examined the subject of European transmigration through Britain between 1836 and 1914. He is a former Caird Fellow of the National Maritime Museum, London, and a Kaarle Hjalmar Lehtisen Researcher of the Institute of Migration, Finland.

William Kenefick lectures in Scottish and British history at the University of Dundee. He has published widely on Scottish maritime and labour history, and the Irish and dock trade unionism and politics in Glasgow, and has a particular interest in the impact of the First World War and the Russian Revolution on the Scottish working class, political radicalism and the Scottish diaspora, and links between immigrant workers and Scottish labour.

Milton Shain is Director of the Isaac and Jessie Kaplan Centre for Jewish Studies at the University of Cape Town. His latest book, *Memories, Realities and Dreams: Aspects of the South African Jewish Experience*, was co-edited with Richard Mendelsohn.

Richard Mendelsohn teaches history at the University of Cape Town. His research interests lie in South African Jewish history and in 'film and history'. He is the author of *Sammy Marks: 'The Uncrowned King of the Transvaal'*, a biography of the pioneering South African Jewish industrial and mining entrepreneur, and is co-editor, with Milton Shain of *Memories, Realities and Dreams: Aspects of the South African Jewish Experience*.

Vivian Bickford-Smith teaches history at the University of Cape Town. He is the author of *Ethnic Pride and Racial Prejudice and Victorian Cape Town* and many other works on Cape Town history.

Tony Kushner is Director of the AHRB Parkes Research Centre for the Study of Jewish/non-Jewish relations and Professor of History at the University of Southampton. He has recently published *We Europeans? Mass-Observation, 'Race' and British National Identity in the Twentieth Century* (2004), and, with Donald Bloxham, *The Holocaust* (2005).

Rainer Liedtke is Assistant Professor in Modern History at the University of Kiel and Lecturer at the University of Giessen. His publications include *Jewish*

Welfare in Hamburg and Manchester, c.1850–1914 (1988), ed. with S. Wendenhorst, *The Emancipation of Catholics, Jews and Protestants: Minorities and the Nation State in Nineteenth-Century Europe* (1999), and ed. with D. Rechter, *Towards Normality: Acculturation and Modern German Jewry* (2003).

Jonathan Goldstein is a Professor of History at the University of West Georgia, where he teaches courses on China, Japan, India, Vietnam and the Holocaust. His books include *Philadelphia and the China Trade* (1978), *America Views China* (1991), *China and Israel, 1948–98* (1999), and *The Jews of China* (2000).

Index

Abensur, Jacob 54
Abraham, Alexander 150
Abraham, John 150
Abraham, Joseph 150
Abulafia, Raphael 14
Aby Tetomim (orphan school) 67
accionistas (share dealers) 105
acculturation 36, 56; Anglo-Jewish 99–100;
  Danish-Jewish 57–8
Act for the Naturalization of Jews (1753) 147
Adelman, Jeremy 21
Adis, Nissim 273–4
Africa, Sephardic enclaves 113, 116; slave trade
  127
Agron, Gershon 276–7
Agudat Israel 284
AHRB Parkes Centre for the Study of
  Jewish/non-Jewish Relations (University of
  Southampton) 1
Aleppo, Levantine port of 37, 41
Alexander III (Tsar) 201
Alexander, Abraham 150
Alexander, Joseph 149
Alexander, Morris 244
Alexander, William Wolf 150
Aliens Act 1905, and Glasgow 223; and Libau
  209
Aliens List (Bevis Marks, 1803) 67
Altona, Jews from 51, 53
Aluzay, Rabbi 102
Alvares, Manuel 80
American Jewish Joint Distribution Committee
  281
Amsterdam, assimilation 36; cosmopolitanism
  95, 96, 97; cultural identity 106; early
  modern 94–9, 104–6; economic life 105;
  Etz Haim Yeshiva 64, 70, 272; growth of
  Jewish community 34; *Mahamad* 7, 62–3,
  70, 98, 99; *parnassim* 63, 64, 69, 70, 72, 97–8,
  99; Portuguese Jews 22, 23, 105; privileges
  for Jews 143, 144; religious
  education/leadership 5–6; 'semi-Jews' in
  100; Sephardim 6, 25, 35, 96, 97, 105; space
  105–6; Stock Exchange, Calvinists in 105;
  synagogues in 35

ancien régime 18, 157, 159, 160
Andreadis, A. 190
Anjou (King of Naples), decrees by 173
antebellum period, Charleston 123, 128, 129,
  130, 131, 135, 136
anti-Semitism, Cape Town 239; Citizenry
  (Hamburg interest group) 81; Corfu 172,
  185, 187–9; Glasgow 217; Hamburg 268;
  Libau 197; Nation of Islam 125, 126; and
  nationalism 188
Apulian Jews 173
Arias, Jeosuah Menahem 63
Aron, Stephen 21
Aryanisation, Hamburg 12, 268
Ashendon, P. 241
Ashkenazi Jews, in Charleston 127, 131; in
  Copenhagen 5, 51, 52; in Hamburg 6; in
  Libau 197; in London 100; and Portuguese
  Jews 51, 52; and Sephardi port Jews 2; in
  Trieste 32
assimilation, 104
Association for Jewish Studies Conference,
  Boston (2003) 293
Atlantic Studies 293
Attar, Ben 14

Baghdad, belief intensification/quasi-secular
  Jewish identity 274–8; communal
  origins/commercial activity 273–4
Baird, J. G. A. 227
Bajohr, Frank 268
Balkans region 21, 34
Ballas, Shimon 277
ballotazione procedure (naturalisation) 8, 33,
  158, 159, 163, 166
Baltic region, economic contribution of Jews
  202–4
Barbados, Jewish population 35
Barnet-Clarke, William 239
'Baroque Judaism' (late eighteenth century)
  55–7
Baruch Carvaglio family, Abraham 31, 38
Bayonne 34, 63
Belilios family 31
Ben Eliezer, Benjamin 277

Recently published by Vallentine Mitchell

Scenes and Personalities in Anglo-Jewry 1800–2000
Israel Finestein

This volume consists of articles by Israel Finestein written over a period of fifty years. These wide-ranging studies graphically present significant features of Jewish public life in Anglo-Jewry or with a bearing upon that community.

Anglo-Jewry in Changing Times: Studies in Diversity 1840–1914
Israel Finestein

'These brilliant studies and individual vignettes illuminate British social history as much as they light up the social history of the Jews in Britain.' Professor David Cesarani

www.vmbooks.com

Recently published by Vallentine Mitchell

Opportunities that Pass:
An Historical Miscellany
Cecil Roth,
edited by Israel Finestein and Joseph Roth

Cecil Roth was the first Anglo-Jewish historian to become a household name. In addition to his numerous books Roth wrote many articles for a wide range of journals in Britain and overseas, notably in America, on Jewish life and history. This volume comprises a substantial collection of them, selected for their special and continuing Jewish appeal and human interest, none of which have appeared in book form before. Roth loved travel and his many journeys to Europe inevitable included visits to regions of post or then current Jewish residence. He was an acute observer of scenes, people, atmosphere and change. Characteristics of his approach are his historical accounts of some, to us, curious observance of familiar Jewish festivals in different localities he visited. Typical of his article titles are 'Was Hebrew ever a Dead Language', 'England and the Ninth of Av', 'Was there ever a Ban on Jews Returning to Spain' and 'Paradoxes of Jewish History'. Of particular interest is the first article in the book, written in 1932, entitled 'Opportunities that Pass: A Plea for the Study of Disappearing Customs and Folklore'. Was it an unwitting prophecy, or did he have an observer's and historian's presentiment of what lay ahead?

Cecil Roth was a unique personality. He gave of his best in whatever he did. He achieved much. This volume is edited with affectionate respect by Israel Finestein and Cecil's nephew, Joseph Roth.

www.vmbooks.com